Human Rights at the Intersections

Human Rights at the Intersections

Transformation through Local, Global, and Cosmopolitan Challenges

Edited by
Anthony Tirado Chase
Pardis Mahdavi
Hussein Banai
Sofia Gruskin

BLOOMSBURY ACADEMIC
LONDON • NEW YORK • OXFORD • NEW DELHI • SYDNEY

BLOOMSBURY ACADEMIC
Bloomsbury Publishing Plc
50 Bedford Square, London, WC1B 3DP, UK
1385 Broadway, New York, NY 10018, USA
29 Earlsfort Terrace, Dublin 2, Ireland

BLOOMSBURY, BLOOMSBURY ACADEMIC and the Diana logo are trademarks of
Bloomsbury Publishing Plc

First published in Great Britain 2023
This paperback edition published 2024

Series design by Adriana Brioso
Cover image © Tierney/Adobe Stock

A catalogue record for this book is available from the British Library.

Library of Congress Cataloging-in-Publication Data

Names: Chase, Anthony Tirado, editor. | Mahdavi, Pardis, 1978– editor. |
Banai, Hussein, editor. | Gruskin, Sofia, editor.
Title: Human rights at the intersections : transformation through local, global, and
cosmopolitan challenges / edited by Anthony Tirado Chase, Pardis Mahdavi,
Hussein Banai, Sofia Gruskin.
Description: London ; New York : Bloomsbury Academic, 2023. |
Includes bibliographical references and index.
Identifiers: LCCN 2022038663 (print) | LCCN 2022038664 (ebook) |
ISBN 9781350268661 (hardback) | ISBN 9781350268678 (epub) | I
SBN 9781350268685 (pdf) | ISBN 9781350268692
Subjects: LCSH: Human rights. | Human rights movements. | Cosmopolitanism. |
Human rights–Case studies. | Human rights movements–Case studies. |
Cosmopolitanism–Case studies.I
Classification: LCC JC571 .H6915 2023 (print) | LCC JC571 (ebook) |
DDC 323—dc23/eng/20220926
LC record available at https://lccn.loc.gov/2022038663
LC ebook record available at https://lccn.loc.gov/2022038664

ISBN: PB: 978-1-3502-6870-8
        eBook: 978-1-3502-6867-8
        ePDF: 978-1-3502-6868-5

Typeset by RefineCatch Limited, Bungay, Suffolk

To find out more about our authors and books visit www.bloomsbury.com
and sign up for our newsletters.

Contents

Editor and Contributor Biographies

Hussein "Huss" Banai is an Associate Professor of International Studies in the Hamilton Lugar School of Global and International Studies at Indiana University, Bloomington, and a research affiliate at the Center for International Studies at the Massachusetts Institute of Technology. He is the author of *Hidden Liberalism: Burdened Visions of Progress in Modern Iran*, and co-author of two volumes on US-Iran relations: *Republics of Myth: National Narratives and the US-Iran Conflict* and *Becoming Enemies: U.S.-Iran Relations and the Iran-Iraq War, 1979–1988*.

Anthony Tirado Chase is a professor at Occidental College and chair of its Young Initiative on the Global Political Economy. Chase has published widely on human rights in the Middle East and globally. His more recent work has focused on city-level action, especially in projects with the L.A. Mayor's office on translating global norms—from human rights, the SDGs, and transitional justice—into local policy.

Sofia Gruskin directs the University of Southern California Institute on Inequalities in Global Health. She is Professor of Preventive Medicine and Chief of the Disease Prevention, Policy and Global Health Division at the Keck School of Medicine, and Professor of Law and Preventive Medicine at the Gould School of Law. Gruskin sits on numerous international boards and committees, including the Lancet Commission on Health and Human Rights. Professor Gruskin has published extensively, including several books, training manuals and edited journal volumes, and more than 200 articles and chapters covering a wide range of topics. She is an associate editor for *Global Public Health*, on the editorial advisory board for *Revue Internationale des Études du Développement*, and a trustee of *Sexual and Reproductive Health Matters*.

Pardis Mahdavi PhD is the Provost and Executive Vice President at the University of Montana. Previously, she was Professor and Dean of Social Sciences at Arizona State University. Before coming to Arizona, she was Acting Dean of the Korbel School of International Studies at the University of Denver (2017–2019), after spending eleven years at Pomona College from 2006–2017 where she most recently served as professor and chair of anthropology and director of the Pacific Basin Institute at Pomona College as well as Dean of Women. Her research interests include gendered labor, human trafficking, migration, sexuality, human rights, transnational feminism, and public health in the context of changing global and political structures. She has published six single authored books and one edited volume in addition to numerous journal and news articles. She is a lifetime member of the Council on Foreign Relations and has been a fellow at the Social Sciences Research Council, the American Council on Learned Societies, Google Ideas, and the Woodrow Wilson International Center for

Scholars. In 2018 she was appointed by Colorado Governor John Hickenlooper and re-appointed by Governor Jared Polis to serve on the Colorado Commission on Higher Education. For more information, please visit www.pardismahdavi.com

Yohanna Abdou is from Niger. He is a child of persons who were affected by Hansen's disease. In 2009, Yohanna founded the local Association of IDEA Niger, with the support of IDEA International and is now acting IDEA's Niger Country Representative and a member of the Board of Directors for IDEA International. Since 2012, Yohanna has worked for The Leprosy Mission Niger as Head of Program and Research. He previously worked for the Danja SIM Leprosy Health Center and with the Ministry of Youth, Sport and Culture.

Pablo Gustavo Abitbol Piñeiro is professor of Social Sciences and Humanities at the Technological University of Bolívar (UTB), coordinator of the Regional Historical Memory Group, and member of the Peacebuilding Space of Montes de María. He conducts basic and applied research projects (with emphasis on participatory action research – PAR) on collective memory, social learning, cultural change, polycentric governance, market design (especially local and regional food systems), democratic development, deliberation, and reconciliation.

Pascale Allotey is a global health leader, working at the intersection of health systems, gender and global health equity. She is the Director of the United Nations University International Institute for Global Health, the UN think tank on global health. Hussein "Huss" Banai is an Associate Professor of International Studies in the Hamilton Lugar School of Global and International Studies at Indiana University, Bloomington, and a research affiliate at the Center for International Studies at the Massachusetts Institute of Technology. He is the author of *Hidden Liberalism: Burdened Visions of Progress in Modern Iran, and co-author of two volumes on US-Iran* relations: Republics of Myth: *National Narratives and the US-Iran Conflict* and *Becoming Enemies: U.S.–Iran Relations and the Iran–Iraq War, 1979–1988.*

Erin Bromaghim serves in the Los Angeles Mayor's Office of International Affairs as the Director of Olympic and Paralympic Development, leading coordination and planning ahead of the 2028 Games. She has also led the City's work to implement the Sustainable Development Goals as the Conrad N. Hilton Foundation Fellow on the SDGs and serves as a visiting senior fellow on State and City Diplomacy with the Truman Center on National Policy. Erin previously spent 14 years as a senior civilian with the U.S. Department of Defense, where she managed interagency defense, intelligence, special operations, and security reform efforts.

Alison Brysk is the Distinguished Mellichamp Professor of Global Governance at the University of California, Santa Barbara. She is the author or editor of fifteen books on international human rights, most recently *The Struggle for Freedom from Fear: Contesting Violence Against Women at The Frontiers of Globalization* (2018) and *The*

Future of Human Rights (2018). Professor Brysk has been selected Distinguished Scholar in Human Rights of the International Studies Association and the American Political Science Association; a fellow at the Woodrow Wilson Center; a Fulbright Professor in Canada, India, and at Oxford; a Taiwan Fellow; and a member of the Council on Foreign Relations.

Mauro Cabral Grinspan is an Argentinian intersex and trans activist and researcher. He co-founded GATE and served as its executive director from 2017 to 2022, coordinating GATE's work on depathologization. Mauro participated in the elaboration of the *Yogyakarta Principles* and of the *Yogyakarta Principles Plus Ten*, being a signatory of both. He currently works at the Global Philanthropy Project, coordinating its task forces on trans, intersex and responding to anti-gender issues.

Morgan Carpenter is a bioethicist, human rights advocate, and creator of the intersex flag. The Executive Director of Intersex Human Rights Australia, he plays an active role in systemic advocacy on legislative, regulatory and clinical reform, seeking to ensure that medical practices on people with innate variations of sex characteristics conform to fundamental human rights norms.

Sergio Chaparro Hernández is an Atlantic Fellow for Social and Economic Equity at the London School of Economics. He holds a BSc in Economics, a BA in Philosophy and a MA in Law at the National University of Colombia. He works as program officer at the Center for Economic and Social Rights.

Cristián Correa is a senior expert at the International Center for Transitional Justice (ICTJ) since 2007. As such, he advises civil society organizations, victims' groups, governments, and state institutions in numerous countries around the world on how to address the consequences of massive human rights violations, and on how to learn from them to build sustainable peace.

Zita Davis is the Executive Officer for Mayor Garcetti's Office of Economic Opportunity. Under the leadership of the deputy mayor, Zita works with policy directors to create employment, education, and community-based initiatives that seek to provide equitable access and opportunity to all Los Angeles residents and their communities. Zita is married, has three adult children and lives in Los Angeles.

Alethia Fernández de la Reguera is an associate researcher at the Research Center for Gender Studies at the National Autonomous University of Mexico. Her work focuses on the study of gender-based subjectivities, bureaucracy, and violence at the Mexican southern border. Currently, she is an elected member of the Conacyt-National System of Researchers (level 1) and leads a research program on gender and migration funded by the UNAM-PAPIIT program.

Kate Gilmore, former UN Deputy High Commissioner for Human Rights, is IPPF's Board Chair, Honorary Professor at Essex University and Professor-in-Practice at LSE.

She is Interpeace's vice chair and a member of the WHO Gender and Human Rights Advisory Panel and of the WHO Immunization Agenda 2030 Partnership Panel.

Michael Goodhart is professor of Political Science and Gender Studies at the University of Pittsburgh; he writes and teaches on human rights, democratic theory, injustice, and globalization. He is author of *Injustice: Political Theory for the Real World* (2018), *Democracy as Human Rights: Freedom and Equality in the Age of Globalization* (2005), and many articles and book chapters. Most recently, Goodhart was a fellow in residence at the Swedish Collegium for Advanced Study in 2021–2 and director of Pitt's Global Studies Center from 2017–21. Sofia Gruskin directs the University of Southern California Institute on Inequalities in Global Health. She is Professor of Preventive Medicine and Chief of the Disease Prevention, Policy and Global Health Division at the Keck School of Medicine, and Professor of Law and Preventive Medicine at the Gould School of Law. Gruskin sits on numerous international boards and committees, including the Lancet Commission on Health and Human Rights. Professor Gruskin has published extensively, including several books, training manuals and edited journal volumes, and more than 200 articles and chapters covering a wide range of topics. She is an associate editor for *Global Public Health*, on the editorial advisory board for *Revue Internationale des Études du Développement*, and a trustee of *Sexual and Reproductive Health Matters*.

LaDawn Haglund is a sociologist, professor, and researcher in the areas of human rights, social and environmental justice, and socially transformative processes. Her research analyzing the social and political dimensions of sustainability and environmental governance has received support from the U.S. National Science Foundation, the J. William Fulbright Foreign Scholarship Board and the Brazilian Fulbright Commission. Dr. Haglund is co-editor (with Robin Stryker) of *Closing the Rights Gap: From Human Rights to Social Transformation* (2015) and author of *Limiting Resources: Market-Led Reform and the Transformation of Public Goods* (2010), as well as articles in *Sustainability*, *Latin American Perspectives*, *Journal of Human Rights*, *Water Policy*, *European Journal of Sociology*, and *The Arrow: A Journal of Wakeful Society, Culture, and Politics*.

Paulo Estevao Hansine is a health professional, resident of Chimoio, Mozambique, and an activist in the fight against discrimination and improving the quality of life of people affected by leprosy and their families. He volunteered to work with patients affected by leprosy in 1982 and in 1984 was appointed as Provincial Supervisor of the national leprosy program. He has studied leprosy in Mozambique, Brazil, and Ethiopia, including working for the WHO. He was a founding member of IDEA Mozambique and elected chair of the Supervisory Board in 2005. He works for AIFO as Leprosy Advisor in the Provincial Health Directorate of Manica.

Bahey eldin Hassan is the director and cofounder of the Cairo Institute for Human Rights Studies (CIHRS), an organization established in 1993 with the aim of spreading and rooting human rights in Egyptian society and across the Arab region. He is also a board member of several international human rights NGOs.

Shareen Hertel is professor of Political Science at the University of Connecticut, jointly appointed with the UConn Human Rights Institute. She is editor of *The Journal of Human Rights*, co-editor of the Routledge *International Studies Intensives* book series, and publishes widely, including *Tethered Fates: Companies, Communities and Rights at Stake* (2019) and *Unexpected Power: Conflict & Change Among Transnational Activists* (2006). Hertel has served as a consultant to foundations, nongovernmental organizations (NGOs) and United Nations agencies in the United States, Latin America and South Asia.

Joe Hoover is senior lecturer in Political Theory at Queen Mary University of London. His work examines questions of global ethics drawing on philosophical pragmatism and agonistic political theory.

Adnan Hossain is assistant professor of Gender Studies and Critical Theory at Utrecht University. He is the author of the monograph 'Beyond Emasculation: Pleasure and Power in the Making of Hijra in Bangladesh' (2021). His second book, 'Badhai: Hijra-Khwaja Sira-Trans Performances across Borders in South Asia' is collaboratively authored by scholars working across boundaries of disciplines, methods and nations (forthcoming).

Jone Andre José is a founding member of IDEA Mozambique in 2005 and is married and father of seven children in Chimoio. He was elected president of IDEA Mozambique—Manica delegation in 2010. He is a person affected by leprosy who has suffered discrimination in his community and in receiving public services. Since 2005 he has been actively involved in the fight against such discrimination and works to capture and support new cases of leprosy in the city of Chimoio.

Kristi Heather Kenyon is associate professor and program director in the Human Rights Program at the University of Winnipeg's Global College. Her work is informed and inspired by more than twenty years of work in, on and with civil society groups in Canada, South East Asia and Southern Africa.

Rajat Khosla is the Senior Director of Research, Advocacy and Policy at Amnesty International. He previously served as Human Rights Adviser for the World Health Organization, managed the global campaign on UDHR@70 at the Office of the UN High Commissioner for Human Rights, and has held a variety of research and policy roles including at the the Centre for the Study of Developing Societies, the International Environmental Law Research Centre.

Angela Kim is a program manager in the City of Los Angeles Mayor's Office of International Affairs where she oversees the development of an inclusive FDI strategy for L.A. and manages the City's SDG online platforms. Angela received her BA and BS from UCLA and her Masters of Environmental Science from the University of Toronto. Pardis Mahdavi, PhD is the provost and executive vice president at the University of Montana. Previously, she was professor and dean of Social Sciences at Arizona State University.

Before coming to Arizona, she was acting dean of the Korbel School of International Studies at the University of Denver (2017–2019), after spending eleven years at Pomona College from 2006–2017 where she most recently served as professor and chair of anthropology and director of the Pacific Basin Institute at Pomona College as well as Dean of Women. Her research interests include gendered labor, human trafficking, migration, sexuality, human rights, transnational feminism, and public health in the context of changing global and political structures. She has published six single authored books and one edited volume in addition to numerous journal and news articles.

Gaea Morales is a PhD candidate in Political Science and International Relations at the University of Southern California. Her research is centered on the question of how global governance ideas translate into local action and the role of sub-national actors in global politics. She received her BA in Diplomacy and World Affairs and French Studies from Occidental College.

Vera Paiva is professor of Social Psychology at the University of São Paulo, where she founded the Interdisciplinary Group for Aids Prevention and co-coordinates the Solidary Research Network to respond to the COVID-19 crisis. She has served on a variety of national and international commissions addressing the psychosocial dimensions of inequality in relation to sexuality, HIV, and health promotion and care.

Momin Rahman is a professor of sociology at Trent University in Canada. His current research is on the conflicts between LGBTQ identities and Muslim cultures, and the experiences of LGBTQ Muslims, including a funded research project on LGBTQ Muslims in Canada. His books include *The Oxford Handbook of Global LGBT and Sexual Diversity Politics* (2020, co-edited with Michael Bosia and Sandra McEvoy), *Homosexualities, Muslim Cultures and Modernity*, (2014), *Gender and Sexuality* (2010, with Stevi Jackson) and *Sexuality and Democracy* (2000).

Nelson Camilo Sánchez is an assistant professor of law, General Faculty, and the Director of the International Human Rights Clinic, at the School of Law at the University of Virginia. He is also a director at the UKRI Gender, Justice and Security Hub.

Shehu S/Fada is from Gusau, Zamfara State in Nigeria and contracted leprosy in his fourth year of primary school. He went to GSS Shinkafi where he finished in 1983. Shehu faced a lot of stigma, discrimination, and isolation in school and in his community. He became the national president of IDEA Nigeria and represented IDEA Nigeria on many occasions including at many events in other countries. He has received numerous national and international awards for his advocacy for people affected by leprosy.

Brenda Shockley is an attorney who worked in the nonprofit community economic development sector in South Los Angeles for over three decades before joining Mayor Garcetti's administration as Deputy Mayor for Economic Opportunity and Chief Equity Officer.

William Paul Simmons is professor of Gender & Women's Studies and Director of the Human Rights Practice program at the University of Arizona. He has more than 25 years of experience as a human rights educator and researcher, including serving as a consultant in a wide range of contexts: in The Gambia, Senegal, Niger, Ghana, Nigeria, Mozambique, Bangladesh, China, Mexico and the United States. His books include *Joyful Human Rights* (2019), *Human Rights Law and the Marginalized Other* (2011), and *Binational Human Rights: The U.S.-Mexico Experience* (2014).

Lara Stemple is the Assistant Dean for Graduate Studies and International Student Programs at UCLA School of Law, where she oversees the law school's LL.M. (masters) and S.J.D. (doctoral) degree programs. Stemple teaches and writes in the areas of human rights, global health, gender, sexuality, and incarceration. Before joining UCLA, Stemple was the Executive Director of the human rights organization Just Detention International and was a Rockefeller Post Doctoral Fellow at Columbia University's Program on Sexuality, Gender, Health, and Human Rights. She also served as the Senior Advocacy Officer at the Pacific Institute for Women's Health. Before that, Stemple worked for the international program at the Center for Reproductive Rights in New York and was a Teaching Fellow at Harvard University. Stemple currently serves as co-Vice Chair of the Board of Directors of the UC Global Health Institute and is a founding faculty member of its Center of Expertise on Women's Health and Empowerment. Stemple has drafted legislation that was signed into law, lobbied members of Congress and United Nations delegates, and testified before legislative bodies. Media commentary has included CNN, National Public Radio, Al Jazeera, the New York Times, the Los Angeles Times, Slate, and The Atlantic.

Dolores Trevizo is professor of Sociology and chair of the Latinx and Latin American Studies Program at Occidental College. She has published articles on protest movements in Mexico since 1968, including those demanding human rights for political dissidents as well as for families of activists disappeared during the dirty war. Her current research on violence and insecurity in Mexico focuses on armed vigilante responses to cartel-related homicides between 2012–2015.

Acknowledgements

We deeply appreciate Noah Yee Yick's invaluable administrative assistance in putting together this volume's manuscript. We also thank Sophia Najafi and Alex Kukura for their editorial assistance. Lastly, we are grateful for the support of the Young Initiative on the Global Political Economy on this project, and most especially for the indefatigable work of its former Assistant Director Chamnan Lim.

Foreword: Reimagining Human Rights

César Rodríguez-Garavito

As the brilliant ethnobotanist Wade Davis has reminded us, despair is an insult to the imagination. He had plenty of data and reason to draw this conclusion. Working with Indigenous peoples around the world, Davis has documented the vast wealth of what he calls the "ethnosphere": the countless inventions – from tools to cuisine to religions to science – that human imagination has produced in order to live in communities and coexist with other forms of life on Earth.[1]

Therefore, the crises that endanger life on Earth today -the climate emergency, the threat of nuclear war, the sixth great species extinction- are also crises of the imagination. The resulting hopelessness is palpable in all fields of human activity, but it is especially poignant in those focused on defending life, such as human rights. While human rights were one of the best human inventions of recent centuries, as the Argentine philosopher Carlos Nino wrote,[2] today they are on the defensive and need to be reinvented.

Although we are certainly not in the "endtimes" of human rights, as some critics have prematurely concluded, it has become patently clear that traditional strategies, narratives, and organizational forms are not always the best fit for the purpose of addressing the mounting existential challenges to human rights. As I have argued elsewhere, although the field is not at a moment of terminal crisis, it is going through a period of profound transition, in which the paradigm of thought and practice that was developed in the 70 years since the adoption of the Universal Declaration of Human Rights is increasingly at odds with the needs of the twenty-first century, to the point that a new paradigm is needed if human rights are to remain relevant and impactful by 2030 and beyond.[3] Yuval Harari has rightly noted that "while human rights movements have developed a very impressive arsenal of arguments and defense against religious biases and human tyrants, this arsenal hardly protects us against consumerist excesses and technological utopias."[4] I would add that it hardly protects us against democratically elected autocrats, planetary risks such as global warming and pandemics, or digital mega-corporations thriving on the accumulation and sale of personal data and the manipulation of human behavior.

---

[1] Wade Davis, *Light at the Edge of the World: A Journey through the Realm of Vanishing Cultures.* Douglas & McIntyre (2007).
[2] Carlos Nino, *Ética y Derechos Humanos* (Astrea, 1984).
[3] *See* César Rodríguez-Garavito, "Human Rights 2030: Existential Challenges and a New Paradigm for the Human Rights Field," in Nehal Bhuta, Florian Hoffmann, Sarah Knuckey, Fréderic Mégret & Margaret Satterthwaite, eds. *The Struggle for Human Rights* (Oxford University Press, 2021), from which this section is partially drawn.
[4] Yuval Harari, *21 Lessons for the 21st Century* (Penguin Random House, 2018) 215.

If imagination is the antidote to despair, it is urgent to reimagine human rights. I believe this involves two interrelated tasks, one practical and the other analytical, to which this book makes notable contributions. On the practical side, reimagining human rights means multiplying, emulating, amplifying and connecting the innovative tactics that movements and organizations around the world create every day, often in the most difficult contexts of the global South. The case studies and "snapshots" in this book are a sampling of the rich repertoire of practices and movements that are giving rise to a new human rights paradigm, from the right to the city movement to the new waves of feminist thought and activism around gender and sexualities to the global explosion of economic and racial justice mobilization. Although not part of the book, it is essential to include among the sources of the new paradigm the youth and Indigenous peoples' movements against ecological collapse, which seek not only the protection of human rights but the preservation of life itself on Earth.

Elsewhere, taking a cue from social innovation studies and initiatives in other fields, I suggest that these and other movements are disrupting the dominant paradigm of human rights in ways that increase the collective capacity and impact of the movement.[5] These constructive disruptions take the form of concrete initiatives that address systemic challenges in human rights and, if successful, have the potential to be scaled to the field level. As shown by the case studies and "snapshots" in this book, they consist of a wide variety of efforts, including novel inter-organizational collaborations, new narratives, the expansion of the concept of rights holder, creative litigation and human rights education that expand the movement's toolkit and knowledge base, and so on. What they all have in common is a deliberate spirit of experimentation and willingness to learn from other fields, and even from failure.

As the title of this volume suggests, these and other innovations are to be found oftentimes at the intersections between movements, disciplines, geographies, generations and tactics. In addition to being *intersectional*, therefore, this book can be seen as *transitional*. In exploring intersectional spaces, it offers evidence and insights that are directly useful for imagining what human rights practice may be beyond the ongoing paradigmatic transition.

The second task that is necessary to reimagine human rights is analytical in nature. In addition to new tactics, we need new concepts and analytical perspectives. A particularly striking feature of the critiques of the human rights movement put forth by authors such as Samuel Moyn and Stephen Hopgood is that it is based on a highly limited view on the practice of human rights. It is a perspective whose eyes are directed largely at the most visible actors in the Global North. For Hopgood, for instance, "Human Rights are a New York-Geneva-London-centered ideology focused on international law, criminal justice, and institutions of global governance. Human Rights are a product of the 1%."[6] As Julieta Lemaitre and Gráinne de Burca have noted in their incisive responses to Moyn's work, his criticisms are almost invariably focused

---

[5]   See "Human Rights 2030," supra n. 1.
[6]   Stephen Hopgood, 'Human Rights: Past Their Sell-By Date' (*Open Global Rights*, 18 June 2013) <https://www.openglobalrights.org/human-rights-past-their-sell-by-date>

on international non-governmental organizations such as Human Rights Watch, as if they were a proxy for the movement writ large.[7]

Documenting and engaging with the everyday life of human rights requires broadening the field of vision well beyond Geneva, London, or New York. This, in turn, calls for two conceptual and methodological moves that capture the circulation of human rights ideas and practices between the local and the global, as illustrated by the chapters in this volume, especially those included in Section 1. First, it entails tracking how the international norms developed in those sites are translated, implemented, indigenized, contested, and even transformed at the national and local levels. Second, it involves looking into the active role of local subjects, including those from subaltern groups, from racially oppressed communities to impoverished classes to women to undocumented migrants to Indigenous peoples and other actors that are lumped together as "victims" in the traditional view of rights. This expanded perspective creates analytical and empirical space to capture the myriad ways in which subaltern actors not only adopt and adapt, but also disrupt, remake, and re-export new norms and frames that challenge the traditional rights paradigm and the rules of neoliberal globalization.

Rather than a homogenous project, the human rights field should be understood as an ecosystem for collaboration, contestation, synergies, and competition among multiple political projects – from the expansion of neoliberal capitalism to anti-capitalist Indigenous peoples' struggles to internet neutrality to gender justice to class-based mobilization for social justice to the youth movement for climate rights and many others. While they all use international human rights as one of their master frames, they do so in a selective and proactive way: they embrace, modify, prioritize, contest, localize, and globalize different pieces of the normative human rights toolkit, thus helping to enforce and transform the master frame in equal measure.

The tradition of law and society studies that this book draws on provides some of the analytical tools that are needed to understand the translation of international human rights into local cultures. For instance, Sally Merry's work on the "vernacularization" of human rights offers a particularly cogent framework for capturing the process running from the global to the local.[8] However, scholars have paid considerably less attention to the process running in the opposite direction, from the local to the global and from the South to the North. Subaltern local actors and their allies not only engage but also contest, transform, and export back to the global arena alternative understandings of those rights.

Put differently, most studies of human rights have been concerned with the *vernacularization of the global* – that is, with the making of the *lingua franca* of

---

[7] *See* Julieta Lemaitre, 'The View from Somewhere: on Samuel Moyn's Not Enough' (*Law and Political Economy Project*, 9 July 2018) <https://lpeproject.org/blog/the-view-from-somewhere-on-samuel-moyns-not-enough/>; Gráinne de Burca, 'Shaming Human Rights' (2018) Jean Monnet Working Paper 2/18 <https://jeanmonnetprogram.org/paper/shaming-human-rights-a-review-of-samuel-moyn-not-enough-human-rights-in-an-unequal-world/>.

[8] Sally Engle Merry, *Human Rights & Gender Violence: Translating International Law into Local Justice* (University of Chicago Press, 2006)

international human rights and its contested adoption at the local scale. We need to be equally concerned with the *globalization of the vernacular* – that is, with the legal and political processes whereby local actors, including subaltern groups, introduce modifications and neologisms into the vocabulary and even the grammar of human rights.[9]

This volume gives us precisely this type of well-rounded and complex account of human rights. Rather than remaining in the comfort of partial views of the movement, it embraces the messiness of the practice of rights and the possibilities of this transitional moment. And it rekindles our imagination at a time when we need it most.

---

[9] See César Rodríguez-Garavito, "The Globalization of the Vernacular: Mobilizing, Resisting, and Transforming International Human Rights from Below," in Philip Alston, ed. *Essays in Honor of Sally Merry* (Oxford University Press, forthcoming), from which this section is partially drawn.

Introduction: Intersections and Transformations

Anthony Tirado Chase, Pardis Mahdavi, and Sofia Gruskin

Human Rights at the Intersections: Transformations through Local, Global, and Cosmopolitan Challenges grapples with two conundrums of global importance. The first is urgent and topical: can human rights invigorate social movements with an alternative, more inclusive vision of the world? The second is more academic and also crucial: can scholars working on human rights contribute to shaping such alternatives in ways that are compelling beyond narrow academic circles? In linking these two conundrums, we underscore the need for meaningful intersections between human rights studies and grassroots action in locales around the world. We take as our call to action the need to build a counterweight strong enough to meet the rising challenge of state-led authoritarian nationalisms.

Our hope is to expand academic intersections with current programmatic and activist efforts to promote and protect the human rights of all people. This is essential to any effort to expand the potential of human rights in all domains, most crucially in the intersections between cultural, economic, political, and social rights. This volume, in short, is a vehicle for a political project: catalyzing debate over key issues that are essential foundations to move toward envisioning compelling alternatives to xenophobic nationalism. It is informed by leading voices in human rights who seek to move beyond their disciplinary silos and engage with other scholarly disciplines and activist realities.

It has been remarkable to observe the number of academic disciplines engaging with human rights in recent years. While the fact of this growth is to be heralded, most often this happens from within isolated disciplinary frames rather than in multi-disciplinary or interdisciplinary ways. As the Sociologist José Julián Lopéz aptly puts it, "the field currently takes the form of an academic archipelago, a series of islands ... relatively isolated from one another."[1] This volume emphasizes, instead, the intersections by deliberately bringing together contributors from many different disciplines, perspectives, and positionalities. The four coeditors come from backgrounds in anthropology, comparative politics, international relations, law, and public health. Each are based at US institutions in ways that inform our positionalities, as does being a refugee from Iran (to Canada), a Colombian American dual citizen, and being children of refugees from Iran and from Nazi-occupied Holland. Contributors come from those

---

[1] José Julián Lopéz, *Human Rights as Political Imaginary* (London: Palgrave Macmillan, 2018), p. 6.

disciplines as well as gender studies, history, philosophy, and sociology and also include practitioners grappling with these issues in real time within both government and civil society spaces. Many work at North American and British academic institutions, bringing to their institutions and to this book voices from twenty countries from the six continents of the world (excluding Antarctica). Most importantly, we bring together a broad number of cases from around the world that highlight transnational connections between the local and the global. It is that transnational positionality that is the essential frame for this volume. The point is always to foreground intersections rather than seeing any particular locality in isolation or as disconnected from global-local currents.

Our hypothesis in bringing together contributors who are diverse in so many senses is that, by intentionally intersecting varied topics, perspectives, contexts, and positions around recurring questions on key human rights issues, we can help move past the field's often tired tropes. This is essential if we are to invigorate what human rights can offer to the cultural, economic, political, and social issues of our time. We recognize that insular academic work has too often failed to learn from activism. By breaking apart disciplinary and geographical borders, we also hope this volume will help rectify some of the disconnects that often exist between academic and activist perspectives. Engaging with fresh approaches is essential if we are to challenge the existential political crises assaulting us on a daily basis.

Our book's four interconnected sections move past monolithic notions of human rights in the hopes of contributing to a more textured, dynamic understanding of human rights' potential. Within each section, contributions from both academics and practitioners break apart the still prevalent assumptions that human rights are a free-floating international regime that should be brought to bear—from the top-down—to locales around the world. This pernicious binary between the global and the local doesn't just mask but also disempowers activism amongst the range of actors that use human rights as a tool toward their empowerment and the creation of more pluralistic social contracts. In short, human rights, as used here, are not a singular regime but, rather, engage a complex set of horizontal and vertical interactions between individuals, communities, and governing entities toward a pressing purpose: re-envisioning our societies.

More specifically, Section 1 ("Exploding the Global-Local Binary in 'Cosmopolitan' Human Rights") challenges assumptions regarding cosmopolitanism, making clear the need for an approach that goes beyond theoretical abstractions to tangibly engage with peoples' lived realities that impel the relevance of human rights. Chapters in this section complicate standard accounts by engaging with how trans-border solidarities and an emphasis on working within local contexts can be mutually empowering rather than contradictory. Section 2 ("Human Rights, the City, and 'Local' Actors") is intimately linked to Section 1. It aims to take Section 1's focus on the "local" one step deeper by highlighting the centrality of cities—as well as other non-state and sub-state actors—in engaging human rights beyond a traditional conceptualization as an international regime constructed by and for nation-states. This section highlights, therefore, how cities as well as other sub-state locales have become key centers for connecting human rights to communities that are constituted transnationally. Human rights can and must engage with governance at the city, nation-state, regional, and global levels, as well as at their intersections.

Sections 3 and 4 take a deep dive into topics that bring to light the issues raised in the previous sections in concrete ways. Sexual rights and feminism were each chosen as a thematic focus because we have observed them as lightning-rod issues within and across disciplinary silos as well as within human rights movements across the globe. Section 3 ("Sexuality and Sexual Rights") illustrates how even efforts to support sexual rights and move toward increasing human rights protections for all people regardless of how they are born, their sexuality, sexual orientation, or gender identity invariably are both constrained and supported by intersections with the same local, national, and global norms, standards and actors brought to light in the chapters above. Section 4 ("Feminism and the 'Triple Bind'") takes on debates around feminism as they have been the center of fractures and fissures in both human rights discourses and feminist movements. Both sections provide examples of what can be learned and applied from these experiences to the overarching questions raised in preceding sections.

Each of the four sections begins with a brief introduction clarifying why the particular thematic issue area was chosen, the particular conundrums it seeks to illustrate, and the issues with which authors are grappling in their chapters and snapshots. We chose these four themes not just because they are each intellectually important and politically urgent (although they are!). We chose them because their intersections speak directly to how we can respond to the dividing and demonizing dark shadow of declining democratic institutions and rising nationalisms. More positively, these intersections show how human rights exist not only in the abstract or as government responsibilities, but as part of grassroots political consciousness and action around the world. These actions must be in synergy with other political and normative impulses that seek to change the unsatisfactory status quo in which we all find ourselves. For human rights to have greater impact in diverse locales and with diverse communities, they must be owned at multiple levels and by multiple actors across the globe. This demands complex ideas of "community" that take as a point of departure that local (and global) communities are neither singular nor insular. Now more than ever they are constituted dynamically in intersectional and transnational contexts. We suggest that, at a time of global, state-led blowback in many parts of the world against human rights, this awareness is essential to opening up new paths for rights activists. And, beyond that, conceptually this volume gives the basis to substantiate in practice the theoretical contention that the human rights regime move past its traditional state-centrism and, instead, forthrightly engage with a blurred world in which identity, community, and governance are plural and multileveled.

Our core argument is that the power of human rights is precisely in the ways in which they are continuously reconstituted and reshaped through interactions amongst those struggling for rights across different domains. We see such mutually empowering conversations as key to ensuring the ongoing relevance of human rights to all struggles. Xenophobic nationalisms always seek to instrumentally target vulnerable communities. And, as is seen in attacks against so-called "gender ideology" by nationalist movements around the world, nondominant sexual and gender communities bear the brunt of that targeting, as do ethnic and racial minorities. But, as well (and bringing us full circle), struggles for sexual and gender rights as well as feminism are also at the forefront of complicating ideas of community beyond the cosmopolitan or the local, hence directly connecting to the contributions in other sections. Sexual rights, gender rights, and feminist struggles have all been at the vanguard of using human rights across multiple levels to challenge the status quo.

Our sub-title of *Transformation through Local, Global, and Cosmopolitan Challenges* flows out of this core argument. It is meant to indicate what we believe to be at the heart of human rights. Human rights must be continuously transformed if they are to be part of challenging exclusionary economic, political, and social structures. This book comes on the heels of the global outpouring of grassroots protests, many seeking to resist state violence in the context of COVID-19 and beyond. Intersections between global and grassroots organizing are essential for human rights to be an effective part of this resistance. We are inspired by these uprisings and how they insist that human rights be envisioned in new and more resonate ways. That is essential if human rights are to be effectively used by social movements to transform our world.

In closing, it is important to note that this book comes out of an ongoing conversation among its contributors; it is not a set of independent chapters chosen by the editors. It flows out of a September 2019 workshop entitled *Cross-cutting Global Conversations on Human Rights: Interdisciplinarity, Intersectionality, and Indivisibility* co-sponsored by Occidental College's Young Initiative on the Global Political Economy, in collaboration with Arizona State University, Indiana University, and the Institute on Inequalities in Global Health, University of Southern California. The results of the workshop convinced us of the need to widen the conversation, including a roundtable series with *Open Global Rights* (September, 2020) and now this book.

Taken together, our hope is to catalyze purposeful action about how we can and must all continuously reimagine what human rights are, and what they potentially can be.

Section One

Exploding the Global-Local Binary in "Cosmopolitan" Human Rights

Introduction

Anthony Tirado Chase[*]

In a world spinning out of control, what is the relevance of this section's discussions of cosmopolitan versus locally oriented politics? Collapsing confidence in international and national governance has led to an inability to deal with global crises—from covid to climate change—and a more general loss of faith in which even the most democratic institutions face popular unrest. In that context, is a theoretical discussion of cosmopolitanism not quaintly archaic?

Perhaps not. This debate is not actually as airily theoretical as it might first appear. The crux of the issue is about if and how human rights might tangibly inform how we engage with these deadly important matters. Contributions in this section have distinct points of entry, take different positions, and illuminate different aspects of cosmopolitanism and exploding a global-local binary in human rights engagements, but each are concerned with a common question: how do we best conceptualize political community in a manner that creates solidarity in confronting the raging issues of the day?

A central lesson to take from these contributions is that conceptualizing community as local versus cosmopolitan makes as little sense as limiting activists' choices to using either local or global political tools in their struggles. Ultimately, we cannot have locally driven politics without a cosmopolitan sense of solidarity, nor can we have a meaningful cosmopolitanism unless it is deeply embedded in local lived realities that impel on-the-ground movements for human rights around the world.

A false binary between cosmopolitan and local is misleading and risks constraining how human rights can empower struggles against status quo power structures. Prioritizing the "cosmopolitan" risks eliding the primacy of the lived realities which motivate political actions. At times discussions of cosmopolitanism conflate critiques of an abstract notion of global community with a critique, at least by implication, of the relevance of global institutions and norms to local politics. Few are seeking cosmopolitanism as an end in itself, but many local communities do see both useful and harmful intersections of global currents with local issues. And, similarly, prioritizing the "local" risks erasing how lived realities are constituted by those

[*] This introduction draws substantially from Chase and Morales, "Cosmopolitanism and lived realities: beyond global-local binaries" (September 2020), available at: https://www.openglobalrights.org/cosmopolitanism-and-lived-realities-beyond-global-local-binaries/. The author acknowledges and very much appreciates Gaea Morales' contributions.

intertwined local, regional, transnational, and global currents. It is not just that it is common to have multiple political identities informed by and connected to multiple communities. It is that to deny that basic reality with a simple idea of "local" is to conceptualize community in an exclusionary manner. Doing so echoes and reinforces xenophobic language that marginalizes minorities and migrants against a mythical notion of "our" singular community.

Moving beyond an abstract local versus cosmopolitan binary is necessary to address human rights crises around the world by mobilizing empathy and solidarity to address distinct yet linked vulnerabilities. Michelle Alexander's *The New Jim Crow* speaks to the urgency of this sort of empathy and solidarity:

> A politics of deep solidarity is beginning to emerge—the only form of politics that holds any hope for our collective liberation .... The future of our democracy may depend on other racial and ethnic groups learning to see that our fates are, in fact, inescapably intertwined .... We must learn to care for one another across all boundaries and borders and build a movement of movements rooted in a love so fierce that when a Mexican child is ripped from the arms of his mother at the border, and when a black child is ripped from the arms of her mother as she's arrested on the streets of New York, and when a white child is ripped from the arms of her mother in a courtroom in Oklahoma, we feel the same pain, the same agony, as though it were our own children.[1]

Social movements, thus, need to recognize that challenging status quo power depends on challenging siloed notions of local versus cosmopolitan ideas of community. Analogously, this also means recognizing that the tools of social struggle should not be siloed either. Instead, organizing in ways that connect across local, national, and global silos is essential to creating the sort of sustainable structural change so needed to counteract the siren song of xenophobic politics.

[1] Michelle Alexander, *The New Jim Crow* (New York: New Press, 2020), p. xliv–xlv.

"A Band Aid on a Bullet Wound": Cosmopolitan Desire in a Pluriversal World

Joe Hoover

We live in unjust times. Yet, as urgent as our current moment feels, it is not unique. Human affairs are inevitably marred by injustice. I offer this pessimistic reminder not to blunt hope our current crises can be addressed, nor to dissuade political action, but to focus on the tension between pursuing an idealized vision of justice and responding to the concrete, disfiguring effects of injustice. To explore the significance of this tension, I draw on Judith Shklar's heterodox reflections on justice. She begins by noting that moral and political philosophers have been more interested in justice than injustice. "They take it for granted that injustice is simply the absence of justice, and once we know what is just, we will know all we need to know."[1] This assumption diverts our attention from the experience of injustice and impairs our analysis of its causes, as it directs our energies to imagining a just order that promises escape from injustice as an act of rational will. Echoes of this idealized understanding can be heard beneath contemporary appeals for a cosmopolitan response to our unjust times. But we should hesitate before we attempt to orient ourselves amidst these resonances.

I am tempted to heed Michael Goodhart's advice in this volume to abandon cosmopolitanism.[2] My instinct is that the concept is inessential to confronting injustice and fighting for our human rights. As I elaborate below, cosmopolitanism has profound limitations as a partisan fighting-creed, diminishing its capacity to confront the resurgence of reactionary ideologies hostile to social difference and democratic equality. In spite of my doubts, I want to resist the inclination to dismiss cosmopolitanism, as it is an ideal valued by many who are committed to the pursuit of justice. My hope is to be a critical friend to those who find meaning and motivation within that tradition. Many contributors to this volume outline a critical vision inspired by cosmopolitan sentiments, such as Shareen Hertel and Kristi Kenyon who both examine how the COVID-19 pandemic has reinforced the importance and complexity of connections

---

[1] Judith N. Shklar, *The Faces of Injustice* (New Haven and London: Yale University Press, 1990), p. 15.
[2] See also, Michael Goodhart, "Forget cosmopolitanism: the future of human rights is local," *Open Global Rights*, November 6, 2020, https://www.openglobalrights.org/forget-cosmopolitanism-the-future-of-human-rights-is-local/.

between the local and global.[3] Hussein Banai puts it most starkly, urging us to cling to cosmopolitan ideals of human equality.[4] Nonetheless, there are practical risks in this clinging, arising from the originary link between cosmopolitanism and the desire for justice as a transcendent ideal order.

Taken impressionistically, cosmopolitanism is an undeniably laudable expression of sympathy for all human beings, especially those in distress. Yet, there are many ways of expressing such concern, many different languages and concepts we might mobilize. It is important to think carefully about what makes cosmopolitanism distinctive, to ask: what other desires does it bring with it? Here I want to focus on the desire for order that haunts cosmopolitanism.[5] But not all ghosts are sinister, and pernicious specters might yet be exorcised. So, my critical investigation is not intended as a categorical rejection.

The desire for order that Shklar identifies is a normal emotional response to life's trials. However, when that desire grows out of an underlying resentment of the world, or a disappointment with the shape it takes, then the longing for order becomes troubling—even destructive. In his essay "Is Life Worth Living?" William James diagnoses what he calls "a nightmare view of life." The nightmare emerges from the gap between the troubles of actual human lives and our hope of finding some deeper truth to our existence, which might provide order. Whether such hope is grounded in faith in divinity or the truth of rational morality, it is the same longing. He writes:

> the visible surfaces of heaven and earth refuse to be brought by us into any intelligible unity at all. Every phenomena that we would praise there exists cheek by jowl with some contrary phenomenon .... Beauty and hideousness, love and cruelty, life and death keep house together in indissoluble partnership; and there gradually steals over us, instead of the old warm notion of a man-loving Deity, that of an awful Power that neither hates nor loves, but rolls all things together meaninglessly to a common doom. This is an uncanny, a sinister, a nightmare view of life, and its peculiar ... poisonousness lies expressly in our holding two things together which cannot possibly agree,—in our clinging on the one hand to the demand that there shall be a living spirit of the whole, and, on the other, to the belief that the course of nature must be such a spirit's adequate manifestation

---

[3]   See also, Shareen Hertel, "Mobilizing empathy for a truly cosmopolitan human rights," *Open Global Rights*, September 30, 2020, https://www.openglobalrights.org/do-sub-state-actors-complicate-how-we-think-of-cosmopolitanism/; and Kristi Heather Kenyon, "Relationship-based cosmopolitanism is key to meaningful but messy rights protections," *Global Open Rights*, October 5–2020, https://www.openglobalrights.org/relationship-based-cosmopolitanism-is-key-to-meaningful-but-messy-rights-protections/.

[4]   Hussein Banai, "Everyday Cosmopolitanism: clinging to the faith of common humanity," *Open Global Rights*, October 8, 2020, https://www.openglobalrights.org/everyday-cosmopolitanism-clinging-to-the-faith-of-common-humanity/.

[5]   The lingering concern with order is seen at the very end of Kenyon's contribution to this volume, where she sensitively explores "the promise and potential of decentralized human rights discourse" but worries about the "perilous unpredictability" of decentralizing the meaning of human rights.

and expression. It is in the contradiction between the supposed *being* of a spirit that encompasses and owns us and with which we ought to have some communion, and the character of such a spirit, as revealed by the visible world's course, that this particular death-in-life paradox and this melancholy-breeding puzzle reside.[6]

The dilemma is not relieved by abandoning faith in a natural order constructed in accord with divine or rational principles. This simply increases our sense of estrangement, leaving us lost in a "multiverse" where we cannot find the communion promised by a just and orderly "universe."[7] Before considering how James's advice for overcoming the nightmare view of life can help us embrace a more critical cosmopolitan orientation, the deep link between the desire for an ordered moral universe and cosmopolitanism needs elaboration.

A word's etymology is not its destiny, but attention to origins can expose the hidden shape of those concepts that shape us. Ubiquitous appeals to cosmopolitanism over the past forty years justify reflection on its ancient origins. However, rather than rendering the ancient Greeks as direct forebears of European modernity, I want to ponder the strangeness of their thought and the tensions it contained. Cosmopolitan, most simply, describes a citizen of the world, which we already know. But what is the world that Diogenes, and others, imagined themselves citizens of? The κόσμος (cosmos) named an orderly arrangement before it referred to the world, describing imposing columns of soldiers in the warring armies of Homer's epic poetry, and the bejeweled garments of rulers and gods, basking in the grandeur of their power.[8] As Greek culture developed, cosmos came to refer to a singular and ordered world, in which the natural and divine were properly arranged—the arrangement a good unto itself, the highest good, in fact.[9] Finally, only with the birth of Greek philosophy did the cosmos become an abstraction, a rational order behind the veil of experience, and a logical necessity to securing true justice.[10] In this transformation, presented in abridged form, we can detect the need cosmopolitanism has long satisfied. Namely, a longing for order in everyday existence, reflecting our dissatisfaction with the crude excess and violence of worldly politics—it becomes a wish to escape from a life beset by disorder, evil, and falseness. But this seeking after a rational and just order does not eliminate the powerful forces causing injustice, which make life difficult and dangerous. The desire for escape from life may inculcate a stoic refusal of power, or inspire utopian attempts to moralize it, but in

[6] William James, "Is life worth living?" *International Journal of Ethics* 6, no. 1 (1895), 8–9. [Emphasis in the original.]
[7] James, "Is life worth living?" p. 10.
[8] Jaan Puhvel, "The origins of Greek Kosmos and Latin Mundus," *The American Journal of Philology* 97, no. 2 (1976), 154–167.
[9] Catherine M. Chin, "Cosmos," in *Late Ancient Knowing: Explorations in Intellectual History*, eds, Catherine M. Chin and Moulie Vidas (Oakland: University of California Press, 2015), p. 99–116.
[10] Paul Cartledge, "Introduction: defining a kosmos," in *Kosmos: Essays in Order, Conflict and Community in Classical Athens*, eds, Paul Cartledge, Paul Millet, and Sitta von Reden (Cambridge: Cambridge University Press, 1998), p. 3–4.

either case, cosmopolitanism has had an intimate and ambiguous relationship to the exercise of unjust power.[11]

A history of cosmopolitanism is beyond my scope here,[12] but it is important to note that its fortunes track the rise and fall of universalizing imperial projects. In the ancient world, cosmopolitanism waxed with the expanding empire of Alexander the Great, as well as Rome's growing dominion. Taking more Manichean form, it influenced Christian ideas of just war and natural law, and returned to prominence during the Enlightenment, as European colonialism spread around the world. And in the contemporary era it reclaimed its prestige, and became indelibly associated with human rights,[13] at the moment US hegemony reached its post-Cold War peak. Imperial projects inherently try to bring the world into a singular order, and as such are necessarily violent and destructive. The supposition I ask the reader to grant is that both the harm and disorder attending imperial projects, as well as the attempt to moralize such overwhelming power, engender a distinctive cosmopolitan desire for *universal* moral order.

In unjust times we dream of a more harmonious world, where suffering, violence, and oppression are unknown. For several decades, as the economic, social, and political changes wrought by neoliberal globalization took hold, we have been told the path to that better world is a liberal cosmopolitan one. The central claim of this renewed universalizing vision is that progress requires the extension of equal moral concern to everyone, regardless of their diverse identities and affiliations. As a political project, it demands a move from exclusive national identities and rigidly bordered states, to a global society of free individuals, an ideal practically expressed in human rights, international law, and global governance. It is a dream promising respect for humanity and a rational, rule-based global order.

But as we survey our world today, such cosmopolitan hopes are tragically unrealized. The power of the state has been expanded by new weapons and tools of surveillance, while the allure of virulent nationalism and vicious xenophobia has returned with surprising force. Human rights and international institutions are hamstrung due to the reassertion of state sovereignty by a new generation of illiberal leaders. The tactics of social movements, instrumental in the creation of human rights, have been co-opted and distorted by brutish campaigns seeking to undermine inclusive democratic politics at the local, national, and global levels. In analyzing the current backlash against globalization and liberal cosmopolitanism, Colin Crouch argues we are seeing a return to exclusive nationalism and the reclaiming of privileged identities, as people reject Enlightenment rationalism and the globalization of economic and social life. He

---

[11] As Haglund notes in this volume, we struggle to identify and understand the structural causes of injustice, the way in which the order of the world is the problem. Cosmopolitanism as conventionally conceived does little to illuminate structural injustice, instead it encourages us to dream of a form of order untouched by injustice.

[12] A brief but insightful overview can be found in Pauline Kleingeld and Eric Brown, "Cosmopolitanism," in *The Stanford Encyclopedia of Philosophy*, ed. Edward N. Zalta (Winter 2019 Edition), https://plato.stanford.edu/archives/win2019/entries/cosmopolitanism/.

[13] Goodhart, in this volume, traces this process of entwinement.

distinguishes two axes of conflict to explain this situation, with the tension between universal individualism and communal tradition on the one hand, and free competition and social equality on the other. Understanding these tensions helps make sense of the unexpected—such as working-class voters electing billionaire autocrats. Taking emotional identification in politics seriously, Crouch asks, "do transnational commitments have enough emotional energy to transcend the nation's demand of a monopoly of loyalty?"[14] His response is to offer a more egalitarian and rooted cosmopolitanism, grounded in the hope that a younger generation, at ease with unbounded and multiple political identities, might realize such a project.

While Crouch provides an attractive cosmopolitan alternative, drawing it away from neoliberalism, and toward democracy and social justice, he misses the central problem. Achieving cosmopolitanism, for Crouch, is a matter of motivating popular attachment to a common human identity—and making it our fundamental moral and political affiliation. It requires that we see all individuals as sharing an essential nature, enabling the inclusion of difference into a single moral order. Therefore, the problem is one of overcoming people's irrational attachment to social tradition and communal identity, so that "they" can desire to be included in "our" rational plans. The path to this better world is through the extension of universal human rights and the creation of institutions that can assure their authority.

The abstraction of liberal cosmopolitanism makes it difficult to see that our most pressing problem is not an irrational attachment to particular identities, but a deeper and more damaging hierarchy of humanity that cannot be reasoned away. The imagined liberal subject, agreeing rational contracts or claiming universal rights, invites us to dream of a new world without addressing the reality of injustice in the actual world,[15] stranding us in a contemporary version of James's nightmare vision of life.

The promise of cosmopolitanism is specious if we neglect the malignant exclusions at its center. To speak against universality now, while violent identity conflicts proliferate, may seem obscene. However, if cosmopolitanism is to provide an escape from the nightmare life of the early twenty-first century, then it must be critically re-examined, as the experience of communities fighting against xenophobia, systemic racism, gender violence, deprivation, and inequality reveal a fundamental inadequacy.[16] Cosmopolitanism is historically intertwined with European modernity and coloniality.[17] As Kimberly Hutchings writes, "[t]his is not just about the explicitly

---

[14] Colin Crouch, *The Globalization Backlash* (Cambridge: Polity, 2019), p. 83.

[15] This intellectual phenomenon, and especially its racialised dimension, is captured by Charles W. Mills in his classic *The Racial Contract*. In this volume, Goodhart, Haglund, and Hertel argue in different ways that contemporary liberal cosmopolitan cannot properly conceive or respond to global inequalities. Charles W. Mills, *The Racial Contract* (Ithaca and London: Cornell University Press, 1997).

[16] Patricia Hill Collin, *Black Feminist Thought: Knowledge, Consciousness, and the Politics of Empowerment* (New York and London: Routledge, 2009), p. 46–48.

[17] Aníbal Quijano, "Coloniality and modernity/rationality," *Cultural Studies* 21, no. 2 (2007), 168–178.

genocidal effects of colonialism but about how even those members of the colonized who are not killed are deprived of the world they previously inhabited,"[18] as the many worlds outside European modernity were annihilated or subjugated. Critics of cosmopolitanism as a form of coloniality focus on its ontological understanding of the world as universal rather than pluriversal. Universality subsumes human differences under an essential moral sameness, which is inadequate to overcome "familiar hierarchical claims about the 'backwardness' of those who do not share Western ways of life,"[19] because that hierarchy is the necessary ground of liberal cosmopolitanism's presumed moral necessity and superiority.[20] This presents many profound challenges for those moved by, and hoping to advance, cosmopolitan ideals. Here I focus on two.

First, as Shklar warned, a love of ideal justice may blind us to everyday injustices arising from the normal operation of our social and political systems, especially those held in place by civic passivity and the silent acceptance of injustice in exchange for a peaceful life.[21] She challenges us, saying, "we do not care as much about justice as we say,"[22] perhaps in part because we want to believe in the inherent goodness of order itself. Further, if we do not engage with the reality of injustice, we willfully ignore that distinguishing between mere misfortune and injustice, as well as who we recognize as a victim of injustice, are deeply political matters. Appeals to humanity, the pronouncement of universal standards, are empty (or worse) if they don't begin with the difficult work of identifying and dismantling the structures of oppression and domination that perpetuate injustice.[23] Planning for a different world, if it is more than utopian fantasy, must address the legacies of existing injustice and embrace democracy in a radical, inclusive form. As the rapper Black Thought wrote, during the difficult and chaotic spring of 2020:

> The murder of black, brown and Indigenous men, women and children is a GLOBAL tradition. A heritage. A long legacy. So . . . news of such carnage is losing its sensation as we grow numb. Sad part is it's likely to get far worse before matters get any better. I do feel a paradigm shift as some truth has come to light but until the greater truth, the one about the real history of the world and how things became the way they are is told, I fear it'll be business as usual. A band aid on a bullet wound.[24]

Justice requires a reckoning with the murder, theft, rape, and displacement of those treated as less-than-human. Didactic commands to recognize our common humanity

---

[18] Kimberly Hutchings, "Decolonizing global ethics: Thinking with the pluriverse," *Ethics and International Affairs* 33, no. 2 (2019), 117.

[19] Hutchings, "Decolonizing global ethics."

[20] Enrique Dussel, "Eurocentrism and modernity," *boundary 2* 20, no. 3 (1993), 65–76.

[21] Shklar, *The Faces of Injustice*, p. 39–45.

[22] Shklar, *The Faces of Injustice*, p. 45.

[23] Iris Marion Young, *Justice and the Politics of Difference* (Princeton, NJ and Oxford: Princeton University Press, 2011), p. 37–38.

[24] Tariq Trotter (Black Thought), "Burning Building," Instagram photo, May 29, 2020, https://www.instagram.com/p/CAxhbszFPjL/.

are insufficient because who gets to be human, and who decides, is the fundamental problem. A cosmopolitanism worthy of our effort must begin with those fighting for their own humanity, who are dedicated to building the new relationships necessary for the realization of true human empathy, otherwise it will remain an ideology of the privileged.

And this brings us to a second challenge cosmopolitanism must face, can it confront and rectify the hierarchy of humanity it is built upon? This question has no easy answer. We might start by confronting the desire for universal order and its accompanying fear of disorder. We see this desire at work in liberal cosmopolitanism's ambiguous relationship to freedom; it venerates the moral equality of all individuals as autonomous actors yet insists the use of our freedom must be constrained by the demands of reason. But what if that rational constraint becomes the source and justification for an unbearable, unjust order? What other desires could motivate cosmopolitanism? I want to briefly consider two accounts of the desire to escape from the orderly, which might provide inspiration.

First, Richard Sennett describes how the women of ancient Athens celebrated an unofficial summer ritual, the *Adonia*.[25] Intended to mourn and celebrate Adonis, as a hero and accommodating lover of women, the ritual took place on the rooftops of Athenian homes. The women gathered, under cover of night and enveloped in the sensuous aroma of burning incense, to celebrate their desires in the company of other women, drinking, joking, and engaging in anonymous amorous activities. The ritual was unrecognized by the city, and philosophers like Plato were baffled by the irrational hedonism practiced in these dark and transgressive spaces, where "women momentarily and bodily stepped out of the conditions imposed on them by the dominant order of the city."[26]

This same desire to escape the order of the world is explored by Saidiya Hartman. In her critical fabulation of the wayward lives of young Black women arriving in northern US cities at the end of the nineteenth century, she traces the limits the social order placed on the oppressed.[27] Fleeing the racial subjugation of the South, these young women arrived in the supposedly progressive North, only to find their freedom brutally restricted. She tells the story of Mattie, arriving in New York from Virginia, seeking liberation and opportunity, but finding constraint and drudgery.[28] Hartman reveals the possibilities opened up by Mattie's discovery and pursuit of sexual desire, which leads to social approbation but also the uncovering of an anarchic form of freedom.

> To esteem her acts, to regard rather than vilify Mattie's restive longing, is to embrace the anarchy—*the complete program of disorder*, the abiding desire to change the

[25] Richard Sennett, *Flesh and Stone: The Body and the City in Western Civilization* (New York and London: W.W. Norton, 1994), p. 73–80.
[26] Sennett, *Flesh and Stone*, p. 80.
[27] Saidiya Hartman, *Wayward Lives, Beautiful Experiments: Intimate Histories of Social Upheaval* (London: Serpent's Tail, 2019).
[28] Hartman, *Wayward Lives*, p. 45–76.

world, the tumult, upheaval, open rebellion—attributed to wayward girls. It is to attend to other forms of social life, which cannot be reduced to transgression or to nothing at all, and which emerge in the world marked by negation, but exceed it.[29]

These glimpses of the desire to evade and surpass the given order, what we might call counter-desires, can inspire a cosmopolitanism moved by different needs, by a desire for disorder as the condition of possibility for the creative, excessive—even unsettling—freedom to change the world. Clinging to conventional cosmopolitanism gets uncomfortably close to a fear of the free, wild, disordered, and creative impulses of humanity. Can cosmopolitans learn to love differently, and more dangerously?

To return to James and how we might overcome the nightmare view of life, he counsels that, in place of a desire for moral order, we might rely upon vital instinct in our fight against the evils of the world, accepting suffering as inherent to the struggle to live. Yet the women celebrating the *Adonia* suggest a richer vitality, as does Millie's anarchic, libidinal pursuit of freedom. And James's own desire to live exceeds the stoic acceptance of suffering, extends to a more protean ethos at home in a pluriverse, even invigorated by it. The uncertainty that attends a desire to escape from too much order is made equally of fear and hope, and as James says, "we are free to trust at our own risk anything that is not impossible,"[30] such that even if a pluriversal citizen is a so far unrealized hope, it nonetheless may be worthy of our effort. But it will not be discovered as a finished ideal, rather it is a possibility struggling to be made real, "something really wild in the Universe which we, with all our idealities and faithfulness, are needed to redeem."[31]

This fight, however, is defined by the difficult politics of building non-hierarchical forms of solidarity, and the challenge of navigating the deep differences that arise when plural worlds coexist. Fighting for a disorderly and pluriversal cosmopolitanism is neither easy nor safe, but there are guides with whom we might travel. As human rights activist Virginia Lee said to me when discussing her longtime work in Washington DC, a more just world must be built "out of the experiences of the oppressed" and seek to create "relationships of solidarity and service rather than dependence and superiority."[32] This work will be painful for those habituated to assume the privilege to define and speak for humanity. As Hutchings notes, it requires working with dissonance as a vital part of creativity, putting "one's own sense of self and entitlement to one side."[33] She continues:

> such work builds a pluriversal ethics not theoretically but in contingent practices of accommodation. Any such practice is fundamentally contingent upon the recognition of which relations are important within a particular context. It leaves

---

[29] Hartman, *Wayward Lives*, p. 62. [Emphasis in the original.]
[30] James, "Is life worth living?" p. 20.
[31] James, "Is life worth living?" p. 23.
[32] Joe Hoover, *Reconstructing Human Rights: A Pragmatist and Pluralist Inquiry in Global Ethics* (Oxford: Oxford University Press, 2016), p. 10–11.
[33] Hutchings, "Decolonizing global ethics," p. 122.

a permanent legacy not in a change in ethical commitments but in the sedimentation of ethical capacities, of self-restraint and humility, to limit the imperial reach of those commitments.[34]

A pluriversal global ethics will be defined by ongoing struggle, constant negotiation, and contingent moments of compromise. Our moral ideals must be built from the material of our actual, messy, and deeply plural world, not on the denial and monistic rationalization of it.

The flash of a more pluriversal ideal can be seen in Walt Whitman's "Song of Myself," where he writes:

> Walt Whitman, a *kosmos*, of Manhattan the son,
> Turbulent, fleshy, sensual, eating, drinking and breeding,
> No sentimentalist, no stander above men and women or apart
> from them,
> No more modest than immodest
>
> Unscrew the locks from the doors!
> Unscrew the doors themselves from their jambs!
>
> Whoever degrades another degrades me,
> And whatever is done or said returns at last to me.
>
> Through me the afflatus surging and surging, through me the
> current and index.
>
> I speak the pass-word primeval, I give the sign of democracy,
> By God! I will accept nothing which all cannot have their
> counterpart of on the same terms.
>
> Through me many long dumb voices,
> Voices of the interminable generations of prisoners and slaves,
> Voices of the diseas'd and despairing and of thieves and dwarfs,
> Voices of cycles of preparation and accretion,
> And of the threads that connect the stars, and of wombs and
> of the father-stuff,
> And of the rights of them the others are down upon,
> Of the deform'd, trivial, flat, foolish, despised,
> Fog in the air, beetles rolling balls of dung.[35]

---

[34] Hutchings, "Decolonizing global ethics," p. 122.
[35] Walt Whitman, *Leaves of Grass* (New York: Bantam Books, [1892] 1983), p. 41–42.

Whitman's final image is, I think, especially apt in our current moment, as we find ourselves struggling for human rights, for a more just world, whatever our particular attachment to cosmopolitan tradition. But to complement Whitman, we might return one last time to ancient Greece. In Aristophanes' comedy, "Peace," the protagonist Tygaeus ascends to heaven on a dung beetle.[36] When his daughter asks why he did not choose Pegasus as a more heroic mount, he practically reflects that he will need half the rations for his journey, as his farcical steed is sustained by excrement. Assured in his choice, Tyageus nonetheless labors to keep the beetle true to its heavenly course, as his coleopteran companion struggles to resist the temptations of the earthly latrines below. A humbled cosmopolitanism could do worse than to trade images of armies, bejeweled finery, and a rational cosmos, for the quotidian figure of a beetle rolling its dung ball up a hill, and to accept that the inescapable shit of the world is part of life as we engage in the difficult work of improving our plural, contradictory, and always unfinished world.

---

[36] Aristophanes, *The Birds and Other Plays* (London: Penguin, 2003), p. 91–46.

Snapshot #1: Localism vs. Globalism: Authoritarianism's Battlefield in the Arab Region

Bahey eldin Hassan[1]

The binary of human rights' universalism or cultural relativism was a central theme that dominated public debate after the first human rights organizations in the Arab region were established. It was a battlefield not only with Arab governments, but also with political and intellectual opposition figures, especially Islamists and pan-Arabists. Five decades later, this heated contention dwindled in favor of the universalist position. This was not only a result of the sustained and creative engagement of human rights defenders from different backgrounds, but also due to escalating repression, the rise of a globalized internet community, and the rise of global solidarity with local demands for rights and freedoms. It became clearer for average "locals" in authoritarian countries that their chance of seizing their rights is far more likely if their local demands are shared globally. This might be an indication of both a rising ethical sense of belonging to a globalized community and an increasing instrumental sense of the value of these types of global connections.

In the early 1990s, the Cairo Institute for Human Rights Studies (CIHRS) was one of the first Egyptian human rights organizations to have a PO Box. Some of the mail we received didn't even have a specific address; the words "human rights" (in Arabic) on the envelopes led the letters to be delivered to the CIHRS. Many of those were addressed to non-existent entities: the International or World Human Rights Organization. I always wished I could interview their authors to better understand how they saw their world. Why did they think that an international human rights organization could help with their local injustices? Why didn't they address themselves to institutions like the Organization of the Islamic Conference or the Cairo-based League of Arab States?

The letters were written by dispossessed people who sought salvation through what might be described as a message in a bottle. It was clear to me that those letters came mostly from outside Cairo,—from underprivileged and seemingly uneducated Egyptians complaining about life's hardships, be those economic, social, religious, or police harassment. Their conception of "human rights" was synonymous with "a better life." Those average Egyptians looked at human rights organizations as "global social protectors" that would deliver on citizens' entitlement to a better, more humane life.

---

[1] Director of the Cairo Institute for Human Rights Studies (CIHRS).

During the January 2011 uprising in Egypt, I saw on CNN a clip that featured someone who could have been one of those who sent the letters that CIHRS received. The clip showed an average Egyptian yelling in Tahrir Square that all he, and the other protestors, want is to live like Western citizens. He was not asking to live like an upper-class Egyptian, nor was he asking to emigrate to Europe. He was asking for his humanity.

For many decades, the regime and the Islamists have—for different reasons—been the actors most resistant to comprehensive human rights progress in Egypt. But since the military coup of 2013, Islamist approaches to the issue became more complex. For instance, Islamists had been antagonistic to the notion of the universalism of human rights and supporters of the implementation of the death sentence in Egypt. Yet, as Egypt experiences the most brutal regime in its modern history and Islamists are among its primary victims, that has changed; Islamists actively avoid public debates on human rights, particularly regarding the abolition of the death sentence. The regime, on the other hand, has doubled down on its attempts to undermine the universalism of human rights. Given the regime's brutality and Egypt's increasing economic hardship, it became clear to the regime that it has lost its moral raison d'être. It has, therefore, resorted to exaggerating the alleged tension between local and global values as its main ideological battlefield with local human rights communities.

President Abdel-Fattah al-Sisi publicly attempts to invalidate the applicability of universal human rights on the Egyptian people. He alleges that those norms are only valid for Westerners and that only the "Egyptian concept of human rights" applies to Egyptians. He never, of course, elaborates specifics of what this "Egyptian concept" might be. In 2018, the Egyptian rubber-stamp Parliament[2] adopted one of the most oppressive pieces of legislation in Egypt's modern history; it purportedly addresses cybercrimes but in fact penalizes anyone who attacks what the law calls "family principles or values of the Egyptian society."[3] The law does not define the so-called "Egyptian family's principles and values." Instead, it imposes a subjective narrow understanding of family's values in a country well known for its multiethnic, multireligious, and multicultural society across diverse rural, urban, Bedouin, and Nubian communities.[4] Moreover, the Public Prosecutor established a monitoring unit that operates under a fascist slogan: "The Purge of Social Media, in collaboration with the department of Morality Police at the Ministry of Interior."[5] It goes without saying, the targeted victims are exclusively women that do not belong to the "upper class."

The regime has understood that the potential for universalism of human rights to operate as a conductor for global–local connections is one of the biggest threats to its

[2]　France 24. 2021. Egypt to vote for new 'rubber-stamp' parliament. France 24. [online] Available at: <https://www.france24.com/en/live-news/20201022-egypt-to-vote-for-new-rubber-stamp-parliament> [Accessed 29 September 2021].

[3]　Cairo Institute for Human Rights Studies. 2021. Egypt: In security campaign to protect family values, Public Prosecution abdicates its duty to protect citizens. Cairo Institute for Human Rights Studies. [online] Available at: <https://cihrs.org/egypt-in-security-campaign-to-protect-family-values-public-prosecution-abdicates-its-duty-to-protect-citizens/?lang=en> [Accessed 29 September 2021].

[4]　Cairo Institute for Human Rights Studies. 2021. Egypt.

[5]　Cairo Institute for Human Rights Studies. 2021. Egypt.

authoritarian project. It accordingly prioritizes isolating Egyptians by attempting to cut them off from the outside world, propagating the idea that due to social context they are not entitled to the same rights as others. Today's Egypt is no longer just a scene of an unprecedented level of impunity and massive human rights crimes. In order to shield itself from criticism, the current military regime has waged a war of ideas on the concept of human rights itself. This aims to woo ultra-conservatives by building an ideological wall between Egyptians and their basic rights and freedoms under the guise of protecting family values.[6] The elite intellectual debate from five decades ago on universalism versus cultural relativism has been transformed into a daily battlefield for individual freedoms of average Egyptians.

---

[6] Al-Monitor: The Pulse of the Middle East. 2021. TikTok girl's detention brings Egyptian human rights into spotlight. [online] Available at: <https://www.al-monitor.com/originals/2021/04/tiktok-girls-detention-brings-egyptian-human-rights-spotlight> [Accessed 29 September 2021].

2

Relishing the Roots: The Promise and Peril of Decentralizing Human Rights Discourse

Kristi Heather Kenyon

"konoway tillicums klatawa kunamokst klaska mamook okoke huloima chee illahie"
(Chinook jargon "everyone was thrown together to make this strange new country.")[1]

The yellow-brown sky smells like a campfire from forest fires hours away. Flags hang limply at half-mast in front of empty schools, and homemade signs in various shades of orange state "every child matters." It is a recognition that has come too late for the hundreds of children whose tiny unlabeled remains are re-discovered this spring and summer at former Indian Residential Schools finally bringing to light the horror that Indigenous people have been recounting for decades.[2] In Winnipeg (Canada), where I live, a statue of Queen Victoria is torn down by a crowd, its pedestal marked with orange handprints. COVID-19 continues to limit in-person interaction. My research projects in Ghana, Botswana and South Africa are conducted by zoom, and my students—moved home to rural areas having lost the jobs that enabled them to live in the city—struggle with the shaky internet access that is now their lifeline to education, services and community. Protestors block hospitals doors to object to mask and vaccine mandates and advocate "accessibility" and references to "human rights" become frequent in the news, on placards, and in social media.

---

[1] Chinook jargon is a trade language from North America's northwest coast. It is formed by and used in cross-cultural interaction. This passage is from Lieutenant Governor Iona Campagnolo's inauguration speech in which she referenced Terry Glavin's poem "Rain Language." This quotation refers to British Columbia and the people who populate it, I use it here with a more ethereal meaning of 'country' that we are all thrown together in, and to make, this unusual time.

[2] Courtney Dickson and Bridgette Watson, "Remains of 215 children found buried at former B.C. residential school, First Nation says," *CBC News*, May 27, 2021, https://www.cbc.ca/news/canada/british-columbia/tk-eml%C3%BAps-te-secw%C3%A9pemc-215-children-former-kamloops-indian-residential-school-1.6043778.

Olivia Stefanovich, "Flags will remain at half-mast until agreement is reached with Indigenous leaders: Trudeau," *CBC News*, September 10, 2021, https://www.cbc.ca/news/politics/canadian-flags-to-remain-at-half-mast-residential-schools-1.6170504.

It is a difficult and important time to be thinking about human rights, solidarity, cosmopolitanism and the promise of broadening the public conversation around human rights. In its form, content and rhythm, this chapter is a product of this uneasy liminal space of connection and disconnection. Drawing on my research in Southern Africa and experiences in pandemic Winnipeg, I focus on the components of emergent human rights discourses informed and shaped by both the local and the global. I argue that community is critical to a robust rooted conceptualization and articulation of human rights.

"motho ke motho ka batho" (Setswana, "a person is a person through other people")[3]

Although often framed in individual terms, human rights are inherently relational. They regulate and guide how we live together. Community is a critical component of human rights in three important ways. First, it is the setting within which human rights are necessary—most human rights relate to our interactions. Second, it is the context where we experience connection and relatedness—it is the sphere where we can become human to each other. Third, it is where we develop meaningful interpretations of human rights that resonate in our cultural, political and historical locales. The second of these components is the glue that binds this trifecta. Community is the place where we experience mutual recognition, interconnection and consequent empathy.[4] As the African philosophical concept of *botho* or *ubuntu*[5] explains, "one cannot be a human being alone, only in community."[6] It is through relationships that we have the potential to create, recognize and honor each other's humanity. The global human rights regime depends on community. The promise and challenge of our current era is to engage in these relationships and nurture community across distance, in virtual spaces, across painful divides, over masked expressions, and through differences in culture, politics and ways of life.

Conceptual Legitimacy and Rootedness

Human rights did not come in a package on a ship which sailed from Europe and docked in Cape Town and I don't know came on either horseback or donkeyback to Botswana. It is a concept which has existed amongst peoples from time immemorial.[7]

---

[3] Augustine Shutte, *Philosophy for Africa* (Milwaukee: Marquette University Press, 1995), p. vi.
[4] Shareen Hertel. "Mobilizing empathy for a truly cosmopolitan human rights," *Open Global Rights*, 30 September 2020. Available via https://www.openglobalrights.org/do-sub-state-actors-complicate-how-we-think-of-cosmopolitanism/
[5] The concept is common in many parts of sub-Saharan Africa, *botho* is the Setswana term, *ubuntu* the isiZulu and isiXhosa term.
[6] M. Munyaka and M. Mothlabi, "Ubuntu and its sociomoral significance," in *African Ethics: An Anthology of Comparative and Applied Ethics*, ed. M.F. Murove (Scottsville, South Africa: University of KwaZulu-Natal Press, 2009), p. 68.
[7] Alice Mogwe, as interviewed in *Botho: LGBT Lives in Botswana*, [film], 2013. https://vimeo.com/69577157.

The relationship between the "international"—understood as global centers of power, and the seat of UN institutions—and the local is often framed as one of unidirectional dependence. In this depiction, information "trickles down" from global to local,[8] bringing with it legitimacy, authority and sometimes funding. Local human rights activists, organizations and movements are portrayed as requiring material and conceptual support from the international. This incomplete depiction obscures and marginalizes the important role that local activists play in supporting human rights in and beyond their communities, not only practically, but conceptually. Although international treaties and mechanisms formalize and codify human rights, their legitimacy is fed from these local roots. These international structures would become stale without regular infusions of local innovation.

Indeed, Hopgood has described global "Human Rights" as "past their sell-by date" arguing that we may be "on the verge of the imminent decay of the Global Human Rights Regime."[9] He adds that although "[g]lobalization means diversity," in practice 'Human Rights' are "a kind of secular monotheism with aspirations to civilize the world."[10] This global evangelism typically engages shallowly at best with existing understandings of human rights. In the words of a participant in my research, "human rights is the new kind of missionary. Back in the day they came and they told us about Jesus. Now they come and tell us about human rights." But, as another research participant noted, "human rights are not new," adding "our ancestors have been singing this song forever," if perhaps with slightly different lyrics. At issue here is not a questioning of the relative newness of state-centric formalized human rights structures, but a questioning of the cultural ownership of human rights' conceptual core. Explaining the importance of local human rights messaging she notes:

> I think a lot of the times in Botswana we link [human rights] to *botho* because it's the easiest way to describe it. [...] Because I think just the concept beyond that has always been linked to something that has been brought from the West. And in order not for people to get caught up in that [...] you try to steep it in culture. And so then—you're bringing it home for them so that they can relate. Because in terms of anyone taking on board any information or you changing a mindset, they must be able to relate, otherwise it's just a foreign concept and they feel that it's being imposed.

---

8   Kristi Heather Kenyon, "Building up vs. tricking down: human rights in Southern Africa," *Open Global Rights*. 16 Nov 2017. https://www.openglobalrights.org/building-up-vs-trickling-down-human-rights-in-southern-africa/; Kristi Heather Kenyon, "Relationship-based cosmopolitanism is key to meaningful but messy rights protections" 5 Oct 2020. https://www.openglobalrights.org/relationship-based-cosmopolitanism-is-key-to-meaningful-but-messy-rights-protections/.

9   Stephen Hopgood, "Human rights: past their sell-by date," *Open Global Rights* June 18, 2013, https://www.opendemocracy.net/en/openglobalrights-openpage/human-rights-past-their-sell-by-date/; Stephen Hopgood, The Endtimes of Human Rights (Ithaca, NY: Cornell University Press, 2015), p. vxi.

10 Stephen Hopgood, "Human rights: past their sell-by date," *Open Global Rights* June 18, 2013, https://www.opendemocracy.net/en/openglobalrights-openpage/human-rights-past-their-sell-by-date/; Stephen Hopgood, The Endtimes of Human Rights (Ithaca, NY: Cornell University Press, 2015), p. vxi.

A growing body of literature examines the ways in which local human rights activists contribute not only to the practice, but also to the conceptualization of human rights. Zwart, for example examines how local culture can, facilitate the meaningful "implementation of international human rights."[11] Merry's work on "vernacularization," focuses on the role of intermediary "knowledge brokers" in both adopting and adapting international language and frameworks.[12] Civil society actors that exist in a middle space between the grass roots and the international can play an important role in interpreting, "framing,"[13] "localizing,"[14] translating,[15] and "vernacularizing"[16] human rights in order to increase their local resonance and advocate effectively. Local approaches, however, are not only about adopting and adapting human rights concepts from the international sphere to the local context. "Local" is not only a destination, nor is it a conceptual void.

Levitt and Merry speak about hybridity and creation as they describe how activists mix international concepts with local "ideological and social attributes," in the process "wrestling" with ideas from near and far to "make something new."[17] Englund argues that locally grounded insights are "more than mere background to the discourse" and "more fruitful perspectives into translation are possible when discourse and its social and political context are understood to constitute one another."[18] It is this mutual constitution that is critical—within it recognition that conceptual "trickling up" provides the lifeblood to international structures without which they can become hollow and disconnected. Interaction with these locally embedded perspectives on human rights are crucial to the international as well as the local. Past debates on culture and human rights have been preoccupied by universalism versus cultural relativism, giving prominence to the idea of culture as an obstacle to true human rights implementation.[19] As Goodhart notes (this volume) localism is often seen as threatening to human rights cosmopolitans heavily invested in universalism. But local perspectives offer the global human rights project a much-needed opportunity for rejuvenation. Engagement with rooted interpretations of human rights can diversify the human

---

[11] Tom Zwart, "Using local culture to further the implementation of international human rights: The receptor approach," *Human Rights Quarterly* 34, no. 2 (2012), 546–569.

[12] Sally Engle Merry, "Transnational human rights and local activism: Mapping the middle," *American Anthropologist* 108, no. 1 (2006), 38–51. http://www.jstor.org/stable/3804730.

[13] Charli Carpenter, "Setting the advocacy agenda: Issues and non-issues around children and armed conflict," *International Studies Quarterly* 51, no. 1 (2007), 99–120; and Clifford Bob, "Dalit rights are human rights: Caste discrimination, international activism, and the construction of a new human rights issue," *Human Rights Quarterly* 29 (2007), no. 1, 167–193.

[14] Amitav Acharya, "How ideas spread: Whose norms matter? Norm localisation and institutional change in Asian regionalism," *International Organization* 58, no. 2 (2004), 239–275.

[15] Harri Englund, "Towards a critique of rights talk in new democracies: The case of legal aid in Malawi," *Discourse & Society* 15, no. 5 (2004), 527.

[16] Peggy Levitt and Sally Merry, "Vernacularization on the ground: Local uses of global women's rights in Peru, China, India and the United States," *Global Network* 9, no. 4 (2009), 441–461.

[17] Levitt and Merry, "Vernacularization on the ground," p. 459.

[18] Englund, "Towards a critique of rights talk in new democracies," p. 303.

[19] See, Jack Donnelly, *Universal Human Rights in Theory and Practice* (Ithaca, NY: Cornell University Press, 2003); and Alison Renteln, "Relativism and the search for human rights," *American Anthropologist* 90, no. 1 (1988), 56–72.

rights canon, invigorate discourse, and help shift "culture" from the margins of human rights conversations. These acknowledgments can, in turn, broaden the community of recognized human rights actors and theorists and, in doing so, aid in building a larger more vibrant network.

Democratizing Human Rights Discourse

The culture of human rights derives its greatest strength from the informed expectations of each individual. Responsibility for the protection of human rights lies with states. But the understanding, respect and expectation of human rights by each individual person is what gives human rights its daily texture, its day-to-day resilience. [...] The culture of human rights must be a popular culture if it is to have the strength to withstand the blows that will inevitably come. Human rights culture must be a popular culture if it is to be able to innovate and to be truly owned at the national and sub-national levels.[20]

A critical part of the conceptual situatedness of human rights is ownership of the language. Yet, a strange and unfortunate paradox of human rights is that its language, ostensibly of struggle and emancipation (see Goodhart this volume), is often legalized, elite and inaccessible.[21] Even initiatives that aim to lessen this divide, and help make, for example, the Universal Declaration of Human Rights a popular document, reinforce the idea of human rights filtering down from "the international" to the local level. Improving the readability of this document or distributing translations, are all versions of what some participants in my research have described as "people coming to tell us what our rights are."

What does a popular language of human rights look like, how is formed, and how can it become a vernacular? In my research with SECTION+ 27, a South African advocacy group named and advocating for the constitutional rights to health and education, participants were frank in stating that "it's not up to us to decide what people demand as their rights." Instead, activists described the Constitution, not as an authoritative document distinct from the people, but as an authoritative document because it was participatory and supported by and infused with meaning by the people. Respondents spoke of the Constitution as providing a framework that needed to be given substance by the population.

---

[20] Statement by Sergio Vieira De Mello, United Nations High Commissioner for Human Rights to the 59th Session of the UN Commission on Human Rights as cited in "UN Secretary-General Remarks at the Funeral of Sergio Vieira de Mello" Rio de Janeiro, 23 August 2003. Available at: http://www.universalrights.net/heroes/display.php3?id=67.

[21] Even if, as Jensen and others argue, freshly independent states of the Global South played a significant role in the construction of the contemporary human rights system the geographic, cultural and linguistic distance between formal human rights codification and human rights activism in the Global South remains vast (see: Steven L. B. Jensen, *The Making of International Human Rights: The 1960s, Decolonization, and the Reconstruction of Global Values*. Human Rights in History, (Cambridge: Cambridge University Press, 2016.) doi:10.1017/CBO9781316282571.

Whether you fill in that outline with color and meaning depends upon the extent to which you engage with the outline and demand that there's some definition that is given to it. So, in the case, for example, of the right to sufficient food in South Africa, the human right to sufficient food or the right to food, it hasn't been touched sufficiently in this country. So, all you've got is a few bland words that says everyone has a right to sufficient food. But go to the right of access to healthcare service and you find that it's a lot of coloring in that has been done. If you go to education, you see that there's more and more coloring in that's being done. In this conceptualization the population determines what the meaning of the secured rights are—if there is the right to education, for example, does that include books, teachers, toilets, curriculum content?

Another component of this constitution of meaning is the use of local materials as interpretive tools. What examples are used, who is referenced as a hero or villain, and how are current events related to or inserted into a historical narrative? Swidler has written on the role of "culture as a 'tool kit'"[22] and the "cultural stock for images of what is an injustice."[23] When in 2015 and 2016, South Africa students mobilized for access to "free decolonized higher education" they drew from their own history in particular ways.[24] They highlighted continuity from apartheid—emphasizing ongoing spatial and socioeconomic divides, they chose their own heroes—many of whom differed from those endorsed by the state, and they repurposed powerful cultural symbols such as apartheid-era protest songs. In South Africa these rhythms and melodies are a recognizable way for groups to assert that "this injustice is like that injustice." Anti-apartheid songs have been repurposed for access to HIV medication, union strikes, and socioeconomic inequity. Alongside domestic heroes, South African student protestors also drew energy from and made parallels to international figures and events, referencing Léopold Senghor and Martin Luther King among others, and drawing likeness to international movements such as US-originated Black Lives Matter. These interpretive strategies communicate clear categorizations ("this, is what this event is an example of") to those within, but also beyond the community and country's borders. They knit current events into particular places in the human rights tapestry in doing so performing emancipatory practices of conceptual ownership.

"We call our own shots"
　　-anti-vaccine placard

---

[22] Ann Swidler, "Culture in action: Symbols and strategies," *American Sociological Review*, 51, no. 2 (1986), 277.

[23] Mayer N. Zald, "Culture, ideology and strategic framing," in *Comparative Perspectives on Social Movements: Political opportunities, Mobilizing Structures and Cultural Framings*, eds, Doug McAdam, John D. McCarthy and Mayer N. Zald, (Cambridge: Cambridge University Press, 1995), p. 266.

[24] Kristi Heather Kenyon, Juliana Coughlin and David Bosc. 2021 "'Born Free': it's cute, but it's a lie": ns#FeesMustFall and youth counter-narratives of continuity in South African history," in *Young People and Popular Culture in Africa*, ed. Paul Ugor, (Rochester, NY: University of Rochester Press, forthcoming October 2021); Kristi Heather Kenyon and Tshepo Madlingozi. "'Rainbow is not the new black': #FeesMustFall and the demythication of South Africa's liberation narrative" Third World Quarterly, 43:2, 494-512, DOI: 10.1080/01436597.2021.2014314.

Unexpectedly, human rights language has "come home" to Winnipeg in new and dramatic ways in the last two years. I now see many examples of local human rights advocacy, with people interpreting human rights through their own lenses, drawing on international networks, and making historical parallels to craft expressions of injustice. Signs, placards and social media posts employ the language of human rights making regular references to the *Canadian Charter of Rights and Freedoms*, international treaties and the *Nuremberg Code*. Some of these references and movements reflect a spirit of mutual recognition and solidarity—a march of unprecedented scale attesting that "Black Lives Matter," and a sea of orange in support of Indigenous rights. The majority, however, of these local expressions of human rights are individualized defenses of "liberty" and "freedom" in the context of the COVID-19 pandemic and emerging mask and vaccine mandates.

Prominent local depictions of human rights in the COVID-19 environment include references to bodily autonomy, the right to non-discrimination, and protection from medical experimentation. Parallels are frequently made between vaccine mandates and a historical canon of egregious human rights abuses. As a scholar of activism and a longtime advocate of democratized, diversified voices on human rights discourse, it is a bit like seeing Frankenstein come to life. This new creation, ostensibly of human rights activism, has familiar facets, but they are pieced together in such a way so as to run contrary to the spirit of human rights. In analyzing whether this is a manifestation of localized human rights discourse, there are two key questions: 1) is this local? and, 2) is this human rights?

Although these movements appear locally and protests are primarily populated by residents, their local human rights grounding is relatively weak. Despite the symbolic use of a Gandhi statue adjacent to the Canadian Museum for Human Rights as a rallying site, they have virtually no links to the city's existing human rights community. Instead, the movement draws strength from a largely virtual non-geographic, community benefiting significantly from international (principally US) reinforcement. Through this network of Facebook and other social media groups advocacy materials and messaging are shared. Borrowing from other jurisdictions is made clear, for example, by the regular quoting of American legislation (*Americans with Disabilities Act, Health Insurance Portability and Accountability Act*) and regulatory bodies (Food and Drug Administration) in protests, homemade or internet-ordered "vaccine exemption cards," and videos of confrontations with store clerks and health officials. In contrast with other non-geographic communities, such as LGBTQ communities (particularly where criminalized), globalized Black Lives Matter movements, and communities united by medical conditions, anti-vax groups are not grounded in a shared experience based on an immutable aspect of identity. Instead, they are connected by an ideological perspective often reflecting mistrust of government and pharmaceutical companies.

Do such groups develop meaningful community-informed interpretations of human rights? In this context, there is a disconnect with slogans largely sourced from the "virtual community" often with limited local community resonance or connection. Domestic human rights instruments are cited (principally the *Canadian Charter of Rights and Freedoms*), but the creativity in interpretation is limited largely to removing rather than adding contextualization (i.e., Charter rights have limitations and are contextualized in a "free and democratic society" both of which are elided in anti-vax representations). Unlike the South African student protestors whose parents suffered under apartheid, Winnipeg protestors are unlikely to have familial or personal links to the images of injustice they are presenting. The "stock images of injustice" used—references to slavery, the Holocaust, and apartheid South Africa—are largely distant false equivalencies. Belle Jarniewski, Executive Director of the Winnipeg-based Jewish Heritage Centre of Western Canada, and the daughter of Holocaust survivors, has decried Holocaust comparisons as "unconscionable" and a "distortion of history."[25] Local protestors who invoke this parallel to "honor" Holocaust victims do so in spite of the local Jewish community's wishes, similarly quoting Rosa Parks and Martin Luther King without engagement with the city's Black community or anti-racist movements,[26] and employing the language of "accessibility" to the anger of local people with disabilities. Canada's own a canon of egregious human rights violations rarely feature in anti-vaccination rhetoric. Similarly, groups who have faced systematic human rights abuses including Indigenous and racialized communities, are not well represented.

In some instances, there is a problematic coincidence of human rights language and hate speech. Prominent national anti-vaccination speaker, Chris Sky, flown in to speak at a Winnipeg rally and subsequently arrested for violating public health orders, has a history of clearly racist and anti-Semitic remarks.[27] Indeed, the Canadian Anti-Hate Network has said there has been a migration of participants, including Sky, from the earlier Canadian iteration of the French-initiated "Gillet Jaune" protests (economic and later anti-immigrant protests) with a related carry-over of racist and anti-Semitic language.[28]

Finally, I argued that community is where we have the opportunity for mutual recognition—that it is the space where we become human to each other. This is the most critical facet of human rights and the piece least easily identified amid this movement. If, as I argued earlier, the global human rights regime can become stale and hollow without infusion from local activism, this is an example of such hollowness at a local scale. It is activism with an imported template and without meaningful "coloring in" at the local level. Yet, for its participants it can have real meaning, and provide a framework through which to see and interpret the world.

[25] Rachel Bergen, "Antisemitic rhetoric continues to be used by some opponents of COVID-19 measures," CBC News, October 10, 2021, https://www.cbc.ca/news/canada/manitoba/vaccine-mandates-holocaust-comparisons-1.6200527?fbclid=IwAR0LkYgz7mSQSbKgTlMUlw8ZckKt1GZ l3kzMRCBOWy3-_yHPxRt7CDS28uo.

[26] Bergen, "Antisemitic rhetoric."

[27] Bergen, "Antisemitic rhetoric."

[28] Peter Smith and Elizabeth Jones, "M-103 to the Pandemic: Evolution of Canadian Islamophobic Activists Show How Hate Movements Adapt," Canadian Anti-Hate Network, October 5, 2021, https://www.antihate.ca/m_103_pandemic_evolution_canadian_islamophobic_activists_shows_how_hate_movements_adapt

One of the ways in which systems of injustice and violence operate most effectively is by disconnecting, disassociating, and dislocating people from their personal and social histories, that is, by disconnecting them from their stories.[29]

Local human rights narratives that are rooted in context are important. They are important locally, as sources of mutual recognition and advocacy, and internationally—as a source of concrete, lived meaning to international conventions, structures and advocacy groups. This is the place where human rights are still, very much alive, and the place from which the international movement can, with respectful engagement, draw strength. But, celebrating the promise and potential of popular human rights discourse and recognizing how individual perspectives give human rights their "daily texture, [and] day-to-day resilience" must be mediated with recognition of the perilous unpredictability of this enterprise. "Letting go of the reins" of human rights conceptualization means that there is a loss of control of who will interpret these ideas, and how, and in what context. Not all interpretations of human rights need to trace the historical trajectory of the contemporary state-based human rights system. All true human rights interpretations must, however, emerge from community and be rooted in a story of mutual recognition and shared humanity. By divorcing stories of suffering from the populations that endured them, some in the Winnipeg anti-vaccination movement are using the experiences of others as opportunistic rhetorical tools and wielding them in ways that inhibit rather than facilitate mutual recognition. "Thrown together" as we are in this "strange new country" of isolated connection and blurred geography, it is more important than ever to be vigilant and attentive to the stories we tell, the slogans we use and the stories we are told. In the words of Thomas King, "The truth about stories is that that's all we are."[30]

[29] Jessica Senehi, Maureen Flaherty, Cyndi Sanjana Kirupakaran, Lloyd Kornelsen, Mavis Matenge, and Olga Skarlato. "Dreams of Our Grandmothers: Discovering the Call for Social Justice Through Storytelling," *Storytelling, Self, Society* 5, no. 2 (2009), 90–106. http://www.jstor.org/stable/41949022.
[30] Thomas King, *The Truth About Stories: A Native Narrative*, (Toronto: House of Anansi Press, 2003).

3

The Future of Human Rights is Local

Michael Goodhart

The local, not the global . . . remains the crucial site of struggle for the enunciation, implementation, and enjoyment and exercise of human rights.[1]

The future of human rights is local. That simple statement is disconcerting to many human rights advocates, as I learned recently when colleagues at two conferences expressed reservations about my efforts to question conventional thinking about human rights by drawing lessons from local and grassroots movements, struggles, and innovations.[2] These colleagues were concerned that foregrounding the local would fuel the current backlash against human rights.[3] More deeply, they seemed to regard cosmopolitanism as somehow essential to, even constitutive of, human rights, key not just to their coherence but to their very ethos. This is a common view, I suspect, but one that should be rejected. We need an alternative conception and politics of human rights, both to make sense of the present backlash and to theorize and advance emancipatory projects that might help to address the structural injustices fueling that backlash.

Cosmopolitanism and the Human Rights Project

Cosmopolitanism is a belief in a form of universal reason or rationality that transcends problematic forms of particularistic attachment and ultimately leads to human emancipation. This belief entails both an egalitarian morality based in, e.g., the dignity

---

[1] Upendra Baxi, *The Future of Human Rights*, 3rd ed. (New Delhi: Oxford University Press, 2008).

[2] Michael Goodhart, "How do human rights matter?" in *Why Human Rights Still Matter in Contemporary Global Affairs*, ed. Mahmood Monshipouri (New York: Routledge, 2020); Michael Goodhart, "Human rights cities: Making the global local," in *Contesting Human Rights: Norms, Institutions and Practice*, eds. Alison Brysk and Michael Stohl (Cheltenham, UK: Edward Elgar Publishing, 2019).

[3] Sanja Dragić, "On the concept of the 'human rights backlash'" (paper presented at the Imagining the Human, Vienna, 2019); Leslie Vinjamuri, "Human rights backlash," in *Human Rights Futures*, eds, Stephen Hopgood, Jack Snyder, and Leslie Vinjamuri (Cambridge: Cambridge University Press, 2017).

or autonomy of individual human beings, and a progressive understanding of history as the unfolding of reason toward human freedom. As Joe Hoover explains (in this volume), cosmopolitanism's fortunes rise and fall with those of the imperial projects with which it is associated. Following the Second World War and struggles for decolonization, ideological divisions quashed the incipient (and now-largely-forgotten) world federalist movement, and cosmopolitan fell out of fashion.[4] It was reborn in the 1990s—its ascendency tied to the rise of a US-led coalition of liberal democratic, capitalistic states to unfettered hegemony—as the ideology for the era "after the end of ideologies, the ideology at the end of history."[5]

This newly configured cosmopolitanism differed importantly from earlier versions in replacing universal reason with an empirical account of "contemporary globalization and its effects" as the driving force of history and moral progress.[6] Thus in contemporary cosmopolitanism:

> globalizing processes, both past and present, objectively embody different forms of normative, non-ethnocentric cosmopolitanism because they rearticulate, radically transform, and even explode the boundaries of regional and national consciousness and local ethnic identities.[7]

This reformulation, as Cheah notes, makes cosmopolitanism more palatable for a purportedly postcolonial world. It also renders globalization's material processes and outcomes impervious to critical scrutiny by making them definitional of cosmopolitanism itself. As one of the conditions of possibility of cosmopolitanism, neoliberal globalization cannot readily be subjected to critique within a cosmopolitan framework; it is effectively naturalized (hypostatized) in this new ideological formation.

Cosmopolitanism and human rights are imbricated historically, a connection that traces to the Enlightenment philosophy of Immanuel Kant, the revolutionary theory and politics of Thomas Paine, and the imperial and colonial projects of European powers.[8] That history notwithstanding, contemporary human rights were not *born*

---

[4]   Luis Cabrera, "Review article: World government: Renewed debate, persistent challenges," *European Journal of International Relations* 16, no. 3 (2010), https://doi.org/10.1177/1354066109346888, https://journals.sagepub.com/doi/abs/10.1177/1354066109346888.

[5]   Costas Douzinas, *Human Rights and Empire: The Political Philosophy of Cosmopolitanism* (New York: Routledge-Cavendish, 2007), 33.

[6]   Pheng Cheah, *Inhuman Conditions* (Harvard University Press, 2009), 18.

[7]   Cheah, *Inhuman Conditions*.

[8]   See, e.g., Immanuel Kant, *Kant's Political Writings*, ed. Hans Reiss, trans. H. B. Nisbet (Cambridge: Cambridge University Press, 1970); Thomas Paine, *The Rights of Man* (online: University of Groningen, 1791/2), http://www.let.rug.nl/usa/documents/1786-1800/thomas-paine-the-rights-of-man/text.php; Anthony Pagden, "Human rights, natural rights, and Europe's imperial legacy," *Political Theory* 31, no. 2 (April 2003); Bonny Ibhawoh, *Imperialism and Human Rights: Colonial discourses of rights and liberties in African history* (SUNY Press, 2008); Gurminder K Bhambra, "Cosmopolitanism and postcolonial critique," in *The Ashgate Research Companion to Cosmopolitanism*, eds, Maria Rovisco and Magdalena Nowicka (Farnam, UK: Ashgate, 2011); Dipesh Chakrabarty, *Provincializing Europe: Postcolonial Thought and Historical Difference* (Princeton, NJ: Princeton University Press, 2000).

cosmopolitan. The existing human rights regime is anchored in the Universal Declaration of Human Rights, which eschews philosophical grounding,[9] and the UN Charter in which it is embedded enshrines state sovereignty and non-interference as pillars of the postwar order. It was only through the construction of the New World Order in the 1990s that human rights *became* cosmopolitan. For the triumphal coalition, the UN human rights regime provided both a clearly articulated account of moral universality and an established legal and institutional framework for international action—substantial assets that enabled the coalition to operationalize its power through already-existing, internationally-sanctioned channels and to restyle itself as *the international community.*

Through this transformation, human rights were apotheosized into a cosmopolitan Human Rights Project, which became the third element of a new cosmopolitan trinity alongside liberal democratization and neoliberal globalization.[10] I understand this Project as the global advancement of an international legal regime of human rights built on liberal political, economic, and philosophical foundations, anchored in UN and regional systems of treaties, councils, tribunals, and monitoring mechanisms, and backed by the militarized power of liberal democratic states and the soft power of those states and their corporate, philanthropic, and international NGO partners.[11]

The Human Rights Project has been enormously successful. Over the past 30 years, human rights discourse has become the normative lingua franca of global politics. New rights instruments have proliferated, and rights NGOs have multiplied. International negotiations on every topic are saturated with rights talk, and rights condition aid, trade, development and diplomacy. Perhaps most significantly and controversially, humanitarianism has become a core modality of global politics and humanitarian intervention commonplace. In short, human rights have become an integral part of the wider project of global governance launched in the 1990s. Stepping back for a moment, it's clear why many proponents—and critics—of human rights associate them so closely with cosmopolitanism.[12]

The Human Rights Project has been widely and roundly criticized.[13] I am mainly interested in the cosmopolitan conceptualization of rights that it has made predominant.

[9] Standard histories treat this as a pragmatic requirement of achieving consensus on the Declaration itself.

[10] Their elevation was confirmed in the 1993 *Vienna Declaration and Programme of Action*, which put the universality of rights firmly "beyond question" (Article 1) and called for the strengthening and enhancement of the international machinery of monitoring and enforcement.

[11] This definition riffs on Stephen Hopgood, *The Endtimes of Human Rights* (Ithaca, NY: Cornell University Press, 2013).

[12] Compare Anne-Marie Slaughter, *A New World Order* (Princeton, NJ: Princeton University Press 2004) and Michael Neocosmos, "Can a human rights culture enable emancipation? Clearing some theoretical ground for the renewal of a critical sociology," *South African Review of Sociology* 37, no. 2 (2006).

[13] E.g., Wendy Brown, "'The most we can hope for...': Human rights and the politics of fatalism," *The South Atlantic Quarterly* 103, no. 2 (2004); Douzinas, *Human Rights and Empire*; Hopgood, *The Endtimes of Human Rights*; Makau Mutua, *Human Rights: A Political and Cultural Critique* (University of Pennsylvania Press, 2002); Eric Posner, *The Twilight of International Human Rights Law* (New York: Oxford University Press, 2014).

Cosmopolitan human rights are configured as universal, transcendent, liberal, and international. The universality of rights means that they apply to everyone, everywhere, a single morality for humanity. Transcendence refers to the quality of rights that elevates them above politics, makes them fixed, nonnegotiable. Cosmopolitan rights are liberal, meaning, they are the familiar civil, political, and security rights—plus property—enshrined in the constitutions and politics of liberal democratic states. Their international character makes them a matter of concern—and enforcement—for the international community.

Again, stepping back, it's clear why local human rights struggles, however laudable their goals, tactics, and aspirations, can seem suspect to proponents of the Human Rights Project. What we might call the ethico-political geography of those struggles contains a latent contradiction and therefore poses an implicit threat. Each of these virtues of cosmopolitan rights—universality, transcendence, liberality, and internationalism—can be positioned as such only in relation to the oppressive (local) vices against which the Human Rights Project is set. Put differently, the specificity of the local is imagined as the problem to which cosmopolitan human rights provide the solution. Thus, the particular moralities of various societies pose the threat of relativism in their variation (deviation) from the universal morality that human rights express. Limited, parochial outlooks and attachments steeped in custom and tradition engender conflict and must be transcended. Illiberal ethnic, religious, and cultural authoritarianisms typical of local politics must be checked through the protection of individual civil, political, and security rights. Finally, the volatile backwardness of the local, which threatens to erupt into religious, ethnic, or nationalist violence, must be policed by the international community. This conceptual matrix is summarized in Figure 1.

Cosmopolitan anti-localism is not new; earlier iterations similarly coded some spaces, and certain "native" bodies associated with those spaces, as uncivilized, savage, brutal, barbaric, etc.[14] Nor is it merely incidental: anti-localism furthers the imperial projects to which cosmopolitanism is always yoked by coloring any opposition to those projects as hostility to universal reason, egalitarian morality, and human progress. Crucially, the substitution of an empirical logic of globalization for universal reason in contemporary cosmopolitanism, discussed earlier, means that resistance to the material consequences of globalization—namely, metastasizing social and economic inequality—registers as backlash within cosmopolitanism by definition.

Figure 1 The conceptual matrix of cosmopolitan human rights

COSMOPOLITAN	LOCAL (OPPRESSIVE)
Universal	**Particular** (relativist)
Transcendent	**Limited** (parochial)
Liberal	**Illiberal** (populist/authoritarian)
International	**Statist** (nativist/xenophobic)

[14] See note 7.

Put differently, the cosmopolitan conception of human rights is indifferent or hostile toward social and economic rights. Not only is globalization naturalized, but the liberal morality of rights defines social and economic questions as *political* questions rather than as appropriate subjects of rights discourse. Thus, the Human Rights Project, as Moyn observes, "[turns] a blind eye to galloping material inequality" because it is politically and theoretically ill-equipped to grapple with it. In the modern era, he argues, human rights have "coexisted with a political economy of hierarchy they didn't disturb," concerning themselves instead with sufficiency—with providing a floor beneath which the poorest should not be allowed to fall.[15] Inequality, or egalitarian measures to address it, are local matters to be resolved through national politics.

Backlash

This indifference or hostility to social and economic rights helps both to explain contemporary backlash and to illustrate why an alternative conceptualization of rights is urgently necessary. Again, cosmopolitanism will by default register any form of resistance to the Human Rights Project or to wider global governance arrangements as a kind of atavism. Rising ethno-nationalism and associated forms of illiberalism and authoritarianism readily fit this script. But popular repudiations of cosmopolitan projects like the EU (Brexit), NATO, the UN, and multilateralism more generally are also colored as rejections of reason, morality, and progress—as was evident in the liberal/cosmopolitan handwringing over Trump's foreign policy.[16] In many liberal democracies, backlash and democratic backsliding are sides of a coin.

Rising ethno-nationalism and illiberal democracy undoubtedly generate real and frightening oppressive measures directed against immigrants and refugees or against "foreigners" and other minoritized resident populations, frequently including racial, ethnic, and religious groups and queer people. (Women are also frequently targeted, somewhat differently, in complex ways that I cannot unpack here.) Such measures are frequently rationalized through appeals to mythic and mythologized claims of communal purity or authenticity and justified as responses to looming threats to a "native" population depicted as besieged. Again, this kind of politics reinforces the storyline about backlash as an outburst of primordial evil, usually (the story goes) summoned and unleashed by unregenerate leaders in fits of toxic masculinity (think Trump, Duterte, Erdoğan, Bolsonaro …). Against this backdrop, criticisms of cosmopolitanism can easily seem counterproductive, even dangerous. They are,

---

[15] Samuel Moyn, *Not Enough: Human Rights in an Unequal World* (Cambridge, MA: Harvard University Press, 2018), 176; 217–218; 193.

[16] See, e.g., Jeanne Morefield, "Trump's foreign policy isn't the problem," *The Boston Review*, 08 January, 2019, https://bostonreview.net/war-security/jeanne-morefield-trump%e2%80%99s-foreign-policy-isn%e2%80%99t-problem; Corey Robin, "Check your amnesia, dude: On the vox generation of punditry," *Crooked Timber*, 21 July 2016., https://crookedtimber.org/2016/07/21/check-your-amnesia-dude-on-the-vox-generation-of-punditry/.

however, necessary—both for understanding backlash and for theorizing what role human rights might play in an emancipatory alternative.

Jacques Rancière has argued that, in the rich countries, there is a widespread feeling that human rights have become empty, useless. This feeling arises, he argues, when rights are depoliticized—by which he means, no longer useful in contesting social exclusion and challenging social hierarchies. For Rancière, the de-politicization of rights helps to explain the replacement of politics globally with a humanitarian ethic.[17] Rancière sees this as a function of consensus, which makes contestation of social and political exclusion impossible. I want to explore this process through which rights come to appear useless further.

The cosmopolitan consensus forged in the 1990s neutralizes or neuters any human rights critique of inequality conceptually, by naturalizing globalization and its effects, and practically, by leaving inequality undisturbed. There is thus no space within the cosmopolitan consensus for egalitarian politics. A transnational egalitarian politics becomes unthinkable in these circumstances, and local egalitarian projects are easily dismissed or overridden as forms of particularism or illiberalism incompatible with reason, morality, and progress. It's at least plausible, in such circumstances, that human rights come to appear useless (in rich liberal democratic states) because the civil and political rights they prescribe are institutionalized and because they are ineffective in theorizing or challenging the social and economic inequalities resulting from neoliberal globalization. Rights become empty insofar as there is nothing for them to contest—or, nothing to contest through them.

This interpretation suggests a particular reading of the contemporary backlash "against human rights" in the richer countries. Contemporary anti-globalism or anti-cosmopolitanism in these countries reflects a popular perception that the global economy unfairly advantages countries with low labor costs. These same countries, in this perception, also benefit from generous aid and nation-building programs funded by the wealthier countries. Ironically, then, (some) citizens of rich countries, who have benefited tremendously from the hierarchical global economic arrangements of the past few centuries, nonetheless feel themselves tremendously aggrieved by contemporary globalization. They are not altogether wrong: neoliberalism has disproportionately benefited a tiny elite while triggering a precipitous drop in living standards and economic security for many other people in the "rich" countries.[18]

This generates backlash "against human rights" in two ways. First, cosmopolitan human rights prove utterly ineffective in analyzing or challenging inequality, even as material conditions worsen for millions. Meanwhile, literally trillions of dollars are directed toward cosmopolitan misadventures, like the "reconstruction" of Afghanistan, and away from domestic programs that might address increasing precarity. These

---

[17] Jacques Rancière, "Who is the subject of the rights of man?" *South Atlantic Quarterly* 103, no. 2/3 (2004).

[18] E.g., Thomas Piketty, *Capital in the 21st Century*, trans. Arthur Goldhammer (Cambridge, MA: Harvard University Press, 2013). Of course, those once comparatively high living standards were themselves predicated on previous injustices.

dynamics can fuel a deep resentment of the Human Rights Project and of the (cosmo) politicians who shill for it. Second, while the liberal rights of the Human Rights Project may appear useless to privileged majority groups, the same is not true of minoritized populations. As victims of multiple and overlapping forms of oppression, they can find civil and political rights valuable in struggles for formal legal equality and recognition— which can be matters of life and death in encounters with the police, the bureaucracy, or their neighbors. Perversely, their ongoing, justified demands for rights and recognition are frequently distorted by ethno-nationalist (ring)leaders looking to distract or deflect attention from material inequality as "divisive" demands for "special treatment."[19] Thus human rights become, in the febrile effervescence of the populist imagination, part of a cosmopolitan conspiracy to shame or replace them.

A cosmopolitan conception of rights cannot connect virulent ethno-nationalism with simmering economic resentment in any productive way.[20] Thus Brexit, Trump's victory, *les gilets jaunes*—none of these can be read in the light of growing social and economic precarity as expressions of frustration with the "cosmopolitan elite" who dominate the economy and the foreign policy establishment that engages in endless humanitarian wars and interventions while paying little heed to the concerns and grievances of those negatively impacted by globalization. Instead, cosmopolitanism can only read this backlash as atavism, regression.[21]

Emancipatory Human Rights

The upshot of my argument so far is that a cosmopolitan conceptualization of human rights is, for related reasons, a poor framework for understanding backlash and an unsuitable vehicle for an emancipatory politics adequate to the challenges of social exclusion and economic inequality that we confront today. In fact, I see it as an obstacle to the theorization and development of such a politics and to the creation of global solidarity in the struggle against inequality, in part because it conceives local politics— the source of much innovation in human rights praxis today—as inherently problematic. Moreover, these problems cannot be fixed through a revised cosmopolitanism or one that does better in staying true to its ideals: cosmopolitan human rights are configured as anti-local and as hostile to egalitarian politics *by virtue of their being cosmopolitan.*

We urgently need a new conception and politics of human rights that rejects cosmopolitanism and embraces an emancipatory understanding of rights, one more

---

[19] For one pertinent and noxious example see The President's Advisory 1776 Commission, *The 1776 Report*, The National Archives (online, 2021), https://trumpwhitehouse.archives.gov/wp-content/uploads/2021/01/The-Presidents-Advisory-1776-Commission-Final-Report.pdf.

[20] The connection needn't be causal: I'm reminded of the early 20th-century German social democratic lament that *anti-Semitism is the socialism of fools.*

[21] Nothing here should be read as excusing or justifying the ugly, violent politics of ethno-nationalism. I am simply interested in understanding it. There is a roiling debate about the respective roles of racism and economic precarity in fomenting ethno-nationalism; I can't join it here, but I am skeptical of simplistic formulations that position these as somehow mutually exclusive explanations.

deeply informed by their history and continuing use as struggle concepts. This emancipatory conception of rights must re-center social and economic injustice and embrace local innovation and experimentation alongside a trans-local and transnational politics of solidarity. What would an emancipatory alternative to cosmopolitan human rights look like? In what follows I offer a preliminary sketch of an emancipatory conception of human rights. This conception is not a theoretical abstraction but rather an extrapolation from the praxis of grassroots human rights struggles.

Emancipatory rights are place-based, by which I mean that they are responsive and adapted to the particular social, cultural, and political contexts in which they operate. As opposed to universal manifestos of rights, which become fixed and have a homogenizing uniformity, place-based rights allow for innovation as activists seek solutions to the problems confronting them.[22] Not only are the meanings of rights reworked in context, but the catalog of rights itself is continually renegotiated as well. This place-based modality of transnational linkages itself implies a novel form of political imaginary and of counter-hegemonic praxis.[23] Emancipatory rights are also political insofar as they are *repoliticized* in the sense implied by Rancière's account. Rights do not shut down politics through consensus but rather open it up through contestation.

The emancipatory conception of rights positions them as a radical alternative to the atrophied, bourgeois understandings that put social and economic rights (except, somehow, for property) off the table. Rights are for challenging all forms of domination, oppression, and exploitation, in whatever form or "sphere." Finally, emancipatory human rights are "people-centered," which means that they empower oppressed people by adopting their epistemological and existential standpoint and enabling them to try to restructure unjust social arrangements. Instead of licensing international interference or promoting externally imposed agendas (neoliberalism), people-centered rights are tools for emancipation through intersectional analysis and bottom-up participation.[24] This conceptual matrix is summarized in Figure 2.

Figure 2 The conceptual matrix of emancipatory human rights

EMANCIPATORY	COSMOPOLITAN (OPPRESSIVE?)
Place-based	**Universal** (fixed, homogenizing)
Political	**Transcendent** (apolitical, impartial)
Radical	**Liberal** (bourgeois, atrophied)
People-centered	**International** (interventionist, neoliberal)

[22] E.g., Shareen Hertel, "A new route to norms evolution: insights from India's right to food campaign," *Social Movement Studies* 15, no. 6 (2016).

[23] Arturo Escobar, "Beyond the third world: Imperial globality, global coloniality and anti-globalisation social movements," *Third World Quarterly* 25, no. 1 (2004/02/01 2004.

[24] Ajamu Baraka, "'People-centered' human rights as a framework for social transformation," (10 December 2013–2013). https://www.ajamubaraka.com/peoplecentered-human-rights-as-a-framework-for-social-transformation.

In the brief space remaining, I want to at least indicate what difference an emancipatory conception of human rights might make across each of these four dimensions, using as my example struggles for the Right to the City.[25] The Right to the City (R2C) was first articulated in the late 1960s as a critique of and political response to transformations in urban life and democracy driven by capitalist development policies and processes of "accumulation by dispossession" in Paris and other European and North American cities.[26] Today it is more commonly associated with movements in the Global South and with a radical politics opposed to neoliberal urban "development"—i.e., displacement and expropriation.[27]

The R2C is not a human right in the conventional sense.[28] While some observers regard it as a demand for the realization of other rights,[29] it comprises both existing rights and the programmatic demand that residents are entitled and should be enabled to shape the futures of their cities.[30] Many proponents characterize R2C as both oppositional and aspirational, predicated upon a form of radical openness that gives it a capacious character and a valuable "strategic fuzziness";[31] others describe it as both a slogan and an ideal, "a right to change ourselves by changing the city."[32]

R2C is evidently *place-based*; it connects local injustice to global structures and processes that condition it. While in particular cities it represents an autochthonous expression of local demands and desires, it is also deeply enriched by transnational networks developed through the World Social Forum process (and with the support of the Rosa Luxemburg Foundation). The global character of R2C makes it fluid and plural, rather than fixed and homogenizing this global frame and discourse provide a further resource for the formulation and articulation of contextually specific programs for social transformation.

R2C is also explicitly *political*. It challenges the commodification of housing and wider neoliberal logics of urbanization,[33] and in doing so problematizes the insulation of social and economic issues from democratic control. R2C is not impartial and does not pretend to ground a consensual morality. It seeks not to transcend politics but

---

[25] These paragraphs borrow from Goodhart, "Human rights cities."

[26] Henry Lefebvre, *Writings on Cities*, ed. and trans. Eleonore Kofman and Elizabeth Lebas (Oxford: Blackwell, 1996); David Harvey, "The right to the city," *The City Reader* 6 (2008).

[27] Eva García Chueca, "Human rights in the city and the right to the city," in *Global Urban Justice: The Rise of Human Rights Cities*, eds, Barbara Oomen, Martha F Davis, and Michele Grigolo (Cambridge: Cambridge University Press, 2016); Peter Marcuse, "Rights in cities and the right to the city?," in *Cities for All: Proposals and Experiences towards the Right to the City*, eds, Ana Sugranyes and Charlotte Mathivet (Santiago, Chile: Habitat International Coalition, 2010).

[28] It does, however, have a charter, the *World Charter on the Right to the City*, adopted in 2004: https://www.hlrn.org.in/documents/World_Charter_on_the_Right_to_the_City.htm

[29] Charlotte Mathivet, "The right to the city: Keys to understanding the proposal for 'another city is possible,'" in *Cities for All.*; cf. Kafui A Attoh, "What kind of right is the right to the city?," *Progress in Human Geography* 35, no. 5 (2011); Michele Grigolo, "Towards a sociology of the human rights city," in *Global Urban Justice*.

[30] Marcuse, "Rights in cities and the right to the city?" p. 90.

[31] Attoh, "What kind of right . . .," p. 678.

[32] Harvey, "The right to the city."

[33] See Jamie Peck, *Austerity Urbanism: The Neoliberal Crisis of American Cities*, Rosa Luxemburg Stiftung (New York: Rosa Luxemburg Stiftung, May 2015).

rather to reinvigorate it by thematizing social and economic inequality and structural injustice in specific urban contexts. Doing so is a way of resisting the invisibilization of poverty and inequality.

This repoliticization is tied to the *radical* nature of the R2C "program." As Hoover has argued, demands for the decommodification of housing (for example) are not simply claims on governments but represent transformative demands for social and economic reorganization.[34] Such demands challenge liberal conceptualizations of human rights by exceeding them; they demonstrate the emancipatory potential of rights as a terrain of social and political contestation.

Finally, the R2C is *people centered*. Following Baraka,[35] I understand this to mean that the impact of injustice on the most vulnerable and oppressed members of society is prioritized in human rights politics, a kind of universality from below.[36] Intersectionality, both as an analytical tool and as a political commitment, facilitates the prioritization of these injustices and their framing in terms that highlight commonality and connection and promote solidarity. This is a democratic politics of connecting the dots between structures and manifestations of injustice that, in different ways and to varying degrees, affect entire communities. Such a politics again prioritizes local needs and desires; it rules out external projects that would define rights universally or intervene in behalf of some universalized program of rights or humanitarian concern—but does so in the name of a general normative commitment to putting people first.

I don't have space to discuss why I believe such a politics might be an effective antidote to at least some forms of backlash, but the re-politicization of human rights and the radical and emancipatory thrust of this approach indicate the shape such an argument might take. In closing, let me reiterate that there is no need to invent this politics; it is thriving all around us. To see and embrace it, we must forget cosmopolitanism, with its inherent hostility to place-based, politicized, radical, and people-centered politics. The future of human rights is local.

---

[34] Joe Hoover, "The human right to housing and community empowerment: Home occupation, eviction defence and community land trusts," *Third World Quarterly* 36, no. 6 (2015).

[35] Baraka, "'People-centered' human rights."

[36] I owe this formulation to my friend and colleague Jackie Smith.

Snapshot #2: Global-Local Intersections to Advance Accountability in Post-conflict Côte d'Ivoire

Cristián Correa

Grassroots mobilization for advancing accountability in post conflict Côte d'Ivoire shows both the opportunities in and the obstacles to successful global-local cooperation to advance accountability for mass human rights violations.

Background

Alassane Ouattara emerged in 2010 as Côte d'Ivoire's new president following years of internal conflict, with rights violations committed on all sides. In 2011, Ouattara promised to implement a series of accountability measures to address the serious human rights violations committed during the conflict. This was inspired by global experiences of transitional justice, as recommended by The Elders[1] and a UN Commission of Inquiry.[2] Soon after, President Ouattara established the Truth, Dialogue, and Reconciliation Commission, a special investigative body at the General Prosecutor's Office (the *Cellule Spéciale d'Enquête*), and a commission of inquiry (the *Commission Nationale d'Enquête*).

The International Center for Transitional Justice (ICTJ) responded to a call to assist in launching this effort. We worked with state institutions and civil society organizations, helping them develop tools to deliver a balanced sense of criminal justice for those responsible of the most serious crimes; for an honest and inclusive dialogue to acknowledge both wrongs committed and lessons learned on how to guarantee their non-repetition; and for responding to the needs of victims to be listened, acknowledged, and receive reparations.

[1] Visit by Koffi Anan, Desmond Tutu and Mary Robinson, May 2011, at https://www. kofiannanfoundation.org/foundation-news/the-elders-to-visit-cote-divoire-to-encourage-healing-and-national-reconciliation-english-francais/
[2] Report of the International Commission of Inquiry to the Human Rights Council, 1 July 2011, A/HRC/17/48.

Opportunities

ICTJ soon discovered that the bulk of the Ivorian victims, especially those residing in remote communities, were not being included in the conversation. Some Abidjan-based NGOs working on reparative justice issues had little or no contact with victims from poor, affected regions far from the capital. The class divide between Abidjan-based NGOs, progressive policymakers, and those affected by the conflict entrenched the geographical exclusion of many victims. Discussions about human rights or gender had little resonance beyond small circles of educated elites. But approaching grassroots victims' groups and community leaders was not easy either. Sometimes we asked ourselves: Are we creating false expectations? Are we bringing abstract ideas that have little meaning to victims? Is it safe for people to examine recent horizontal violence in a civil war characterized by the manipulation of interethnic conflicts?

An opportunity came when the truth commission began talking about reparations for victims, and President Ouattara announced the creation of a trust fund for victims' reparations. The commission needed to define what reparations should entail and how to distribute them among victims. We realized that victims could be afforded the opportunity to more directly advocate for their rights and influence policy if they were first able to share their experiences and bring proposals based on them. Opening possibilities for acknowledgment, justice, and, eventually, some symbolic and material reparations could help improve their lives, and most importantly, their agency.[3]

Grassroots organizations and victims' groups developed a clear agenda based on their own views about the consequences of the violations suffered. Female victims also brought their claims, affirming their partnership with, but also their independence from male leaders. Even victims of intercommunity violence saw an opportunity to work together, despite a history of violence and mistrust, presenting a common front demanding that the national government listen. The backing of a transnational civil society organization like the ICTJ helped these groups gain access and valuable experience from transitional processes in other parts of the world about how to strategize to advance their demands.

Obstacles

Despite early promises, state institutions did little to advance investigations about violations, provide any form of acknowledgment and reparations to victims, or address the causes and consequences of the conflict. On the contrary, as President Ouattara entrenched his hold on his power, he moved to using prosecutions and pretrial detention to persecute opponents. As a result, the country's political divisions and responsibility for rights violations remain unaddressed. In the context of authoritarian rule, deep

---

[3] See Cristián Correa, "Operationalizing the right of victims of war to reparation," in *Reparations for Victims of Armed Conflict*, Max Planck Trialogues on the Law of Peace and War, Vol III, eds, Cristián Correa, Shuichi Furuya and Clara Sandoval (Cambridge: Cambridge University Press, 2020).

polarization, fragile détente, and the persistent exclusion of the historically who are also affected by the conflict, calls for social cohesion by the Ivorian authorities were vacuous. Initial victim access to authorities seemed to be valued, but ultimately the government did not want to acknowledge wrongdoing, investigate violations committed by their own, or find the disappeared. Distribution of reparations was done without identifying victims in transparent ways and exploited for electoral purposes.

Global–local cooperation had its limits, especially when much of the international community chose to support Côte d'Ivoire's supposed "economic miracle" and its strongman's assistance for the West's war on terror. Thus, the UN Security Country saw an opportunity to declare victory and close its mission, validating Ouattara's strategic manipulation of global actors. Without international pressure, grassroots groups demanding truth, justice, and reparation were left without crucial support.

Conclusion

Côte d'Ivoire's national transitional justice institutions failed to achieve their goals of truth, justice, and effective reparations. That failure, however, neglects the positive changes that engaging in this process had, nonetheless, on Ivorian society. Something has changed when victims are now leading rights' advocacy efforts, when youth groups are working to transform grievances into demands for reform, and when women's groups are engaging local leaders in addressing gender issues. Victims and affected communities have gained a sense of empowerment that comes from demanding change. For example, *Femmes Debout pour la Paix et le Progrès en Côte d'Ivoire*, a grassroots women's organization in Bouaké, now joins traditional male leaders in their monthly discussions about reparations and other local development policies. The *Réseau Action Justice et Paix*, a multiregion coalition of youth groups use media, songs, and theater to encourage their peers to be suspicious of politicians manipulating their grievances to recruit them for violent actions. Instead, they encourage them to demand that those grievances be addressed. The *Confédération des Organisations des Victimes de la Crise Ivoirienne*, which includes victims from different regions and sides, launched a monitoring project which published several reports about the implementation of reparations local governments to improve the living conditions of the most vulnerable and to get their help protecting mass graves.[4]

---

[4] For a comprehensive analysis of transitional justice in Côte d'Ivoire and the roles played by different actors, see M. Suma, *Resetting the Agenda: A reflection of the past and proposals for Justice and Social Cohesion in Côte d'Ivoire* (ICTJ forthcoming).

4

Human Rights at the Intersections of Structural and Cultural Violence

LaDawn Haglund

Human rights and democracy are always in need of protection. Yet, the sheer number of authoritarian heads of state in recent years—Trump, Bolsonaro, Modi, Erdoğan, and other right-wing demagogues—is stunning. The creative machinations they have used to hold onto power, moreover, makes the current moment in history seem dangerously unique. But to turn a classic saying on its head: all that seems new is actually old. Prejudice and fear have been manipulated for political ends repeatedly throughout history, and the social conditions that make this possible are not unique to our time.

More than a decade ago, while the United States was reeling from a mortgage lending crisis that quickly went global, I wrote a short piece invoking Karl Polanyi to explain how market fundamentalism and a disconnect between the economy and societal well-being had helped spawn and deepen the crisis.[1] Though Polanyi was describing the "stark utopia" of economic liberalism at the beginning of the 20th century, our experience in the first decade of the 21st was eerily similar. Also similar, though few suspected it at the time, was the "ever-given political possibility" of a "fascist situation" arising out of the societal pain caused by this dominating market logic.[2]

Now, after an attempted takeover of the US Capitol in 2021, we must marvel again at the prescience of Polanyi's warning:

> If a "revolutionary situation" is characterized by the psychological and moral disintegration of all forces of resistance to the point where a handful of scantily armed rebels were enabled to storm the supposedly impregnable strongholds of reaction, then the "fascist situation" was its complete parallel except for the fact that here the bulwarks of democracy and constitutional liberties were stormed and their defenses found wanting in the same spectacular fashion.[3]

---

[1] Karl Polanyi, *The Great Transformation* (Boston: Beacon Press, 1944); LaDawn Haglund, "Fear, hope, and great transformations," Blog, *Rethinking Development Economics*, 18 September 2008.

[2] Polanyi, *The Great Transformation*, p. 247; see also Hertel, this volume.

[3] Polanyi, *The Great Transformation*, p. 247.

Although most defenses have held for the time being, the astonishing rise of illiberal forces both in the US and globally should lead us to ask: What in the world is happening?

Answers to this question can be made plainer utilizing what C. Wright Mills called a "sociological imagination."[4] Commenting on a related 20th century upheaval, the Great Depression, Mills argued "there was little doubt—except among certain deluded business circles—that there was an economic issue which was also a pack of personal troubles."[5] The link between personal suffering and "structural contradictions ... seemed plain."[6] But in the post-War period, "many great public issues as well as many private troubles" were individualized, "in a pathetic attempt to avoid the ... problems of modern society."[7] This cultural framing that blames individuals rather than socioeconomic systems for social problems remains strong, at least in the United States, and can be readily observed in the backlash against efforts to address systemic racism, structural inequality, and immigration (among other things).

It can be difficult to see with the human eye the *structure* of injustice—the relatively enduring patterns of behavior, relationships, institutions, and rules that reproduce political, economic, environmental, and social harm. The COVID-19 pandemic and a variety of other upheavals laid bare the consequences of these structural factors in ways that are unprecedented in recent times.[8] Workers essential to our food, health, and well-being are undervalued and underpaid, yet expected to put themselves at the front line, in harm's way, to keep our systems running.[9] Meanwhile, the CEOs of the companies for which they work are launching rockets into space and seeing large increases in their personal assets.[10] Large sectors of the population have so little wealth that they depend exclusively on the next paycheck to avoid eviction while wealthy investors drive up housing prices across the world.[11] And global inequality directs vaccines and lifesaving equipment to the wealthiest countries and populations rather than to the most vulnerable or sick.[12]

---

[4] Charles Wright Mills, *The Sociological Imagination*, (Oxford University Press, 2000 [1959]).

[5] Wright Mills, p. 11.

[6] Wright Mills, p. 12.

[7] Wright Mills, p. 12.

[8] "US: Systemic rights failings - capitol attack, pandemic, police killings, racial injustice, migrants' rights, economic disparities," Human Rights Watch, January 13, 2021. https://www.hrw.org/news/2021/01/13/us-systemic-rights-failings

[9] World Health Organization, "Impact of COVID-19 on people's livelihoods, their health and our food systems," Joint statement by ILO, FAO, IFAD and WHO 13 October 2020, https://www.who.int/news/item/13-10-2020-impact-of-covid-19-on-people%27s-livelihoods-their-health-and-our-food-systems

[10] Neil Vigdor, "Bezos thanks Amazon workers and customers for his vast wealth, prompting backlash," *The New York Times*, July 20, 2021, https://www.nytimes.com/2021/07/20/science/bezos-amazon.html.

[11] Greg Lacurci and Annie Nova, "They lived paycheck to paycheck before the pandemic. Then their worst nightmare came true." CNBC, 7 November 2020, https://www.cnbc.com/2020/11/07/they-lived-paycheck-to-paycheck-then-the-pandemic-hit-.html; "Push: The Global Housing Crisis," Documentary on Leilani Farha. *Al Jazeera*, https://www.aljazeera.com/program/witness/2021/9/30/push-the-global-housing-crisis.

[12] UNGA, "Decrying COVID-19 vaccine inequity, speakers in General Assembly call for rich nations to share surplus doses, patent waivers allowing production in low-income countries," General Assembly, Seventy-sixth Session, 10th & 11th Meetings, GA/12367, 23 September 2021, https://www.un.org/press/en/2021/ga12367.doc.htm.

Similarly, the massive resistance to systemic violence—against mainly Black but also Indigenous people and people of color—revealed a well-documented but not widely acknowledged legacy of cruelty, in a continuous line from colonization and slavery through Jim Crow and the Civil Rights Movement to modern police brutality, marginalization, and dispossession.[13] The consequences of systemic racism for BIPOC communities go far beyond racist policing to encompass inadequate housing, an aging basic services infrastructure, unequal access to health care, struggling schools, and continued segregation.[14]

Finally, climate change continues to wreak havoc on those communities which contributed very little to global emissions while those who contributed most are also more able to escape the consequences.[15] Similarly, those who have most to lose in terms of maintaining their livelihoods as they and their ancestors once had, particularly Indigenous and tribal peoples in the Global South, are often least able to influence decisionmakers who could stem planetary crises.[16] Our entire global economic system—upon which we all depend but that allocates resources with extreme inequity—is structured to be mostly indifferent to ecological impact, relying heavily as it does on cheap fossil fuels, massive shipping networks, and dirty production.[17] We are, collectively, on a treadmill in support of capital accumulation that we cannot seem to get off.[18]

The handmaiden of this "structural violence"[19] is "cultural violence"[20]—the ideologies, narratives, myths and assumptions about race, class, gender, and human nature that allow people to obfuscate systemic injustice, avoid responsibility, or make excuses for the violence these structures perpetuate.[21] In the common vernacular, *violence* is often understood to be something physical, sudden, and unforeseen. The slow violence of insecurity, exposure to risk, chronic hunger, deprivation, and countless other injustices is largely invisible to those not experiencing or intentionally seeing it.

[13] David Lyons and Michael K. Brown, *Redress for Historical Injustices in the United States: On Reparations for Slavery, Jim Crow, and Their Legacies* (Duke University Press, 2007); Rebecca Solnit, "As the George Floyd protests continue, let's be clear where the violence is coming from," *The Guardian*, 1 June 2020, https://www.theguardian.com/commentisfree/2020/jun/01/george-floyd-riots-violence-damage-property-police-brutality.
[14] John Eligon and Julie Bosman. "How Minneapolis, one of America's most liberal cities, struggles with racism," *The New York Times*, June 1, 2020, https://www.nytimes.com/2020/06/01/us/minneapolis-racism-minnesota.html.
[15] Sarah Al-Arshani and Kelsey Vlamis, "Countries contributing the least to the climate crisis are feeling the worst of its effects," https://www.businessinsider.com/climate-change-worst-places-in-the-world-hardest-hit-2021-10. 13 November 2021.
[16] David Harvey, "The 'new' imperialism: Accumulation by dispossession," *Social. Regist.*, 40, (2004), 63–87.
[17] Daniel Faber, "Global capitalism, reactionary neoliberalism, and the deepening of environmental injustices," (2018), 8–28. https://doi.org/10.1080/10455752.2018.1464250.
[18] John Bellamy Foster, Brett Clark, and Richard York, *The Ecological Rift: Capitalism's War on the Earth* (New York University Press, 2011).
[19] Johan Galtung, "Violence, peace, and peace research," *Journal of Peace Research* 6 no. 3 (1969), 167–191.
[20] Johan Galtung, "Cultural violence," *Journal of Peace Research* 27, no. 3 (1990), 291–305.
[21] Matthew Mullen, "Reassessing the focus of transitional justice: the need to move structural and cultural violence to the centre," *Cambridge Review of International Affairs* 28, no. 3 (2015), 462–479.

Similarly, the cruelty with which we destroy the natural world or endanger and kill animals is rarely visible to those not directly witnessing. Indeed, cultural violence is like a deliberate blinding process, designed to obscure these violent processes from our potential outrage.

The events of 2020–2021 have once again awakened the possibility that our sociological imaginations could grasp the structural and cultural violence of the modern capitalist political economy and the geography of 500 years of colonialism and slavery upon which it was built. It is becoming nearly impossible *not* to acknowledge how these interlocking systems have recklessly exploited planetary resources to feed imperial and industrial ends; forced or lured laboring bodies to fields, factories, and other front lines to produce value for scraps; and shamelessly allocated the bounty of these processes to a small number of largely already-well-off beneficiaries.

Even for those who were not directly victimized by these longer-standing legacies, globalization has extended and intensified the environmental and social disruption of capitalist production to maximize accumulation. As these depredations become visible, it's no wonder that anger and fear are on the rise (see Hertel, this volume), reactivating and giving new life to the scapegoating that has been with us since time immemorable. Dominant cultural narratives that challenge the structural violence of capitalism itself are rare and actively disputed by hegemonic actors who stand to benefit from the maintenance of business as usual. In this context, cultural backlash in the form of tribalist scapegoating is to be expected and has come with a vengeance.

What role might human rights play in defending democratic institutions and basic human dignity not only from the onslaught of right-wing xenophobia and racism but also from the ravages of capitalism? Human rights discourses and practices must be stable and well-defended to withstand the active resistance that they attract from those who benefit from the status quo. But they also must be radical enough to confront reactionary dogmas and the deeper structures that feed them. Goodhart and Hoover (both in this volume) show quite clearly that narrow cosmopolitan human rights are misaligned with the challenges that face us today. In particular, a cosmopolitanism that doesn't acknowledge and incorporate the reality of structural and cultural violence, instead striving for a mythic shared humanity, contributes to and reifies this violence.

Because structural and cultural violence are never wholly global or local, so must be human rights struggles. Like wildfires, floods, and hurricanes, structural threats to human rights are unimpeded (and in fact exacerbated) by borders; they shape the fortune of individuals, communities, and nations; and they leave their wreckage in urban and rural areas alike. Similarly, human rights, though embodied in an international canon, are crafted and reworked through national constitutions, regional NGOs and advocacy organizations, and local policies and struggles. The idea that international law and geopolitics is "where the action is" represents a particular cosmopolitan blind spot. In actuality, some of the most exciting and consequential efforts to defend human rights happen on the ground, where people live.

Cities are a helpful lens with which to view these efforts, in part because human beings cluster there, threats to well-being are ubiquitous, and solutions can reach far more people. Cities are also powerful nodes of capital accumulation and private property, and thus provide clear examples of how capitalist enclosure of public space can clash with human rights.[22] As international human rights norms are embedded in national constitutions and laws and anchored in local struggles, projects, and imaginaries, local state actors become important duty bearers in areas such as policy, regulation, and service provision.[23] As a result, sub-national actors, both state and non-state, are crucial to the realization of human rights, even in their most cosmopolitan framing.

Human rights instruments, in particular as formulated in the Sustainable Development Goals (SDGs) and the New Urban Agenda, are increasingly utilized by city administrators to articulate and set policy and urban planning goals.[24] They can provide guidelines for establishing minimum standards, strategies for engaging populations and changing hearts and minds, tools for dismantling harmful structures and constructing alternatives, or weapons against violators. But despite the proliferation of "SDG Cities," how transformative are these efforts?

A useful tool for unpacking this question is the "MAPs" (mechanisms, actors and pathways) framework, which draws attention to actors at global, regional, and local levels who utilize both generalized and targeted mechanisms to forge pathways toward rights realization.[25] The MAPs framework calls our attention to *which actors*, with *what beliefs and perspectives*, are taking *which actions* (and *incentivized how*), toward *what kind of social transformation*. This latter question is crucial: "human rights" as individual claims may stop short of addressing the structural and cultural underpinnings emphasized above that could truly transform society. Yet, they also imply (and sometimes explicitly *demand* in the form of state obligations) examination of the structural and systemic factors that facilitate or thwart rights realization. *This is where the radical potential of human rights lies.*

As Figure 1 illustrates, in the first "moment of social transformation," prevailing structural and cultural realities, as well as "belief formation" processes shape actors' *beliefs and perceptions*. The second moment is when desires and beliefs translate into *action*—or, in the absence of particular beliefs or perceptions, incentives or coercion compel action. The third moment is the culmination of actions and interactions into broader *structural and/or cultural change*, setting the stage for new beliefs and perceptions to emerge.

Operating at each analytic "moment" (1–3) are multiple mechanisms through which change can occur: legal, legislative, and administrative (international, national, or local), informational (data and indicators, shadow reports, monitoring), symbolic (framing, meaning-making—visual or imagined), power-based (protest, political pressure, international pressure), and cooperative (community building, alliances, shared projects).

[22] Neil Brenner, Peter Marcuse, and Margit Mayer, eds, *Cities for People, Not for Profit: Critical Urban Theory and the Right to the City* (Routledge, 2012).

[23] Varun Gauri and Daniel M. Brinks, eds, *Courting Social Justice: Judicial Enforcement of Social and Economic Rights in the Developing World* (New York: Cambridge University Press, 2010).

[24] United Nations Sustainable Development Goals, https://sdgs.un.org/goals.

[25] LaDawn Haglund and Robin Stryker, eds, *Closing the Rights Gap: From Human Rights to Social Transformation* (Oakland: University of California Press, 2015).

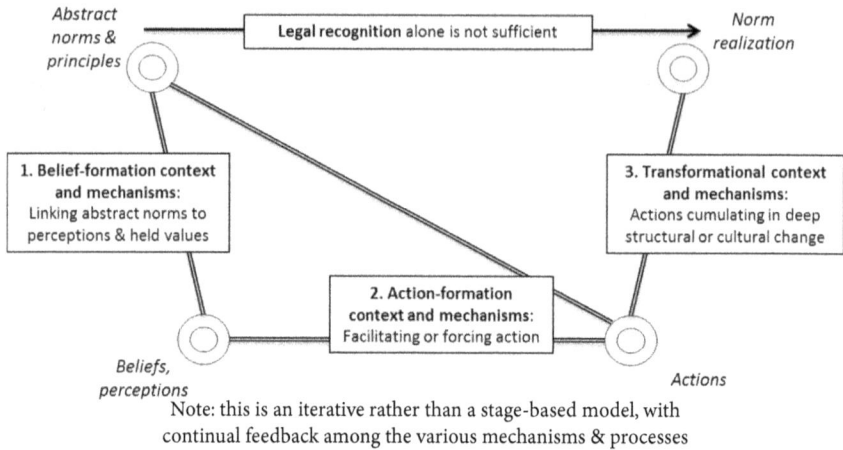

Abstract norms & principles — Legal recognition alone is not sufficient → Norm realization

1. Belief-formation context and mechanisms: Linking abstract norms to perceptions & held values

3. Transformational context and mechanisms: Actions cumulating in deep structural or cultural change

2. Action-formation context and mechanisms: Facilitating or forcing action

Beliefs, perceptions

Actions

Note: this is an iterative rather than a stage-based model, with continual feedback among the various mechanisms & processes

Figure 1 Moments of social transformation. Haglund and Stryker 2015.

Local governments have utilized this full range of mechanisms to promote the SDGs. Law and policy infused with human rights imperatives have been able to recolonize institutional spaces and pry open specific alternatives to structural violence. There are many examples of these "double movements"[26]—citizen review boards designed to protect civil rights and hold police accountable;[27] public goods created to achieve universal social rights in health, education, water, and sanitation;[28] and safety nets that decommodify workers and shield them from the ravages of structural unemployment and for-profit housing markets.[29] In the realm of the experimental and aspirational are a "Pluriverse" of other state and non-state initiatives that prioritize rights-based economic, social, cultural, civil, and political rights.[30] It is not difficult to imagine how such measures of social protection, universalized, would lessen the pain of insecurity and the appeal of reactionary demagogues.

The main structural barrier to these kinds of initiatives are capitalist social relations—legally supported concentration of ownership, decision making, and capital in the hands of a few—accompanied by cultural narratives of "job creation," "Nanny States," "Welfare Queens," and "There Is No Alternative." These narratives took on new life in the US and UK under Reagan and Thatcher, respectively, were globally disseminated starting in the 1980s, and still dominate economic discourse. Nevertheless, in recent years human rights have been important tools in fighting this cultural

---

[26] Polanyi, *The Great Transformation*.
[27] The Opportunity Agenda: n.d. https://transformingthesystem.org/criminal-justice-policy-solutions/create-fair-and-effective-policing-practices/promoting-accountability/.
[28] LaDawn Haglund, *Limiting Resources: Market-led Reform and the Transformation of Public Goods* (Pennsylvania State University Press: University Park, 2010).
[29] Jody Heymann and Alison Earle, *Raising the Global Floor: Dismantling the Myth That We Can't Afford Good Working Conditions for Everyone* (Stanford University Press, 2009).
[30] Ashish Kothari, Ariel Salleh, Arturo Escobar, Federico Demaria, and Alberto Acosta, *"Pluriverse": A Post-Development Dictionary*, (New Dehli: Tulika Books 2019).

violence, not only by reframing the normative impetus for law and policy,[31] but also by reimagining alternatives utilizing other mechanisms of social transformation: information, symbolism, political and social pressure, and cooperative initiatives.

For example, planning, reporting, and voluntary local review integrating SDG goals and benchmarks have provide new ways to understand and monitor progress, raise awareness of where action is needed, and provide roadmaps for action.[32] They also have provided opportunities for sharing and comparison among cities.[33] Inclusion of community-based organizations and civil society in these plans and reports allows for more robust flows of information and monitoring, shapes community feelings of efficacy, creates linkages among the multiple issues facing cities, and builds alliances for deeper change.[34] Institutionalizing human rights in local policy decisions can further strengthen accountability to the SDGs in the absence of binding obligations.[35] Coalitions such as the US National Human Rights Cities Alliance mobilize a range of mechanisms—data gathering, reporting, organizing, and pressure on public administrators—to do just this embedding of local policies and processes in social values.[36]

Human rights are also used as symbols by both state and non-state actors to reframe attempts to legitimize the unhealthy and unjust status quo as morally repugnant.[37] Here, a "sociological imagination" is crucial to make the linkages between what are framed as individual failings and the historical and systemic drivers of human suffering. Rights-based narratives can also create a sense of shared humanity, compassion, and community (see Kenyon, this volume) based on the ontological frailty of human life and the precarity of social institutions.[38] However, this symbolic sympathy cannot assume a cosmopolitan sameness that glosses over structural violence and diversity of

---

[31] Gillian MacNaughton, and Diane F. Frey, eds, *Economic and Social Rights in a Neoliberal World* (Cambridge University Press, 2018).

[32] Emily Hosek, "Global trends in integrated sustainable urban development for the 2030 agenda." United National Department of Social and Economic Affairs, n.d., https://sustainabledevelopment. un.org/content/unosd/documents/4209Session%204-1%20Emily%20Hosek.pdf; Sustainable Development Solutions Network, "2019 US Cities Sustainable Development Report," 8 July, 2019, https://www.sustainabledevelopment.report/reports/2019-us-cities-sustainable-development-report/; SDGs Partnership Platform, "Achieving SDGs—one city at the time- towards local authority voluntary review," n.d., https://sustainabledevelopment.un.org/partnership/?p=30537.

[33] Thematic Research Network on Data and Statistics, "Local action to global replication: How sub-national data efforts support SDG achievement," April 2019, https://www.sdsntrends.org/research/2019/4/15/local-data-action-microgrant-insights.

[34] United Nations University, Macau, "Data Intermediation and Collaboration with Community-based Organizations," https://cs.unu.edu/research/sdgs-cbo, https://www.mdpi.com/2071-1050/7/2/1651.

[35] Jackie Smith and Joshua Cooper, "Bringing human rights home: new strategies for local organizing," Blog, *Open Global Rights*, 1 August 2019, https://www.openglobalrights.org/bringing-human-rights-home-new-strategies-for-local-organizing/.

[36] US National Human Rights Cities Alliance, http://wiki.humanrightscities.mayfirst.org/index.php?title=Main_Page

[37] Andrea Ballestero, "The ethics of a formula: Calculating a financial—humanitarian price for water," *American Ethnologist* 42, no. 2 (2015), 262–278; Brianne McGonigle Leyh, "Imperatives of the present: Black Lives Matter and the politics of memory and memorialization," *Netherlands Quarterly of Human Rights* 38, no. 4 (2020), 239–245.

[38] Bryan S. Turner, "Outline of a theory of human rights," *Sociology* 27, no. 3 (1993), 489–512.

experiences. Instead, it must embrace a "Pluriverse" of possible futures that incorporate a range of life- and rights-affirming alternatives.[39]

Paradoxically, one of the challenges of narration is that multiple narratives *are* possible. Indeed, this discussion of structural and cultural violence narrates history in ways that are uncommon in mainstream discourse. Similarly, Black Lives Matter, #MeToo, Occupy, QAnon, and countless other narratives vie for public attention and are supported by people with varying access to the more powerful means of communication. The institutionalization of human rights in legitimate institutions helps boost their utility in forming counternarratives, while human rights stories have the advantage of invoking a broadly legitimized core set of standards that can be "vernacularized" to resonate with specific communities.[40]

Human rights as cooperative mechanisms can create humane space for a variety of alternatives, whether or not human rights are the key symbolic framing. But these do not necessarily have to be "polite spaces" without conflict. In fact, they may need to be brave spaces, where we not only make room for each other but also challenge each other to be better and commit to socially just values (see Hoover, this volume).[41] "Order" may not be possible and may in fact be dangerous for those at risk in the current order. In fact, urban protest may be the other side to the cooperative coin, invoked when spaces for dialogue and negotiation are closed to those whose rights are being violated. Protestors' use of human rights imperatives can often be the catalyst pressuring intransigent duty bearers to act.

To summarize, the transformative potential of human rights mechanisms and strategies in urban areas depends on the capacity to shift beliefs and perceptions as well as foster or force action (see Figure 1); but to be truly transformative, they must interrupt the structural and cultural violence perpetuating urban decay, exclusion, and state failure. This may mean introducing new discourses and ideas that shift societal goals and values, as well as individual and collective identity [what Stryker and Haglund (2015) call *symbolic or ideational transformation*]. On the plane of *material transformation*, it may entail reforming institutions and policies to improve service delivery and socioeconomic well-being. Finally, transformation may need to be *political*, with a redistribution of power and opening of decision-making processes to previously disadvantaged or marginalized groups.[42]

The SDGs cities movement may or may not lead to the deep transformations signaled above. Efforts to ensure a "Right to the City" illustrate the challenges and promise of transformative urban reform. At its most general, a Right to the City calls for burdens, benefits, and decisions that affect city life to be shared equally among

---

[39] Kothari et al., "*Pluriverse*," see also Hoover, this volume.

[40] Sally Engle Merry, *Human Rights and Gender Violence: Translating International Law into Local Justice* (University of Chicago Press, 2009).

[41] Brian Arao and Kristi Clemens, "A new way to frame dialogue around diversity and social justice," in *The Art of Effective Facilitation: Reflections from Social Justice Educators*, ed. Lisa M Landreman (Stylus Publishing, 2013).

[42] Stryker and Haglund; see also Siri Gloppen, "Social rights litigation as transformation: South African perspectives." in *Democratising Development: The Politics of Socio-economic Rights in South Africa*, eds, Peris Jones and Kristian Stokke (Amsterdam: Nijhoff 2005), pp. 153–180.

inhabitants. Cities do not "belong" to everyone equally; law and policy can be wielded by powerful actors in defense of an unjust status quo. Calls for a right to the city are demands not only for basic human rights but also a radical reconfiguration of the underlying political economy.[43] Unfortunately, the rhetoric of "the right to the city" can be co-opted in ways that not only do not challenge injustice but actually attempt to erase any such challenges. The SDG Cities movement bears the same risk of becoming another project of reimagining the city in the image of capital without rooting out structural and cultural barriers to rights realization.

Achieving urban human rights must be seen as a process of social transformation, where visions beyond profit, interests beyond elites, and actions beyond growth and job creation are valorized and vested with power. Challenging capitalism, property rights, power relations, and/or long-standing elite privilege requires a sociological imagination to envision why structural change is both possible and necessary. Luckily, people already are imagining alternatives, some based in human rights discourses and practices, some not.[44] This work is not easy and in fact can be dangerous, as repression of recent movements for social, environmental, and racial justice attests.[45] A key contribution of human rights may actually be to protect these voices and prevent repression of alternatives so that space can be created for new social logics to govern our world.

---

[43] Peter Marcuse, "Whose right(s) to what city?" in *Cities for People, Not for Profit: Critical Urban Theory and the Right to the City,* eds, Neil Brenner, Peter Marcuse, and Margit Mayer, (Routledge, 2012).

[44] Kothari et al., "*Pluriverse*"; Arturo Escobar,"Una minga para el posdesarrollo." *Signo y pensamiento* 30, no. 58 (2011), 278–284.

[45] Hank Johnston and Pamela Oliver, eds, *Racialized Protest and the State: Resistance and Repression in a Divided America* (Routledge, 2020); Philippe Le Billon and Päivi Lujala, "Environmental and land defenders: Global patterns and determinants of repression," *Global Environmental Change* 65 (2020), 102163.

5

Everyday Cosmopolitanism and Human Rights

Huss Banai

My principal aim in this chapter is to describe a mode of human interaction that is at once locally contingent (i.e., its content differs from one context to another), universally in evidence (i.e., can be observed across different societies around the globe), and complementary to, if not purposefully supportive of, human rights work (i.e., direct and indirect efforts that respect human dignity as an end in itself). I call this mode of human interaction *Everyday Cosmopolitanism*. It is an "everyday" activity in the sense that it is a mundane, often banal occurrence between individuals within and/or across societies on a daily basis. It may turn on harmony, contentiousness, or indifference depending on the context; but its scope only concerns relations between fellow human beings (and not objects or other beings in nature). It is "cosmopolitan" in the limited Stoic conception of the term that recognizes the moral priority of equal human dignity in social interactions. The political implications of this moral quality—which is almost an afterthought in many daily human interactions across the globe—are immense for human rights, however much the justificatory basis for them remains contested.

I wish to be clear from the outset, however, that the conception of "cosmopolitanism" I have in mind in this chapter differs from liberal-cosmopolitan visions that tend to sublimate divergent ways of life into an abstract universal identity (often premised on a shared rationality). In contrast to the latter notions, Everyday Cosmopolitanism is not a *justificatory* view of human rights, but merely a mode of social interaction—a way of life—complementary to securing the conditions for the observance of human rights. It may reasonably be asked, then, why the term "cosmopolitan" should be used to describe this ostensibly ordinary activity at all. My preference for hanging on to the term is twofold. First, the etymology of the term points to a central truth about the character of such commonplace interactions that is worth preserving. The phrase *kosmopolitês* first appears in the fourth century BCE philosophical rhetoric of Diogenes the Cynic who, in response to a question about his origins, is said to have responded, "I am a citizen of the world" (Diogenes Laertius, VI 63). By declaring himself thus, Diogenes was neither arguing for rootlessness nor belonging to a universal community of humankind; rather—and, alas, this subtle distinction is too often overlooked by champions of cosmopolitanism today—he was insisting on the *priority of recognizing human dignity above all other attachments*. Although a citizen of Sinope, he interpreted his local loyalties, attachments, and duties within this inclusive normative framework that underlined the incidental nature of communal belonging.[1]

My second reason for holding on to the term is to rescue it from precisely the sorts of normative projects that see in cosmopolitanism either a new metric for remaking the world in the image of Western modernity, or a demonic universalist conspiracy hatched by rootless fund managers and/or liberal professors bent on destroying national belongings. Neither of these associations remotely resembles everyday interactions that prioritize understanding and coexistence above exclusivist commitments (be they local or global). Contra conventional liberal depictions of cosmopolitanism, such everyday cosmopolitan engagements are not ideal-typical encounters—they constitute daily realities. Understood in this way, reactionary opponents of cosmopolitanism and its liberal champions equally obscure the commonplace reality and unremarkable nature of everyday cosmopolitanism. Dispensing with the label "cosmopolitanism," therefore, would be more than just parting ways with a serially abused concept, for it would also lend credence to caricatures of an otherwise critical aspect of daily cooperation and coexistence. To be sure, this ingredient is not universally the same, nor in evidence everywhere; all the same, it attests to a preference for—however thinly, tacitly, or contentiously—universal recognition of human beings as ends in themselves.

That a basic acknowledgment of this preference undergirds human rights discourse and practice is, in fact, uncontroversial. Whether at the local, regional, national, or global level, struggles on behalf of human rights proceed on the assumption of equal respect for human dignity.[2] What is less agreeable is whether this shared understanding ought to also serve as the ultimate justification for human rights regardless of their content, scope, and location.[3] I do not believe that it should, but that is an entirely different subject matter on which considerable time and intellectual energy has already been spent (and which I do not wish to revisit here).[4] For my purposes, what I am interested in here is the extent to which concern for, and the recognition of, human rights are aided by interactions I classify as Everyday Cosmopolitanism. In the following, I examine two categories of empirical cases that illustrate what I mean by the intersection of Everyday Cosmopolitanism and human rights. I then consider the

---

[1] For comprehensive examinations of this particular reading of cosmopolitanism that especially eschew Eurocentrism, see Kwame Anthony Appiah, *Cosmopolitanism: Ethics in A World of Strangers* (New York: W.W. Norton, 2006); Farah Godrej, *Cosmopolitan Political Thought: Method, Practice, Discipline* (New York: Oxford University Press, 2011); and Martha C. Nussbaum, *The Cosmopolitan Tradition: A Noble but Flawed Ideal* (Cambridge, MA: Harvard University Press, 2019).

[2] George Kateb, *Human Dignity* (Cambridge, MA: Harvard University Press, 2011).

[3] For a succinct summary of, and thoughtful reflections on, these disagreements, see Carol C. Gould, *Globalizing Democracy and Human Rights* (Cambridge: Cambridge University Press, 2004).

[4] For some prominent examples in normative political theory, see Charles R. Beitz, *The Idea of Human Rights* (New York: Oxford University Press, 2009); Seyla Benhabib, *Another Cosmopolitanism* (New York: Oxford University Press, 2008); Michael Ignatieff, *Human Rights as Politics and Idolatry* (Princeton, NJ: Princeton University Press, 2001); and Mathias Risse, *On Global Justice* (Princeton, NJ: Princeton University Press, 2012), Part I. The substantive core of the debate is best represented in the exchange between Michael Goodhart and Jack Donnelly in *Human Rights Quarterly* 30, no. 1 (February 2008), 183–204.

implications of these intersections for how we might think about the inequities that both enable and undercut human rights at the local level. I conclude the chapter by explaining the key differences between the categories of interactions I describe and rationalist-cosmopolitan conceptions of emancipation and consensus.

Allies and Critics

Everyday Cosmopolitanism is not limited to a particular domain of activity—i.e., cultural, political, economic, etc.—rather, it is distinguished by a particular mindset that is, depending on the circumstances, either instinctive or a fruit of reflection across many different spheres of activity. This frame of mind, as I noted above, has to do with recognizing human beings as ends in themselves and not as instruments of other forces (be they human or nonhuman). Of course, this does not mean that everyone's views and actions must be equally respected; rather, that by virtue of being human, their *personhood* is entitled to respect. This basic respect for the dignity of individuals as moral beings forms the basis of countless interactions every day, even as fierce disagreements over basic beliefs and facts still persist. Everyday Cosmopolitanism attests to the ordinariness of such dynamics in daily life. But the moral import and political implications of Everyday Cosmopolitanism become especially apparent when considering the promotion and quest for human rights in particular contexts. In this section, I consider two broad classifications of activities—one positive, another negative—that best demonstrate the crucial connections between Everyday Cosmopolitanism and human rights. The first, what could also be called *positive* Everyday Cosmopolitanism, is an exercise in inclusion through affirmation of a particular struggle for human rights or mitigation of an injustice. The second, *negative* category of engagements are no less inclusive in their implications, but instead of affirming existing rights-based struggles or movements they engage in constructive criticisms of their aims, strategies, and tactics. To be clear, these categories are not mutually exclusive, and, in most cases, they constitute different dimensions of the same overall normative project. For the purposes of brevity and clarity, I will resort to shorthand monikers "allies" and "critics" in this section to illustrate the connections between these different dimensions of Everyday Cosmopolitanism in relation to human rights discourse and practice.

In the wake of prominent gender- and race-based social justice movements across the globe (the Women's March, #MeToo, Black Lives Matter protests, most prominent among them), the concept of "allyship" has garnered much attention in the public imagination and among scholars. "Allyship" or "ally behavior" is ascribed to members of advantaged groups who take action in support of, or express solidarity with, members of disadvantaged groups in local and/or global communities.[5] At the core of

---

[5] The term has become a staple of institutional efforts around diversity, equity, and inclusion, with many public institutions—especially in the United States—defining and touting their own allyship on various matters. For an historical overview of the term's resonance with issues of social justice, see, Meredith D. Clark, "White folks' work: Digital allyship praxis in the# BlackLivesMatter movement," *Social Movement Studies* 18, no. 5 (2019), 519–534.

this concept is the question of responsibilities and moral obligations owed to those among us who are at a disadvantage due to historical and/or contemporaneous factors. While allyships are fraught with ethical dilemmas in relation to systemic and large-scale issues with layered socioeconomic, cultural, and political factors—e.g., What are the motives that lie behind advantaged groups' participation? Are they ultimately performative exercises that merely signal awareness but don't yield any tangible or substantive changes in the underlying structures of domination and disempowerment? Who benefits from allyship more if only discourses change without corresponding changes in structural inequities?[6]—they also exemplify the thin, mundane, and micro-level nature of an affirmative social engagement characteristic of positive Everyday Cosmopolitanism.

At both the individual and group levels, the recognition of one's advantages and privileges relative to those of others'—and, most significantly, perhaps as a symptom of others' systemic marginalization and suffering—is critical for establishing the links between injustice and human dignity. Affirming the underlying grievances of disadvantaged persons and groups through social movements and political mobilization by advantaged groups can be a powerful means to political change both symbolically and in concrete policy terms. This is evidenced, for instance, in the case of *Estallido Social* protests in Chile between 2019 and 2021 that began as a series of small gatherings against the fare hikes of the Santiago Metro, but then soon ballooned into nationwide demonstrations against widespread corruption, social inequality, privatization, and political unaccountability.[7] The harsh crackdown by the Carabineros security units further inflamed public grievances and resulted in more resilient bonds of solidarity between various local and national networks of activism that continue to struggle against multiple violations of human rights. The protests formed an intersection between Women's and Girls' rights, Indigenous rights, labor rights, refugee and migrant rights, disability rights, children's rights, prison reform, and anti-corruption movements.[8] Indeed, this welling up of everyday grievances into affirmative coalitions of activists and ordinary citizens also had parallels in Colombia (over increased taxes, widespread corruption, inadequate healthcare, and police brutality), Hong Kong (the Anti-Extradition Law Amendment Bill movement and protests in

---

[6] For empirical examinations of some of these ethical issues, see Wendy S. Hesford, "Reading the signs: Performative white allyship," *Quarterly Journal of Speech* 107, no. 2 (2021), 239–244; Haneen Shafeeq Ghabra, "Don't say his name: The terror attacks in New Zealand and the ethics of White allyship," *Journal of International and Intercultural Communication* (2020), 1–16; Kelsey Blair, "Empty gestures: Performative utterances and allyship," *Journal of Dramatic Theory and Criticism* 35, no. 2 (2021), 53–73; Helena R. M. Radke, Maja Kutlaca, Birte Siem, Stephen C. Wright, and Julia C. Becker, "Beyond allyship: Motivations for advantaged group members to engage in action for disadvantaged groups," *Personality and Social Psychology Review* 24, no. 4 (2020), 291–315; and J. E. Sumerau, TehQuin D. Forbes, Eric Anthony Grollman, and Lain AB Mathers, "Constructing allyship and the persistence of inequality," *Social Problems* 68, no. 2 (2021), 358–373.

[7] Amanda Taub, "'Chile Woke Up': Dictatorship's Legacy of Inequality Triggers Mass Protests," *The New York Times*, November 18, 2019, https://www.nytimes.com/2019/11/03/world/americas/chile-protests.html.

[8] "Chile: Events of 2020," *World Report 2021*, Human Rights Watch: https://www.hrw.org/world-report/2021/country-chapters/chile.

2019–2020), and Iran (ongoing protests against water mismanagement, widespread corruption, and labor rights, and political repression), among other places. In each case, the resilience and efficacy of the protest movements are derived from the affirmative bonds of solidarity between groups with disparate grievances and agendas, but whose everyday travails and struggles allow them to empathize with each other. These everyday interactions can be in the form of conversations with neighbors and family members, observing interactions between others in public and private spaces, reading about personal hardships or achievements on social media, listening to complaints or accolades, or simply reflecting in silence on how best to support one's peer or loved one. These mundane engagements, however variable in levels of intensity, force us to contemplate fellow human beings in their own terms by affirming their personal imprint in our own lives. In other words, these daily interactions contribute to our becoming allies to others by compelling us to see our own personhood implicated in the personhood of others, and vice versa.

To reiterate, this does not necessarily mean that such expressions of allyship will yield meaningful political changes or succeed in overcoming the ethical dilemmas that underpin the motivations behind them. Nonetheless, they do provide an important resource for reflective understanding, which is necessary for affirming the plights of others. The progress that is yielded by this positive variant of Everyday Cosmopolitanism can be slow, halting, even frustrating, as witnessed in the cases of privileged White allies of Black and Brown activists within the Black Lives Matter (BLM) movement.[9] This is why active engagement with the flaws and motivations behind such acts of solidarity are so crucial.[10] As many in the BLM movement have noted, reactive, symbolic, and episodic expressions of solidarity may well attest to a salutary shift in the social conscience of White allies, but they are not remotely enough for addressing acute structural inequities that would require deep economic and political concessions by advantaged groups. Indeed, this is where the negative or critical category of everyday cosmopolitan interactions become relevant.

Constructive scrutiny and moral criticism are as much a part of our everyday activities, as are affirmative expressions of empathy and solidarity. This aspect of Everyday Cosmopolitanism, however, is less a matter of intuition and nearly always arises out of a philosophical predisposition toward contextual thinking. In this mode, it is not enough to merely identify with, and pledge support to, disadvantaged persons, but also to actively work toward rooting out the sources of indignity. This, in turn, requires scrutiny of existing practices and conditions. The motivations behind critical Everyday Cosmopolitanism, therefore, are fundamentally emancipatory: they seek to identify and remove the sources that trample on human dignity. This emancipatory aim is self-reflexive in that it begins with an account of one's own positionality (be it in a domestic setting, or more broadly concerned with socioeconomic, cultural, and

---

[9] For a critical assessment, see Matthew W. Hughey, "How Blackness matters in White lives," *Symbolic Interaction* 44, no. 2 (2021), 412–448.

[10] Adam Szetela, "Black Lives Matter at five: Limits and possibilities," *Ethnic and Racial Studies* 43, no. 8 (2020), 1358–1383.

political matters), identity-formation, and ethical commitments. The critical subject, therefore, confronts the world not with a solidified, immutable sense of the past or self, but with an awareness of the tentative hold that identity and socioeconomic circumstances have on individuals and social groups in society. This particular critical disposition, too, is present in mundane, everyday interactions between people, even as it differs from more affirmative acts of solidarity by—once again, either instinctively or through reflective thought—taking a critical measure of not merely an instance of injustice, but the permissive circumstances that perpetuate cycles of violence and indignity.

A good example of this critical manifestation of Everyday Cosmopolitanism was the divergent everyday life experiences of different cohorts of women (based on class, race, religious affiliation, nationality, education, etc.) that informed their participation in, and subsequent criticisms of, the "resistance" movement that took shape after the 2016 US election. The first Women's March took place one day after the inauguration of Donald J. Trump as president of the United States, and garnered worldwide attention as a result of massive marches held in major metropolitan cities across the US and the globe. From the outset, however, there were glaring discrepancies between the aims of the founding organizers of the March (who were mostly women of color) that endeavored to focus attention on the intersections of gender, racial justice, immigration, labor rights, environmental concerns, etc. and the singular focus of the white female majority on Trump and his myriad misdeeds and misogynistic pronouncements against women.[11] The reactions to the criticisms that followed were notable for two reasons. First, rather than dismissing such contradictions as necessary sacrifices for maintaining unity against Trumpism and rising authoritarianism around the globe, the movement was reoriented back toward intersectional activism. This certainly diluted the specific gender-based focus of the resistance against the Trump presidency, but more significantly opened up the space for cross-cutting activism and solidarity across a range of issues that made the broader movement against rising xenophobia and autocracy more resilient.[12] The second noteworthy aspect of the responses to the

[11] For criticisms, see Jia Tolentino, "The Somehow Controversial Women's March in Washington," *The New Yorker*, January 18, 2017, https://www.newyorker.com/culture/jia-tolentino/the-somehow-controversial-womens-march-on-washington; and Mabinty Quarshie, "Is the Women's March More Inclusive This Year?" *USA Today*, January 18, 2018, https://www.usatoday.com/story/news/2018/01/18/womens-march-more-inclusive-year/1038859001/. The organization's leaders also had to address charges of anti-Semitism leveled at two of the founding organizers, Tamika Mallory and Carmen Perez, who were accused of having "berated" other organizers for their Jewish heritage on account of their "special collective responsibility as exploiters of brown and black people." (Anna North, "The Women's March Changed the American Left. Now Anti-Semitism Allegations Threaten the Group's Future," *Vox*, December 21, 2018. https://www.vox.com/identities/2018/12/21/18145176/feminism-womens-march-2018-2019-farrakhan-intersectionality.

[12] As one study of the movement found after, "the Women's March has made good on its commitment to intersectional activism. By creating a diverse leadership and talking about intersectionality at events, it has attracted people with a commitment to this cause—or persuaded people in its movement to care more deeply about intersectionality." See, Michael T. Heaney, "IS the women's march focused on white women—or does it promote intersectional activism?" Monkey Cage, *The Washington Post*, July 8, 2019. Also, see Heaney, "Intersectionality at the Grassroots," *Politics, Groups, and Identities* 9, no. 3 (2021), 608–628.

criticisms relate directly to the everyday critical manifestations of cosmopolitanism. The intersectional criticisms of the March resonated mostly because of how well they corresponded to the daily experiences of disadvantaged groups and the knowledge of the enabling structures and circumstances that formed the roots of their specific grievances. Although the mode of engagement was different (critical as opposed to affirmative), the operational mechanism behind negative Everyday Cosmopolitanism is the same: to appreciate one's personhood implicated in the personhood of others and rendered through complex intersections of myriad factors, structures, and contingent circumstances.

Contra Rationalism

Taken together, the positive and negative categories of Everyday Cosmopolitanism I have briefly discussed above certainly aim for enhanced shared understandings of what injures and might fulfill human dignity. But it is important to note here that these objectives are still quite different from rationalist-cosmopolitan perspectives that conceive of self-reflection and critical thinking mostly in instrumental terms for achieving consensus.[13] This latter of thought is best exemplified in the Habermasian notion of universal critique based on "rational autonomy" and the emancipatory project of the Frankfurt School. According to Habermas, emancipation can only come about as a result of a process of rational self-reflection, whereby "... interest in the way one's history and biography has expressed itself in the way one sees oneself, one's roles and social expectations .... Insights gained through critical self-awareness are emancipatory in the sense that at least one can recognize the correct reasons for his or her problems."[14] For Habermas, then, universal autonomy would come about in the form of a "rational consensus," where constant communication and argumentation would lead to an "ideal speech situation."[15] In concrete terms, this would mean that mundane, everyday disagreements between persons must necessarily yield to a consensus for meaningful emancipation to be achieved. But this is hardly the case in real life, when emancipatory potentials are realized precisely because they make visible the alternatives to mainstream consensuses.

Negative or critical manifestations of Everyday Cosmopolitanism diverge greatly from such rationalist understandings of universal autonomy, consensus, and

---

[13] Acknowledgement of intersectionality, for instance, does not yield any consensus on the priorities or strategies that a social movement ought to pursue, any more than our everyday critical awareness of our own complicity in structures of inequity could cohere around a public consensus.

[14] J. Habermas, *The Theory of Communicative Action, vol. 1: Reason and the Rationalization of the Society* (Cambridge University Press, 1984), p. 285.

[15] This second universal element of Habermas's rationalist proposition, however, ultimately finds itself on a slippery slope. Critics of this approach have rightly pointed to the difficulty in accommodating difference under the conditions of miscommunication, ambiguity of language, and in relation to the existing diversity of thoughts and beliefs. See, Chris Brown, "'Turtles all the way down': Antifoundationalism, critical theory, and international relations," *Millennium: Journal of International Studies* 23, no. 1. (1994), 221–222.

emancipation. Under negative Everyday Cosmopolitanism, emancipation is not measured against any readily discernible "rational consensus," but is rather derived from an everyday understanding that "not all values have a single measure,"[16] and that for emancipatory interest to be meaningful it must be both self- and other-critical. Armed with this emancipatory interest, critical cosmopolitans do not look for a way out of contestation and disagreement—to the contrary, they seek them out. The objective is not to stir conflict and foment hostility, however, but rather to broaden one's cultural, historical, political, economic, and social vocabularies, and to detect among them zones of cooperation, commonality, and reflection. Yet, this is not necessarily representative of some of the more conventional liberal-cosmopolitan writings that believe a mere exchange of ideas, goods, and histories will suffice. Kwame Anthony Appiah's recent meditation is very much representative of this conventional perspective:

> I am urging that we should learn about people in other places, take an interest in their civilizations, their arguments, their errors, their achievements, not because that will bring us to agreement, but because it will help us get used to one another. If that is the aim, then the fact that we have all these opportunities for disagreement about values need not put us off. Understanding one another may be hard; it can certainly be interesting. But it doesn't require that we come to agreement.[17]

Critical manifestations of Everyday Cosmopolitanism certainly exemplify the dialogic dimension of this laudable objective; but they also embody—owing to the positive dimensions of Everyday Cosmopolitanism explained above—a built-in capacity for self-reflection, empathy, and solidarity that could be exercised even prior to provocation by others. Exchanges of argument and information alone will not convince individuals and groups from different backgrounds and socioeconomic conditions to suddenly give up their grievances. It is only through a process of sustained self-examination and critique that one can go beyond arguments about the "self-ness" of "self" and the "otherness" of "others" to a more constructive, humane, and ethical mode of contestation about matters of justice and equality.

In this sense, critical instances of Everyday Cosmopolitanism help to prepare the ethical foundation for a just, egalitarian, and democratic society unburdened by the stereotypical weight of inflated histories and false distinctions. It does so by recognizing the constitutive role played by individuals in the processes of cultural (re)production and identity-formation. Indeed, such a disposition does not treat marginalized and disadvantaged groups as stable or homogeneous entities, but rather finds from within these group myriad instances of dissonance and convergence, of deep-seated resentment and love. Of course, this is hardly an enjoyable exercise, for it almost requires of one a sort of ascetic zeal with which to guard against the encroachment of comfort and self-affirmation that could in an instant transform one into a mere

---

[16] Appiah, *Cosmopolitanism*, p. 166.
[17] Appiah, *Cosmopolitanism*, p. 78.

contrarian, or worst yet, a relativist. Yet, here too, the emancipatory interest can lead the way. In the process of interrogating the utility of their observations, a person may come to understand their own identity from the point of view of an Other first, and then proceed with that understanding to contemplate the world beyond.

As regards human rights, the differential manifestations of Everyday Cosmopolitanism are, in aggregate, as much a *mood* as they are *normative commitments* to emancipation, which grapple seriously with what William Connolly has called the "identity/difference paradox": the notion that "identity requires difference in order to be, and it converts difference into otherness in order to secure its own self-certainty."[18] Everyday, mundane, and ordinary expressions of cosmopolitanism that I have described above speak to a self-reflexive disposition that does not simply seek to engage in endless critique/affirmation for critique's/affirmation's sake, but rather to work within specific spatial-temporal frameworks—as one has no choice by to do in everyday life in one's household, local community, region, state, or global society—in order to address particular social-historical configurations and to point to future possibilities. Human rights, with their intersectional, cross-cutting, trans-regional, and global consciousness are directly tied to these at once ordinary, resonant, and very much consequential interactions.

---

[18] William Connolly, *Identity/Paradox: Democratic Negotiations of Political Paradox* (Minneapolis, MN: University of Minnesota Press, 1991), p. 64.

6

Who Cares? Exclusion, Empathy and Solidarity

Shareen Hertel

Broken Hearts

Early in the COVID-19 pandemic, red hearts emerged as a collective expression of gratitude to healthcare and other frontline workers, particularly in the United States. Hearts in windows and on doors served as an invitation to conversations—about who those workers are, why they are vulnerable, and what can be done to keep them safe. Symbolically, the heart offered a potential tool for forging solidarity and for exploring "deeper patterns of exclusion at the 'heart' of the spread of COVID-19" within the US and globally.[1]

Today, nearly two years later, the red hearts have faded. The space they may have created for mobilizing empathy across social or political or racial divides has shrunk, replaced by deepening division in the US over whether or not people will vaccinate against COVID-19[2] and by a widening gulf in access to vaccines globally.[3] I focus on the *political economy of resistance to vaccination* to help us better understand why overt rejection has become a symbolic gesture of empowerment for some people in the United States. At the same time, I explore the *political economy of the inability to access vaccines globally* which further deepens the experience of economic exclusion that many people in the Global South experience daily.

Framing these issues in terms of economic rights helps center questions of relative economic power. It situates discussions of personal rights and duties against the backdrop

---

[1] Shareen Hertel, "Mobilizing empathy for a truly cosmopolitan human rights," *Open Global Rights*, 30 September, 2020, Available online: https://www.openglobalrights.org/do-sub-state-actors-complicate-how-we-think-of-cosmopolitanism/.

[2] Michael Daly, Andrew Jones, and Eric Robinson, "Public trust and willingness to vaccinate against COVID-19 in the US from October 14, 2020, to March 29, 2021," *JAMA*, 325(23), 2397–2399. doi:10.1001/jama.2021.8246.

[3] As of this writing, 82 percent of all COVID-19 doses had been administered to people in high and upper-middle-income countries; less than one percent had been administered in low-income countries. See Duke University Center for Global Development (2021), *US Emergency Plan for Global COVID-19 Relief: Urgent Action to End the Pandemic Globally and Accelerate US Recovery and Security* (Durham, NC: Duke University), available online: https://healthpolicy.duke.edu/sites/default/files/2021-08/US%20Emergency%20COVID%20Plan_FINAL_For%20Distribution.pdf.

of broader state and corporate responsibilities in relation to health systems,[4] the drug industry,[5] and economic policy choices that have deepened inequality dramatically since the 1980s within the USA and globally.[6] The structural roots of economic and social exclusion underlie the symbolic content of resistance to COVID-19 vaccination for a subset of people who are the focus of this chapter. Lack of vaccination by choice or circumstance can often be yoked to the sense of powerlessness that people—differentially situated around the world—experience daily. Vaccines have moved to the forefront of our collective symbolic vocabulary, yet a lack of solidarity[7] often prevents us from reckoning with the injustice[8] that has made vaccines a lynchpin of symbolic politics.

Symbols, Strife, and Economic Rights

This chapter is an invitation to think in new ways about how to better understand not only vaccine hesitancy but also access to vaccines for those who want them globally—and offers a framework for addressing the structural roots underlying both challenges. We have another "opportunity to harness emerging symbols and re-imagine their scope and depth"[9] by focusing on the symbolic power that the decision to vaccinate (or not) has taken on.

As of this writing, more than seven in ten US adults (72 percent) had received at least one dose of a COVID-19 vaccine. Those who remain unvaccinated are concentrated among a subset of "uninsured adults, Republicans, rural residents, white Evangelicals, those without college degrees, and young adults."[10] Their grounds for resisting vaccination vary, with some pointing to the speed with which the vaccines were developed or the supposed effects of vaccination as evidence of potential harm. Others oppose the COVID-19 vaccination politically, in the name of manifesting their freedom to resist government control over their bodies or movement. Some reject both vaccination and masking because of a personal aversion to shots or the discomfort or appearance of masks. For others, who work in low-wage, hourly jobs with minimal to no paid sick leave, determining when and if to be vaccinated means calculating the lost wages or near impossibility of scheduling time off for vaccination and potential recovery against the potential risk of becoming infected with COVID-19.

[4] Lisa Forman and Jillian Clare Kohler, "Global health and human rights in the time of COVID-19: Response, restrictions, and legitimacy," *Journal of Human Rights* 19, no. 5 (2020), 547–556, DOI: 10.1080/14754835.2020.1818556. See also Wendy H. Wong and Eileen A. Wong (2020), "What COVID-19 revealed about health, human rights, and the WHO," *Journal of Human Rights* 19, no. 5, (2020), 568–581, DOI: 10.1080/14754835.2020.1819778.
[5] Santoro, Michael and Robert Shanklin, "Human rights obligations of drug companies," *Journal of Human Rights* 19, no. 5, (2020), 557–567, DOI: 10.1080/14754835.2020.1820315
[6] S. Galea and S. M. Abdalla, "COVID-19 Pandemic, Unemployment, and Civil Unrest: Underlying Deep Racial and Socioeconomic Divides," *JAMA* 323, no. 3, (2020), 227–228. doi:10.1001/jama.2020.1113
[7] Kathryn Libal and Prakash Kashwan, "Solidarity in times of crisis," *Journal of Human Rights* 19, no. 5, (2020), 537–546, DOI: 10.1080/14754835.2020.1830046.
[8] Michael Goodhart, "Revisiting interdependence in times and terms of crisis," *Journal of Human Rights* 19, no. 5, (2020), 520–527, DOI: 10.1080/14754835.2020.1814709.
[9] Hertel, "Mobilizing empathy."
[10] Kaiser Family Foundation, *KFF COVID-19 Vaccine Monitor: September 2021*, (2021), available online: https://www.kff.org/coronavirus-covid-19/poll-finding/kff-covid-19-vaccine-monitor-september-2021/.

Debates over vaccination are driving a wedge further into a polarized US society, with doses of vaccine going unused even as only a fraction of the world's population is vaccinated.[11] I concur with journalist Jamelle Bouie,[12] who has observed that shifts in the US economy have played a role in making vaccination salient on multiple levels:

'If American society has been reshaped in the image of capital, then Americans themselves have been pushed to relate to one another and our institutions as market creatures in search of utility, as opposed to citizens bound together by rights and obligations … this is the society we have built, where individuals are left to carry the burdens of life into the market and hope that they survive. This so-called freedom is ill suited to human flourishing. It is practically maladaptive in the face of a pandemic …. When you structure a society so that every person must be an island, you cannot then blame people when inevitably they act as if they were. If we want a country that takes solidarity seriously, we will actually have to build one.'[13]

Economic rights theory serves as a lens through which to explore the individual and collective aspects of rights at stake in the COVID-19 vaccine debate. Such rights include access to basic subsistence (i.e., food, clothing, shelter, health), labor rights, and social welfare safety nets for people who cannot provide for themselves.[14] Each one of us can claim such rights, but they are bound up with our individual and collective duties to one another. Recognition of our mutual interdependence is thus linked to creating the stable systems that make equitable economic rights fulfillment possible. Without that stability, we are all at risk.

The Political Economy of Vaccine Hesitancy

Recent national survey data has shown a correlation between income and willingness to vaccinate against COVID-19,[15] and while income alone is not the sole driver of such

---

[11] A. Christie, J. T. Brooks, L. A. Hicks, E. K. Sauber-Schatz, J. S. Yoder, M. A. Honein and CDC COVID-19 Response Team, "Guidance for implementing COVID-19 prevention strategies in the context of varying community transmission levels and vaccination coverage," *MMWR/Morbidity and mortality weekly report* 70, no. 30, (2021), 1044–1047, https://doi.org/10.15585/mmwr. mm7030e2. See also Luca Li Bassi, "Allocating COVID-19 vaccines globally: An urgent need," *JAMA Health Forum* 2, no. 2, (2021), e210105. doi:10.1001/jamahealthforum.2021.0105

[12] Jamelle Bouie, "If you skip the vaccine, it is my 'damn business,'" *The New York Times*, 14 August 2021, A18.

[13] Bouie, "If You Skip the Vaccine." See also Mike Konczal, *Freedom from the Market: America's Fight to Liberate Itself from the Grip of the Invisible Hand* (New York: New Press, 2021).

[14] Shareen Hertel and Lance Minkler, *Economic Rights: Conceptual, Measurement, and Policy Issues* (New York: Cambridge University Press, 2007).

[15] Jennifer D Allen, Wenhui Feng, Laura Corlin, Thalia Porteny, Andrea Acevedo, Deborah Schlidkraut, Erin King, Keren Ladin, Qiang Fu and Thomas J. Stopka, "Why are some people reluctant to be vaccinated for COVID-19? A cross-sectional survey among US Adults in May-June 2020," *Preventive Medicine Reports* 24 (101494), (2021), https://doi.org/10.1016/j.pmedr.2021.101494, see Table 2. There have been highly educated and high-income anti-vaccine advocates for decades in the United States, long before the advent of the COVID-19 vaccine. The class composition of the US anti-vaccine movement, however, is less uniform; for details on the evolution of the movement in the USA, see James Colgrove, *State of Immunity: The Politics of Vaccination in Twentieth Century America*, (Berkeley, CA: University of California Press, 2006).

decisions, the economic underpinnings of alienation and lack of empowerment that give rise to this position among a segment of the US population also underpin the ongoing global inequity in access to basic vaccine supplies. I engage a framework for social transformation which focuses on mechanisms-actors-pathways integral to *transforming* normative understandings and accountability structures—the "MAPS" framework[16]—because tackling the vaccination crisis involves transforming both a subjective individual-level sense of powerlessness and objective structural-level forces that perpetuate inequality. This transformation is grounded in the act of reframing vaccination both as a *choice that protects all of our freedoms*, not one that violates freedom,[17] and as a *duty that we have to one another* in order to safeguard and advance our collective well-being.

Understanding why a portion of people in the US say no to vaccination requires us to confront the numbers underlying their sense of precarity. Those same numbers, in turn, help explain why some people who feel economically or socially precarious are reluctant to support global development assistance or trade reforms that would enable *other* people in *other* countries to access vaccines or related basic public health services. Since the 1980s, income inequality in the USA has widened steadily in tandem with decreased rates of unionization, casualization of labor, welfare state retrenchment, tax and investment reforms favoring high-net worth individuals—a policy mix that has led to stagnant wages coupled with increased cost of living and the erosion of the middle class.[18]

Carnes and Lupu have explored the role of white working-class voters in former President Donald J. Trump's election, arguing that the election was not the outcome of "recent" factors, purely based on Trump's political discourse. Rather, white working-class voters have been shifting toward the Republican Party for several decades.[19] More Republicans are now "*calling themselves working class on surveys*"[20] Carnes and Lupu note—even when their education or income may not match the label (i.e., a combination of no college degree and a household income below the US Census Bureau's 2016 median of $60,000). A politics of "nostalgic deprivation"[21] rooted in the threat to or loss of

---

[16] LaDawn Haglund and Rimjhim Aggarwal, "Test of our progress: The translation of economic and social rights norms into practice," *Journal of Human Rights* 10, no. 4, (2011), 494–520, DOI: 10.1080/14754835.2011.619409. See also LaDawn Haglund, and Robin Stryker, *Closing the Rights Gap: From Human Rights to Social Transformation* (Berkeley, CA: University of California Press, 2015); see LaDawn Haglund, LaDawn, "Human rights pathways to just sustainabilities," *Sustainability* 11, no. 12, (2019), 3255. https://doi.org/10.3390/su11123255.
[17] David Cole and Daniel Mach, "Vaccine mandates protect freedom," *The New York Times*, 5 September 2021, SR 5.
[18] Robert Reich, *Saving Capitalism: For the Many, Not the Few* (New York: Penguin, 2015); William H. Felice and Diana Fuguitt, *Human Rights and Public Goods: The Global New Deal* (Lanham, MD: Rowman & Littlefield, 3rd edition, 2021), p. 215–219. See also Galea and Abdalla, "COVID-19 Pandemic, Unemployment, and Civil Unrest," p. 227.
[19] Nicholas Carnes and Noam Lupu, "The white working class and the 2016 election," *Perspectives on Politics* 19, no. 1, (2021), 55–72.
[20] Carnes and Lupu, "The white working class," p. 63, footnote 15, emphasis added.
[21] Justin Gest, Tyler Reny, and Jeremy Mayer, "Roots of the radical right: Nostalgic deprivation in the United States and Britain," *Comparative Political Studies* 51, no. 3, (2018), 1694–1719.

status—both economic and social—is in part driving the growing political polarization in the USA and with it, the increasingly divisive debate over COVID-19 vaccination. Widening inequality *overall* exacerbates underlying racialized inequality while at the same time exacerbating the lack of solidarity that Bouie so graphically describes above, leaving people islands unto themselves in increasingly racially hostile archipelagos.

At a global level, widening absolute inequality across nations *even prior* to the COVID-19 pandemic underscored the precarity of people's lives at the margins[22] and the inability of many governments in the Global South to compete for access to medicines and medical technology.[23] Long-standing patterns of unequal development across countries, together with corruption and inequality in developing countries themselves, have all intensified the effects of the pandemic in countries throughout the world.

But the structural nature of global poverty is not at the forefront of public consciousness in the USA. Year-on-year public opinion data reveals a lack of attention to, understanding of, or interest in development policy by many people surveyed in the United States, and a hardening of attitudes regarding social welfare across many industrialized countries.[24] Many of the same people who have felt socially alienated or economically precarious (or both) have experienced an intensification of precarity during the pandemic.[25] From this position, latching onto a resurgent sense of isolationism to justify "not caring" about the effects on COVID-19 on others or "not investing" in problems in "those countries" seems to make sense.

Yet COVID-19 and its even more highly transmissible Delta variant are borne on the wings of globalization: transmitted as people travel, as international commerce intensifies, as more foreign laborers move from place to place. The blockages in supply chains and slowdowns in commerce in the Global North are directly tied to worker sickness, sclerotic transportation, shipping backlogs, container shortages—all of which are reflective of crisis in developing countries like Bangladesh or China.[26] The discourse

---

[22] Miguel Niño-Zarazúa, Laurence Roope, and Finn Tarp, "Global inequality: Relatively lower, absolutely higher," *The Review of Income and Wealth*, Special Issue 63, 4 (2017), 661–648. See also Katharine G. Young, "The idea of a human rights-based economic recovery after COVID-19," *International Journal of Public Law and Policy* 6, no. 4, (2020), 390–415. DOI: 10.1504/IJPLAP.2020.114810.

[23] Forman and Kohler, "Global health and human rights in the time of COVID-19." See also Li Bassi, "Allocating COVID-10 vaccines globally."

[24] Lyle Scruggs, "Public opinion and economic human rights: Patterns of support in 22 countries," *Journal of Human Rights* 17, no. 5, (2018), 568–588, DOI: 10.1080/14754835.2017.1422705.

[25] Wen-Jui Han and Jake Hart, "Job precarity and economic prospects during the COVID-19 health crisis," *Social Science Quarterly* 102, no. 5, (2021), 2394–2411, available online: https://onlinelibrary.wiley.com/doi/full/10.1111/ssqu.13031.

[26] Jeanna Smialek Jeanna and Madeleine Ngo, "Top Fed officials say the labor market needs more time to heal," *The New York Times*, 27 September 2021. Available online: https://www.nytimes.com/2021/09/27/business/economy/fed-labor-market-interest-rates.html. See also International Labour Organization/ILO, *Research Brief: The effects of COVID-19 on trade and global supply chains* (Geneva: ILO, 2020), available online: https://www.ilo.org/wcmsp5/groups/public/---dgreports/---inst/documents/publication/wcms_746917.pdf and see Workers' Rights Consortium Report, "'My children don't have food. I can withstand this hunger, but they cannot': What the crisis means for people who make collegiate apparel," Washington, DC: Workers' Rights Consortium, (2020), Available online: https://www.workersrights.org/wp-content/uploads/2020/06/My-children-dont-have-food_June-2020.pdf

of economic isolation passes over such interconnections in favor of a language of blame (e.g., for the "Wuhan virus") or a zero-sum framing that equates help for the other person abroad with decreased resources to tackle domestic inequality in the USA.

The Challenge of Forging Solidarity

The policy response to US-based (domestic) reluctance to vaccinate may seem on its face different from the steps that would be necessary to tackle lack of access to vaccines globally. But the cross-cutting nature of inequality and the psychological roots disempowerment are common to people pushing back against vaccines (in the US) and those clamoring for access to vaccines (in developing countries).

Returning briefly to Haglund and Aggarwal's mechanisms[27] for understanding and promoting awareness of economic rights gives us a place to begin: a framework for rethinking the nature of desperation *and* a vehicle for focusing on the transformative potential of vaccination as integral to our individual and collective well-being. Haglund and Aggarwal focus on "situational mechanisms" that constrain people as well as the "action-formation mechanisms" that link people's "desires and beliefs to their actions," while at the same time exploring how advocates can create "transformational" mechanisms. If, early in the pandemic, the red heart served as a belief-formation mechanism that led some individuals to engage in new forms thinking and action animated by a sense of solidarity (e.g., by bringing people together to focus on shared appreciation for healthcare and frontline workers), then what are the steps involved in reframing the symbolism of vaccination?[28]

The first is to move beyond a politicized standoff toward a searching exploration of the sense of powerlessness that has been turned on its head by saying "no" and "pushing back" against vaccination in the United States. Second is the step of re-visioning the lack of access to vaccines in the developing world not as an inevitable outcome but as *something that can be changed* through commitment to equitable distribution of the vaccine in the interest of shoring up collective security. Third, is the step of more clearly specifying the nature of shared fate intrinsic to stemming the ability of the COVID-19 virus and its variants to mutate and spread.

Fourth is the step of reframing the discourse of vaccination in order to emphasize the linkages between freedom, rights and duties. As David Cole and Daniel Mach (respectively, the National Legal Director of the American Civil Liberties Union (ACLU) and the Director of the ACLU Program on Freedom of Religion and Belief) argue, vaccine mandates "actually further civil liberties. They protect the most vulnerable among us ... safeguard those whose work involves regular exposure to the public ... offer the promise of restoring all of us to our most basic liberties ... we all

---

[27] Haglund and Aggarwal, "Test of our Progress," p. 496.
[28] I focus on informational and symbolic mechanism integral to the MAPs framework. Other mechanisms (such as pressure- or power-based actions and legal advocacy) are emerging among pro- and anti-COVID-19 vaccine networks but are not analyzed in this chapter.

have the fundamental right to bodily integrity and to make our own health care decisions. But these rights are not absolute. They do not include the right to inflict harms on others."[29]

Transforming the symbolic power of (not) vaccinating also means finding scientifically grounded ways of discussing vaccination that are paired with active modes of listening and new ways of framing solutions (beyond the medical to encompass the economic and social dimensions of the issue). Haglund and Aggarwal's MAPS process pivots around social transformation—which I use to analyze the challenge of building consensus on a minimal level of universally available *access* to economic goods and services and on baseline criteria for the *quality* of health, education, employment, housing and economic rights.[30]

Saying no to vaccinating against COVID-19 ultimately makes individual people and all of us more insecure. Given the increasingly strident (and negative) equation of social welfare with "socialism" in US political discourse, it will not be easy to expose the economic insecurity underpinning COVID-19 vaccine rejection for some people, or the economic isolationism which pushes vaccines further out of reach in developing countries. But "turning inward"[31] is not an option if we want to stop the spread of COVID-19. Beginning the transformative work of reframing vaccine rejection's symbolic power is the first vital step toward a safer future.

---

[29] Cole and Mach, "Vaccines protect freedom."
[30] Haglund and Aggarwal, "Test of our progress," p. 512–513.
[31] Thomas J. Bollyky, Lawrence O. Gostin and Margaret A. Hamburg (2020), "The equitable distribution of COVID-19 therapeutics and vaccines," *JAMA* 323, no. 24, (2020), 2462–2463. doi:10.1001/jama.2020.6641, p. 2462.

Section Two

Human Rights, the City, and "Local" Actors

Introduction

Anthony Tirado Chase*

Human rights' translation into international law and treaties has been in many ways state led. The United Nations—that so-called "temple of states"—has played a leading role in the elaboration of human rights law and norms, and continues to be the focus of many of its key institutions. Ironically, however, rising global xenophobia has also been largely state led. This has meant states pushing back against both human rights legal obligations within their domestic jurisdictions and constraining the ability of global institutions to advance human rights norms and their on-the-ground policy implementation.

This is a conundrum for human rights activists who have tended to look to both international law and global institutions as a useful counterweight against state attempts to monopolize power within their borders. States most often do so, of course, in favor of dominant elites and to the detriment of marginalized communities who have seen in human rights a useful tool in their empowerment. How to respond to the conundrum that the global environment that has played a part in advancing human rights is now increasingly hostile?

Responding to that conundrum is what animates how Section 2 builds off Section 1. Section 1 had a broad global-local framing, including references to cities and other local actors, for its discussions of cosmopolitanism. Section 2 deepens that by specifically engaging with how human rights are increasingly part of governance beyond the nation-state. At this time of state-led hostility to the international rights regime, activists are having some success with using local sites as a point of entry for the implementation of human rights and other global norms. This trend includes work at sub-state levels within and across state borders and is most evident among stakeholders in the wave of so-called "human rights cities." This is a project which, in short, attempts to use international norms to inform more effective city policy on issues that range from homelessness to economic inequity, LGBTQI rights, police reform, tax policy, truth and accountability, climate change, and just transitions.

In that context, it is key to consider how we conceptualize human rights' relationship to governing institutions. Is that solely about the state, as in a traditional

---

* This introduction draws substantially from Chase and Morales, "Cosmopolitanism and lived realities: beyond global-local binaries" (September 2020), available at: https://www.openglobalrights.org/cosmopolitanism-and-lived-realities-beyond-global-local-binaries/. The author acknowledges and very much appreciates Gaea Morales' contributions.

conceptualization? Or can grassroots communities and sub-state governing institutions—including but not limited to the city—take on human rights obligations to advance their ability to confront not just the specific issues mentioned above (and many more!) but, more broadly, human rights as a tool to inform and invigorate grassroots struggles against populist xenophobia around the globe?

It is an essential premise of this book that, while state-led international law has been a key anchor for human rights' place in politics around the globe, their essential impulse lies in how they connect to lived realities around the world. Do human rights have reason to matter to the struggles to give agency to disempowered communities?

In that sense, it's really not so ironic to displace the state and global institutions as the heart of human rights. The lived realities of human rights explored centrally in this book have always existed vibrantly outside of human rights' traditional state centrism. Thus, the increasing engagement of local jurisdictions with human rights—examples of which are found in each of this section's contributions—is more than just a backstop during a period of globalized state hostility to human rights. It is an invitation to more participants into the necessarily constant reimagination of human rights. Such reimaginations are a vital element if human rights are to be part of pushing back against increasingly exclusionary politics in so many parts of the world. This reimagining must begin but not end with more horizontal, representative governing structures that use human rights not as a gift from on high but, rather, as a tool toward the empowerment of traditionally marginalized populations.

1

From Rebels to Rocks: Cities as Anchors in Turbulent Times

Gaea Morales

Introduction: The City as Local and Global

During the 2019 High-Level Political Forum on Sustainable Development at the United Nations (UN), the UN-wide Local2030 network hosted its third session on local (public, private, and non-governmental sectors) contributions to the achievement of the Sustainable Development Goals (SDGs). City representatives from across the globe presented the first set of "voluntary local reviews": measures of data-driven, city-level progress on the various goals and indicators. Though the SDGs were initially intended for national-level implementation and measurement, cities have taken center stage on reporting on sub-national advances on sustainable development.

But what exactly happens between "think global" and "act local"? What transformations or adaptations occur, when grounding nationally oriented frameworks in locally driven policy? These questions are not only made possible by centering cities as institutional agents, beyond mere sites of action.[1] They are also particularly urgent in a period of concurrent crises, from the rise of nationalist leaders to the persistent COVID-19 pandemic and the increasing frequency and intensity of natural disasters. Though research in recent decades have moved beyond the nation-state, these have focused largely on non-state actors, bypassing the city as a force for and *of* change.

It is urgent that we investigate the role of sub-national or sub-state governance actors in global systems. Cities serve as the missing link between what has become a mantra across both academic and policy spheres: thinking globally *and* acting locally. There is extensive literature on cities adopting values from both the international (top-down), and grassroots (bottom-up) levels, but less on a systematic investigation of what factors have enabled their participation in the global sphere. The element of city-

---

[1] Jonathan Barnes, "Politics." In *Aristotle's Politics: Writings from the Complete Works: Politics, Economics, Constitution of Athens* (Princeton University Press, 2016); Stephen D. Krasner, "Approaches to the State: Alternative Conceptions and Historical Dynamics," *Comparative Politics* 16, no. 2 (1984): 223–46; Jefferey M. Sellers, "State-Society Relations." In The *SAGE Handbook of Governance* (London: SAGE Publications Ltd, 2011) p. 124–41.

state dynamics becomes particularly important when envisioning how cities—for better or worse—may pursue contradictory values to those held above at the national level, and below at the grassroots level.

Thus far, there has been a wealth of literature on localizing global regimes, but less on understanding the process by which local level support translates into the adoption of cross-cutting, cross-sectoral sustainable development initiatives. How do cities adopt and implement international norms and standards? I argue that, especially where national governments either withdraw from international commitments, or simply fall short in the protection of people and the environment, cities act not just as rebels, but as rocks. Cities can simultaneously revolutionize sustainable development approaches, while also grounding and anchoring international norms at the sub-national level. They are able to achieve this through both horizontal ties and vertical pressure: vast networks of inter-city partnerships, and the joint weight of political will within local government institutions and civil society activism and advocacy.

This chapter therefore serves two purposes: first, it provides a brief overview of the literature on the (re)emergence of the city in global politics; and second, it proposes both a preliminary and partial response to the puzzle of city-level adoption of national-oriented policy instruments, as well as the tensions that this process may provoke. By centering cities in the case of sustainable development, I, alongside colleagues in this section, illuminate the micro-level impact of international frameworks. These include both the benefits of translating nationally oriented policies, *and* the tensions that arise when local institutions adopt standardized international language that may conflict with either or both state- and civil society-held positions.

The Urban Lens: Cities in Global Context

Scholarship on the city as a global, political actor spans multiple fields and disciplines, ranging from politics, economics, and sociology to the natural and spatial sciences. This transdisciplinarity is in itself indicative of the complex processes operating within the sub-national institution, and the variety of ways in which the city is conceptualized: as a space, actor, institution, and system.

Challenging the primacy of the state in analysis[2]–especially as having monopoly over politicking—is not inherently radical.[3] The comprehensive literature on state formation sheds light on how the "city" or the "city-state" in many contexts (e.g., Mediterranean, European) served as the prototype, and eventually the "nucleus" for the modern state. This evolution occurred through processes of urban development and the creation of networks across these cities via trade and migration flows over time.[4]

[2] Max Weber, "Politics as a Vacation," *American Journal of Cultural Sociology* 5, no. 3, (2017): 307–321, 84.
[3] Weber, "Politics as a Vacation," p. 78.
[4] Krasner, "Approaches to the State", p. 241; Hendrik Spruyt, "War, Trade, and State Formation." In *The Oxford Handbook of Comparative Politics* (Oxford University Press, 2009), p. 2.

Neil Brenner and Saskia Sassen were two of the earliest scholars to formalize the concept of the "global city," through what has come to be broadly known as the phenomenon of "glocalization." Brenner forwarded a re-scaling of territorial organization in the context of an expanding global scale, producing what he calls the "glocal state."[5] Sassen centers the "global city," suggesting that cities are strategic points for localizing global economic processes,[6] and in ways serve as conduits for global non-state networks that enable individuals to experience the global in the micro-spaces of daily life.[7] Some scholars even go so far as to claim that not only are cities on the rise, but also that the nation-state is in decline.[8]

More recent scholarship highlights what a magnification of the city or urban unit of analysis enables and reveals, and what earlier "glocal" scholars do not fully explore. These include global connections that begin within city spaces, such as the influence of university communities,[9] the reverberations of social movements, and a rapidly expanding and evolving technology sector.[10] These considerations are key when dealing with fundamentally transnational issues such as environmental protections and combating climate change.[11] The recent contribution of Sellers, Lidström and Bae for instance speaks to how cities' historical exercise of powers on land use and development and environmental quality has been critical to the very development of local governance and its policy sectors.[12] Cities' historical embeddedness in the policy coverage of topics of global concern present them with a unique vantage vis à vis international policymaking, and transnational policy diffusion and learning more broadly.

The empirical literature paralleling these developments have focused predominantly on the city in the context of global environmental governance and climate action networks.[13] Scholars focus heavily on transnational city networks that seek to mobilize against climate consequences and share best practices, and what this phenomenon

[5] Neil Brenner, "Global Cities, Glocal States: Global City Formation and State Territorial Restructuring in Contemporary Europe," *Review of International Political Economy* 5, no. 1 (1998): 1–37; John Eade, *Living the Global City: Globalization as a Local Process* (Routledge, 1997).

[6] Saskia Sassen, "The Global City: Strategic Site/New Frontier," *American Studies*, (2000): 79–95, 3.

[7] Saskia Sassen, "Local Actors in Global Politics," *Current Sociology* 52, no. 4 (2004): 649–670, 651.

[8] Benjamin R. Barber, *If Mayors Ruled the World: Dysfunctional Nations, Rising Cities* (Yale University Press, 2013).

[9] Jefferey M. Sellers, *Governing from Below: Urban Regions and the Global Economy* (Cambridge University Press, 2002).

[10] Yale H. Ferguson and Richard W Mansbach, "Technology and the Transformation of Global Politics," *Geopolitics* 4, no. 3 (1999): 1–28; Sellers, *Governing from Below*.

[11] Kent E. Calder and Mariko de Freytas, "Global Political Cities as Actors in Twenty-First Century International Affairs," *SAIS Review of International Affairs* 29, no. 1 (2009): 79–96; Peter Newman, "Global City Planning." In *Future of Sustainable Cities: Critical Reflections*, edited by J. Flint and M. Raco (Policy Press, 2011); Janne Nijman, "The Future of the City and the International Law of the Future." In *Law of the Future and the Future of the Law*, (Torkel Opsahl Academic, 2011); Janne Nijman, "Renaissance of the City as Global Actor", In *The Transformation of Foreign Policy* (Oxford University Press, 2016).

[12] Jefferey Sellers, Anders Lidström and Yooil Bae, *Multilevel Democracy: How Local Institutions and Civil Society Shape the Modern State* (Cambridge University Press, 2020).

[13] Michele M. Betsill and Harriet Bulkeley, "Cities and the Multilevel Governance of Global Climate Change," *Global Governance* 12 (2006).

demonstrates about the continued blurring of the domestic and international divide.[14] Key networks noted in the literature include the C40 Cities Climate Leadership Group (C40), Local Governments for Sustainability (ICLEI), and (thematically) broader organizations such as United Cities and Local Governments (UCLG)–institutionalized networks that have the capacity and resources to shape policy norms.[15] Put simply, the interdisciplinary literature demonstrates that scholars are coming to terms with the growing role of cities, relative to states, in the global arena. They are nodes at which multiple social, political, and economic systems intersect. However, cities do not only act in ways that shape domestic and international systems—their very actions are also shaped by their constituents. This recursive relationship is critical when considering the question of "localization," i.e., what factors enable cities to not only publicly support, but also meaningful engage with international frameworks to inform and transform local policy? The following section begins to grapple with this question—and by conceptualizing the "city" broadly—provides a preliminary theoretical framework for further empirical research.

Developing a City-based Agenda: What does "Localization" Entail?

Recognizing the city as its own actor within the state certainly pushes the boundaries of statist assumptions dominating both international relations and earlier comparative work. Noticeably absent in the literature on global–local linkages however are references to, and use of, institutionalist theory or framing cities as institutions (or organizations). In this approach, policy decisions are institutional effects, and these effects are transmitted via relational mechanisms. Tools from historical institutionalism, such as path dependence (e.g., in case study analysis), may enable the generation of temporally-sensitive hypotheses and outcomes pertaining (local) institutional development.[16] At the same time, historical institutionalist approaches are particularly suited to illustrating the interaction between global level phenomena and local processes in politics.[17] Sociological institutionalism allows scholars to integrate the notion of social legitimacy (with respect to a broader cultural environment) as grounds

---

[14] Vanesa Castán Broto and Harriet Bulkeley, "A Survey of Urban Climate Change Experiments in 100 Cities," *Global Environmental Change* 23, no. 1 (2013): 92–102.; Milja Heikkinen, Aasa Karimo, Johannes Klein, Sirkku Juhola, and Tuomas Ylä-Anttila, "Transnational Municipal Networks and Climate Change Adaptation: A Study of 377 Cities," *Journal of Cleaner Production* 257 (2020); Taedong Lee, "Global Cities and Transnational Climate Change Networks," *Global Environmental Politics* 13, no. 1 (2013); Frank Nevens, Niki Frantzeskaki, Leen Gorissen, and Derk Loorbach, "Urban Transition Labs: Co-Creating Transformative Action for Sustainable Cities," *Journal of Cleaner Production* 50 (2013): 111–122.

[15] Barber, *If Mayors Ruled the World.*

[16] Andrew Bennett and Colin Elman, "Society for Political Methodology Complex Causal Relations and Case Study Methods: The Example of Path Dependence," *Political Analysis* 14, no. 3 (2006): 250–267; Scott E. Page, "Path Dependence," *Quarterly Journal of Political Science* 1 (2005): 87–115.

[17] Thomas Rixen, Lora Anne Viola, and Michael Zürn, *Historical Institutionalism and International Relations* (Oxford University Press, 2016).

for the diffusion, learning, and adoption of certain (local) institutional practices.[18] Combining these institutionalist approaches allows for an integration of the social features of the phenomenon, with the historical, structural (and likely constraining) features of state and local policymaking. In other words, this approach allows for an investigation of specific cases in their temporal and structural context,[19] while engaging the cultural context (e.g., ideas and norms).

Below, I present initial theoretical assumptions, informed by these research traditions, on how cities "localize" international norms. Together, these assumptions can serve as a theoretical foundation for further research exploring both inter-city and intra-city relationships in the process of localization.

1. Cities (i.e., city governments) possess some degree of agency and autonomy vis à vis the state, and participate in networks within the international community

Both the localization of sustainable development and internationalization of cities blur the lines between the local and global spheres, and raise important questions about where the city—as an organization—stands relative to the state.[20] While cities are unable to, for instance, sign or ratify treaties, they may still seek and acquire (social) legitimacy through alternative sources of cultural authority by signaling adherence to rules of the international bureaucracy.[21] We can see this most clearly in various cities' embeddedness in global networks, and participation and presence in international forums such as the United Nations.

Cities are plural at best and divided at worst. But contrary to Peterson's perspective,[22] cities are not monolithic, or necessarily less effective than federal mechanisms in achieving social outcomes. Instead, in order to understand the city as an *actor* and both the horizontal and vertical institutional effects of local governance systems, we must recognize the city as an aggregate entity—one that is in constant engagement with its constituents. Engagement in this case does not necessarily suggest that the city government is consistently representative of or aligned with constituent needs, especially of those historically marginalized in formal and informal avenues of agenda setting. Rather, the city does not act in isolation from its societal environment. City

---

[18] Michael Barnett and Martha Finnemore, *Rules for the World: International Organizations in Global Politics* (Cornell University Press, 2004); John W. Meyer, John Boli, George M Thomas, and Francisco O Ramirez, "World Society and the Nation-State," *American Journal of Sociology* 103, no. 1 (1997): 144–81; John W. Meyer and Brian Rowan, "Institutionalized Organizations: Formal Structure as Myth and Ceremony," *American Journal of Sociology* 83, no. 2 (1977): 340–363.

[19] Stefano Bartolini, "On Time and Comparative Research," *Journal of Theoretical Politics* 5, no. 2 (1993): 131–67; Kathleen Thelen, "Historical Institutionalism in Comparative Politics," *Annu. Rev. Polit. Sci.* 2 (1999): 369–404.

[20] Ileana M. Porras, "The City and International Law: In Pursuit of Sustainable Development," *Fordham Urban Law Journal* 36, no. 3 (2008): 537–601.

[21] Barnett and Finnemore, *Rules for the World*; Peter A. Hall and Rosemary C. R. Taylor, "Political Science and the Three New Institutionalisms" *Political Studies* 44, no. 5 (1996): 936–957; Paul Pierson, *Politics in Time* (Princeton University Press, 2004).

[22] P. E. Peterson, *City Limits* (University of Chicago Press, 1981).

decisions and actions are subject to scrutiny not just by grassroots and community actors, but also other cities.

2. Cities (i.e., city spaces) host a diverse and vibrant community of international and grassroots stakeholders that can act to pressure government actors

Societal actors are not powerless in shaping or influencing the process of localization, or local policy more broadly. Local communities expect city *government*, as an organization, to address the needs of different groups and communities with potentially competing interests. These interests can be normative (e.g., asserting key rights and raising issues of accountability), policy driven (e.g., from demands on strengthening environmental protections to calls for more robust affordable housing programs), or economic (e.g., seeking support for businesses, sufficient employment opportunities, managing trade relations, range of private-public partnerships, etc.). These communities and actors—civil society and advocacy groups, non-profit, non-governmental organizations, academic institutions, or private industries—neither act independently nor on a single plane. They too, similar to the city, and with advancements in global communication technologies, are inextricably connected to vast global networks. They may themselves have a stake in ensuring cities are aligned with globally held or transnationally shared norms, standards, or regulations.

As a result of this environment, city administrators may be more responsive (relative to the state) to both the demands of local community and sensitive to standards posed by (what it views as) like-cities. I raise this assumption in efforts to further understand the relationship between proximity (in levels of governance, to individual constituents) and responsiveness in terms of policy adoption. There are two assertions embedded in this assumption. First, city administrators are more likely to respond to the demands of local actors. Second—assuming these actors will leverage progress in like-cities as points of comparison, city administrators are consequently more responsive to the standards of like-cities.[23] Cities may also be pressured to take on the characteristics and structures of other like-institutions (i.e., institutional isomorphism), e.g., other prominent cities, especially when seeking to be viewed as socially legitimate actors not just by the international community, but also by their local constituents.[24] Where bottom-up pressure align with the proliferation of city innovations worldwide, and where there is political will from the bureaucracy, localization can occur as a means to respond to the demands of constituents while integrating into a broader system of city actors.

---

[23] Porras, "The City and International Law."
[24] Hall and Taylor, "Political Science and the Three New Institutionalisms"; Pierson, *Politics in Time.*

3. City officials are able to leverage partnerships with private actors in order to respond to demands from both the international and local levels, and localize international norms in times of political uncertainty

Localization is not a mere signal of support for an international norm or framework: it entails a great deal of (re)imagination and data-collection on one end, and fundraising and promotion on another. The support of private institutions is critical especially where cities choose to pursue values that may not be directly aligned with national-level decision-making. In the United States, we saw this occur with a wave of city-level support for the Paris Climate Accord amidst the Trump presidency's withdrawal. At the national level, we saw a similar phenomenon with the declaration of sanctuary cities amidst federal immigration raids around the country. Partnerships with non-profits or foundations, think tanks, and academic institutions more broadly (including colleges and universities), can and have been ways for cities to generate financial and intellectual support for endeavors such as adopting, selecting, and translating nationally oriented norms and criteria for sustainable development, where federal support falls short (or is nonexistent).

Through these assumptions, I argue that the city is a legitimate international actor that is embedded in global networks but is accountable—and responsive—to local demands. Where international frameworks align with bottom-up demands, and where city officials have the will and capacity, localization of an international framework can occur. Localization then is a form of internationally informed, but locally sourced innovation. It is a process produced by the confluence of local level interests, facilitated through local government institutions.

A Clash of Localizations: Rights, Ownership, and Distributive Justice in the Agenda

By establishing that cities are autonomous agents, I argue that inter-city networks and the alignment of political and civil society actor interests enable the process of localization. Localization in this case consists of not just support of an international framework, but also a translation of its very principles and indicators to the urban scale. While cities may act to ground international norms in times of political instability, the very process of localization also highlights tensions that scholars and local practitioners alike must acknowledge. Here, I raise these tensions more narrowly through the localization process of the Sustainable Development Goals.

1. Re-centering Human Rights in the City

Human rights activists have critiqued the vague, implicit presence of human rights in the sustainable development agenda. The localization process is also at risk of perpetuating this gap, particularly in its data-driven conceptualization of progress. In the same way we ask what the SDG indicator data can tell us, we must also ask what narratives or perspectives we might be missing from the data. Human rights narratives and measures of equity and justice must not be seen as at odds with developmental outcomes, but deeply embedded in how cities measure progress.

2. Who Owns Localization?

At present, the development of SDG voluntary local reviews is very much owned by city government: various mayor's offices of international or public affairs. The imaginative force of the localization process however requires collaboration: it calls for a participatory process. City actors must meaningfully engage not just private actors, but also civil society and community members—especially communities that have been historically excluded. Community engagement is necessary not only to identify key issue areas for which international norms can serve as tools for repair and growth, but also to be able to concretely define "sustainable development" in terms consistent with community values and expectations. In order to generate citywide transformation, and holistic sustainable development, the communities must see their stake in the process of localization and own the language of sustainable development.

3. Bridging Urban-rural and North-south Divides

Finally, it is important to recognize that the study of cities requires careful and deliberate consideration of national and regional contexts. When answering questions on structures of power and inequities within cities, what happens beyond city limits are equally relevant to understanding these internal dynamics. Much of the literature, addressed even in this volume, recognizes the relationship between the "urban" and the "rural," and the concentration of economic and political power both regionally in Global North cities, and nationally in northern metropolitan areas. Cities across the globe are neither created nor act equally, and cities—especially capital cities—are not representative of nation-states. With this understanding, we can complicate how we construct city incentives, whom cities consider as members of their constituencies, and the asymmetrical power dynamics of inter-city networks. At the same time, we can better highlight both the tensions that arise when cities engage with civil society actors acting locally, particularly those with networks across rural areas or less dense, smaller cities, and when Global South cities participate in international forums vis à vis those from the Global North.

Conclusion: Reimagining the City

David Harvey writes in *Rebel Cities: From the Right to the City to the Urban Revolution*:

> [T]he question of what city we want cannot be divorced from the question of what kind of people we want to be, what kinds of social relations we seek, what relations to nature we cherish, what style of life we desire, what aesthetic values we hold. The right to the city is, therefore, far more than a right of individual or group access to the resources that the city embodies: it is a right to change and reinvent the city more after our hearts' desire[25].

---

[25] David Harvey, *Rebel Cities: From the Right to the City to Urban Revolution* (Verso Books, 2013), p. 4.

Put in context of the process of localization, localization allows city governments to act on its right to reimagine a city as not only part of a broader global network, but as an institution that embodies the values of its communities. The broad propositions presented here serve a preliminary role of consolidating the study of cities and localization in international politics and global regimes. Further, the tensions I identified here are not arguments against localization. On the contrary, they highlight why it is so important to take the process of localization seriously: capturing the tensions that persist when global meets local and opening up conversations on how we can overcome them.

I close with one potential approach to addressing the key tensions that persist between the innovating city and constraints posed by national government infrastructure: framing cities as anchors. Cities, in processes of localization, ground the vessel of the state in the broader conversations of the international community, especially in times of turmoil and instability. The anchor however is inextricably tied to (and at times, an extension of) the state—linked by a chain of actors, from non-governmental organizations to grassroots advocates, and the dynamic processes that govern their relationships. It is these very questions concerning city agency and political, economic, and social autonomy, in the context of an international community increasingly receptive to non-state and sub-national voices, that deserve further theoretical and empirical exploration, especially when linking frameworks such as the SDGs to the broader realm of the human rights regime. In order to advance these theoretical foundations and develop further empirical approaches, scholars must not work within academic silos. The work of urban-global governance is as much about investigating linkages as it is about fostering connections—not just across the local, national, and the international—but also across academia, city government, private actors, and civil society.

Snapshot #3: Global Human Rights Norms and City Policy in Los Angeles

Angela Kim and Erin Bromaghim

Los Angeles has the third biggest metropolitan economy in the world, with a thriving $1.1 trillion market, and a port complex through which a third of the goods shipped to the US enter. And LA is a global city, where 37 percent of its four million residents are foreign born, hundreds of languages are spoken, and deep connections exist with cities and other governments around the world. This should make it unsurprising that Los Angeles is also directly engaged in implementing global agendas, demonstrating our ownership of, and responsibility to, international agreements. LA is taking the lead in pushing cities to not only adopt global human rights norms but to contribute in turn to global norm setting. Local governments cannot ignore global norms because our communities are where these norms become real.

As populations and resources are increasingly concentrated in urban centers, we must recognize that local and regional governments are key to effective implementation of global norms at the grassroots. Local governments are the engines of change, rapidly testing and redesigning systems and infrastructure to confront the global challenges of our time, from climate change to racial and gender equity. Solving these problems depends upon the active engagement of cities, and the continuous application of these values to the systems, services, and infrastructure they deliver.

In Los Angeles, we engage with global rights norms and frameworks every day, with city staff bringing these commitments into practice. We have grouped these practices into three categories: (1) local adoption of international agreements; (2) public support for human rights protections; and (3) norm setting and advocacy through city networks.

Adopting International Agreements Locally

LA has adopted, through mayoral or city council action, several international norms including the Convention on the Elimination of All Forms of Discrimination against Women (CEDAW), the Paris Climate Agreement, and the Sustainable Development Goals. In 2019, the city adopted Ordinance 186084, establishing the Los Angeles' Civil and Human Rights Law, now enforced by the Civil + Human Rights and Equity Department. Los Angeles has shown that local leaders can lay claim to international norms and translate these ideas into practice. Adopting these frameworks and commitments is not just a political statement, but a means by which global agreements become a part of city policies and programs. CEDAW adoption was followed by Executive Directive #11, which mandates that city departments appoint a gender equity liaison and prepare gender equity action plans and measurable goals. The city's commitment to the Paris Agreement is incorporated into local targets set in LA's Green New Deal.

Public Support for Human Rights Protections

The Los Angeles region is home to at least eight of the world's largest foreign-born populations outside of their country of origin, including Mexico, Vietnam, Korea, and Iran. LA also has the third largest Consular Corps in the world, representing more than 100 nations. In a city so connected to the world, LA's residents are impacted by human rights abuses, state-sponsored violence and repression, and increasing authoritarianism abroad. Speaking out against these abuses, in support of diaspora communities and human rights protections, is a means by which Los Angeles can officially express our values and solidarity. The city has issued statements, passed resolutions, and openly condemned human rights violations, and advocated for action or recognition by the US government. In 2009, the City Council passed a resolution denouncing the inhuman treatment of lesbian, gay, bisexual, and transgender (LGBT) people in Iraq. In 2018, the City Council passed a resolution in support of the Iranian people's right to political protest. And in 2021, the City Council introduced a resolution in response to the Taliban's takeover of the Afghanistan Government, requesting support from the US government to resettle Afghan refugees in LA.

Norm Setting and Advocacy Through City Networks

Los Angeles' Mayor Eric Garcetti chaired the C40 network for Climate Action and the City Hub and Network for Gender Equity (CHANGE). Los Angeles is a founding city member of the Mayors Migration Council (MMC) and the Urban20, and has sister city or bilateral relationships with more than 50 cities around the world. These city networks and connections bring together the world's largest and most diverse urban areas to tackle transnational challenges like climate change, gender equity, and human migration. Working together, cities learn and share from one another, develop new standards and progressive commitments, and advocate for more ambitious action, often setting goals for themselves that exceed the international consensus. For example, in April 2020, Mayor Garcetti convened a COVID-19 Recovery Task Force of C40 mayors, and in July 2020 they released the Agenda for a Green and Just Recovery, outlining bold steps to deliver an equitable and sustainable recovery from the pandemic. The agenda identifies actions mayors can take to prioritize jobs and an inclusive economy, resilience and equity, and health and well-being.

Through these three means—translating global norms into local practice, publicly engaging on rights issues, and advocating through city networks and partners—cities like Los Angeles bring human rights home. While these norms may be universal, most were written and adopted by national governments or in multinational settings. Adapting them to fit a local context demands that local leaders and residents see value in doing so; value that manifests as safer, sustainable, and more equitable places to live, work, and play. This translation from norm to action often demonstrates where real tensions exist. The response to such tensions, and local ownership of these shared commitments, can and should inform their continued evolution.

2

Resourcing Rights: How Sub-state Actors Can Use Local Fiscal Policy to Counteract Democratic Erosion

Sergio Chaparro Hernández and Nelson Camilo Sánchez

The principles of solidarity, responsibility, and care—both between human beings and between peoples and nations—have been severely tested with COVID-19's global spread. The massive failures in the international and individual states' responses to this test are indicative, in turn, of deeper problems in national political, economic, and social systems that have gradually drifted away from such principles. Therefore, it is not surprising that the recent rise of nationalist and authoritarian discourses has been linked to the dissatisfaction of millions of people with an exclusionary political system and an economic model co-opted by an uber-rich minority.

In recent years, the human rights community has responded to this authoritarian upsurge in a variety of ways, including two we would highlight. On the one hand, several initiatives have sought to promote scenarios of solidarity and rights-building at the local level—to address dissatisfaction with the failures of cosmopolitanism and globalization.[1] On the other hand, activists have called for a redoubling of efforts to make material justice and the struggle against inequality a priority of the human rights movement.[2]

Two spaces have been particularly active and innovative in this line of resistance to authoritarianism: the "Human rights cities" movement and the Initiative for Human Rights Principles in Fiscal Policy. It is urgent these two movements work toward deepening their interactions in order to advance their interconnected projects. This chapter argues that a local discussion of fiscal policy from a human rights perspective has enormous potential for creating more democratic, ecologically responsible, social local polities with sufficient capacity to respond to authoritarian attacks on democracy and rights. However, for this potential to be unleashed, sub-national entities must fill a

---

[1] Koldo Casla and Kath Dalmeny, "What Does that Mean Here? Localizing Human Rights in the UK.," *OpenGlobalRights* (October 31, 2019). Available at: https://www.openglobalrights.org/localizing-human-rights-in-the-UK/.

[2] Philip Alston, "The Populist Challenge to Human Rights," *Journal of Human Rights Practice* 9, no. 1, (February 2017), 1–15, https://doi.org/10.1093/jhuman/hux007.

gap that nation-states have so far failed to fill: shifting fiscal policy from the periphery to the center of the global human rights movement's agenda.

The Movement for Fiscal Justice and Human Rights

State capacity is critical for the realization of human rights. And, to a large extent, the state's ability to fulfill its functions—including the protection of human rights—rests on its strength in mobilizing economic resources.[3] However, for decades commentators and activists have lamented the human rights field's "historical ambivalence" toward addressing the material and financial requirements for realizing human rights legal commitments.[4]

This passive attitude has begun to change. There is increasing recognition of how current economic systems impact increasing inequality and failures to respect, protect and fulfill human rights.[5] Particularly, a group of human rights advocates joined the efforts of social justice experts and activists to urge the creation of an international tax justice movement and address the capture of national tax systems by wealthy elites.[6] Furthermore, the need for human rights to have a stronger voice on how public resources are best gathered, spread, and invested became more evident after the economic crisis of 2008 and the worldwide explosion of austerity and fiscal consolidation measures.[7]

Based on an interdisciplinary assessment of the social and other implications of fiscal policy, the tax justice movement has identified four desirable purposes for tax systems that intertwine seamlessly with human rights objectives: i) *raising revenue*-- which focuses on generating funds to deliver essential services; ii) *redistribution*—as a vehicle to address poverty and inequality; iii) *representation*—seeking to build accountability of governments to citizens and reclaiming public space, and, iv) *repricing*—as a mechanism to change behaviors for the public good.[8] More recently,

---

[3] In this spirit, article 2 of the International Covenant on Economic, Social and Cultural Rights calls on state parties to take steps "to the maximum" of their "available resources" to achieve the realization of the rights recognized in the covenant.

[4] Nicholas Lusiani and Mary Cosgrove, "A Strange Alchemy: Embedding Human Rights in Tax Policy Spillover Assessments." In Philip Alston and Nikki Reisch, *Tax, Inequality, and Human Rights* (Oxford University Press, 2019), p. 162. See also Samuel Moyn, *Not Enough: Human Rights in an Unequal World* (Cambridge, MA: Belknap Press, 2018).

[5] Brinks, Daniel, Julia Dehm, and Karen Engle, "Introduction: Human Rights and Economic Inequality," *Humanity: An International Journal of Human Rights, Humanitarianism, and Development* 10, no. 3 (2019): 363–375.

[6] According to the State of Tax Justice 2020 Report: "the world is losing over $427 billion (USD) in tax a year to international tax abuse. Of the $427 billion, nearly $245 billion is lost to multinational corporations shifting profit into tax havens to underreport how much profit they made in countries where they do business and consequently pay less tax than they should." Global Alliance for Tax Justice et al. The State of Tax Justice 2020: Tax Justice in the time of COVID-19, 4 (2020).

[7] Center for Economic and Social Rights, Assessing Austerity. Monitoring the Human Rights Impacts of Fiscal Consolidation (2018).

[8] Liz Nelson, *Tax Justice & Human Rights: The 4 Rs and the Realisation of Rights* (Tax Justice Network, 2021); Matti Kohonen et al., "Creating a Human Rights Framework for Mapping and Addressing Corporate Tax Abuses." In Alston and Reisch, *Tax, Inequality, and Human Rights*, p. 385.

two complementary aims were added: v) *recovery*—emphasizing the counter-cyclical role of fiscal policy, and vi) *remedying* the legacy of social exclusion and ecological damage—by implementing effective affirmative budgetary measures.[9]

Moreover, while the movement has recognized that tackling tax abuse is a top priority, the strategy would not be complete without analyzing how available resources are invested. In this sense, "Fiscal Justice" comprises all the measures whereby States "acquire and allocate resources, including taxation, public debt, income from public companies, macro-fiscal planning and all the processes associated with the budgetary cycle."[10]

As stated in the preamble of the recently adopted Principles for Human Rights in Fiscal Policy, the potential of a human rights-based fiscal policy is twofold. On the one hand, it has a "transformative potential" to combat poverty, inequalities, power asymmetries, and other structural factors that hinder the full realization of rights.[11] On the other hand, a socially just fiscal policy (one that "distributes revenue and wealth more equitably") can reduce polarization, marginalization, and social discontent by "confronting the current historic levels of inequality.[12]

The wealth and breadth of the progress of this process are impressive. First, thanks to these efforts, we now have sophisticated conceptual reflections on the relationship between fiscal policies, democracy, and rights.[13] Second, beyond being limited to a discussion of a closed circle of experts, the organizations and voices part of this movement represent a plural array of thoughts, agendas, and identities.[14] And finally, the movement has had a main priority to develop concrete tools that can be used by both the fiscal policymaking community and specialized human rights bodies. Among these instruments are the Principles for Human Rights in Fiscal Policy, which develop detailed guidance to governments on producing and monitoring fiscal policies that respect human rights.[15]

However, due to the global scale of this problem and the historical prominence of national regulators in budget and tax decisions, most discussions on this issue focus on proposals for changes to the international tax system and central national taxation systems.[16] Without ignoring the importance of continuing to advance on these two fronts, in the remainder of this chapter, we will defend the importance of promoting a

---

[9] The Initiative for Human Rights Principles in Fiscal Policy, Principles for Human Rights in Fiscal Policy (2021). Guideline 1.2.

[10] The Initiative for Human Rights Principles in Fiscal Policy. Op cit.

[11] The Initiative for Human Rights Principles in Fiscal Policy. Preamble.

[12] The Initiative for Human Rights Principles in Fiscal Policy.

[13] See, for instance, T. Pogge and K. Mentha (eds.), *Global Tax Fairness* (Oxford University Press, 2016); P. Beckett, *Tax Heavens and International Human Rights* (Routledge, 2017); Alston and Reisch, *Tax, Inequality and Human Rights*.

[14] For a comprehensive account of the organizations, alliances, spaces, and initiatives that are working on this topic, see Nikki Reisch, "Taxation and Human Rights: Mapping the Landscape" In Alston and Reisch, p. 33–57.

[15] The Initiative for Human Rights Principles in Fiscal Policy. Op cit.

[16] R. Mason, "The Transformation of International Tax," *American Journal of International Law*, 114, no. 3 (2020), 353–402. doi:10.1017/ajil.2020.33.

more decisive inclusion of this issue in the agendas of sub-state actors, especially in so-called "human rights cities."[17]

The Existing Connections Between the Two Movements

As recognized by members of the human rights cities' movement, "there is neither a common framework nor a methodology to become a human rights city."[18] Instead, the movement has focused on identifying and sharing lessons learned and existing promising practices to promote human rights cities better. Some of these lessons—and of the basic principles that the various declarations on the subject have structured— connect implicitly to concerns of the fiscal policy movement. For example, the preamble to the Gwangju Guiding Principles for a Human Rights City, adopted in May 2014, notably recognizes that "the right to the city" considers "the common interests for socially just and environmentally balanced use of urban space over individual right to property."[19] Moreover, principle 6 maintains that a "Human Rights City" must "ensure a long-term continuity through the institutionalization of adequately-resourced programs and budget."[20] Finally, principle 7 emphasizes that a human rights approach should be implemented in government and administrative activities in all phases of policy, including planning, policy formulation, implementation, monitoring, and evaluation.[21]

However, there is little explicit mention of the role of fiscal policies in the scaffolding of the human rights city. To begin with, the Gwangju Principles do not explicitly refer to taxation or fiscal policies. On the other hand, in the minds of those promoting this exchange of best practices, fiscal policy issues are not yet identified as human rights priorities. This is clear, for example, from the recent report "Local Government and Human Rights," presented by the Office of the United Nations High Commissioner for Human Rights to the Human Rights Council in July 2019.[22] While the report seeks to systematize "lessons for local governments seeking to align further their legal framework, policies, and programmes with human rights norms," none of the examples presented directly address legal, policy, or institutional frameworks related to tax or spending policies in sub-national entities.[23]

---

[17] A paramount meeting point for the global human rights cities is the World Human Rights Cities Forum of Gwangju, which has been promoting debate an action on the subject for almost a decade. The Cities Forum process has been facilitated in partnership with civil society organizations such as the Gwangju International Centre, the Raoul Wallenberg Institute, INIFID NGO and Asia Democracy Network (ADN21). http://www.whrcf.org/en/whrcf.php

[18] Human Rights City Network, Report to the Office of the United Nations High Commissioner for Human Rights (2018).

[19] WHRCF - World Human Rights Cities Forum. Gwangju Guiding Principles for a Human Rights City, 2014 (online) [Accessed October 11, 2021].

[20] Id. at Principle 6.

[21] Id. at Principle 7.

[22] OHCHR, Local Government and Human Rights. A/HRC/42/22. 2 July 2019.

[23] A sole mention to financial resources is found at the end of the report in a section on "challenges faced by governments in the promotion and protection of human rights." In that chapter, the report notes that "Financial resources and economic constraints are major challenges for local governments." In our opinion, the report's drafters do not appear to understand the potential that a fiscal policy approach can bring to the field under study.

This is not to say that tax policy issues have been entirely absent from the activism and practice of the cities and human rights movement. On the contrary, there is an array of concrete and inspiring examples of how subregional entities can make their human rights initiatives a reality by reorienting their tax and fiscal practices.[24] The argument we want to make in this chapter is that it is critical for the human rights and cities movement that fiscal issues are articulated as key to its agenda rather than a side issue.

An effort in a similar vein—although not expressly based on an international human rights law framework—is proposed in the report "Unmasking the Hidden Power of Cities," the product of extensive research across more than 100 cities in the United States.[25] This report starts from a compelling idea that we fully share: "Cities have a set of governing powers that, if used to their fullest, could have significant national-scale effects on economic inequality, racial and social justice, and climate change."[26] In addition, the report develops what it calls "seven core legal powers or local governments to identify the potential scale of impact," which are nothing more than seven core fiscal policy issues.[27]

The Potential of a Rights-based Fiscal Policy for Sub-national Entities

Cities play a fundamental role in protecting, promoting, and fulfilling human rights. The agglomeration of heterogeneous individuals in the urban space creates advantages for local governments that, when adequately used, might help them to comply with their human rights obligations.[28] One of these advantages lies in the fact that the dynamics of urban agglomeration generate sufficient resources to finance the city's needs and its inhabitants.[29] This is particularly relevant for contexts of authoritarian rule at the national level. Cities with more democratic electoral preferences might play

---

[24] Matti Ylönen, for example, has articulated a persuasive call for a reorientation of public procurement policies based on analysis of the City of Helsinki's initiatives seeking to advance its free trade policies and its tax haven-free initiative by using procurement decisions. See, Ylönen, M. V. S. "Cities as world-political actors? The "tax haven-free" cities initiative and the politics of public procurement," (Palgrave Communications, 2016), p. 2, [16041]. https://doi.org/10.1057/palcomms.2016.41.

[25] R. Tynan, N. Fortunato and D. Cohen. *Unmasking the Hidden Power of Cities* (Partnership for Working Families, 2018).

[26] Id. at p. 2.

[27] The seven powers identified in the report are: 1) direct spending, 2) Procurement and Contracting; 3) Economic Development and Sectoral Strategies; 4) Proprietary Power; 5) Land Use; 6) Regulation; and 7) Taxation.

[28] Agglomeration can also have negative effects such as congestion, pollution, and crime. People voluntarily stay in or migrate to cities because they perceive that the positive effects outweigh the negative ones.

[29] This proposition is known as the George-Hotelling-Vickrey theorem (GHV theorem) or the "golden rule of local public finance." According to a specific interpretation of this theorem, under certain conditions the costs of public services in the city can be financed with the surpluses derived from urban agglomeration, see Dirk Löhr, "Provision of Infrastructure: Self-financing as Sustainable Funding," Dialogue of Civilizations Research Institute (2016).

a counterweight role as spaces for democratic contestation.[30] However, their ability to effectively do so strongly depends on their capacity to fund more inclusive policies.

Therefore, fiscal policy is crucial for sub-national city governments to gain sufficient capacity to respond to authoritarian attacks on democracy and rights. This approach poses a set of interesting questions to explore: what kinds of conflicts on fiscal matters usually arise between authoritarian national governments and more democratic city governments? How do these conflicts, the negotiation power of these actors, and the scope of policies that cities can propose change across diverse institutional fiscal arrangements (e.g., fiscal federalism, fiscal decentralization, centralized regimes)? In light of institutional fiscal constraints, how much fiscal space do cities have to fund more progressive policies and resist authoritarian rule? How can the principles of participation, transparency, and accountability be implemented throughout the tax and budgetary cycles at the local level? How do inter-states and intra-states fiscal equality rules, as well as national and city political dynamics, impact the ability of municipalities to advance more progressive policy alternatives?

We contend that taking a more extensive use of rights-based tax and budgetary policy alternatives is a critical strategic step for city governments seeking to oppose authoritarian tendencies of national governments that can compromise the rights of their inhabitants, particularly those of marginalized groups. Moreover, these policy alternatives can help overcome some of the challenges posed by the potential constraints that cities may face in their fiscal policy space stemming from the issues raised by the questions posed above. To this end, we discuss three potential ways city governments could enshrine human rights principles by implementing tax/fiscal policies. This analysis is not intended to address the abovementioned questions comprehensively but, rather, to argue for a greater emphasis on fiscal issues on the agendas of movements such as the Human Rights Cities Movement, civil society initiatives linking budgets and human rights, as well as that of the Doughnut Economics Action Lab.

The first application we would like to discuss is the potential of right-based tax policies such as progressive property taxes and the collection of urban development charges for Latin American countries to overcome the restrictions to fiscal space faced by sub-national governments more broadly. After decades of neoliberal reforms initiated in the '80s, sub-national administrations in Latin America acquired increasing responsibilities, such as providing essential public services and emergency assistance. In most cases, decentralization did not come with the expected process of strengthening sub-national governments' fiscal capacities to perform their new responsibilities adequately.[31] This has led to a situation in which, on the one hand, the revenues collected by sub-national governments remain low as a percentage of total revenues and, on the other hand, indirect taxes based on economic activity or royalties for the

---

[30] For concrete case studies of the emergence of progressive cities as spaces of contestation to opposite trends at national level, see Mike Douglass, *The Rise of Progressive Cities East and West* (Springer, Singapore, 2019).

[31] See, for instance, Iván Finot, *Descentralización en América Latina: teoría y práctica* (CEPAL, 2001); D. Arroyo, "Estilo de gestión y políticas sociales municipales en Argentina." In J. C. Venesia, (comp.) *Políticas Públicas y Desarrollo Local* (Fundación Instituto de Desarrollo Regional de Rosario, 1998).

exploitation of non-renewable natural resources—whose tax bases are vulnerable to fluctuations in macroeconomic variables—remain as the most common financing sources.[32] In contrast, revenues from more stable sources such as property or real estate tax are widely underutilized. In 2019, while, on average, OECD countries collected 1.9 percent of GDP in property taxes, revenues collected by Latin America through this type of tax accounted only for 0.9 percent of GDP.[33]

In addition to property taxes, city authorities can also strengthen their capacities over urban planning regulation, which plays a significant role in the current regressive allocation and distribution of real estate profit increases. As part of their territorial planning and management, cities should include mechanisms to control and regulate the local land market to recover part of this real estate wealth as a source of revenue. The betterment levy, for instance, is a type of taxation based on the principle that those who benefit from a value increased in their property by public investments must pay for it (principle of benefit). Yet, it can incorporate the principle of contributive capacity and help sub-national governments deal with the chronic lack of adequate infrastructure and services in progressive manners. Although Latin America has innovative local experiences in territorial taxation, they are still isolated cases, and there is plenty of room for extensive use of these tools.[34]

The second application we will discuss is budgetary policy. In recent decades there has been a proliferation of civil society initiatives to generate accountability for budget decisions from a human rights standpoint.[35] Some cities remain at pace for more democratic experiments for fiscal decision-making despite shrinking civic space at the national level. That is the case of Porto Alegre in Brazil, which in 2019 marked the 30th anniversary since *participatory budgeting* in the city began.[36] More broadly, Brazil has seen intensifying civil society demands around fiscal justice issues after a constitutional amendment to establish a 20-year public expenditure cap was approved in 2016.[37] The Brazilian civil society organization Instituto de Estudos Socioeconômicos (INESC)

[32] Juan Pablo Jiménez, and Teresa Ter-Minassian. "Política fiscal y ciclo en América Latina: el rol de los gobiernos subnacionales," *Serie Macroeconomía y Desarrollo*. División de Desarrollo Económico—CEPAL y Agencia Española de Cooperación Internacional para el Desarrollo (AECID) (2016).
[33] OECD/ECLAC/CIAT/IDB (2021). Revenue Statistics in Latin America and the Caribbean 2021, https://www.oecd.org/tax/revenue-statistics-in-latin-america-and-the-caribbean-24104736.htm.
[34] Catalina Molinatti., Eduardo Reese., Julieta Rossi., Luna Miguens. Aspectos generales y estándares aplicables a las políticas fiscales subnacionales y a los instrumentos tributarios y no tributarios de base territorial. Serie Documentos Complementarios a los Principios de Derechos Humanos en la Política Fiscal Nº 6 (2021).
[35] United Nations Office of the High Commissioner for Human Rights & International Budget Partnership, Realizing Human Rights Thought Government Budgets. HR/PUB/17/3 (2017).
[36] Boaventura de Sousa Santos, "Participatory budgeting in Porto Alegre: toward a redistributive democracy," Politics & Society 26, no. 4 (1998): 461–510. For a more recent take see: Oliver Escobar, "Transforming lives, communities and systems? Co-production through participatory budgeting." In *The Palgrave Handbook of Co-Production of Public Services and Outcomes* (Palgrave Macmillan, Cham, 2021), p. 285–309.
[37] See, for instance: INESC, CESR, Oxfam Brazil, "Human Rights in Times of Austerity" (2016), at https://www.cesr.org/sites/default/files/Brazil%20Austerity%20Factsheet%20English%20FINAL.pdf; Ana Luíza Matos de Oliveria., Pedro Rossi., Esther Dweck, (Coord.) *Austeridade e retrocesso: impactos sociais da política fiscal no Brasil*. 1ª ed. São Paulo: Brasil Debate e Fundação Friedrich Ebert Stiftung (2018).

created and has consistently applied a methodology for budget analysis both at national and sub-national levels based on human rights norms. Although human rights organizations have faced an increasingly hostile context since the beginning of Jair Bolsonaro's government, INESC and allies have used this powerful tool to hold the national government accountable for the human rights impacts of austerity policies.[38] In addition, INESC has developed complementary tools that could be useful for local governments to design and implement budget policies in line with their human rights obligations.[39]

Finally, the third application we would like to discuss is the potential for further development of how substantive policies and decision-making processes in the area of public resources management might look like in the context of the application of innovative city planning tools, as is the case of Doughnut Economics. The Doughnut is a robust social progress framework that envisions a world in which the essentials of life for everyone (which constitutes the inner circle of the Doughnut or "social foundations")—ranging from food and water to gender equality and having a political voice—can be met while respecting planetary boundaries (the outer circle of the Doughnut).[40]

Cities worldwide are using this framework in alliance with the Doughnut Economics Action Lab—an initiative whose aim is to help create 21st-century economies that are regenerative and distributive by design—to explore how to turn it into more sustainable policies in urban spaces.[41] Amsterdam, for instance, is implementing a strategy to halve the use of new raw materials by 2030 and achieve a fully circular city by 2050.[42] Although initiatives developed by the Doughnut Action Lab are in the early stages of implementation, the Doughnut Economics framework has an enormous potential to inform decisions on how to collect, distribute and use public resources for prioritizing the fulfillment of basic needs while cities contribute to respecting planetary boundaries. Moreover, this framework connects urban planning with pressing global aims in ways that might allow cities to find international allies when national governments are hostile to such ideas.

Concluding Remarks: The Way Forward and the Promises of Cross-movement Collaboration

There is transformative potential in a dialogue between two emerging movements: fiscal justice and human rights and the human rights cities movement. The recently

[38] Livi Gerbase, "The Fight for Human Rights in the Context of COVID-19: a tough ride for Brazilian civil society organizations," (Sept 28, 2020). Available at https://www.cesr.org/confronting-covid-how-civil-society-responding-across-countries-brazil-0.

[39] See https://www.inesc.org.br/acoes/principios-de-direitos-humanos-na-politica-fiscal/.

[40] Kate Raworth, *Doughnut Economics: Seven Ways to Think Like a 21st-Century Economist* (Chelsea Green Publishing, 2017).

[41] Kate Goodwin, "Designing the Doughnut: A Story of Five Cities," (April 19th, 2021), at https://matchboxstudio.medium.com/designing-the-doughnut-a-story-of-five-cities-8bad04ded5e3.

[42] City of Amsterdam. Amsterdam Circular 2020–2025 Strategy (2019), available at https://www.amsterdam.nl/en/policy/sustainability/circular-economy/.

launched Principles for Human Rights in Fiscal Policy include some policy guidelines for sub-national governments that might become a good starting point for finding common ground. On the one hand, they call on local authorities to extensively use property taxes' revenue collection and redistributive potential. But, on the other hand, they urge them to promote equity in the distribution of the burdens and benefits of urbanization, primarily through the ability of sub-national governments for land regulation.[43] In tandem, by inserting the rights-based fiscal policy initiative's postulates into the human rights city movement, the global human rights movement can advance two parallel modes of resistance to anti-cosmopolitan populism. First, fiscal policy discussions are vehicles for building democratic agreements at the local level, demonstrating that human rights can be operationalized in everyday practice. Second, more effective and inclusive municipal decision-making processes on fiscal matters might strengthen institutions' legitimacy, translating treaty rights into reality.

---

[43] The Initiative for Human Rights Principles in Fiscal Policy. Op cit. Guidelines 3.5 and 12.2.

3

Truth-in-Los Angeles: "Reimagining and Rejuvenating Global Norms at the City Level"

Anthony Tirado Chase

Every day I learn about some new truth-telling or racial healing initiative.... [that is] bubbling up all over the [United States]. ... For example, the Black Women's Truth and Reconciliation Commission, Bridging the Divide (between Chicago police and communities they serve), Universities Studying Slavery, the work at Georgetown, Harvard and Brown Universities, Ferguson's Truth-Telling Project, Northeastern University Law School's Civil Rights and Restorative Justice Institute, Coming to the Table, Equal Justice Initiative, Richmond's Initiatives of Change, the Kellogg Foundation's Truth, Racial Healing, Transformation Enterprise, The Mass Slavery Apology, the emergence of slavery and lynching museums and so many others.

Fania Davis[1]

Background

"Truth and Reconciliation." Post-Apartheid South Africa may have branded that phrase in our global consciousness but, in fact, it had a prior history in truth-telling processes in Latin America (Argentina, Bolivia, Chile, Uruguay) and Africa (Uganda, Zimbabwe). And, while not under the Truth and Reconciliation brand as such, similar concepts had previously informed other post-conflict transitions starting with the Nuremberg trials. Per Fania Davis' epigraph above, we are now seeing a dramatic rise of such processes to reckon with histories of racial injustice in locales across the United States.

That spread is due to the simple but powerful idea that has come to be institutionalized in truth and reconciliation commissions: that truth-telling about historical human rights violations is essential to the emergence of a new, more just political order. The irony this chapter explores is that, even as we see a growing appeal of such commissions,

---

[1] "Is the United States Ready for a Truth Process?" available at: https://www.ictj.org/news/united-states-ready-truth-telling-process.

we are seeing their foundations transformed as they spread to non-traditional jurisdictions such as cities in the US. Can the powerful appeal of this type of historical reckoning thrive as they are adapted to these new contexts? And might such adaptations actually address many of the flaws in the traditional truth commission formula and, thereby, rejuvenate their effectiveness around the globe?

This formula is well-developed: truth commissions link truth-telling to accountability, reparations, and guarantees of non-repetition via institutional reform as the path to social-political reconciliation in divided societies. As Andrieu Kora puts it regarding the Nuremberg precedent, "the trials were also used for larger, more ambitious, purposes: issuing a detailed narrative of past atrocities, documenting the history for future generations, acting as a deterrent for the future, giving victims a voice, strengthening the rule of law, and promoting reconciliation on the ground."[2] Zvobgo cogently summarizes the promise that has continued as truth commissions have developed from such early precedents, arguing that they are not just cathartic for victims but, "for the broader society, commissions can help individuals and communities grapple with the truth of past violence, a process many consider crucial to social and political reconciliation, peace, and stability....In terms of national politics, truth seeking can have a positive effect on human rights respect, democratization, and democratic consolidation."[3]

These are powerful promises. Nonetheless, this formula has also been subject to skepticism.[4] Criticism of the reconciliation element in the "Truth and Reconciliation" formula has been particularly withering. It is not just that there have been disappointing results from many truth and reconciliation commissions, from South Africa to (as Cristián Correa discusses in his "Snapshot" in Section 1 of this volume) Côte D'Ivoire. More fundamentally, the simplicity of a notion that truth-telling somehow could or even should lead progressively to reconciliation is problematic. Ethically, it can be perceived as putting the burden on victims to forgive their more powerful victimizers. Conceptually, a focus on reconciliation regarding responsibility for mass atrocities— even if there is some degree of individual accountability—can be seen as avoiding coming to grips with more structural forces that impel such violence.[5] Even after a truth-telling process, the powerful ideologies that justify and the political-interests that profit from structural violence often remain in place and, ironically, continue to thrive off such structures.[6] This can make "reconciliation" a potentially bitter pill. The critique

---

[2]   Andrieu Kora, "Transitional Justice: A New Discipline in Human Rights, Mass Violence & Résistance," *SciencesPo* [online], January 2010: http://bo-k2s.sciences-po.fr/mass-violence-war-massacre-resistance/fr/document/transitional-justice-new-discipline-human-rights, ISSN 1961– 9898.

[3]   Kelebogile Zvobgo, "Demanding Truth: The Global Transitional Justice Network and the Creation of Truth Commissions," *International Studies Quarterly* (2020), 1–17.

[4]   David Mendelhoff, "Truth-Seeking, Truth-Telling, and Postconflict Peacebuilding: Curb the Enthusiasm?" *International Studies Review* 6, no. 3 (September 2004), 355–380.

[5]   Mahmood Mamdani, "Amnesty or Impunity? A Preliminary Critique of the Report of the Truth and Reconciliation Commission of South Africa (TRC)," *Diacritics* (Autumn–Winter, 2002), 32–59.

[6]   William Gumede, "Failure to Pursue Economic Reparations Has and Will Continue to Undermine Racial Reconciliation" in Mia Swart and Karin van Marle (eds), *The Limits of Transition: The South African Truth and Reconciliation Commission 20 Years on* (Brill: Leiden, 2017), p. 59–93.

of reconciliation as a goal has led to that specific word often being dropped as an immediate goal in many recent truth-telling processes. That has, not, however, led to change in what I would argue is the flawed formula that has informed the creation of truth commissions across the globe. Indeed, increasing doubts that these processes have produced long-term results indicates that a more far-reaching critique is needed.

We can begin that critique by looking at the commonly accepted bases of truth commissions. Priscilla Hayner lays these out as follows:

> A truth commission (1) is focused on the past, rather than in ongoing events; (2) investigates a pattern of events that took place over a period of time; (3) engages directly and broadly with the affected population, gathering information on their experiences; (4) is a temporary body, with the aim of concluding with a final report; and (5) is officially authorized or empowered by the state under review.[7]

These five foundational elements are, I would argue, problematic in a way that is not easily rectified by simply changing terminology from "reconciliation" to "accountability." One, does a focus on "the past" mean we exclude attention to ongoing systemic exclusion? Two, does a focus on "a pattern of events" mean that underlying structures of political-economic domination are left untouched? Three, does engaging with affected populations imply a top-down approach that is brought to the grassroots rather than owned at the grassroots? Four, does an insistence that such bodies be "temporary" cripple the need for ongoing, continuous self-reflection and implementation? And five, does a reliance on official state authorization center too much power in government elites rather than in marginalized communities?

There are dimensions and caveats to each of those critiques I just made, and each are worthy of a long discussion. I am by no means arguing that truth commissions should be dismissed; indeed, despite their identifiable flaws, I would nonetheless argue that they continue to have great potential. What I am trying to do, instead, is highlight the conundrum that is at the heart of this chapter. On the one hand, transitional justice's truth-telling processes have had inadequate results due, I suggest, to the flaws I highlight above. On the other hand, per Davis' opening quote, the idea at their center— that to change a state-society there needs to be a collective reckoning with the past rather than forgetfulness and "moving on"—is so powerful that we are continuing to see its resonance as a way to productively address past histories.

This spread continues to occur at the more traditional level of nation-states undergoing post-conflict transitions but is also extending to unexpected locales. Unexpected in that many are in established, stable democracies that are not "transitioning" out of violent conflict. And unexpected in that many are taking place at the sub-state level—particularly in major cities—rather than within the typical domain of the nation-state. As we see with such truth-telling initiatives across the United States, at times they are taking place within both of these non-traditional domains. We see,

---

[7] Priscilla Hayner, *Unspeakable Truths: Transitional Justice and the Challenge of* Truth Commissions (Routledge, 2010).

therefore, that standard parameters of a transitional justice truth process are, from the grassroots, already being reconfigured to make them more relevant to communities making claims for historical reckonings.

Are there ways to push that further—to more profoundly change that formula in a way that will better fulfill the flawed promise of what, from here on, I will call truth and accountability processes? Cities in the United States developing truth and accountability processes to envision an overdue reckoning with past injustices gives us a chance to test the possibility of such productive evolutions. Can these local experiments in truth and accountability processes impact not just those specific locales, but also inform processes in other parts of the country and the world with innovative re-imaginings that make more real their promised potential?

These processes in different communities across the United States tend to focus on how racial injustice is deeply embedded in the US's foundations and, more importantly, its ongoing structures. This is often being done with a recognition of intersecting patterns of structural violence against other marginalized communities, not just Black Americans. Davis' epigraph lists a number of such efforts and to that list can be added other truth-telling experiments, such as those in Providence RI, Iowa City, Greensboro NC, Long Beach and San Francisco CA, Brownsville MD and the broader Maryland Lynching Truth & Reconciliation Commission. Posthumus and Zvobgo count 20 "past, present, and proposed official US truth commissions"[8] and that number seems to be increasing by the month. There are variations in the approaches in each of these initiatives, but they are inspired by a common notion: that global norms of truth and accountability processes can inform local reckonings with the ongoing impacts of racial injustice across the United States. To be clear, there are also proposals for this to take place at the federal level, but those in local jurisdictions around the US are pushing these processes from the community and city level.

Key Questions Raised by Los Angeles' Proposed Truth and Accountability Process

I have been engaged with a team developing a proposal for a truth and accountability work in Los Angeles—Truth-in-LA[9]—that gives insight both on these conceptual flaws and the potential promise of locally grounded truth commissions. Time will tell if these initiatives in Los Angeles and other parts of the US will be successful or even if they might bubble up into informing a comprehensive federal level initiative. It is too early to answer such questions now (in the case of a LA, it's not even clear if there will be such a local process). It is not, however, too early to use this work as a basis on which to reflect on some key practical and theoretical questions that flow out of working on

[8]   Daniel Posthumus and Kelebogile Zvobgo, "Democratizing Truth: An Analysis of Truth Commissions in the United States," *International Journal of Transitional Justice* (forthcoming), 1.
[9]   Full details of this project, included proposals for an LA truth-telling process, is here: https://truthinla.org.

global truth-telling norms in a local context. Specifically, work in Los Angeles gives the basis for addressing the following interlinked questions:

1. Might the increasing use of global norms in local politics invigorate the imagination of grassroots activism to help stimulate responses and inform new, more pluralistic conceptions of our social contracts? In short, in the context of Los Angeles, do global truth-telling norms open up new paths for facing old issues?
2. Flipping that, does local engagement with global norms—be those human rights, the Sustainable Development Goals or transitional justice and truth-telling—give space to re-conceptualize those global norms in a way that addresses critiques of such putatively international, "state-owned" norms? In short, in the context of a sub-state actor like Los Angeles, does adaptation at local levels open paths to reimagine global truth-telling norms?
3. And, more theoretically, does the increasing number of intersections between "local" sub-state actors and international norms complicate how we think of the traditional binary between local action vs. cosmopolitan impulses? In short, what is a local/cosmopolitan binary when there are so many intersections that make categories of city-level "local" and global level "cosmopolitan" problematic?

Los Angeles' exploration at a city level of global transitional justice and truth-telling norms gives context in which to engage those questions. Does bringing global norms to a city show the relevance to global norms outside a state-based framework? Do they also show how such global norms can be strengthened through diffusion of local adaptations? And, lastly, does it show that working within the framework of a local/city vs. cosmopolitan/global binary does an injustice to the complexity of interactions and intersections in a transnationalized world?

From Global Norms in Local Politics to Local Adaptations Informing Global Re-imaginings

In the context of Los Angeles, global norms have a particular reason to be seen as relevant. LA has a long history of racial eruptions—most famously in the 1965 Watts riots and the 1992 Rodney King explosion, as well as the 2020 Black Lives Matter demonstrations (as noted in this volume by Shockley and Davis). Obviously, there is a national dimension to these eruptions, as with all racial matters in the United States. But there are also past and ongoing histories of racial hierarchies and exclusion specific to Los Angeles. What is more, local attempts in Los Angeles—from court consent decrees regarding the LA Police Department practices to post-riot commissions such as the McCone and Christopher Commissions (and the national Kerner Commission)— have singularly failed to address core causes of these eruptions. Both city officials and community groups recognize that there has been a breakdown in trust between communities and city government. Local mechanisms, whatever their good intentions, have had little success in resolving those breakdowns and there is little faith that they can do so in the future.

In that context, it is fair to ask if global norms offer new ideas for addressing issues on which local action is stagnant. Indeed, it should not be a surprise that some in Los Angeles look to international mechanisms as a way to address city-level issues. Again, there is a national dimension to this. As already noted, Los Angeles is not unique in the US in seeking to learn from global truth-telling norms to inform local truth and accountability processes. More broadly, there is a long history of African Americans reaching out to international mechanisms to circumvent national and local patterns of human rights violations based in racial identity. From Fannie Lou Hamer to W.E.B. Du Bois to Ralph Bunche (in their very distinct ways, of course), there was a pre- and post-WWII impulse from Black leaders to look to using global norms as a way to address racial issues in the US.[10] Carol Anderson is most comprehensive in this regard in her critique of the ways in which the post-WWII civil rights leadership deliberately weighed the internationalist option versus working within US-specific institutions. The decision to work within a US civil rights tradition rather than a more comprehensive international human rights framework is critiqued by Anderson as, in part, responsible for the civil rights movement's gains being limited to the formal political sphere rather than taking on broader social and economic structures within the United States. Nonetheless, internationalist impulses never entirely disappeared in African American activist spaces and, within that historical tradition, recently a "New Black Internationalism" has emerged. Specifically, in the wake of the Ferguson unrest following the murder of Michael Brown and the BLM protests of summer 2020, the Movement for Black Lives has constituted itself firmly within an internationalist frame based in global solidarities.[11]

The relevance of global norms to local struggles is obviously nothing new. Per Keck and Sikkink's so-called "boomerang effect,"[12] global norms most often come into play when local structures are unwilling or unable to address ongoing human rights issues. As Fionnuala Ní Aoláin comments regarding truth processes in the US, this is a matter of global norms "filling in" when local, national structures are insufficient to provide truth and justice—when even democracies are not "self-correcting."[13] The impulses are, of course, always local, but the tools are whatever can be most effective—local, regional,

[10] Keisha Blain, *Until I am Free: Fannie Lou Hamer's Enduring Message to America* (Beacon Press, 2021); Adom Getachew and Jennifer Pitts (eds), *Du Bois' International Thought* (Cambridge University Press, 2022); Kal Raustiala, *The Absolutely Indispensable Man: Ralph Bunche, the United Nations, and the Fight to End Empire* (Oxford University Press, 2022).
[11] Adom Getachew, "The New Black Internationalism," *Dissent* (Fall 2021). Getachew writes that "The global mass mobilizations in the wake of George Floyd's murder last year, and the revival of the decades-long history of black solidarity with Palestine earlier this year, illustrated how overlapping experiences of state violence have created material grounds for new solidarities." For more detail on the substance of what Getachew's "New Black Internationalism," specifically M4BL's "A Vision for Black Lives: Policy Demands for Black Power, Freedom & Justice," see Robin D. G. Kelley, "What Does Black Lives Matter Want?" *Boston Review* (Aug 17, 2016) available at: https://bostonreview.net/books-ideas/robin-d-g-kelley-movement-black-lives-vision.
[12] Margaret Keck and Kathryn Sikkink, *Activists beyond Borders* (Cornell University Press, 1998).
[13] Fionnuala Ní Aoláin "The Relevance of Transitional Justice Twenty Years after 9/11"—webinar on September 30, 2021, available at: https://mediaspace.illinois.edu/media/t/1_6pefh0d4.

national, or international. In the case of truth and accountability processes around racial injustice in a location such as LA, global norms are being proposed as a way to move past a static and unsatisfactory status quo. In developing a potential framework for such a process, practitioners from across the globe were interviewed. This was done in order to inform a process that benefits from global precedents, from other US local truth-telling initiatives, and from the community impulses and engagements underlying their current fluorescence.

The most basic lesson from global truth-telling processes is that what *sort* of truth-telling process is as important a question as *if* there should be a truth-telling process at all. Best practices from both successes and struggles in global experiences led to the proposal in Los Angeles that its process address three intersecting frames: recognition (changing dominant historical narratives via art and memorialization projects); responsibility (having governing institutions take active responsibility for past action and future reform); and repair (engaging in both symbolic and substantive reparative actions that both acknowledge and help heal past wrongs).

Within each of these three intersecting frames are a number of underlying principles, again drawing from numerous case studies from around the globe. The first of these is that a truth and accountability process must be holistic and comprehensive—i.e., recognition means little unless accompanied by active responsibility and true reparative action just as reparation means little in the absence of substantive recognition and responsibility-taking. A second is that truth and accountability must be based in a community partnership that recognizes intersectionalities among affected communities—i.e., it is not just that, rather than a government-led top-down process, there must be ownership by the directly impacted community, but also a recognition of connections to other vulnerable communities if a process is to be impactful and unifying rather than pitting communities against each other. And third, that they must be grounded in ongoing institutional commitments and accountability-based outcomes—i.e., contrary to common practice, a truth and accountability process should be long-term rather than temporary and must be accompanied by substantive implementation authority.

While, again, each of these principles can be broken down and discussed at length, the point here is a theoretical response to the initial question I am addressing: do global norms have the potential to open up new paths in local politics? In this case, global norms are informing a potential truth-telling processes in Los Angeles just as they are doing across the United States. And they are doing so in unprecedented ways given the US's insular history when it comes to global norms. What is remarkable is that, even at this early stage, it is clear that these global norms are opening imaginations to different and potentially more productive ways to address issues on which progress has long been stagnant or even regressive.

Given the political obstacles, there is no assurance that proposed processes will accomplish their goals. What is clear, however, is that global truth and accountability norms have ignited movements to address the US's long history of racial injustice in ways that are comprehensive rather than piecemeal; that are structural rather than reformist; and that are about re-envisioning the social contract in a more pluralistic manner rather than being limited to begrudging recognition of past discrimination and violence. To give one example regarding reparations, Davis and Geddes ask:

How do we create a multi-dimensional, complex reparations process that includes transformative economic measures? ... [We are seeing] a transformation of reparations moving from something that is just focused on a "hand-out" or cash from the government to the means by which communities build sustainable ways of living. So when we think about economic dignity for example: what does it mean for everyone to have access to housing, access to food?[14]

In Los Angeles, this has led to a key point regarding global norms informing innovative new approaches. Beginning to think about how international human rights—such as the right to adequate housing—can be part of how truth and accountability processes are conceptualized came about as one way of addressing the issues Davis and Geddes raise. Substantive rather than rhetorical human rights obligations have traditionally been absent from truth-telling processes around the world. Integrating reparative elements based in substantive economic human rights obligations in one possible corrective. This comes from a realization that truth and accountability should not be just about putting a band aid on old wounds (in Hoover's phrase), but rather that they risk doing more harm than good unless they simultaneously recognize, take responsibility for, and help repair those wounds.

The proposed innovation in Los Angeles that draws on a separate category of global norms—human rights—that has generally been, at best, merely rhetorical in truth processes, raises our next question: do adaptations of global norms at local levels open paths to, in turn, reimagining global truth-telling norms? We have seen that global norms are impacting local truth-telling initiatives in Los Angeles and around the United States. The ways in which they are doing so have the potential to bridge distinct global policy frameworks and use them to expand how truth and accountability processes are practiced across the globe. This might include constituting a truth and accountability process by using other global norms, as with the notion that international human rights can give great substance to obligations to address structural economic disparities in the proposed Truth-in-LA process. Another is linking the process to the Sustainable Development Goals (SDGs) by integrating in SDG-specific targets from within each goal (i.e., the targets embedded in SDG 10 on reducing economic inequality; SDG 11 on sustainable cities and communities; and SDG 16 on justice and strong institutions) to, again, add substance to the proposed LA process. These SDG-based global norms can give not just specific policy targets to inform what a truth and accountability process should substantively address, but also make clear intersections with a broad range of issues. One last example is the proposal that restorative justice practices—as modeled at a national level with the Australian and Canadian truth processes or, regionally, with the Maine Wabanaki Truth and Reconciliation Commission—be used to facilitate community engagement and overcome marginalized communities' entrenched suspicions of local government, as in Los Angeles. If the aim of truth and accountability processes is to mobilize communities to collectively recognize past harms and take active responsibility for their repair, such restorative justice practices may be key to future successes.

---

[14] ICTJ interview.

This leads to the point that there is much to learn from these local adaptations of truth process norms. Norm diffusion is not just a one-way, top-down process in which global norms filter down to the local level. To the contrary, just as we see how global norms have invigorated searches for racial reckonings in the US, the manners in which such norms are being adopted may have innovations to offer those in other jurisdictions (see Kenyon in this volume). More specifically, sub-state engagement with global norms is doing so in ways that rectify many of the issues that have plagued truth and accountability processes.

Going back to my critique of Hayner's summary of truth-telling process' five foundations, we are seeing in local adaptations corrections to the problematic elements I noted. Notions of integrating obligations to center specific human rights of affected, vulnerable populations, for example, are part of an attempt to move beyond merely recognizing specific events and toward addressing these underlying hierarchies of power that maintain the structures that systemically marginalize some populations. Similarly, ideas of integrating restorative justice practices are meant to engage from the start affected populations in the definition of what truths are at play and how they should be best recognized and repaired. This is something that must happen as truth and accountability processes are constituted, rather than as an add-on at the end of a process as has too often been the case. And we are also seeing that jurisdictions are moving past the notion of these as necessarily "temporary bodies" and, rather, seeing the need for either permanent or semi-permanent truth commissions or, alternatively, designating a follow-up mechanism that takes on continuing implementation work. Lastly, by definition these sub-state processes run contrary to the notion that truth processes must be state authorized. Moving even further beyond traditional state-centrism, we are seeing more recognition that, even when we are speaking of sub-state governmental entities, it remains critical that truth and accountability processes be co-created with affected communities.

Conclusion: Entangling the "Cosmopolitan" Global and the "Local" City Levels

Truth and accountability initiatives at local levels, such as that proposed for Los Angeles, have the potential to show that global norms and national and international models can engage old problems in new ways. As well, these initiatives in cities and other sub-state jurisdictions show that such local adaptations can be part of a two-way street, re-invigorating through local experimentation the globalized model of truth and accountability processes that has, of course, been evolving in its use among nation-states, too.

Beyond these two arguments, it is worth concluding both with a caution and with an opening to a broader theoretical question. The caution is that the "local" is not some sort of silver bullet any more than global norms are a magical solution. Political challenges and structural obstacles to a more pluralistic social contract exist at global, state, sub-state, and non-state levels. It is a mistake to think of them as distinct spheres. Problematic power structures are interwoven at all of these levels and given the turbulent times in which we live there is no reason for optimism that such power structures can be fundamentally changed. And this leads into a concluding argument that, if there is to be tangible change, it is essential to move past prioritizing working at one of these spheres over others.

This chapter has used terms like "local," "city-level," "sub-state," "national," and "global" levels. In some sense those are, indeed, distinct levels, but they are also vague descriptors that are misleading to the degree they imply each variable exists in some sort of silo. To conceptualize possibilities of change, we need to break down these categories. For example, regarding cities, which are the cities that are engaging in truth and accountability processes based on global norms? Which are those engaged in "human rights city" networks? They are not cities as such, but a specific class of cities: larger, more diverse, and more globalized cities. Smaller, more homogenous cities located in rural zones—both within the United States and around the world—have tended to be the heartland of rising xenophobic politics that fears pluralism and reacts against the empowerment of marginalized populations. These are not the local city jurisdictions that are engaging global norms. Using "city" as a determining variable flattens distinctions between different types of cities and different ways in which they engage the national and the global (see Morales in this volume).

If "city" is a problematic variable, it is equally important to also challenge the notion of "local." Los Angeles is a city but, as with other global megapolises, describing it with terms such as local is vaguely quaint. As Kim and Bromaghim note in their "Snapshot" in this volume, "LA is a global city, where 37 percent of its four million residents are foreign born, hundreds of languages are spoken, and deep connections exist with cities and other governments around the world." Further, depending on varying calculations of Los Angeles County's GDP, it would rank between the 19th and 21st largest in the world if it were nation-state—more or less the same as countries like Turkey, Saudi Arabia, and Switzerland. Whatever the specific ranking, Los Angeles' economic size, ethnic complexity, and its population's transnational roots challenge the notion of a city as coterminous with the local. Los Angeles is a globalized, transnational city, just as are many of the cities at the forefront of engaging with global norms. Delimiting its politics as "local" is to miss that complexity.

What does this challenge to conceptualizing politics as existing within these distinct levels and spheres imply? It leads to moving past the traditional notion of a binary between practicing politics at the local, city level as necessarily distinct or even contrary to working at the cosmopolitan, global level. A "global city" such as Los Angeles blurs the idea of identifying cities with the local and the global with cosmopolitanism. What is the point of such a binary when identities are as much defined at border-crossing interstices as by singular roots? When "local" cities are transnationally constituted, the local becomes an insufficient conceptualization of grassroots practices. These practices are often informed by global "cosmopolitan" norms, just as such norms can be (and must be) informed by grassroots practice. New truth and accountability initiatives are just one example of the need to work at multiple levels if we are to create more pluralistic social compacts that address the ghosts of the past that continue to haunt our present.

Snapshot #4: Racial Justice in Los Angeles: What Can Global Truth-telling Norms Offer?

Brenda Shockley and Zita Davis

The demonstrations for racial justice in Los Angeles in 2020 laid bare the urgent and overdue demand to end institutional and structural racism. Mayor Eric Garcetti issued Executive Directive 27—Racial Equity in City Government—to affirm the city's commitment to addressing the cumulative impact of local social, economic and political forces that perpetuate a shamefully disparate and stratified society. Mayor Garcetti called for municipal government to redouble its efforts to promote equity, beginning with his own government, the City of Los Angeles. The mayor's directive has forced study of whether there are disparate impacts in the city's hiring, promotion, and contracting practices. Mayor Garcetti also appointed the city's first Chief Equity Officer to help lead, coordinate, and drive these efforts. The issuance of ED 27 was an important first step to ensure that racial justice is a core value that informs the city's governance. For example, it provided the basis for the Mayor's Office to engage Occidental College's Young Initiative on the Global Political Economy for a city-academic research partnership on how global norms could inform city-level policy to advance racial equity. The resulting Young Initiative Task Force report—"Truth, Accountability, and Transformative Justice"—offers a globally informed and community-driven framework of tremendous utility given the potential of the policies it details.

The City of Los Angeles is one of many municipalities across the country that has indicated its intentions to grapple with its history of racial disparities, inequity, and exclusion. In nearly every social and economic category, there is numerical evidence that demonstrates that the city's long-standing inequities in housing, income, and wealth may have roots in policies and practices established by federal, state, and local governing institutions. LA's high rates of poverty and limited access to quality healthcare for vulnerable individuals and families were laid bare by the coronavirus pandemic. COVID-19 provided an unexpected public discussion about enduring disparities. Occidental's Young Initiative offered the city a blueprint based on global best practices about how to reckon with Los Angeles' distinct history of injustices and how they connect to current disparities.

The task force recommendations include that the city needs new approaches to bring traditionally marginalized communities into the political conversation about how to address past social and economic harms. Based on comparative models of restorative justice from around the globe, student researchers identified a best practice that would help to change dominant, and often false, narratives about the history of Los Angeles. A best practice that would require an open process for re-discovery or "truth-telling" that would be specific to Los Angeles and be inclusive of city communities and city institutions as part of the structure necessary to develop trust and relevant solutions.

The framework from the Occidental Young Initiative Student Task Force provided the city with a guide by which to identify local strategies for community-based efforts to reduce, and ultimately, eliminate structural and institutional racism through intentional, inclusive truth-telling processes. The task force's research identified key lessons that can be learned from national and global experiences with truth-telling processes, and they developed a template for the city to re-imagine itself as an equitable and inclusive city. In brief, if we can truthfully acknowledge our collective history, create the space for honest conversations about the city's role in past actions and future reform, and if we can engage in reparative actions that help heal past wrongs—together we will create a new Los Angeles, a City of Belonging.

4

Localizing International Human Rights Norms through Participatory Video with People Affected by Leprosy in Niger, Nigeria, and Mozambique[1]

Yohanna Abdou (IDEA Niger[2]), Shehu Sarkin Fada (IDEA Nigeria), Paulo E. Hansine, (AIFO and IDEA Mozambique), Jone A. José (IDEA Mozambique), William Paul Simmons, (University of Arizona)

International human rights treaties and declarations have mixed and limited effects on macro-level national policies and practice, especially involving marginalized communities[3]. But a growing body of studies has shown that when translated into local social and cultural conditions, a process known as vernacularization[4] or localization[5], human rights documents can have profound impacts on the rights consciousness and empowerment of marginalized groups.

In this chapter we describe a project to vernacularize a little-known UN document for the rights of a marginalized and stigmatized group, those affected by leprosy. Our transnational team, which included several people affected by leprosy, developed a participatory video protocol for vernacularization in Niger, Nigeria, and Mozambique that could be applied with appropriate modifications in other contexts with other

---

[1] We would like to thank Anwei Skinsnes Law, Mary O'Friel, and Dr. H. Joseph Kawuma for their assistance throughout this project. Thanks also to the many people affected by leprosy who took leadership roles in making this project happen as well as religious and government leaders that helped to facilitate the logistics for the workshops. Special thanks to Danja hospital in Niger. This project was supported by a grant from the Leprosy Research Institute.
[2] Authorship is listed alphabetically to reflect equal contributions to this project.
[3] e.g. Geisinger, Alex and Michael Ashley Stein. 2007. "A Theory of Expressive International Law" *Vanderbilt Law Review* 60: 77–131; but see Risse, T., S. C. Ropp and K. Sikkink. Eds. 1999. *The Power of Human Rights: International Norms and Domestic Change.* Cambridge: Cambridge University Press.
[4] Goodale, Mark, and Sally Engle Merry, eds. 2007. *The Practice of Human Rights: Tracking Law Between the Global and the Local.* New York: Cambridge University Press; Chua, Lynette J. 2015. "The Vernacular Mobilization of Human Rights in Myanmar's Sexual Orientation and Gender Identity Movement" *Law & Society Review* 49 (2): 299–332.
[5] Destrooper, Tine. 2018. "Localization "Light": The Travel and Transformation of Nonempowering Human Rights Norms" in *Human Rights Transformation in Practice,* edited by Tine Destrooper, and Sally Engle Merry. Philadelphia: University of Pennsylvania Press.

international human rights norms. Our experience shows that human rights instruments can resonate with marginalized peoples' lived experiences and can be important, though not perfect, tools for advancing social justice.

Brief Background on Leprosy

Leprosy is little known in the popular or academic imagination with many myths still widely held. Also called Hansen's disease, leprosy is a bacterial disease (mycobacterium leprae) that is not as contagious as many fear. It takes prolonged exposure to someone with an untreated case to catch it and those with a robust immune system cannot contract the disease. Also, a two or three-drug antibiotic regimen over six months of treatment will totally cure the individual. However, if untreated the bacterium will attack peripheral nerve cells, especially in the fingers and toes, and then the individual will not feel cuts and burns, which can lead to permanent damage. In the past, people affected by leprosy have been ostracized and forcefully segregated and placed in leprosaria such as Kalaupapa in Hawaii, Carville in Louisiana, and Culion in the Philippines. Discrimination against people affected by leprosy remains rampant, with individuals and their families often shunned by their community.[6] They often lose employment opportunities, are expelled from schools, and have difficulty getting medical treatment. And, because of the loss of fingers, in many countries they are not able to vote or get proper identifications, as these often require fingerprints. Because of this long-standing stigmatization, the term "people affected by leprosy" should be used instead of the term "leper."

Because of the fear of discrimination including by medical personnel, many affected individuals will not seek treatment. Thus, leprosy is a disease of the stigmatized that could be all but wiped out with effective education and destigmatization campaigns. And yet approximately 200,000 new cases are diagnosed each year especially in resource poor countries that suffer from poor sanitation and nutrition and other factors that weaken the immune system.

Notably, people affected by leprosy including those relegated to leprosaria have been at the forefront of destigmatization efforts for decades[7] and this has led to the creation of numerous international NGOs. Their activism led to the adoption of the UN Principles and Guidelines for the Elimination of Discrimination against Persons Affected by Leprosy and Their Family Members as well as the establishment of a Special Rapporteur on the issue by the Human Rights Council in 2017.[8]

---

[6] IDEA, The International Association for Integration, Dignity, and Economic Advancement, IDEA. 2008. "Report on Stigma and Discrimination Facing People Challenged by Leprosy: A Compilation of Submissions from IDEA Members from Sixteen IDEA Branches" On File with the Authors. See also, *International Leprosy Association—History of Leprosy at* https://leprosyhistory.org/about.

[7] Law, Anwei Skinsnes. 2012. *Kalaupapa: A Collective Memory.* Honolulu: University of Hawai'i Press.

[8] Cruz, Alice. 2020. Factsheet of the Special Rapporteur on the Elimination of Discrimination against Persons Affected by Leprosy and Their Family Members. Available at: https://www.ohchr.org/Documents/Issues/Leprosy/Factsheet_ACruz2021.pdf.

The UN Document: The Rights of People Affected by Leprosy

The UN Principles and Guidelines is a progressive human rights document that emphasizes rights, dignity, participation, and empowerment. It addresses stigmatization by emphasizing that states should eliminate the use of the term "leper" (Guidelines 9) and that those affected should be portrayed "with dignified images and terminology" (Guidelines 13(c)). Not only should their rights be protected, but people affected by leprosy and their works should be at the forefront of rights struggles. They "can be powerful agents of social change" (Principles 9) and should "make a contribution to awareness-raising through their specific talents" (13(e)). Though General Assembly declarations are not binding on states, this declaration was seen as an important step that could significantly reduce stigmatization and thus lead to the elimination of the disease.

Nonetheless, previous leprosy destigmatization campaigns have had mixed results with some reporting little change even after significant investment of resources.[9] But studies that emphasize empowerment and are based upon "careful situational analyses on existing sociocultural beliefs and practices relating to leprosy" have had significant impacts on destigmatization and inclusion.[10] These include adult literacy programs, socioeconomic rehabilitation, and self-help groups.[11] The anecdotal evidence is quite powerful. A participant in a socioeconomic rehabilitation program in Nigeria reported, "before they will separate my plate, but now we are eating together. Since I don't have to beg from them [any longer], they are now recognizing me as a member of the family."[12]

Our project is the first to connect these grassroots empowerment strategies directly to the UN Principles and Guidelines. How do we localize or vernacularize the UN document to advance the rights of people affected by leprosy?

Vernacularization

Localization of human rights norms happens in two general ways: through the upstreaming of local norms to shape the drafting of human rights instruments and institutions and the translation or vernacularization of the document into local contexts.[13] The UN Principles and Guidelines was consciously shaped by on-the-

9   Barkataki, P. S. Kumar, and PS Rao. 2006. "Knowledge of and Attitudes to Leprosy among Patients and Community Members: A Comparative Study in Uttar Pradesh, India." *Leprosy Review* 77 (1): 62–68.
10 Barkataki, P. S. Kumar, and PS Rao. 2006. "Knowledge of and Attitudes to Leprosy among Patients and Community Members: A Comparative Study in Uttar Pradesh, India." *Leprosy Review* 77 (1): 62–68, p. 67, cf. Sermrittirong and Van Brakel 2014.
11 Sermrittirong, Silatham, et al., 2014. "The Effectiveness of De-stigmatising Interventions" *International Journal of Tropical Disease and Health* 4 (12): 1218–1232.
12 Ebenso, Bassey, Aminat Fashona, Mainas Ayuba, Mike Idah Gbemiga Adeyemi, Shehu S-Fada. 2007. "Impact of Socio-Economic Rehabilitation on Leprosy Stigma in Northern Nigeria: Findings of a Retrospective Study" *Asia Pacific Disability Rehabilitation Journal* 18 (2): 98–119.
13 Destrooper, "Localization 'Light.'"

ground actors, with the input of every major leprosy NGO as well as representatives from dozens of countries, many of them people affected by leprosy. Here we focus on the vernacularization of the resulting document into local contexts in Niger, Nigeria, and Mozambique.

Two nuances from the recent vernacularization literature need to be stressed. First, human rights norms do not get imposed from on high onto a tabula rasa society.[14] They are enacted in localized situations that already have norms in place. Community leaders had been exposed to international human rights norms for years through conferences and workshops and had already translated these norms into their communities and leveraged these discourses for change. For instance, the community in northern Nigeria led by Shehu Fada had already previously conducted successful campaigns to gain the right to vote and to a passport to travel for Hajj. In both cases, previous Nigerian policy had required thumbprints to obtain the necessary documents which many individuals affected by leprosy could not provide.

Secondly, human rights norms travel in a rhizomatic fashion, horizontally as well as vertically and various iterations in between. They "move through complex, multilayered, and juxtaposed networks of rights users."[15] In our case, the people affected by leprosy routinely interact with disability rights advocates and government and religious actors. They had already found ways to influence the system and had access to people in power. And they were in touch with other communities of people affected by leprosy in their countries and beyond through international networks.

When we understand that a community is already imbued with its own rights language, with its own networks, and already dealing with its own power dynamics, the expectations for any given intervention must be tempered. Human rights are not some magical pill brought from outsiders.[16] Further, human rights interventions are not discrete activities that begin or end on specified dates but are part of a continuum of interventions that will live on in various ways beyond the scope and control of outside investigators.

Participatory Video for Vernacularization

This participatory video project was grounded in community-based participatory action research (CBPAR), which is a collaboration between researchers and community members to address a community problem. Community members are not subjects to be studied, but full partners in the research project. All research decisions are made jointly between the community and the researchers, and they work together to co-generate knowledge to solve a problem.[17] Thus, the researcher's main task becomes

---

[14] Destrooper, "Localization 'Light.'"
[15] Destrooper, "Localization 'Light.'"
[16] Urueña, René. 2012. *No Citizens Here: Global Subjects and Participation in International Law.* Leiden: Martin Nijhoff.
[17] Simmons, William Paul. 2012. "Making the Teaching of Social Justice Matter" in *Real Social Science.* Cambridge University Press, edited by Bent Flyvbjerg, Todd Landman, and Sanford Schram.

facilitating arenas where researchers and community members can learn from each other.[18] The final research outputs are a product of the entire group, and the intended audience includes the community and well as researchers and others outside the community.[19]

Participatory video (PV) is closely related to CBPAR as it involves a community creating their own videos about a specific issue with assistance from researchers. Usually, the investigator brings video equipment to a community and does basic training on the equipment and filmmaking. Then, the investigator works with the community to develop stories that the community wants to tell who then act out and film the various scenes. In the most time-intensive PV workshops, community members use software to edit the various scenes into a coherent whole. The finished product can then be shown to the same community to elicit further discussion about the topic and the process. It can then be disseminated to other communities, policy makers, and more widely.

The technique has quickly caught on in international development. It is relatively simple, inexpensive, and can be done fairly quickly. It fits dominant participation and empowerment narratives with community members quickly taking over the video production process to tell their own stories and amplify their own voices. Individuals are not othered, they present themselves as subjects capable of telling their own stories. PV harnesses the power of personal testimonies to convey important messages and it often produces very compelling outputs. PV projects can also be a lot of fun for the researchers and the community members with workshops often including laughter, music, and dancing.

PV though shares many of the dangers of other participatory techniques.[20] Many participatory projects only give lip-service to participation, enlisting the community to execute projects that have already been developed by elites from developed countries. More specific to PV, are the investigators influencing the process so that the results do not reflect the community's viewpoint but has the community telling stories that they think the investigators want to hear?

The most intractable issues revolve around power relationships especially considering the very marginalized nature of these communities. The veneer of participation may elicit a good conscience for outsiders but often disempowers marginalized groups by exacerbating inequalities. Are we privileging certain voices and reinforcing current power structures? Did some individuals feel coerced to participate? Did we reach everyone in the community or were some so stigmatized that they did not appear? Similarly, the investigator often has the final say or editing pass in the final product and how it is disseminated so they are really in charge of the final product. This type of extractive storytelling is all too common as researchers parachute into a community and leave with mountains of compelling video. These power issues

[18] Greenwood, Davydd J. and Morten Levin. 2007. *Introduction to Action Research: Social Research for Social Change*. Thousand Oaks, CA: Sage.
[19] Nagar, Richa. 2015. *Muddying the Waters: Coauthoring Feminisms across Scholarship and Activism*. Urbana: University of Illinois Press.
[20] Cooke, Bill and Uma Kothari. 2001. *Participation: The New Tyranny?* New York: Zed Books.

might be even more of a threat with PV as it is so compelling that researchers can get caught up in the moment and not seriously deconstruct what is happening. The method can also be led by inexperienced researchers who might not be attuned to such pitfalls.

Such issues are difficult to navigate, and we may never be sure that the process did not exacerbate existing inequalities, though we can take steps to mitigate them. We follow Simmons (2012) that CBPAR is an ideal and one is always striving to meet that ideal but will always fall short. This project was intentional in involving people affected by leprosy in all aspects of the project design from developing research questions to development of the protocol, through the dissemination of final products. We provided very broad prompts to lessen the influence of the project leaders on the videos. We had only very broad expectations for our projects so that our expectations did not affect the final project.[21] Most importantly our expectations about the overall impact of the project were tempered from the beginning. As Shaw (2012) writes, "it is clearly unreasonable to imagine that a person is definitively empowered after participating in a video."[22] The country directors live and work in these communities. They know firsthand that sustained change will not happen because of one workshop.

The issue we struggled with the most and could not overcome was the lack of women among the core research team and this surely influenced our protocol and its outputs. Some women contributed significantly at various stages but were not involved in a sustained way. This is a problem endemic to activist groups advocating for rights of people affected by leprosy especially in more traditional societies.[23]

Vernacularization of the UN Principles and Guidelines

The international NGO IDEA received a grant through the Leprosy Research Initiative to develop a protocol to vernacularize the UN Principles and Guidelines. IDEA was the first international NGO to be led mostly by people affected by leprosy and is known for privileging the voices of those affected by the disease. Three of the four (2 in Mozambique) country coordinators are directly affected by leprosy, while one has worked with communities of people affected by leprosy for decades. All of them have years of working and living in the affected communities and have experienced numerous instances of discrimination. All are fluent in several local languages and three of the four are fluent in English. They all had experience in participatory methods. The fifth member of the team is a professor of human rights from the US who has

[21] Shaw, Jacqueline. 2012. "Beyond Empowerment Inspiration: Interrogating the Gap between the Ideals and Practice Reality of Participatory Video" in E. J. Milne, C. Mitchell, and N. de Lange (eds) *Handbook of Participatory Video*. Altamira Press, p. 230.

[22] Sampson, Lyneette. 2018. "Critical Pedagogy Through Participatory Video: Possibilities for Post-Colonial Higher Education in the Caribbean" in *Democracy 2.0: Media, Political Literacy and Critical Engagement*. edited by Paul R. Carr, Michael Hoechsmann, and Gina Thésée. London: Brill.

[23] Cruz, Alice. 2020. Factsheet of the Special Rapporteur on the Elimination of Discrimination against Persons Affected by Leprosy and Their Family Members. Available at: https://www.ohchr.org/Documents/Issues/Leprosy/Factsheet_ACruz2021.pdf.

implemented CBPAR and PV projects in several countries and has taught extensively about participatory research methods.

Niger, Nigeria, and Mozambique were chosen based upon several factors. First, IDEA has strong country leaders in each who had good working relationships with related NGOs. The countries are diverse in experiences with leprosy. Mozambique and Nigeria are classified as "high leprosy burden countries" while Niger is listed as a "medium burden country with low risk of expansion" (WHO, n.d.). Each country has a high prevalence of stigmatization but there have been notable successes in each country. Northern Nigeria is known from their robust socioeconomic rehabilitation programs while Niger has a very active and powerful group of activist women affected by leprosy. Grassroots activists in Mozambique drafted the Mozambique Declaration in 2005 with its 15 principles outlining steps for empowerment, inclusion, and dignity.

Our Protocols

The first phase of the project aimed to develop and implement protocols for vernacularization. A second phase that has not been completed[24] would expand the training to other areas within these countries and eventually to other countries. This second phase would involve formal assessment and hypothesis testing. After consultation with the Institutional Review Board at the University of Arizona it was decided that human subjects' approval was not needed for this first phase as it did not involve systematic research. Such approval would be needed before any type of formal assessment.

The researchers first engaged in numerous brainstorming exercises via videoconferences that included lengthy briefings on the conditions in their countries and specific communities. From this brainstorming and a thorough literature review we decided to adopt a participatory video methodology and adapt it to the study population and to each context. Then the co-researchers met in the Nigerien capital of Niamey and piloted the PV protocols with a group of people affected by leprosy, leading to revised protocols.

The resulting protocol was tweaked for each context but in general it involved two days in each community. During that time, the project leaders hung out with the communities as much as possible, joining them for meals, enjoying the local culture, and hearing from community leaders.

The first day included meeting local leaders and gaining permission for the study. It also involved a thorough explanation of the project to the communities involved and obtaining oral consent. In several places, especially where Sharia law was observed discussions with men and women were conducted separately. The second day was a full day beginning by explaining the project again to the group and discussion any questions from the community.

---

[24] Unfortunately, the work in Nigeria ground to a halt as ethnic conflict and banditry increased and continues to this day. Also, each member of the research team endured serious medical issues which prevented expanding the project.

Then, the communities of 40–60 individuals were split into groups of 4–7 individuals. We first covered the use of the video equipment with a researcher or assistant training one person from the group who would then train the next community member who would then train the next and so on. There was some initial trepidation about this process as many people affected by leprosy have limited use of their fingers and hands, and some are visually impaired. However, everyone was quickly able to run the video equipment, with the help of a partner when needed, and were experimenting with the video equipment. The community members then took turns video recording each other while they gave testimonies about their experiences with the disease. Then, the entire group reconvened to discuss the UN document and what it means in their specific context. In several communities we distributed the first ever translation of the UN document in their own language. The researchers deferred to the community members to lead the discussion about the document. These robust discussions were then followed by small group discussions. In time, additional testimonies were recorded as to how the UN document related to their lives including their challenges in realizing their rights. A typical testimony is provided by a man from Niger who said:

> We have taken our medicines, we are healed, we want to enjoy our rights, in order to be able to live among the people, to get involved in all spheres of public life. We have healthy children, who if they notice the discrimination to which we are the object, they will not be at all happy, therefore we implore God and the technical and financial partners to consider us so that they can help us so that we rub shoulders with society as all other healthy persons.

The groups were then instructed to craft a story related to their human rights and film it.

The prompt was to think of an instance where their rights were denied and then what it would be like if their rights were respected. The participants decided the specific topic, created the story, and did the acting and filming. A group of women in Niger re-enacted a recent incident where one of them visited a medical clinic. She was shunned in the waiting room and the doctor would not touch her or even come close to her. For the ideal scene, we see her in the waiting room mingling with the other patients and the doctor giving her a full examination and asking informed questions about her ailments stemming from her previous bout with leprosy. In an especially sad skit by a group of men, one of them acted out a scene where he carried his very sick young daughter to a clinic for treatment. The doctor shooed him away and tended to all of the other patients despite the increasingly frantic pleas from the father. In the end, the young girl died in the man's arms in the waiting room without receiving medical care. We were extremely concerned that re-enacting such a scene would be traumatizing for the man, but in extensive debriefings we found that it was a catharsis for him, especially being able to act out the scene with his peers who had experienced similar forms of discrimination.

Overall, we held fifteen PV workshops involving 754 individuals in the three countries. Approximately 250 video testimonies were collected in six different languages (Zarma, French, Hausa, Portuguese, Ndau and Macua) and over 50 skits were produced. We took special care to involve more marginalized community

Figure 1 Village elders in northern Nigeria with the first Hausa translation of the UN Principles and Guidelines.

Figure 2 Community members in Nigeria enacting a scene in a medical clinic.

members including women (about 35 percent of the participants), those with visible physical effects, ethnic minorities, and those with low literacy. One workshop in Mozambique included 21 individuals who were formally diagnosed on the day of the workshop as it was paired with monthly self-care meetings.

At the end of the two-day workshops, we held group reflection sessions where hundreds of participants reflected positively on their experiences. Many said they felt empowered by the process. They were very excited and somewhat surprised that the

UN had devoted an entire document to their rights and that the UN stated that people affected by leprosy should lead the charge to realize their rights by mobilizing their talents. Other positive comments centered on the increased feelings of unity among the people, and the recognition of everyone's right to contribute. Many women commented on the communal nature of the PV protocol with each participant being heard. The skits crafted by community members were especially helpful in allowing groups to reflect on their current and past experiences alongside what their idealized future would look like.

The communities that had a previous track record of successful advocacy noted that they now realized that they still had a long way to go to fully realize their rights. Others remarked that through the group discussion they gained skills and strategies to advocate for their rights. Many participants learned about IDEA the NGO leading the project and in Mozambique that led to formalizing an IDEA network at the provincial levels.

The next steps varied between the countries. The project stopped in Nigeria due to widespread violence. In Niger, the videos were professionally edited and shown to the affected communities spurring further discussion about steps to advance their human rights. The community settled on improving their living conditions by promoting income generation, vocational training, and increasing literacy. An advocacy message was formulated by these groups and shared with government representatives. In Mozambique, the country coordinators have continued to take video testimonies and hold discussions about human rights during self-help groups and as part of economic empowerment interventions.

Project Assessment

Was this project a success? The UN document was translated into several new languages, and we developed a PV protocol to localize the rights into the lived experience of people affected by leprosy. Dozens of participants were moved just by being asked to be part of the project and to give their video testimonies. Several expressed that nobody had asked them to tell their story before. Especially interesting was how little other community members in these tightly knit communities knew about the experiences and feelings of their neighbors and friends. Most impacted might have been those with physical effects of leprosy, many of whom were initially skeptical that they could film videos. But even those with severe visual disabilities and with limited use of hands or fingers were able to use the video equipment and help in developing the scripts and video production.

Another indicator of success was the reactions by the country coordinators. One of them exclaimed that he finally understood what participatory methodologies should look like and he was amazed by how passionate and attentive the community members were. Since the project required approval from numerous community leaders (emirs, imams, local chiefs, government officials, chief medical officers, etc.), many new grassroots collaborations were cemented. These contacts have been especially helpful in disseminating the results of the project and will no doubt increase the power of future advocacy.

Simmons (from the US), reflecting on the project six months after the workshops thought it had fallen far short of being a success as formal research had not been conducted and the project was unlikely to continue. He had almost a thousand videos and images on his computer in the US and was unsure if the communities that had produced them even had access to them or felt ownership of them. This felt like a perfect example of extractive storytelling. However, he learned that each of the country coordinators had been working with their communities to continue this project creating more videos and disseminating them in ways that they thought would be most effective. So, instead of this being extractive storytelling, the fact that the outside researcher was not aware of what was being done on the ground in these countries was a further example of empowerment. The project did not need him to continue and develop in exciting directions.

Many attributes of the project team contributed to its success. The researchers bonded and developed substantial trust between themselves, and each made important contributions to the project. The researchers, in part from their years of conducting participatory interventions, were adept at patiently listening to marginalized voices. Since the project was being developed while being implemented, none was the recognized expert on the protocol. We were all co-learning from each other and the context, and this served as a model for the participants. Finally, we were all willing to admit when we were wrong, that is, we practiced radical vulnerability, willing to expose our weaknesses.[25]

We end by quoting three youths reflecting on a CBPAR project in New York City that applies directly to this project:

> It was "a process that was profoundly personal, sometimes painful, and, in the end, definitively political. None of us knew quite what we were getting into when we signed on the dotted line and decided to be part of this project; we didn't know where our journey would take us ... Along the way we not only learned how to do research, but also we learned a lot about ourselves and our community."[26]

---

[25] Nagar, Richa. 2015. *Muddying the Waters: Coauthoring Feminisms across Scholarship and Activism.* Urbana: University of Illinois Press.

[26] Cahill, Caitlin, Indra Rios-Moore, and Tiffany Threatts. 2008. "Different Eyes/Open Eyes: Community- Based Participatory Action Research" in Julio Cammarota and Michelle Fine, (Eds.). *Revolutionizing Education: Youth Participatory Action Research in Motion.* New York: Routledge, p. 28.

5

The Complex Intersection of Legacies of Violence and Legacies of Resistance in Montes de María, Colombia

Pablo Abitbol Piñeiro

I

On February 21st, 1971, thousands of *campesinos* (peasant farmers) occupied more than 800 large estates all over Colombia. The action was coordinated by the National Peasant Farmers' Association in response to the persistent obstacles, delays and reversals imposed by the recently enacted Conservative government against the agrarian reform that had been initiated by two Liberal presidents in the early and late sixties. This was not the first nor the last, but the largest social mobilization of its kind, and it triggered a violent backlash of landowners and local political elites against the peasant farmers' organizations. The police and the army were deployed against the occupiers, many were blacklisted and arrested, and hitmen assassinated and threatened their leaders.

Less than a year later the national government and a coalition of lawmakers and landowners subscribed the *Pacto de Chicoral*: an agreement to put an end to the agrarian reform and the peasant farmers' social mobilization, as well as intended to implement a rural modernization strategy focused on industrializing farms and increasing land productivity mainly for the exportation of commodities.[1] Coupled with the violence against the *campesino* social movement, this reaction produced a radicalization of some organizations, the continuation of land occupations, and the emergence and arrival of left-wing guerrillas attracted toward the contexts of social turmoil.[2]

One of the epicenters of this process was *Montes de María*, a fertile region in northern Colombia, located between the cities of Cartagena and Sincelejo, and where the gentle slopes of the San Jacinto Mountains are flanked by the Caribbean Sea and the Magdalena River.

---

[1] Grupo de Memoria Histórica—CNRR, *La tierra en disputa. Memorias del despojo y resistencias campesinas en la Costa Caribe: 1960–2010* (Taurus, 2010).
[2] Rodrigo Uprimny, "Las enseñanzas del Pacto de Chicoral" (*El Espectador*, January 23, 2022).

As narrated by one of the peasant farmers' movement historic leaders, Jesús Pérez, after that violent backlash the grassroots organizations in *Montes de María* suffered enormous losses to murders, threats and exiles, faded, and had to adapt and morph into less notorious community action organizations. However, violence against the *campesinos* not only did not subside, but also mutated and grew increasingly harsh.[3]

A law from 1968 allowed private citizens to form self-defense groups which were armed and trained by the army; and the police-state enacted nationwide in 1978 in order to counteract the escalation of left-wing guerrillas, facilitated and legitimized actions against any perceived threats to the social order and private property, such as "subversive" individuals and organizations. These were the seeds of the self-defense groups which were formed by coalitions of landowners, politicians and narcotraffickers during the nineteen eighties and nineties, and that at the dawn of the new millennium, by then organized as large illegal paramilitary armies, confederated around the United Self-defense Forces of Colombia.[4]

While the guerrillas kidnapped, extorted, committed selective murders and produced the forceful displacement of many individuals and families, the paramilitaries committed massive massacres, selective and indiscriminate homicides and disappearances, with brutal repertoires of violence that terrorized and displaced whole communities.[5] Displacement and dispossession allowed for large armed structures to exert territorial control on strategic corridors for drug and weapons trafficking, as well as to launder money by increasing their land, agro-industrial and commercial assets.[6]

The logic of paramilitary violence—i.e., the instrumentalization of para-statal counterinsurgency operations as a means to impose a counter-agrarian reform[7]—in *Montes de María* and many other rural regions of Colombia was succinctly captured by the confession of an ex-paramilitary operative, *alias Pitirri*: "It was a conspiracy. One came killing, then others came buying, and then others came legalizing."[8]

Memories from the harshest period of violence, in the early twenty-first century, when millions of families were being forcefully displaced in Colombia, tell stories of paramilitaries arriving in plain daylight to rural communities and executing selective homicides while holding the same blacklists which public authorities used to identify and arrest the leaders of the land occupations and the *campesino* movement decades earlier.[9]

---

[3] Jesús María Pérez, *Luchas campesinas y reforma agraria: memorias de un dirigente de la ANUC en la Costa Caribe* (Centro Nacional de Memoria Histórica, 2010). See also, Centro Nacional de Memoria Histórica, *Campesinos de tierra y agua* (CNMH, 2017).

[4] Centro Nacional de Memoria Histórica, *¡Basta ya! Colombia: memorias de guerra y dignidad* (CNMH 2013).

[5] Grupo de Memoria Histórica, *La masacre de El Salado. Esa guerra no era nuestra* (Ediciones Semana, 2009).

[6] FUCUDE, CODHES, OPDS, Opción Legal and Grupo Regional de Memoria Histórica de la Universidad Tecnológica de Bolívar (2018) *Los Montes de María bajo fuego, voces de las víctimas de la violencia* (Contribuciones a la Verdad, 2020).

[7] Armando José Mercado Vega, "Contrarreforma agraria y conflicto armado: Abandono y despojo de tierras en los Montes de María, 1996—2016" (*Economía & Región*, Vol. 11, No. 2, 2019), pp. 197–248.

[8] Jhenifer Mojica, "Para sembrar la paz, hay que aflojar la tierra" (*El Espectador*, November 11, 2021).

[9] Grupo Regional de Memoria Histórica, *Fortalecimiento de las bases y las capacidades territoriales para la reconstrucción participativa de la memoria histórica del conflicto armado en los Montes de María* (Universidad Tecnológica de Bolívar, 2017).

II

In traditional clientelist settings with peasant populations and tenant-based estate labor, large-scale land ownership is a source not only of economic but also of political power, because it entails territorial control, and territories include persons whose votes can be co-opted under the social order imposed by that kind of political economy. In turn, violence and terror not only procure territorial control, but also political (including electoral) power and access to large-scale land ownership. The formation of this feedback cycle, which gives rise to path-dependent trajectories that sustain and engrain extractive and exclusionary social orders over time, thus characterizes the historical emergence and reproduction of rural economic and political power structures in contexts of protracted violent conflict such as *Montes de María*.

Amid the United Self-defense Forces of Colombia's peace agreement and demobilization process, a paramilitary commander declared in an interview that more than 35 percent of the congressmen and women were "friends" of the organization.[10] Subsequent academic research and judicial investigations revealed the enormous magnitude of the paramilitaries' infiltration and capture of much of Colombian politics and the state.[11] Further research has shown that, even though hundreds of high-ranking politicians and public officials were convicted between 2006 and 2013, their political power structures remained in place and even expanded, particularly at the local and regional levels.[12]

In territories such as *Montes de María* another complex feedback cycle emerged from state capture: public funds were diverted by corrupt officials and politicians toward the coffers of paramilitary groups and clientelist organizations, including private sector contractors who, in turn, used diverted public funds to finance those corrupt officials and politicians' political campaigns. As the political power structures that emerged from that process remained in place and expanded, a sub-product of this logic turned out to be the continued exclusion and systemic impoverishment of the rural population, much of which, precisely because of that deprivation, was easily captured by clientelist and vote-buying electoral organizations.[13]

Thus, in these territories, the interplay of violence and corruption tragically turned electoral politics into an insidious poverty trap.

[10] Semana.com, "Habla Vicente Castaño" (*Revista Semana*, June 4, 2005).

[11] Claudia López Hernández, ed., Y *refundaron la patria. . . De cómo mafiosos y políticos reconfiguraron el Estado colombiano* (Debate, 2010). Mauricio Romero Vidal, ed., *La economía de los paramilitares. Redes de corrupción, negocios y política* (Debate, 2011).

[12] León Valencia and Ariel Ávila, *Herederos del mal. Clanes, mafias y mermelada, Congreso 2014–2018* (Ediciones B, 2014).

[13] Grupo Regional de Memoria Histórica, *Metodologías participativas para la interpretación y la apropiación territorial de la construcción de paz en Montes de María* (Universidad Tecnológica de Bolívar, 2015).

III

Since the deactivation of the guerrillas that operated in the region and the national demobilization of the paramilitaries by the mid-2000s, *Montes de María* lives under levels of violence within the national average, but with way below average and stagnant levels of economic growth and well-being, mostly due to the encroachment of clientelist, extractive and criminal networks of actors that intersect and interact with each other, thus structuring a path-dependent persistent sub-national limited access order[14] characterized by institutional rules in use[15] which can be traced back to the local and regional dynamics legated by the armed conflict.

Several factors account for the institutional legacies of violent conflict in the *Montes de María* region.

(1) State capture: corruption, macro-criminality, and private interests finance clientelist political networks that compete electorally to control the extraction of rents and the use of administrative powers to encroach themselves in office to benefit themselves and their allies. Law and contract enforcement agencies, such as prosecutors' and comptrollers' offices, notaries, judges, and police forces, are easily and systematically co-opted, corrupted, and intimidated.[16]

(2) Extractive economies: the presence of extractive enterprises in the region—such as extensive cattle ranching, agro-industrial monocultures, and mining operations—is correlated with the presence of armed groups whose violent activities tend to favor those industries' interests.[17] Additionally, those industries' interests are more prevalent in governmental development plans, than are those held by the communities.[18]

(3) Adaptative structures of macro-criminality: robust, highly specialized, and very violent networks of actors formed within the armed conflict, preserve, transmit, innovate, and produce variation of criminal technologies, business connections, strategic corridors and infrastructures for drug trafficking (both in local and international markets), contraband, extortion, and money laundering.[19]

---

[14] Douglass North, J.J. Wallis & Barry Weingast, *Violence and Social Orders. A Conceptual Framework for Interpreting Recorded Human History* (Cambridge University Press, 2009).

[15] Elinor Ostrom, *Understanding Institutional Diversity*, (Princeton University Press, 2005).

[16] Armando José Mercado Vega, "¿Posconflicto electoral? Nuevos y viejos riesgos electorales en zonas de transición: el caso de los Montes de María", in *Mapas y factores de riesgo electoral. Elecciones nacionales Colombia 2018* (Konrad Adenauer Stiftung, 2018). Armando José Mercado Vega, "Elecciones locales en Montes de María, 2019: riesgo electoral persistente y violencia política de baja intensidad", in *Mapas y factores de riesgo electoral. Elecciones de autoridades locales Colombia 2019* (Friederich Ebert Stiftung, 2019).

[17] Diana Ojeda, et al., "Paisajes del despojo cotidiano. Acaparamiento de tierra y agua en Montes de María, Colombia" (*Revista de Estudios Sociales*, No. 54, 2014), pp. 107–119. Eloísa Berman, "Mapping violent land orders - Armed conflict, moral economies, and the trajectories of land occupation and dispossession in the Colombian Caribbean" (*The Journal of Peasant Studies*, 2019). Instituto de Estudios Interculturales, *Entre paramilitares y guerrillas—la desposesión territorial en los Montes de María 1958—2016* (Pontificia Universidad Javeriana, 2019). Luis Castellanos, *Paramilitarismo, agroindustria de palma de aceite y reconfiguración del territorio en el municipio de Maríalabaja* (Universidad Tecnológica de Bolívar, 2020).

[18] Pablo Abitbol, "La visión comunitaria del desarrollo rural en Montes de María" (*La Silla Vacía*, October 16, 2018).

[19] Luis Fernando Trejos, *Situación de los actores armados en el Caribe colombiano: del orden armado a la anarquía criminal* (Instituto Colombo-alemán para la Paz—CAPAZ, 2020).

(4) Criminalized family ties and social networks: in contexts which are highly permeated by criminal and corrupt activities, the problem of trust is solved by informal institutions that support, and are supported by, family ties and tight social networks, thus producing dynasties and clans that compete and cooperate to dominate clientelist politics and illegal markets.[20]

(5) Failed reintegration processes of ex-combatants and military personnel: highly trained and martially encultured young and adult men return to their communities without proper psychosocial care, as well as no educational and employment opportunities; they are therefore valued by criminal organizations and easy targets for recruitment.[21]

(6) Social norms and political culture: democratic governance is further eroded by the impairment of civil society; community leaders and social organizations are threatened, silenced, divided, and ignored, and citizens' hopelessness and distrust impede significant levels of informed participation and independent voting.[22]

(7) Psychosocial traumas affecting individuals and communities: pain, hate, revenge, as well as torn social bonds, legate emotionally and socially vulnerable persons and group processes that can easily fall in tragic spirals of violence.[23]

The interaction among these different types of mechanisms allows path-dependent formal and informal institutions—that both stem from and support corrupt, criminal, authoritarian and violent social repertoires—to persist and adapt over time, connecting the past armed conflict with present limited access local and regional orders.

IV

The socio-psychological normalization of clientelist, corrupt and violent practices in rural territories is a natural by-product of these complex dynamics imposed by a long-standing and degraded armed conflict.

First, because viewing such practices as normal, socially accepted, behavioral repertoires is a psychological coping mechanism that helps individuals deal with the moral dissonances that those behaviors ensue. Second, because that constellation of practices determines the parameters whereby individuals and groups are able (or not) to adapt, survive and possibly prosper within such institutional context. In turn, the

---

[20] Mauricio Romero Vidal, ed., *La economía de los paramilitares. Redes de corrupción, negocios y política* (Debate, 2011). Luis Jorge Garay & E. Salcedo, *Narcotráfico, corrupción y Estados. Cómo las redes ilícitas han reconfigurado las instituciones en Colombia, Guatemala y México* (Debate, 2012). Jorge Giraldo, ed., *Economía criminal y poder político* (Universidad EAFIT, 2013).

[21] Centro Nacional de Memoria Histórica, *Nuevos escenarios de conflicto armado y violencia. Panorama posacuerdos con AUC: Región Caribe, Antioquia y Chocó* (CNMH, 2014).

[22] Grupo Regional de Memoria Histórica, *Metodologías participativas para la interpretación y la apropiación territorial de la construcción de paz en Montes de María* (Universidad Tecnológica de Bolívar, 2015).

[23] Unidad para la Atención y Reparación Integral a las Víctimas, *Reconciliación en Montes de María, Canal del Dique y Cartagena* (UARIV, 2013). Centro de Investigación y Educación Popular / Programa por la Paz—CINEP/PPP, *Aprendizajes para la reconciliación. Experiencias de reconciliación entre excombatientes y comunidades receptoras* (CINEP/PPP, 2015).

social norms that constitute the normalized constellation of cultural practices constitutes a self-sustaining equilibrium.[24]

Finally, massive forced displacement of rural populations, the crescent urbanization of rural municipalities and the interconnection of geographically nested urban centers with high levels of informal economies and extremely precarious social services, such as quality education, as well as the electoral and economic success of clientelist and corrupt rural elites, together contribute to the transplantation of the rural political culture legated by the armed conflict into the cities, thus deepening, strengthening and perpetuating the grasp of those elites on power.

V

Nonetheless, the *campesino* social movement in *Montes de María* struggled and managed to survive, resist and rekindle itself. By adapting and morphing into less notorious community action organizations, as well as by building social networks of mutual care, Jesús Pérez and many of his companions within the *campesino* social movement were able to pull through four decades of armed conflict and political violence aimed at the extermination of the peasant farmers' leadership and organizations.

While the enactment of a new national constitution in 1991—catalyzed by civil society's demands for peace, human rights, and social, cultural, economic and political inclusion—gave way to innovative institutional resources and enabled the emergence and incorporation of novel and diverse actors in the democratic arena, it's emphasis on decentralization also triggered a fierce (electoral and violent) competition by part of traditional and nascent elites, aimed at capturing the state at the local and regional levels in the midst of a degraded armed conflict, by then fully fueled by the gigantic narcotrafficking economy created by the war against drugs. Thus came, paradoxically, not only the harshest years of violent conflict, but also the most dynamic years for the flourishing of new social movements and civil society organizations.

By the mid-nineties, *Montes de María* saw the creation of some non-governmental and civil society organizations, such as the *Colectivo de Comunicaciones Línea 21* and *Sembrando Paz*, that offered renewed cultural, political and spiritual possibilities of resistance to violence and conflict. The existence of such organizations, in contact with a more engaged international community, brought significant financial and human resources to the region. The *campesino*, and by then also ethnic afro and Indigenous, organizations were able to take a breath and slowly (re)weave local and regional social networks of resilience.

In 2005, with the enactment of the *Ley de Justicia y Paz*, an incipient transitional justice system was put in place in parallel with the paramilitaries' opaque peace agreement and tortuous and imperfect demobilization process. That institutional

---

[24] Christina Bicchieri, *Norms In the Wild. How to Diagnose, Measure, and Change Social Norms* (Oxford University Press, 2017).

infrastructure nevertheless gave further impulse to the reorganization of civil society, mainly via the victims' participation in truth, reconciliation and reparation programs.

Two years later, the strongest guerrilla group in the country, FARC-EP, abandoned operations in the *Montes de María* region, mainly due to military defeat, and in 2012 entered a peace process with the national government that ended in 2016 with a final peace agreement.[25]

The essential core of the peace agreement lies in the intersection of the transitional justice institutional architecture that it puts in place, and its mandates for a reorientation of drug policy, democratic aperture, and rural reform.

All four of these essential elements that constitute the structural peace-building core of the peace agreement have faced persistent obstacles, delays and reversals imposed by the recently enacted Conservative government, just as five decades ago.[26]

VI

The social movement of *Montes de María* faces a new critical juncture.

The peace agreement opened the possibility for grassroots organizations from the sixteen regions most affected by the armed conflict to participate in democratic politics without the interference of traditional parties and political structures, by creating a transitory electoral jurisdiction for two legislative periods in the national legislative body in which only they can participate.

But local political elites have the upper hand—financial resources, clientelist networks, and knowhow—and may capture those posts in the national congress.

The challenge is to quickly and efficiently generate broad and deep dialogues between a plurality of organizations and social platforms, in order to structure fundamental political agreements to overcome this risk, since only by arriving in an articulated manner at the elections will it be possible to politically consolidate a peace-building social movement that can firmly take the opportunity to balance the historical nefarious equilibrium of political power in the territory.

Weaving conversations between the organizations and leaderships that want and can mobilize votes that are not captured by the traditional electoral machines and that sincerely seek to represent of the interests and aspirations of the victims and rural citizens in congress is possible and is being achieved. But it is necessary and urgent to advance in the challenge of materializing a regional dialogue that articulates this diverse, powerful and interesting range of visions and priorities, not only around a robust and unified electoral strategy and legislative agenda, but also invoking and defending a transformation of the engrained political culture legated by the armed conflict and its interactions with clientelist politics.

---

[25] Gobierno de Colombia y FARC-EP, *Acuerdo final para la terminación del conflicto y la construcción de una paz estable y duradera* (Bogotá, 2016).

[26] Kroc Institute, *Five Years of Peace Agreement Implementation in Colombia: Achievements, Challenges, and Opportunities to Increase Implementation Levels* (University of Notre Dame, 2021).

If a significant number of people agree, not only in thinking and saying that politics should be done differently, but also in *doing* politics differently, based on true citizenship and community leadership, the cyclical logic of the political poverty trap could begin to break. And that is the challenge, how to achieve a transformative collective action, especially within a still fragmented social context where everyone thinks that each other is going to act individually.

The transformation of certain customs that are considered normal but are harmful happens, both by changing our expectations about the behavior of others, and by changing the expectations of others about our own behavior.[27] This reflection invites a political exercise of true social transformation that arises from the way in which people and their leaders *commit to express* who they are and who they want to be through their own actions and organizations.

It is in the hands of the leaders of the territory to decide whether it is feasible, based on a transparent and sincere commitment, to set up a coalition that can arrive with a winning list on election day and structure a collective process that in subsequent years conquers several successes in local and departmental elections.

And it is of vital importance that the media, international and non-governmental organizations, academia, and civil society pay special attention to and decisively support this unprecedented political process, which is crucial for the irreversibility of peace in Colombia.[28]

---

[27] Pablo Abitbol, "Lo normal no es inmutable: cómo transformar prácticas culturales nocivas," reseña de Bicchieri, C. (2019) *Nadar en contra de la corriente* (*Economía & Región*, Vol. 13, No. 1, 2019), pp. 254–261.

[28] I wish to thank my former students and now colleagues in the Regional Historical Memory Group of the Universidad Tecnológica de Bolívar, Yessica Blanco and María José Martínez, for their outstanding research assistance in *Montes de María*.

Section Three

Sexuality, Sexual Rights, and Reproductive Rights

Introduction

Sofia Gruskin

The last few years have seen unprecedented progress toward sexual rights around the globe, at both societal and legal levels. The change from social stigma and invisibility to increasing public visibility and rights protections over the course of a few decades in countries across the globe has been nothing short of amazing. One need consider only the record number of countries decriminalizing homosexuality; the growing recognition of sexual assault as a serious crime regardless of where it takes place and against whom; the decriminalization of heterosexual sex outside of marriage for persons over 18; as well as the recent change to the International Classification of Diseases moving transgender health out of the chapter on mental and behavioral disorders into a new chapter on sexual health.

At the same time, the huge and growing backlash against sexual rights across the globe has at times felt like a tidal wave. This includes government sanctioned, or tolerated, violence because of people's real or perceived sexual orientation or gender identity, openly expressed articulations of homophobia and transphobia by government officials and public figures, as well as retrenchment on commitments to comprehensive sexuality education, abortion, and other sexual rights across every continent. Alongside these actions by governments, sit broader ideological attacks against gender equality and sexuality, increased conservatism, a lack of trust or support for multilateralism, and a growth in fascist tendencies and populist anger more generally.

It is this disconnect and what it can teach us about transformation of the human rights enterprise that motivates each of the pieces in this section. Sexuality, and a person's ability to manifest their sexuality consensually, is by now generally understood to be a matter of human rights but is nonetheless enmeshed in a wide variety of cultural norms, attitudes and values, as well as hostage to economic, social, legal and, in particular, political realities. Sexual rights provide an important lens for thinking about how human rights more generally evolve within and beyond institutional spaces (i.e., in linking the civil and political to the economic, social and cultural), as well as the ways in which the interactions between lived realities and the legal, technical, and political spheres allow human rights norms and standards to develop and change.

As the pieces here make clear there is a need to engage more deeply with the full global architecture needed to support sexual rights, and to deliberately engage with the economic, social, cultural, and political contexts that lie beneath what may, at times, seem only somewhat abstract expressions of rights claims. Human rights standards provide a touchstone, but their mere articulation, while essential is far from sufficient. Strong, active and organized resistance to state-sponsored regression is fundamental, as is the use of human rights norms and standards to expose, assess, challenge and systematically address inequalities connected to sex, to sexuality, and ultimately to the health and well-being of all people. Taken together, these pieces ask what challenges to human rights do sexual rights bring to the fore? And, importantly, what value do human rights offer for advancing protections related to sexuality for all people in the current moment?

1

Sex, Sexuality and Reproductive Health: The Role of Human Rights?

Rajat Khosla and Kate Gilmore

Introduction

What is it about sex?

Sex! Its pleasures and its intimacies. Its excitement and dread. The uncertainties of it; the silences and the taboos.

The cruelty of sex when deployed as if a weapon; when, through abuse of power, it is simply put, violence.

The joy sex can bring, and our longing for it. Its unwelcome consequences: its mild infections and the life-threatening ones. Its longed-for experiences, and the unintended, the dreaded even.

Expressions of sexuality go to the very heart of our identities, and are core to our dignity, as human beings. They are not merely optional, nor are they to be shaped only by fad or fashion or, for that matter, by fiat. Sex and sexuality rather, give intimate dimensions to our physicality, shape our search for and secure our sense of belonging. They draw us into among the closest of connections—one with another. Matters of life, and preventable death too, sex and sexuality, in other words are, about all human rights and all about human rights for all.

Albeit grossly uneven in its observance, there is nonetheless broadening acceptance that sex and sexuality are human rights matters: that freedom to manifest our sexuality safely and consensually, and to enjoy the highest attainable standard of sexual and reproductive health as we do so, is our human right.[1] And yet, efforts continue to be mounted—by states and within the international community—to impede and reverse implementation of the promises made by the Cairo Programme of Action and affirmed at the Vienna Human Right Conference and more recently in Sustainable Development Goals.[2] Those promises that autonomy, agency, and choice will determine policies on

[1] United Nations Committee on Economic, Social and Cultural Rights, "General Comment 22: The right to sexual and reproductive health. E/C.12/GC/22," *United Nations*, 2016.
[2] United Nations General Assembly, "UN Transforming our World: The 2030 Agenda for Sustainable Development. A/RES/70/1," *United Nations*, 21 October 2015. See Goals 3.7 and 5.6.

population and developmental and not targets and quotas. The promise that human rights will be upheld as the cornerstone of sexual and reproductive health and well-being; that coercion, threat or violence in this context will eliminated.

Despite progress, or, perhaps, because of it, regressive efforts are intensifying in international, regional and national settings to constrain the capacity of duty bearers to uphold their legal and normative obligations to sexual and reproductive rights, corrode the applicable normative standards and allow clamp down, even on those providing lifesaving, essential sexual and reproductive health services. Among many examples are: the recent US Supreme Court decision to overturn abortion rights; measures in Hungary attacking sexual and reproductive rights;[3] and the decisions of Poland and Turkey to withdraw from the Council of Europe's "Istanbul Convention" on preventing and combating violence against women and domestic violence.[4,5]

Those push backs do not line up along the Global South-North divide, nor track global inequalities alone, but are found in countries the world over—in the constitutionally democratic and in those that make no such pretense. Whether the USA, UK, Turkey, Saudi Arabia, Poland, Indonesia, or the Philippines, what connects them all is their push back on human rights in the context of sex, sexuality, and gender in all its diverse expressions.

Such barriers, among others that non-State actors too mount to our dignity in sexual intimacy erode our rights to express sexuality without fear or harassment undermine our rights to experience pleasurable, sexual intimacy safely and consensually; derail our rights to enjoy access to the assets we need—information, services and support—for positive sexual and reproductive health outcomes—provision of which resources should be to quality standards—not to mention, also affordable, acceptable, and available.[6]

The obstacles that authorities of various kinds and caliber use to corral our sexual and reproductive freedoms and expression are not set up in some kind of a "natural" or "God given" order, although that is a justification averred by many such would-be custodians. Rather, they are constructed barriers, most often, with racist and misogynist intent hard wired into them.

They are social, political, and economic constructions—public choices—that

---

[3]   Bianka Vida, "New waves of anti-sexual and reproductive health and rights strategies in the European Union: the anti-gender discourse in Hungary," *Sexual and Reproductive Health Matters* 27, no. 2 (2019): 13–16.

[4]   Council of Europe, "Text of the Istanbul Convention," Available online: https://www.coe.int/en/web/istanbul-convention/text-of-the-convention.

[5]   See for example: Gabriela stanimirova, "The domino effect of normalizing violence against women: Why Turkey's withdrawal from the Istanbul Convention has become the norm rather than the exception,"Gglobal *Risk Insights*, 21 May 2021. available online: https://globalriskinsights.com/2021/05/the-domino-effect-of-normalizing-violence-against-women-why-turkeys-withdrawal-from-the-istanbul-convention-has-become-the-norm-rather-than-the-exception/; and Sandrine Amiel, "Istanbul Convention: Poland moves a step closer to quitting domestic violence treaty," *Euronews*, 4 January 2021. Available online: https://www.euronews.com/2021/04/01/istanbul-convention-poland-moves-a-step-closer-to-quitting-domestic-violence-treaty (accessed 29 June 2021).

[6]   United Nations Committee on Economic, Social and Cultural Rights, "General Comment 22."

are pushing the very worst of gendered, sexual, and reproductive stigma, intimidation, deprivation and violence onto the poorest; onto Black persons and persons of color; onto minorities—persons with disability; the LGBTIQ+ and on the sex worker too. Those public choices wreak havoc on personal choice for individuals and groups for whom multiple and intersecting discriminations erect unique and often impassable barriers to realization of their sexual and reproductive health, desires and well-being. In other words, gender, sex, and reproductive realities are constituted by, reflect and reinforce the ebbs and flows of power across the politics, cultures, religions, and commerce too that are the stuff of our daily lives.

Formed in our personal human development journeys, and emerging in adulthood as our gendered identities, the interplays between our sexuality and pleasure, between reproduction and health, are not mere questions of physiology, or even preference, but palpably about power and powerlessness: who has power and who is denied it. Why else would an unholy communion of state and non-state actors—the priest, the profiteer, the populist, the patriarch—orchestrate and resource campaigns whose goal, in the context of sex and sexuality, is to exploit our fears, diminish exercise of our freedoms, and erode human rights protections? Spinning a vicious web of mis- and dis-information, a miasma of stigma, threat, intimidation, and fear is manufactured. The very language of human rights is co-opted to disguise their targeting of those whose sex, sexuality, and sexual and reproductive health intent they seek to suppress and repress. The result? The so-called "rights" of the unborn are pitted in false contest with those of a woman; cultural rights are used as premise of permission to mutilate and cut girls' bodies; the language of family-rights is used to deny rights to non-heteronormative families; the right to religion or belief is exploited to "justify" imposition on others regardless of their right to religion or belief.

Exercise of power against others is the aim of those who, via a toxic interplay of masculinity, misogyny, and patriarchy, seek to control and subjugate manifestations of sex and sexuality by other genders. Exercise of power purchased at cost to others is evident in market behaviors of the profiteers who, veneering their business as if providing "choice," instead commodify lifesaving sexual and reproductive health care and redefine the human body as a marketplace. Exercise of power over others is in the authority assumed by faith leaders who claim "divine" inspiration for their championing of rights-violation restrictions on women's freedoms and bigotry against LGBTQI+ persons.

In this paper, we spotlight the role of power in the contexts of sex, sexuality, and sexual and reproductive health. We aim to show how hierarchical power may be challenged and inverted—turned upside down including in the context of SRHR programming. A multi-directional understanding of power, which the human rights framework overlaid on sex, sexuality and reproduction helps to reveal, provides important insights for the promotion of intimate dignity, also in provision of sexuality and sexual reproductive health services and information.

The Powers of Powers

Many theorists, of course, have addressed the workings of power in everyday life, but for the purposes of this paper, we use Steven Luke's three-dimensional approach.[7] Lukes suggests we think of power as coming in three main varieties: i) the capacity to force people to do what they don't want to do; ii) the ability to stop them doing what they want to do; and iii) the power to shape the way they think, and (we would add here) who they love.

The power of *"must do," "don't do"* and *"don't even think about it (or believe it or feel it)"* defines, imposes and enforces the rules of the road, income tax regulations and the lockdowns imposed under pandemics. But varietal power drives farther, and more clandestinely, into the highly gendered, and deeply intimate, domains of sex and sexuality. And, when deployed under the State's coercive authority, if unrestrained by rule of law or wielded without regard to human rights standards, those power tools readily become weapons—an arsenal fought over and fought with by all manner of power brokers, be they church, corporation, culture, community, or clan.

Intersecting and intermingling, the combined intensity of formal and informal power's grip on the intimate body and on sex, sexuality and reproduction, works hierarchically. Its instructions run down a long chain of command from authority to authority, hand to hand, law to faith, policy to social more, culminating in action and inaction that effectively shields the relatively powerful and exposes the relatively powerless: shields the violent intimate partner;[8] protects the priest who sexually abuses;[9] sides with the sports doctor who violates;[10] excuses the health provider who denies women access to safe abortion;[11] sanctions the stigma and contempt that troll gay youth.[12]

The *"must do," "don't do"* and *"don't even think about it (or believe it or feel it)"* that in exercise of power over others, authorities would impose on sex and sexuality, are habitually submerged in claims as to what is "natural" and what is not; as to who is credible and who is not; as to who is deserving and who is not. As a result, such

---

[7] Steven Lukes, *Power: A Radical View* (New York: New York University Press, 1974). Other notable works on power include: Suerie Moon, "Power in global governance: an expanded typology from global health," *Global Health* 15, 74 (2019); Veena Sriram et al., "10 best resources on power in health policy and systems in low- and middle-income countries," *Health Policy and Planning* 33, no. 4 (2018): 611–621.

[8] Mahima Jain, "The 'shadow pandemic' of domestic violence," *BMJ*, 374, no. 2166 (2021).

[9] Claudia Lauer and Meghan Hoyer, "Almost 1,700 priests and clergy accused of sex abuse are unsupervised," *Associated Press*, 4 October 2019. Available online: https://www.nbcnews.com/news/religion/nearly-1-700-priests-clergy-accused-sex-abuse-are-unsupervised-n1062396 (accessed 17 September 2021).

[10] Tierney Sneed, "McKayla Maroney: FBI made 'entirely false claims about what I said,'" *CNN*, 16 September 2016. Available online: https://edition.cnn.com/2021/09/15/politics/gymnasts-senate-judiciary-committee-larry-nassar-hearing/index.html; (accessed 17 September 2021).

[11] Michelle Truong and Susan Y. Wood, "Unconscionable: When providers deny abortion care," *International Women's Health Coalition*, 2018.

[12] Kafkadesk Budapest Office, "Hungarian Parliament speaker's homophobic comments spark outrage," *Kafadesk*, 19 May 2019. Available online: https://kafkadesk.org/2019/05/19/hungarian-parliament-speakers-homophobic-comments-spark-outrage/; (accessed 17 September 2021).

essentialisms hover threat over all but the narrowest versions of sexual expressions. In so many places, and under a wide range of circumstances, if our expressions step us outside those would-be confines, then condemnation, exclusion, exile, even incarceration follows. It stalks your existence if not married; if as a woman, not demure or submissive; if sexually active by your choice, but single or too young an adult; if deemed "promiscuous" or found offering sex commercially. Arbitrary, discriminatory, judgementalisms lend an ideological cover to punitive policies and bigoted practices directed at sex and sexuality—layering abuse on top of denial, punishment on top of shame, and all in the names, variously, of law and policy, tradition and culture, religion and patriarchy too. That layering compounds. In addition to direct batterings and bruisings of the body intimate and desirous, a chilling effect is spread far and wide; not only on those who seek non-conformist expression of their gender, sex, sexuality today, but on those who would do so tomorrow.

There is no ambiguity of intent in that. It is not only about political and other ruling ideologies rendering insubstantial, marginal, fragile, exposed whichever aspects of gender and sexuality they wish to make "other," but to make sure the range of expressions do not survive.

Those "*do's, "don't's,* and "*stop even thinking/feeling about it*"'s span and reinforce the micro to macro levels: from the levels of the interpersonal to the institutional; from the institutional to the intra-State and on to the inter-State and the international. They sustain widespread tolerance for intimate violence in the home,[13] and enable the shame visited upon adolescents who would explore their emerging sexuality.[14] They are exhibited in denial of school students' access to age-appropriate comprehensive sexuality education,[15] and they purchase gay-conversion's cruel therapies[16] and provide public stigmatization of same-sex attraction.[17] Powers' cruel tools are behind the shackling and imprisonment ordered for the woman miscarrying, on the off chance that she induced abortion herself.[18] They are why draconian restrictions on access to safe abortion are in place.[19] They are evident in failures to legislate against child

[13] LynnMarie Sardinha and Héctor E. Nájera Catalán, "Attitudes towards domestic violence in 49 low- and middle-income countries: A gendered analysis of prevalence and country-level correlates," *PLOS ONE* 13, no. 10 (2018).

[14] Emmanuel Asampong et al., "Adolescents and parents' perceptions of best time for sex and sexual communications from two communities in the Eastern and Volta Regions of Ghana: implications for HIV and AIDS education," *BMC Int Health Hum Rights* 13, no. 40 (2013).

[15] "Campaigns to undermine sexuality education in the (US) public schools," *American Civil Liberties Union*, n.d. available online: https://www.aclu.org/other/campaigns-undermine-sexuality-education-public-schools (accessed 17 September 2021).

[16] Shancel Lal, "It is time for New Zealand to end gay conversion practices," *The Guardian*, 5 September 2021. Available online: https://www.theguardian.com/world/commentisfree/2021/sep/06/it-is-time-for-new-zealand-to-end-gay-conversion-practices (accessed 17 September 2021).

[17] Kahofi Jischvi Suy, "Homosexuality: a crime in several African countries," *BBC*, 12 November 2019. Available online: https://www.bbc.com/afrique/region-48618256 (accessed 17 September 2021).

[18] "Women unjustly imprisoned in El Salvador," *Center for Reproductive Rights*, 26 January 2021. Available online: https://reproductiverights.org/center-reproductive-rights-women-unjustly-imprisoned-el-salvador/ (accessed 17 September 2021).

[19] "Draconian abortion laws kill women and girls," *Amnesty International*, 18 August 2015. Available online: https://www.amnesty.org/en/latest/news/2015/08/draconian-abortion-laws-kill-women-and-girls-1/; (accessed 17 September 2021).

marriage and to force a victim of rape to reconcile with the perpetrator.[20] Power is behind the employer who refuses their staff health insurance for contraceptives;[21] present when, as part of a country's development goals, the government adopts target-driven approaches to reproduction;[22] in play when development aid is not only conditioned on how people of an aid providing country are said to manifest their sex and sexuality but on how it is claimed people receiving countries wish to.[23]

They are in play as delegations to the UN General Assembly, in session after session, on resolution after resolution, go line by line seeking to eradicate all and any references to "*gender*."[24] Written into the claims that LGBTQI rights are "*neo-colonial impositions*," a "*virus*" brought to Africa "*to divide Africans*,"[25] those tools are wielded, as if divinely honed, by the Cardinal who cries: "*Gender ideology is a Luciferian refusal to receive a sexual nature from God*."[26]

Exercise of varietal power for control and containment of our sexualities and reproductive choices is present at every turn: in development's global policy dialogues; in the international alliances and partnerships that are formed, and those that are not; and in decisions about the distribution of aid and supply of commodities. It is present in decisions affecting national laws and public budgets. It influences the ways in which SRH services and information are positioned and provided. It decides which of us is empowered to seek and receive, the assets, services and support we need to sustain our sexual and reproductive health and well-being, and who among us are to be denied exactly that. It determines who is granted the space and opportunity to exercise sexuality without fear and who is to be deprived that, no matter how consensual and loving are their preferred expressions.

Who benefits and who loses as a result of power exerted over gender, sex and sexuality is the outcome of multiple levels of decision making—of links in a long and winding chain of powers' choices that confine, constrain and condemn ours—our choices.

[20] Emma Batha, "Post-Soviet countries urged to fix laws that let rapists off hook," *Reuters*, 16 January 2019. Available online: https://www.reuters.com/article/us-europe-asia-law-women-idUSKCN1PB00Q (accessed 17 September 2021).

[21] Cheryl Alkon, "5 things to know about this summer's birth control ruling," *Everyday Health*, 17 July 2020. Available online: https://www.everydayhealth.com/womens-health/things-to-know-about-this-summers-birth-control-ruling/ (accessed 17 September 2021).

[22] Manish Gupte, "Women's experiences with family planning," *Health Millions* 2, no. 3 (1994):33–6.

[23] Jyotsna Tamang, "Foreign ideology vs. national priority: impacts of the US Global Gag Rule on Nepal's sexual and reproductive healthcare system," *Sex Reprod Health Matters* 28, no. 3 (2020):1831717.

[24] Apoorva Mandavilli, "A U.N. declaration on ending AIDS should have been easy. It wasn't." *The New York Times*, 8 June 2021. Available online: https://www.nytimes.com/2021/06/08/health/unaids-declaration-patents.html; (accessed 22 August 2021).

[25] Naureen Shameem et al., "Rights at risk—time for action: The Observatory on the Universality of Rights report," *Association for Women's Rights in Development*, 2021.

[26] Robert Sarah, "Herald Top 10: Cardinal Sarah: 'As a bishop, it is my duty to warn the West,'" *The Catholic Herald*, 31 December 2019. Available online: https://catholicherald.co.uk/herald-top-10-cardinal-sarah-as-a-bishop-it-is-my-duty-to-warn-the-west/ (accessed 22 August 2021).

Human Rights Invert Power

Human rights values and concepts amount to a quest to radically transform those power relations. Through law, policy and practice, human rights norms and standards seek and require a profound inversion of powers' instructions to the relatively powerless; a turning of Lukes' framework on its head. This is the constructive role of power about which Cornwall and Gaventa write.[27] Under human rights, the "*must do*"s, that power would otherwise impose on us, are transformed into obligations placed back on power itself, and on the State in particular, to positively *respect* and *uphold* our rights. It is the State that "*must do*" that. It is incumbent on the State to ensure, for example, that individual consensual expressions of sexuality are not met with punitive sanctions; that a woman is not incarcerated for either miscarriage or because she sought an abortion; that a young girl does not have to live with stigma so often associated with menstruation at school; that we have the essential information, commodities and services we need for sexual and reproductive confidence, health and well-being.

The "*don't do*"s that power would wield against the relatively powerless, are transformed under human rights, into duties for which the powerful must be made accountable, namely their duties to *protect* our rights. Under the terms and conditions of human rights treaties, norms and standards, it is the State that must comply with "*don't do*"s. And it is the State that must exercise the diligence to prevent others too from doing harm to us. It is therefore the responsibility of the State to take all reasonable measures to ensure no woman dies while giving birth; that quality obstetric care is available and affordable; that contraception and other commodities for safer sex are not left as if a luxury for the few but, instead, are available as a choice for all. The State further must take all reasonable steps to ensure no other authority interferes, prevents, obstructs access to those assets.

And against mind control? With regard to the "*don't even think about it*"s? Well, perhaps it is a stretch to draw neat human rights equivalency to Lukes' third variety of power but, nonetheless, in *fulfillment* of our human rights, the State *is* obliged to actively create the conditions in which we all—in all our diversity, difference and distinction— have equal opportunity to flourish: to think, feel and freely express, associate, and assemble, including in exercise of our sexual intimacies and our pleasures, so long as our doing so deprives none other those same freedoms. The State must take all reasonable measures to ensure that education and information on sexuality are well founded, not censored and available to both boys and girls; to ensure that girls are not mutilated in the name of culture or religion; that they are not married while still children; and, when things do go wrong, the relatively powerless are empowered so that

---

[27] Celestine Nyamu-Musembi and Andrea Conrwall, "What is the human rights-based approach all about?: perspectives from international development agencies," *Institute of Development Studies*, 2004. Available online: https://opendocs.ids.ac.uk/opendocs/handle/20.500.12413/4073; John Gaventa, "Linking the prepositions: using power analysis to inform strategies for social action," *Journal of Political Power* 14, no. 1 (2021):109–130.

they can take action also to demand accountability. It is incumbent upon State to take all action necessary for transforming the deleterious effects of power, such that that dominant power can be challenged by those who are subjugated by hierarchies and identity-based subordination.[28]

An ultimate test of the extent to which human rights-based inverted power relations are daily realities, is the extent to which you, I, and all others are able to decide freely and equally what we will do in exercise of our own dignity.

It is why Lukes' "varietal" power framework has particular poignancy for sex, sexuality, and gender. Under its typology, illegitimate constraints on and denials of our dignity as agents in our intimate lives are revealed. So too are the spaces where greater dignity in sexuality would flourish; spaces where, without harm to others, sexual expression, preference and pleasure too may be explored and expanded.

As in myriad other dimensions of human existence, in the intimate realm too and in expression of our identities, dignity is shaped by what choices are ours to make without fear; by what agency we can exercise without undue penalty; by the prospects we have—the opportunities we have to flourish equally, without discrimination: in other words, by what we can choose "to do," what we can choose "not to do" and our degree of freedom to choose "to think, believe or love" as we will, without harm to another and without being harmed.

Human rights-based policy and programming for SRH must have these matters at its core.

Practice, Programming and Leadership Implications

Looking out over the full schema of varietal power, and its exercise by micro to macro authorities—the practitioner and the programmer must ask first not "What are the public policy choices and constraints?" not "What are the choices for formal power?" but ask instead "Where can greater choice and agency for rights holders flourish?" "Where must it flourish more equally, without discrimination, threat or fear and for greater equality?"

From that basis, fully human rights-based SRH programming would tackle to the ground, the intimate-space invaders of faith, fear and shame. It would work to defend and expand in law and policy, the terrain for non-exploitative expression and exploration of sexual pleasure, not only prevention of its pains and penalties, as important as that is.

It would call upon the institutions of accountability to operate and preserve their independence from the necro-politics that underpin varietal power and provide remedies for violations of rights in the intimate realm, whether or not the powerful agree.

---

[28] Gita Sen et al., "When accountability meets power: realizing sexual and reproductive health and rights," *International Journal for Equity in Health* 19, (2020): 111.

It would insist on provision and access, as essential public services, to the full range of assets—services, tools, and information—necessary to underpin equal opportunity for sexual and reproductive health, without discrimination as to gender identify, sexual orientation, reproductive preferences or on any other grounds prohibited by international law.

SRH needs-assessments would be rooted in human rights and analyses of where and by whom choices are so far are denied, and where and at whose hands, inhibitions and prohibitions trap and limit persons' agency. Donors and policy makers too would endorse efforts to ensure accountability for those whose expectations and requirements cause constraint and stricture to land most heavily on the "other"—on those whose possibilities for personal agency are stripped away by misogyny, racism, hate, bigotry and fear.

SRH interventions would be fully situated in a broader context of intersecting gender and race and other inequalities and discriminations, on the understanding that no advance in the realm of SRH alone can succeed as intended, without tackling the larger, all-encompassing, gendered, racialized and other-ing contexts of economic and social inequality and injustice.

Under the logic of the "demographic dividend" for example, access to modern contraceptives is rightly advocated as an essential step for the fuller release of women and girls' talent and contribution to their societies. But that access is little more than window dressing instrumentalization, where the only "additional" contributions open to women and girls, have little to do with respect for all their rights and has more to do with ensuring their ongoing subordination and control, for instance as workers reliably available for exploitative, low paid labor.

What human rights-based approaches demand, in other words, is redistribution of power, not merely greater access to a limited range of assets. They also demand that the greater the power, the more comprehensive the accountability. Impunity would be openly targeted wherever it is lent to those who use their cultural, economic and political power to exclude, to deprive, to shame and intimidate on the grounds of sex, sexuality and gender. SRH programming itself would be made directly accountable to those whose choice and agency it promises to up lift.

Yet, to date, in so much SRH programming, rights holders whose agency should be enabled and whose choices should be enlarged, have been approached instead reductively: meaning that millions of girls are now a little freer to learn the facts of sexual intercourse but still have little space to freely refuse it or choose it? Meaning that investments may have increased for maternal health but are still fiercely contested for safe abortion. Meaning millions of women have greater access to the commodities needed to make practical choices about when to have children but are constrained still by male partners whose behavior has not been challenged. Meaning international standards, and increasingly national laws, are protecting same-sex love, but still hateful social norms and mores that would meet with that love with violence, are taken as somehow acceptable because they are defended as elements of culture or tradition or faith.

As Wei Chang has reminded us "Abortion legalization, free access to contraceptives, and HIV testing services all enable women and girls to make more informed decisions by expanding their choices. However, these interventions do not remove all barriers to exercising agency or equally benefit all women and girls, highlighting the importance of addressing multiple intersecting constraints."[29]

That is what we are still to tackle comprehensively—those of us working for SRHR: the narrowing reductionisms that our own technical specialisms bias us toward; the silo-mandates of our organizations that means we fail to collaborate with others for coordinated multi-level, multi-component interventions; the counterproductive compromises reached with donor and recipient governments; the instrumentalizations for political gain of fear and misinformation about gender, sex, and reproduction that are not challenged; the failure to stand up coherently against power-monopolies whose interests trump the interests of rights holders themselves. At our worst, the results have seen SRHR programming contorted into population control policies or into pro natalists' fertility drives—all for nativist, populist purposes rooted in misogyny, xenophobia, racism and other bigotries.

It is essential that we understand power to be as central in the field of SRHR as energy is in the field of physics.[30] When we fail to account for its role—in all its dimensions and at all its levels; when we fail to assess and disrupt where power is held and by whom; when we don't review whose power our programs serve, then it is the unequal sexual and reproductive status quo that is advantaged—invariably, a misogynist, racist and homophobic stasis.

In the intimate realms of sex, sexuality, and reproduction, who holds and exercises power matters.[31] True realization of SRHR requires often profound inversions of power in favor of rights holders. It demands that those transformations be championed, instigated, and advanced, even in the face of opposition at the highest levels. Programming that is more intentionally and courageously oriented to challenging unequal power differentials and making the powerful more accountable for their human rights obligations, must be supported, including by the international community.[32] That in turn, requires greater boldness from leaders, at the global, national and the local levels; a whole-of-government approach from line-ministries responsible for gender equality, and health, to those in charge of financing. It demands boldness too from those who run the organizations that provide the SRH programs and services, including bold solidarity with their frontline staff who so often bear the brunt of the pushback from power when it is challenged.

---

[29] Wei Chang, "Decision-making power for women and girls: Evaluating interventions in sexual and reproductive health in sub-Saharan Africa" (PhD diss., Gillings School of Global Public Health, University of North Carolina at Chapel Hill, 2020). Available online: http://search.proquest.com. ezp-prod1.hul.harvard.edu/dissertations-theses/decision-making-power-women-girls-evaluating/ docview/2436898223/se-2?accountid=11311.

[30] Borrowing the analogy used by Wiebren J. Boonstra, "Conceptualizing power to study social-ecological interactions," *Ecology and Society* 21, no. 1 (2016): 21.

[31] Ann K. Blanc, "The effect of power in sexual relationships on sexual and reproductive health: An examination of the evidence," *Studies in Family Planning* 32, no. 3 (2001): 189–213. Available online: http://www.jstor.org/stable/2696304.

[32] See for example, Wei Chang et al., "What works to enhance women's agency: Cross-cutting lessons from experimental and quasi-experimental studies," *J-PAL Working* Paper, 2020: 87. Available online: https://www.povertyactionlab.org/sites/default/files/research-paper/gender_womens-agency-review_ 2020-march-05.pdf (accessed 19 September 2021).

Lukes' power framework provides inspiration for those additional programming and leadership efforts for transformation of power relations, suggesting critical points to be amplified and exercised. In the interests of rights holders, their protection and pleasure; for their physical and mental well-being—not only reduction in injury, illness or mortality, those of us in the human rights, health, political and sectors must do all we can—with courage and conviction—i) to resist efforts to make us do what we don't want to do; ii) to resist efforts to stop us from doing what we want to do; iii) to think (analyze, adhere to, and affirm) and believe just as we must, with human rights our core values and their realization our ultimate goal, no matter what power says to the contrary.

Snapshot #5: Global-Local Intersections to Change Politics and Public Policy on Sexuality in Brazil

Vera Paiva

Since the 1980s, human rights activism has changed politics and public policy design and implementation in Latin American countries. Political mobilization against military dictatorships was the opportunity to use human rights language to express shared necessities. Human rights defined an ethical-political horizon to mitigate the consequences of the despots that had sustained and normalized inequalities across the region. Moreover, human rights shed light on the discrepancy between social experience (the present) and social expectations for a better, more just, and more positive future. As Souza Santos[1] has put it, human rights conveyed a notion of equality transcending "a never-ending uncovering of oppressions from inequality."

Brazil is now suffering an extreme backlash against all that was gained over the last decades of human rights-based public policies, including free universal access to justice and public education, as well as a national health care system. As a result of implementing policies based on human rights but skipping transitional justice and accountability for all that had taken place under the dictatorship, the sense that human rights are about "human rights people defending against the punishment of bandits" ("communists") and that "human rights should protect straight persons/people only," as used by Brazilian military dictators from 1964 to 1988, is again at the heart of the backlash.

As Always, Sexuality is Emblematic and Representative.

A review of Brazilian ethnography describes the emergence of the centrality of the concept of sexual rights starting in 1988, which changes the traditional sexual-gender regime and apparatus—the sexuality *dispositif* itself.[2] As in many other Latin American countries, in the past three decades, people had come to embrace women's rights, reproductive rights, rights to sexual and reproductive health, and the right not to be

---

[1] Boaventura de Sousa Santos, "Human rights as an emancipatory script? Cultural and political conditions," in *Another Knowledge is Possible? Beyond Northern Epistemologies*, ed. Boaventura de Sousa Santos (London: Verso, 2007).

[2] Sérgio Carrara, "Moralidades, racionalidades e políticas sexuais no Brasil contemporâneo," *MANA* 21, no. 2 (2015): 323–345.

discriminated against based on sexual orientation. The dynamic relationship between activists, policymakers, politicians, lawyers, and researchers produced a new secular regime of sexuality in Brazil, using human rights language and accompanied by a regulatory mode that supports the dignity of different ways to experience sexuality. Christian moralists never went away, even as legal protections for the sexual rights of all people continued to grow, and a secular socio-judicial language largely substituted for biomedical language, organizing new policies and medical-psychiatric-psychological discourses. Carrara suggests that these changes would make Gayle Rubin's[3] hierarchic system a halfway photograph.

The internet reflects and produces tension—disseminating old and new sexual *dispositifs* through social networks in distinct bubbles that do not interact. In the field of HIV/AIDS prevention and sexuality education where I stand, we observe how access to different framings of sex can change how young people experience sexuality wherever they sit ideologically. The same person may enact and combine sexual discourses in various scenes, particularly as the smartphone has become an extension of their body since 2016—they feel "mutilated" without it.[4]

In the first 18 months of the COVID-19 pandemic, the impacts of two decades of successful free reproductive care policies and AIDS prevention governmental programs, that put sexuality and human rights at their center, were still strong. Throughout Brazil, during these months sex business and apps use exploded. And yet, social media, TV, and the radio (including some Christian stations) engaged in vigorous discourse against sexual health and well-being, the harms of sex tourism, sexual harassment, and sexual abuse against women and children.

The language of rights has always been contested. As sexuality became integral to elections in 2014 or so, the Brazilian extreme right challenged the constitutional integrality of human rights, repeating sexual-moralistic discourses, and stigmatizing and discriminating against sexual-gender diversity.[5] The result froze inclusive gender and sexuality policies in all sectors—most especially in education and health. Bolsonaro's presidency since 2019 has destroyed it, piece by piece, using tactics from the dictatorship. Fake news and social media now manipulate the notion of "gender ideology," accuse "Human Rights people" and candidates of defending pedophilia and of violating religious and children's rights, and of offending the nation's Christian morality. Only the family should talk to teenagers about sexuality. At the start of his presidency, the president and some elected governors ordered every state school to destroy interdisciplinary booklets that include illustrations of the human reproductive system.

---

[3] Gayle Rubin, "Thinking sex: notes for a radical theory of the politics of sexuality," in *Deviations: A Gayle Rubin Reader* (London: Duke University Press, 2011), 137–181. First published in Carole Vance, *Pleasure and Danger: exploring female sexuality* (Boston: Routledge, 1984).

[4] Vera Paiva and Valeria N. Silva, "Facing negative reactions to sexuality education through a Multicultural Human Rights framework," *Reproductive Health Matters* 23, no. 46 (2015): 96–106, 20; Vera Paiva et al., "Youth and the COVID-19 crisis: lessons learned from a human rights-based prevention program for youths in São Paulo, Brazil," *Global Public Health. An International Journal for Research, Policy and Practice* 16, no. 8–9 (2021): 1454–1467.

[5] Benjamin A. Cowan, *Securing Sex: Morality and Repression in the Making of the Cold War in Brazil* (Chapel Hill: The University of North Carolina Press, 2016).

Local and Peripheral Responses to Human Rights Attacks will Emphasize its Future Value

Local historical processes and political contexts matter. Government, government discourses reinvent their use of human rights language and practices. In Brazil, recent history shows these terms used to endorse and normalize state violence, torture, assassination, and terror against "national enemies." Politicians and public servants dispute notions of dignity and autonomy for those who go against the norm, and validate unpunished police violence, even during the COVID-19 crisis.

The intellectual project of denaturalizing the processes that transform differences into inequality must recognize global traits but be aware of their local specificity. As sexualities and genders, inequalities are embodied and lived with different tones, rhythms, power structures, voices, and noises. Intersectionality is contingent on each context, scenario, and interpersonal scene. We can observe different dynamics producing gender and sexuality inequalities in each region and territory.

In the right-wing attack on human rights everywhere, gender and sexual rights reinforce the notion that human rights are only for certain people. The Brazilian case can serve as an example of how local contexts can sustain (or not) the efficacy and legitimacy of emancipatory approaches for human rights. Three decades of democracy produced *sujeitos*—persons who hold embodiment and a concept of themselves also as "human rights holders" (*sujeitos de direitos*).

The history of human rights in the Global South, as well as the Global North, can inform resistance to current attacks on human rights at the local level. To strengthen human rights-based policies and politics that support sexuality in this increasingly complex and difficult time, shared knowledge can increase attention to multiple sources of wisdom, and thereby enable cognitive and historical justice within and between our worlds.

2

Navigating Homocolonialism in LGBTQ2+ Rights Strategies: Sexual and Political Possibilities beyond the Current Framing of International Queer Rights

Momin Rahman and Adnan Hossain

Introduction

LGBTQ2+ rights have reached a threshold of international attention and promotion and, concurrently, provoked widespread resistance from many governments, intergovernmental organizations (IGOs) and socially conservative and religious movements, both in the Global North and Global South.[1] This process of contention between homophile proponents and homophobic opponents, results in what we call "homocolonialism": a political process through which LGBTQ2+ human rights are deployed and then resisted as part of both an actual and perceived neo-colonial dynamic (Dellatolla 2020, Rahman 2014; 2020). This dynamic consists on one side of a globalized but yet modular strategy of promoting LGBTQ2+ rights and, on the other, political homophobia consisting of particular forms of social stigma and legal oppression, led by the state but often in alliance with conservative social movements (Bosia and Weiss 2013) and targeted at the full range of non-heterosexualities. Below, we explain the homocolonial dynamic and then suggest pathways to disrupt its negative effects. To illustrate the potential of these disruptions, we focus on a case study of the

---

[1] LGBTQ2+ refers to the range of non-binary non-heterosexual identities and genders, primarily lesbian, gay, bisexual, transgender, queer or questioning, and 2-spirit indigenous in the North American context, with the + aiming to capture other forms not included in the list. This term is often used synonymously with "queer" to capture the same range. Rights associated with these identities are also increasingly referred to as SOGIESC rights because they address issues of sexual orientation, gender identity and expression, and sex characteristics. In all cases, the abbreviations refer to socially marginalized sexual and gender behaviours and identities, often in implicit contrast to socially dominant forms of binary heterosexual gender and sexual identities or "heteronormativity". For simplicity, we use the term "homophobia" to capture political resistance to LGBTQ2+ even when that may be specifically focused on one population such as transgender (trans*), for example.

queer movement in Bangladesh, a South Asian Muslim-majority nation that has retained legal homophobia from the British colonial era. We then conclude with a discussion of the implications of such examples for a different approach to queer human rights beyond a focus on "known" sexual identities and the prioritization of legal rights-based strategies.

The Homocolonial Dynamic

July 2016 saw the appointment of the UN's first dedicated human rights official for LGBTQ2+ issues as a direct result of the 2012 report *Born Free and Equal*. These rights remain contentious in many parts of the UN but have gradually expanded across many countries since the 1990s, although the European Union (EU) and the Organization of American States (OAS) remain the only intergovernmental organizations to directly incorporate LGBTQ2+ within their human rights framework (Ayoub and Paternotte 2020, ILGA 2020, Thiel 2021). Furthermore, the promotion of LGBTQ2+ rights has been at times part of the official foreign policy of many within the EU, such the Netherlands, as well as countries like Brazil, Canada, the UK and the USA.

It may seem that the global acceptance of LGBTQ2+ rights is on the horizon. Indeed, LGBTQ2+ political organizations such as ILGA (International Lesbian, Gay, Bisexual, Trans, and Intersex Association), as well as the governments and intergovernmental organizations mentioned above, often portray this recent emergence of international rights strategies as the logical next stage in the historic expansion of LGBTQ2+ protections *as* human rights. At the level of everyday experience, it also makes sense to many who live in places where LGBTQ2+ rights are codified—we have gone from complete social stigma and invisibility to increasing public visibility and social rights over the course of a few decades, most visibly in the rich Global North that stretches across North America and Europe but also in some outside this Euro-begotten zone, such as Taiwan and Argentina.

There remains, however, a global divide on the acceptance of LGBTQ2+ rights and identities, and many well-cited analyses seem to suggest that many non-Western countries are depicted as lagging behind (ILGA 2020; Pew 2013). Research has also come to focus on new waves of opposition to LGBTQ2+ rights (Corrales 2020), including states that have implemented harsh legal and social restrictions against an alleged "gay peril" even in the absence of significant LGBTQ2+ related social or political organizing. These have often involved global networks of anti-LGBTQ2+ agitation connecting actors hostile to sexual and gender minorities from the Global North with similar movements in the Global South, such as the leading role that American Christian churches took in anti-gay campaigns in Uganda, for example (Bosia 2015) or more recently, alliances across European nations, both within and outside the EU (Thiel 2021). In assessing this resistance, there is a danger in assuming that countries simply need to "catch up" to those perceived as the most pro-LGBTQ2+ jurisdictions through an expansion of LGBTQ2+ rights frameworks and, more pertinently, that

LGBTQ2+ identities look the same across cultures. An approach to sexual and gender minority organizing that is based in current western understanding of LGBTQ2+ identities as inevitable or the result of logical progress could actually *prevent* LGBTQ2+ human rights frameworks from serving as effective equality resources where sexual diversity is yet to be culturally and politically normalized. On the other side of these politics, there is also a danger of simply accepting state homophobia as a legitimate exercise of postcolonial or anticolonial autonomy. This global divide represents a new wave of homophobia, one that claims resistance to homophile movements as a cultural defense against "alien" but mostly "western" forms of gender and sexual organization and culture that are being *imposed* on a country, in an apparent replay of colonial era cultural and legal domination, but state homophobias are also not innocent of using the anticolonial argument to accrue power to the state or specific political parties. We describe this dilemma of promotion and resistance as one of *homocolonialism* (Rahman 2014; 2020). Let us unpack the stages of this political process and the assumptions it contains.

First, as in the UN report noted above (2012), LGBTQ2+ rights are conceptualized as universal, implying a transhistorical and trans-cultural understanding of sexual and gender identities and their social regulation. In opposition to this perceived universalism, the internationalization of LGBTQ2+ human rights is criticized by many governments and local conservative/religious social movements as being based on *western* experiences of LGBTQ2+ identities and the non-traditional organization of gender relations (Human Rights Watch 2020). Moreover, this identification of LGBTQ2+ as "western" then justifies resisting such human rights as *neo-colonialist* impositions from "outside" the national and/or regional ethnic and religious culture. Homocolonialism thus represents a dilemma for LGBTQ2+ rights because it potentially replays the historical colonialism of western imperialism in contemporary times by forcing a contemporary western understanding of sexual and gender identities, thus provoking resistance framed as anticolonial cultural autonomy. The framing of sexual diversity based on western ideas is evident in many corridors of the UN, EU and in the foreign policies of those countries that both promote LGBTQ2+ rights and provide refugee pathways for LGBTQ2+ peoples. Effectively, the rights are assumed to "attach" to sexual identities that are public (or need to be to claim those protections), individual, and stable across biography, time, and location. This universal characterization of sexual and gender diversity is being deployed in the space of international relations and operates dialectically toward "traditional" cultures; those that are less economically "developed," both within and outside the "west," such as Poland, Hungary, and Russia; often the Global South in general but most regularly Muslim-majority countries and minority immigrant populations, as well as many countries in sub-Saharan Africa.

Through this dynamic, western governments, western queer political organizations—as well as the general public on behalf of which these organizations may claim to speak—are provided with a reassurance of their civilizational superiority, manifested by citizenship rights allied to increasingly normalized versions of homosexuality such as same-sex marriage and increasing public visibility in media and culture and, increasingly, trans* rights. Moreover, and most crucially, this is then contrasted with the apparent absence of apparently universal sexual and gender identity rights in non-western communities worldwide, including minority immigrant groups in the west, creating "others" abroad *and* at home: a classic colonial tactic of creating a respectable norm and foreign others. This homocolonialism then encourages local and transnational cultural resistance to LGBTQ2+ rights by reinforcing the notion that they are "western" and, therefore, somehow incompatible with anti-colonialist politics and cultural autonomy, *even* (and often) at the expense of recognizing local, pre-colonial, traditions of gender and sexual diversity.

This framing of resistance is evident in political campaigns from across the globe, within many minority immigrant communities in the west, and from various Caribbean nations, to Poland, Russia (including Chechnya), Egypt, Uganda, Iran, to name but a few (Bosia 2020). Within this homocolonialist dynamic, *both sides* of the divide accept the premise that LGBTQ2+ rights are western, but one side sees the western as universal because human rights are a 'universal, while the other sees these rights as particular, profoundly western and colonialist. This reinforcing homocolonial dynamic makes it extremely difficult to argue for a rights framework that both recognizes and protects the universal rights of LGBTQ2+ individuals *and* recognizes differences in how sexual identities are understood and socially regulated. To be effective, any deployment of LGBTQ2+ rights must acknowledge this dynamic, particularly when the very deployment could *provoke* a focus on LGBTQ2+ individuals that harms their ability to stay safe from harassment, violence and death. See, for example, the backlash against raising rainbow flags at the embassies of Canada and the UK in Iraq in May 2020 (Nabeel 2020).

Navigating Homocolonialism: Bangladesh in Focus

We discuss here the difficulties of operationalizing this complex conceptual understanding. In doing so, we argue the need to think through how rights strategies may either reinforce or disrupt the equation of sexual and gender diversity with western culture and political power, and thus undermine or support attempts to identify sexual and gender minority concerns with a local, rather than neo-colonialist agenda. Many transnational queer organizations and allied governments may assume that there can or should be a "model" of LGBTQ2+ rights based on western experiences of identities, progress, and human rights. The UN report (2012), for example, nods to cultural differences but asserts a universal existence of queer identities and, moreover, prioritizes strategic deployment of rights frameworks, as do many governmental or IGO policies such as those promulgated by the EU (Thiel 2021). There may be, however, much to learn from local groups about the national specificities of sexual and gender minority movements and identities, the depth of heteronormativity that they face, and what opposition they encounter across cultural and political realms, as well as the differences between queer groups in terms of what they see as important for their lives and what capacities they have to engage in political activity.

Exploring these issues in detail through a case study, we turn to the context of Bangladesh, a Global South Muslim-majority country that was formerly part of British India. Bangladesh is not an exemplary case study of any particular success or failure, but rather illuminates the complexities of the homocolonial dynamic and the difficulties in disrupting its negative effects. While it was the colonial administration that introduced the criminalization of homosexuality, these laws have been retained by the postcolonial state, first as part of Pakistan from its 1947 independence from British rule, and subsequently since Bangladesh became independent from Pakistan in 1971. More recently in this region, we have seen rights advances for trans* identified people, while anti-homosexual laws and attitudes have often remained (Munhazim 2020), although the largest country in the region, India, decriminalized homosexuality in 2018 after many years of activism by queer communities. Varied forms of same-sex sexualities and intimacies exist in Bangladesh that are neither culturally recognized nor linguistically marked. The homosocial configuration of social life—two persons of same-sex/gender characteristic being together in both private and public space—is not accorded any homoerotic connotations and is often conducive for the efflorescence of same-sex intimacies. For example, people of same sex/gender can spend time or live together without provoking any cultural anxieties about same-sex sexualities while similar kinds of heterosocial interaction are frowned upon and can lead to social controversy. Furthermore, same-sex intimacies are often dismissed as "frivolous play," fun and/or a passing phase that one is expected to overcome as one engages in marriage with an opposite gender partner, although most of our knowledge of such diversity is derived from studies focused on "men" rather than women (Hossain 2019). A strong patriarchal sociocultural framework ensures that males are often able to take advantage of such homo-sociality in ways that females cannot. For example, while it is relatively easier for men to stay outside and away from their home, women do not enjoy similar freedoms. Such differential treatment plays a critical role in shaping the cultural expressions of same-sex sexual intimacies. This is particularly evident in the relative lack of public visibility and cultural discussion of female-to-female same-sex sexualities in contrast to male-to-male sexualities.

Public discourse on same-sex sexualities emerged in Bangladesh with the advent of HIV/AIDS activism and intervention in the late 1990s (Hossain 2017). Acknowledging the fact that men who were not gay-identified engage in sexual intimacy with each other, an alternative framework of men who have sex with men (often truncated as "MSM") was proposed as culturally more appropriate by public health specialists and community activists. Both the government of Bangladesh and NGOs worked hand in hand to address sexual health needs of these "MSM" communities without generating any cultural backlash. Over time, "MSM" became part of the standard policy documents, briefs and instruments of the government, even while same-sex sexualities remained (and continue to remain) a criminal offense under section 377 of Bangladesh penal code, the British colonial era inheritance.

NGO initiatives to cater to "MSM" communities across the country resulted in the setting up of DICs (Drop-in Centers) in many major urban and semi-urban areas in Bangladesh. These DICs served not only as sexual health clinics that taught these same-sex loving and attracted men about safe sex and STI and HIV, but also served as sites where community building took place (Hossain 2019). Predicated on a *kothi-Panthi* (insertee-insertor) model, it was and continues to be the *kothis* (effeminate males literally translated) who are most visible in public space. In this gendered sexual cartography, men who take on a penetrative role in sexual encounter with other men are framed as *panthis* while those who are sexually receptive are labeled as *kothis*. While *kothi* also is used as a label for self-identification, *panthi* is a word used by *kothis* to designate their penetrative sexual partners. In other words, there is no community of men who claim themselves to be *panthi* as is the case with the *kothis*.

While these *kothi-panthi* groups predominantly emanate from working class backgrounds, middle-class gay-identified groups began to emerge as online communities from at least 2000 onwards. These more affluent gay communities were critical of health-focused models and epidemiological categorizations of same-sex attracted men as "MSM." They also positioned themselves as part of a transnational LGBTQ2+ movement. A testament to their cosmopolitan aspiration and transnational alliance building was their launching of various international activities including the celebration of international day against homophobia (now IDAHOT, the International Day Against Homo and Transphobia) in public space. In the years that followed, several members of gay-identified groups participated in various regional and international LGBT-themed conferences and platforms, most notably ILGA conferences. In 2015 the largest network of gay men in Bangladesh and abroad, then called Boys of Bangladesh (BOB), working with several lesbian identified content developers, launched Project Dhee, a lesbian themed comic strip as an advocacy tool in Bangla with support from the US Department of State, challenging the male-dominated LGB activist scene in Bangladesh generating social awareness about female same-sex sexuality (Khan 2016). Thus, what started off as a loose network of online based diasporic and local Bangladeshi gay men over time morphed into a more inclusive space that also included women who identified as lesbians.

On the heels of the activism spearheaded by community-based NGOs working with the "MSM" communities as well as the middle-class gay men, *Roopbaan* was launched as a new magazine and platform in 2014. Pitched towards the middle-class queer populace, *Roopbaan* covered issues ranging from gay tourism in Thailand, to campaigning for the repeal of section 377, to male underwear hygiene (Hossain 2019). *Roopbaan* became publicly linked to homosexuality and LGBTQ2+ rights after two prominent activists associated with this platform were brutally killed on 25 April 2016 in Dhaka. A local Islamist organization with links to al-Qaeda claimed responsibility for the killing. A significant event under the banner of *Roopbaan* was the launching of a rainbow rally in 2014 as part of the Bengali New Year celebration. The intent of the rally was not to send any explicit message to the wider society about the presence of the LGBTQ2+ community. Instead, it was designed as part of the wider celebration of the Bengali New Year. Yet the rally brought *Roopbaan* into mainstream view after an online news outlet reported the event as a "gay parade," giving rise to vitriolic public reactions and death threats to many associated with *Roopbaan* and the rainbow rally. The killing of these two activists brought homosexuality into the mainstream public view in Bangladesh for the first time in history, as the media reported the death with explicit reference to same-sex sexual activism and LGBTQ2+ rights. Previously unintelligible to the mainstream populace, the initialism LGBTQ2+ is now often transliterated in Bangla media reporting (Hossain 2019). The killing of Xulhas and Tonoy two years following threw into sharp relief the long-standing tension between the putatively Western-fabricated gay style identity politics and the behavioral model of male-to-male sexuality described as "MSM." Today many mainstream civil society actors, including LGBT groups, view the *Roopbaan*-led queer movement as a strategic suicide that has done a disservice to a nascent community, while the NGOs focused on men who have sex with men see the wider social reaction to *Roopbaan's* emergence and the gruesome murders that ensued as yet another proof of sexual health-focused model being culturally more appropriate than an identity-based approach (Hossain 2019). This brief history illustrates two key points: first, that formations about sexual and gender diversity vary from assumed western categories and identities and second, that nonetheless, the impact of "foreign" aid structures and politics force an engagement with more western categories to secure resources and support, via development monies and targeted funding and organizational support from pro-LGBTQ2+ diplomatic missions. Moreover, the national government may endorse the former, if it is politically palatable under a "health" discourse, and will even turn a blind eye to the latter, unless the issue becomes caught up in a homocolonial dynamic that forces the state to disavow "western influence."

Let's add another layer to this complexity. Another social group internationally known as the third sex/gender of South Asia is publicly institutionalized in Bangladesh. This is very different from most Western experiences and can only be explained by "local" traditions of *hijra* or "third gender" in South Asia, that has been "translated" into the western idea of trans* from local identities that are seen as culturally resonant and authentic, rather than "foreign." Popularly described as neither men nor women, hijras are people typically assigned a male gender at birth who often surgically remove their penis and the scrotum and identify themselves as either non-men or as women (Hossain 2021). However, there are both hijras with a penis as well as those without and both groups are part of the hijra subculture in Bangladesh. While hijras have conventionally been seen as asexual and above desire, the image of hijra asexuality has been challenged with the advent of HIV/AIDS activism (Hossain 2017). The epidemiological framework that propounded the MSM model in the context of targeting male-to-male sexual behavior discussed above also encompassed the hijras, though soon enough it dawned on the activists and public health specialists that hijras represented a separate constituency and could not be reached through DICs (Drop-in Centers) set up to cater to an "MSM" population. Separate interventions in the form of "transgender" DICs ensued, singling out hijras as an at-risk transgender population.

Following HIV/AIDS focused activism came a social campaign for the legal recognition of the hijras as a third gender/sex in Bangladesh. Unlike MSM and gay identities, hijras are culturally seen as "local" and the demand for the legal recognition of hijras was seen as culturally legitimate (Hossain 2017). More importantly, conventionally hijras were seen as special people with the ability to confer blessings and curse the mainstream society. As specialized ritual performers, hijras rendered music and dance on special occasions namely childbirth and weddings in exchange for gifts in both cash and kind (Hossain 2021). Against this backdrop, the government of Bangladesh legally recognized the hijras as a distinct sex/gender in 2013 through a policy decision and a gazette notification to that effect was issued later in 2014. While the legal recognition has been hailed both nationally and internationally as an example of a progressive politics, hijras have been defined as "hormonally, genitally, genetically and sexually disabled" in official parlance (Hossain 2017). Thus, while the public visibility and legal acceptance of hijra may seem to open a door to wider recognition and organization for the full range of LGBTQ2+ identities and rights, it is not clear that this will happen, given the circumscribed definition of medical dysfunction that hijra rights depend upon. Nonetheless, the public discussion of hijras does permit community organizing that links gender and sexual diversity, often with the help of western missions and transnational organizations that does not always or immediately provoke a homocolonial reaction from the Bangladeshi state or public culture. Somewhat similarly to the homonormative trajectory of lesbian and gay rights strategies in many western countries, this example may, above all, illustrate the conditional and tactical necessity of engaging with whatever opportunity structure becomes possible in a heteronormative society.

Conclusion

Resistance to LGBTQ2+ globally varies from political discourses to legislation and organized violence. Across all these realms it is important to assess whether a demand for LGBTQ2+ rights is an *enabling* resource for local movements or whether it creates disabling levels of resistance. Perhaps a more effective strategy would be to focus on community building through services and clinics that focus on sexual health or online community platforms, rather than expecting people to publicly identify through rights claims that might provoke a harsh response. Not only could such a response avoid prompting homocolonialist outrage from national governments and cultural/religious movements that further narrows the possibilities of identifying sexual diversity with local forms, but it could also further avoid the devaluing of rights institutions and freedoms for civil society organizing in general. It may still be that one of the most effective areas an outside government or NGO can work in is to build the infrastructure to support human rights overall, rather than focus on LGBTQ2+ specifically and if a policy-driven focus has for some reason to be on LGBTQ2+ populations, to recognize rights are not necessarily the most effective organizing principle. Many non-Western nations and groups have led the recent activism on LGBTQ2+ rights internationally, but too often, these rights claims are caught up in a regressive dynamic within national polities because they are seen as imposing a Western view of sexual identities. Crucially, we must move toward some decolonial reformulations of the concepts of sexual diversity, if such rights are to be a genuine resource for equality. Otherwise, they are held hostage by this homocolonial dynamic that disempowers *both* universal LGBTQ2+ rights and local, non-western, versions of sexual diversity.

Snapshot #6: Glocalization and Sexual Rights

Pascale Allotey

Glocalization refers to the simultaneous coexistence of the universal and the particular through adapting global principles, products and practices to the local context. The concept often underlies global engagement across several sectors, including trade, international development, and health. It has also been the basis for negotiating and implementing international human rights norms and standards within states. This simultaneity is a critical juncture illuminating many of the tensions in how the protections of sexual rights evolve.

Ghana, considered one of the more stable democracies in sub-Saharan Africa, is a perfect illustration of the complexity of glocalization when it comes to sexual rights. Ghana has built a reputation of tolerance, friendliness and hospitality. In recent years, in an effort to reverse the brain drain, the government has promoted initiatives to encourage the return of Ghanaians in the diaspora. In addition, the year of return, hosted in 2019, commemorated the 400th anniversary of African slaves to America and attracted hundreds of thousands of visitors to Ghana for the spiritual and birth right journey, injecting close to US$2bn into the economy.[1] While the scale of "beyond the year of return" has been limited by pandemic restrictions, the initiative remains a priority.

Alongside this initiative, in July 2021, *The Promotion of Proper Human Sexual Rights and Ghanaian Family Values Bill 2021*, a private members bill, was introduced in the Ghanaian Parliament by the political opposition.[2] The bill proposes far-reaching legislation to, interalia, criminalize sexual minorities, with five years of imprisonment for being LGBTTQQIAAP+.[3] Flexible sentencing is recommended contingent on a request for conversion therapy. Citizens will have a legal "duty to report" any LGBTTQQIAAP+ activity or advocacy and advocating for the rights of LGBTTQQIAAP+ would result in up to 10 years imprisonment.

---

[1] Reality Check Team, "African diaspora: Did Ghana's year of return attract foreign visitors?" *BBC News*, 30 January 2020. Available online: https://www.bbc.com/news/world-africa-51191409.

[2] Matthew Opoku Prempeh (2021), "Promotion of Proper Human Sexual Rights and Ghanaian Family Values Bill, 2021." Available online: https://cdn.modernghana.com/files/722202192224-0h830n4ayt-lgbt-bill.pdf.

[3] LGBTTQQIAAP+ is the initialism for lesbian, gay, bisexual, transgender, transsexual, queer, questioning, intersex, asexual/aromantic, agender, and pansexual used in the documentation of the proposed bill.

The memorandum to the bill states:

Globalization and its attendant acculturation are supposed to augment the strength and values of states and not to compromise the cultural and moral values therein. The right of states to self-determination is a peremptory rule of international customary law that recognizes the sovereignty of states and their power to make laws to protect their values and identity, provided that the laws do not infringe on fundamental human rights.... In a vastly globalized world where the threat of infiltration of foreign cultures is ever-present, states rely on the right to self-determination to preserve their sociocultural values by enacting legislation to minimize the effect of unacceptable foreign influence.

Within Ghana, there have been extensive responses to the bill from local human rights scholars, advocates and prominent academics,[4] contesting the veracity and logic of several of the claims made.[5] Arguments note, for instance, that the description in the bill of LGBTTQQIAAP+ as "inhuman" incites hatred and violates Article 15 (1) of the constitution which provides for the dignity of all persons. At a press conference, the local academic community highlighted that protecting the beliefs and interests of the majority does not justify violations of fundamental human rights, noting particularly the dangers in enacting laws that remove protections for vulnerable and "unpopular" minorities. Notable, as well in their response to the government is Article 39(2) which ensures that customary and cultural values are adapted as an integral part of the evolving needs of the society. A further critical point raised was the need to correct the inaccuracy that binary sex is unequivocally determined at birth.

Externally, an analysis of the human rights violations and potential harms of the bill as proposed was commissioned by the UN Office of the High Commissioner for Human Rights and submitted to the Ghanaian government.[6] The responses eloquently outline the various points in the bill where rights would be violated under existing Ghanaian Law and International Human Rights Law, establishing a system of state-sponsored discrimination and violence. Legal concerns are also raised about setting precedence within Ghana for "duty to report" and restrictions on freedom of speech and right to assemble.

---

[4] JoyNews, "Group of 18 lawyers and academic mount spirited attack against anti-LGBTQ bill (4-10-21)," 4 October 2021, video, 10:37. Available online: https://www.youtube.com/watch?v=TK19g3UCGc8.

[5] Amal Atrakouti, "GHANA: 'The "anti-gay" bill will have far-reaching consequences if we do not fight it now,'" *Civicus*, 27 October 2021. Available online: https://www.civicus.org/index.php/media-resources/news/interviews/5406-ghana-the-anti-gay-bill-will-have-far-reaching-consequences-if-we-do-not-fight-it-now.

[6] Office of the High Commissioner for Human Rights, "Draft Bill on "Proper Sexual Rights and Ghanaian Family Values Bill 2021"—An Analysis by UN Independent Human Rights Experts United Nations in Ghana," *United Nations*, 9 August 2021. Available online: https://ghana.un.org/en/139914-draft-bill-proper-sexual-rights-and-ghanaian-family-values-bill-2021-analysis-un-independent; https://ghana.un.org/en/139914-draft-bill-proper-sexual-rights-and-ghanaian-family-values-bill-2021-analysis-un-independent.

The bill, nonetheless, has had significant local support, championed primarily by religious bodies, including Christian churches in general and the popular Charismatic churches in particular. The bill illustrates the ongoing challenge of navigating the global and the local when sexuality, culture, values and the law come into play.

The dilemma faced by the Ghanaian government, whether to give in to local populist pressures from the church or risk alienating some local actors and a significant international community, is not unique to Ghana. In Africa alone, despite some advances, sexual rights and freedoms in countries like Uganda and Nigeria are severely limited by law and discrimination, hate crimes are rarely prosecuted. Religion, rather than cultural values, appears to exercise the most influence in the politicization of homophobia.[7] A Pan-African survey on tolerance across 34 countries suggests little cause for optimism—there is very little reported tolerance for sexual differences.[8] Homosexuality is illegal in 36 of the 54 countries in Africa—four of these carry the death penalty. There would be significant value to drawing on lessons from the 18 countries in Africa where same-sex relations are legal, or at the very least, not criminalized, and where communities are able to live in some semblance of peace and tolerance.

Ironically, for countries like Ghana, glocalization also results in religious dogma fueled by growing global religious conservatism, particularly from the far-right religious influences in North America.[9] In addition, the opportunities to garner and "trade" support in conservative values-based decisions from the global to the local are increasingly common. Consensus building processes within the multilateral system are rife with examples of negotiations for one global outcome traded off against local considerations.[10] The cognitive dissonance expressed in a national identity of tolerance alongside an expressed need to protect local values and the fervent adoption of prejudice and discrimination is a stark illustration of the complexities of glocalization.

---

[7] Adriaan van Klinken and Ezra Chitando, *Public Religion and the Politics of Homosexuality in Africa*, (New York: Routledge, 2016); Sarah K. Dreier, James D. Long, and Stephen J. Winkler, "African, religious, and tolerant? How religious diversity shapes attitudes toward sexual minorities in Africa," *Politics and Religion* 13 no. 2 (2019): 273–303. Available online: https://doi.org/10.1017/S1755048319000348.

[8] Brian Howard, "AD362: Africans tolerant on ethnic, religious, national, but not sexual differences," *AfroBarometer*, 19 May 2020.

[9] JoyNews, "Group of 18 lawyers."

[10] Courtney B. Smith, "The politics of global consensus building: A comparative analysis," *Global Governance* 5, no. 2 (1998): 173–201.

Intersex Human Rights in a Time of Instrumentalization and Backlash

Morgan Carpenter

Abstract

Intersex variations comprise a set of innate biological characteristics. The bodies of people with intersex variations are routinely subjected to medical interventions intended to make them function or appear more typically female or male, reinforced through a modern clinical construction of intersex traits as "disorders of sex development." For nearly thirty years, an intersex movement has challenged these interventions. Since 2013, the international human rights system has supported demands for an end to forced and coercive medical practices driven by social and cultural norms, and for access to resourced peer and family support, and redress. Few jurisdictions have yet to adequately meet these demands. Over this period, an LGBT movement and an opposing anti-gender movement have instrumentalized claims about the existence and categorization of intersex people in a dehumanizing debate. Human rights bodies, scholars and advocates can help to address these circumstances by attending to the specific circumstances of intersex people, disentangling misconceptions, and focusing attention on practical reforms to implement human rights protections.

Nomenclature

Definitions and terms used to describe the intersex population are contested, as is true for all stigmatized populations. The UN Office of the High Commissioner for Human Rights[1] provides a standardized definition, where intersex is an umbrella term referring

---

[1]   Office of the High Commissioner for Human Rights (2019), "Background note on human rights violations against intersex people," *United Nations*. Available online: https://www.ohchr.org/EN/Issues/Discrimination/Pages/BackgroundViolationsIntersexPeople.aspx (accessed 25 October 2019).

to innate variations in sex characteristics that differ from medical and social norms for female or male bodies, and that give rise to risks or experiences of stigma or harm. In clinical spaces the umbrella term "disorders of sex development" is widely adopted since 2006 but presupposes the necessity of "fixing" intersex bodies. Attempts have been made to ameliorate the clinical reference to "disorders," and refer instead to "differences" or "diverse" sex development. Intersex traits are also described in clinical settings using diagnostic language, including references to particular kinds of anatomical traits, developmental and structural variations, and sex chromosome variations. Traditional terms, such as the word hermaphrodite, come with a different kind of baggage, such as reductive and constraining associations with particular kinds of physical characteristics and identities.

The population is diverse in age and agency. Diagnosis can occur prenatally, during infancy or adolescence, for example, due to physical development or appearance, or later, such as when attempting to conceive a child. Due to a history of limited disclosure,[2] and widespread misconceptions, many individuals may lack any language to describe their characteristics and related lived experiences. Differing access to healthcare means that access to diagnosis is more challenging in some countries and regions. Individuals use the terms available to them, typically taught by clinicians or parents, and these may reinforce the medicalization of intersex bodies. Lack of access to affirmative language may limit access to peers and affirmative understandings of their bodies. Individuals with agency may choose different language in different settings, termed code switching, in order to avoid misconceptions or stigma, or to access peers, community, and affirmative self-conceptions.

Generalizable Issues Affecting the Population

The intersex population is not definable by sex, gender identity, sexual orientation, disability or ethnicity, but experiences of groups defined by these characteristics share some commonalities with experiences of having intersex variations, and higher proportions of people with intersex variations appear to be LGBT or have a disability.[3] Together with LGBT populations, intersex people can experience stigma associated with sex and gender norms, including pressure and medical interventions to ensure conformity with normative ideas about female or male bodies, including appropriate forms of sexual activity and genital appearance. Together with disability populations, intersex people can experience discriminatory social attitudes and pathologization in order to conform to ideas about normal function, including appropriate forms of urination or appearance, such as the idea that boys need to be able to stand to urinate. Together with women, intersex people experience lack of attention to specific health needs, and even risk human rights abuses such as unnecessary medical interventions

[2] Peter A. Lee et al., "Global disorders of sex development update since 2006: Perceptions, approach and care," *Hormone Research in Paediatrics* 85, no. 3 (2016): 170.
[3] Tiffany Jones et al., *Intersex: Stories and Statistics from Australia* (Cambridge: Open Book Publishers, 2016).

due to gender stereotypes, or in order to be seen as marriageable members of society. For example, psychosocial justifications for early surgeries have included reference to marriage and relationship prospects.[4] Sex and gender norms as they impact intersex people are also racialized.[5]

Generalizable health issues include experiences of trauma, loss of sensation and sexual function arising when harmful practices occur in medical settings; limited or absent disclosure of health information, and a lack of ability to make informed decisions about treatment, including lack of access to resourced peer support; potential for cancer risks, which are known to have been exaggerated or interpolated with social and cultural factors in surgical decision-making;[6] and infertility or limited fertility. Some traits are associated with significant health issues, including adrenal and neurodevelopmental issues.[7] Increasingly, prenatal and preconception diagnosis of intersex traits is associated with discrimination in the application of assisted reproductive technologies.[8]

Attempts to reform clinical practices seek to distinguish interventions associated with urgent physical health issues or personal informed consent from medical interventions intended to make bodies fit normative ideas about appearance and function. Forced and coercive medical interventions affecting people with intersex variations have been variously described as clitoral recessions or clitoroplasties, vaginoplasties, phalloplasties and hypospadias repairs, gonadectomies, "gender assignment" or "reassignment," genital "enhancement," "normalization" surgeries, and associated genital examinations, hormone treatments, vaginal dilation treatments, genital sensitivity testing and medical photography. The UN Office of the High Commissioner for Human Rights notes that "loose conceptions of medical necessity or therapeutic treatment may facilitate social and cultural rationales" for such interventions.[9] Without personal informed choice, such practices can violate rights to security, bodily and mental integrity, health, privacy, exercise of legal capacity, non-discrimination, sexual and reproductive rights, and freedom from torture, ill-treatment and violence.[10]

Social and cultural norms and gender stereotypes remain at the heart of clinical practice. A foundational 2006 clinical "consensus statement" identified family distress as well as the possibility of "gender-identity confusion" as rationales for early surgical

---

4 Office of the High Commissioner for Human Rights, "Background note," 14–15.
5 Katrina Karkazis and Rebecca M. Jordan-Young, "The powers of testosterone: Obscuring race and regional bias in the regulation of women athletes," *Feminist Formations* 30, no. 2 (2018): 1–39.
6 Erica M. Weidler et al., "A management protocol for gonad preservation in patients with Androgen Insensitivity Syndrome," *Journal of Pediatric and Adolescent Gynecology* 32, no. 6 (2019): 605–611.
7 Department of Health, "Newborn bloodspot screening condition assessment summary Congenital Adrenal Hyperplasia (CAH)," 2020. Available online: https://www.health.gov.au/sites/default/files/documents/2020/02/newborn-bloodspot-screening-condition-assessment-summary-congenital-adrenal-hyperplasia_0.pdf (accessed 4 August 2021).
8 Edwin P. Kirk et al., "Gene selection for the Australian Reproductive Genetic Carrier Screening project ('Mackenzie's Mission')," *European Journal of Human Genetics* 29, (2021): 79–87.
9 Office of the High Commissioner for Human Rights, "Background note," 13.
10 Office of the High Commissioner for Human Rights, "Background note," 13.

interventions "for reasons of appearance."[11] Today, clinicians identify "surgical options" (i.e., likely outcomes from masculinizing or feminizing surgery),[12] exposure to prenatal androgens and "potential adult gender identity" as rationales in determining sex where assignment is a "dilemma."[13] These indicate an attempt to construct future cisgender, heterosexual adults. Clinicians also refer to "stigma associated with growing up with atypical genitalia" and "[p]arent's wishes and desire to align the genitals with the gender of rearing" as arguments for early surgery.[14] Appearance is prioritized over sensitivity. Community organizations and clinicians have expressed concern regarding an absence of non-surgical treatment pathways and models of care, such as psychological support and standards of care.[15] Medical interventions appear routine everywhere that healthcare is accessible. Such medical interventions may be facilitated in laws that otherwise prohibit female genital mutilation. For example, legislation prohibiting female genital mutilation in Australia prohibits "cultural, religious or other social" rationales for surgery, but exempts procedures to give "a person whose sex is ambivalent [sic], the appearance of a particular sex."[16]

Social and cultural norms also impact perceptions of who intersex people are supposed to be. Specific intersex traits are typically associated with female or male sex registration, for example, someone with XXY sex chromosomes is typically registered male,[17] someone with XY sex chromosomes and complete androgen insensitivity syndrome is almost always registered female, and someone with XY sex chromosomes and seventeen-beta hydroxysteroid dehydrogenase three deficiency might be assigned female or male depending on the anticipated outcomes of masculinizing surgeries.[18] Clinical constructions regard people with intersex variations as either female or male with "disorders of sex development" that can or should be "fixed" while, at the same time, intersex people are often associated with often mythologized third sex or gender categories and regarded as neither female nor male[19] Even where third categories exist,

---

[11] Christopher P. Houk et al., "Summary of Consensus Statement on Intersex Disorders and Their Management," *Pediatrics* 118, no. 2 (2006): 755.

[12] See for example, Morgan Carpenter, "Intersex variations, human rights, and the international classification of diseases," *Health and Human Rights* 20, no. 2 (2018): 205–214, 209.

[13] Komal Vora and Shubha Srinivasan, "A guide to differences/disorders of sex development/intersex in children and adolescents," *Australian Journal of General Practice* 49, no. 7 (2020): 418.

[14] Mark Woodward and Kate Burns, "Disorders of Sex Development," *Surgery* (Oxford) 37, no. 11 (2019): 646–52. https://urldefense.com/v3/__https://doi.org/10.1016/j.mpsur.2019.09.009__;!!JkGB RS3n8cDS!gfT_oQdoCZSFyWb1PdJ-ec9wnsSl9HHq4JqtmjoKlS-iKyAEECSg2W8qYbNuE1Mck3Too_ JbJUWdg0MQb-OHl4LJeleb22I$.

[15] AIS Support Group Australia, Intersex Trust Aotearoa New Zealand, Organisation Intersex International Australia (2017), "Darlington Statement". Available online: https://darlington.org.au/ statement (accessed 10 April 2018).

[16] Attorney General's Department (2013), "Review of Australia's Female Genital Mutilation Legal Framework - Final Report".

[17] Most humans have two sex chromosomes, where XY sex chromosomes are typically associated with being male, and XX sex chromosome are typically associated with being female.

[18] Morgan Carpenter, "Intersex variations, human rights, and the international classification of diseases," *Health and Human Rights* 20, no. 2 (2018): 205–214.

[19] Morgan Carpenter, "The 'normalisation' of intersex bodies and 'othering' of intersex identities," In *The Legal Status of Intersex Persons*, ed. Jens M. Scherpe, Anatol Dutta, and Tobias Helms (Cambridge: Intersentia, 2018b), 445–514.

people with intersex variations are still, in almost all situations, routinely observed or assigned female or male at birth. Any positioning of intersex as a third sex category is opposed by key community statements (such as AIS Support Group Australia et al. 2017) as this disregards the diversity of the population, and specifically the lived experience of cisgender and transgender women and men with intersex variations. Constructions of intersex as a third sex category have nevertheless been co-opted by medicine in, for example, World Athletics "DSD" guidelines that incentivize consent by women with intersex variations to unnecessary medical interventions.[20] It is as if medical intervention is implicitly understood to be the means by which intersex people become validly female or male.

The Intersex Human Rights Movement

While some support groups were established as early as the 1980s, the first advocacy-focused organization, announced in 1993, sought to reform clinical practices:

> Intersex children would be given preliminary gender assignments as boys and girls (recognizing that all gender assignment is preliminary and does not require surgery); hormonal and surgical interventions would be limited to those that were needed to treat clear and present medical problems, with all elective interventions waiting until patients could consent for themselves; intersex children and adults (and their loved ones) would be provided professional, non-shaming psychosocial support and peer support.[21]

The members of that first advocacy organization were denounced as zealots and "the unhappy ones" in the New York Times in 1996[22], but these proposals remain today in community declarations. The period since has seen retrenchment and redefinition by clinicians of the population, in what can only be understood as attempts to maintain clinical authority and practices. These are accompanied by claims of improved surgical techniques, expressed to support existing practice, and circumvent questions on disclosure, necessity and timing of treatment. Appeals for more clinical research date back to the mid-1990s, but evidence to support these practices remains lacking[23] and typically relies on case studies and small samples where clinicians study their own patients. Such studies are prone to ascertainment and confirmation bias.[24] Clinicians have by and large failed to address their complicity in human rights violations.

---

[20] Katrina Karkazis and Morgan Carpenter, "Impossible 'choices': The inherent harms of regulating women's testosterone in sport," *Journal of Bioethical Inquiry* 15, no. 4 (2018): 579–587.

[21] Alice Dreger, "Twenty years of working toward intersex rights," in *Bioethics in Action*, ed. Françoise Baylis and Alice Dreger (Cambridge: Cambridge University Press, 2018), 55–73.

[22] Natalie Angier, "Intersexual healing: An anomaly finds a group," *The New York Times*, 4 February 1996. Available online: http://www.nytimes.com/1996/02/04/weekinreview/ideas-trends-inter sexual-healing-an-anomaly-finds-a-group.html (accessed 2 December 2014).

[23] Lee et al., "Global Disorders of Sex Development Update," 176.

[24] Carpenter, "The 'Normalisation' of Intersex Bodies."

While still poorly resourced, the intersex movement has become a global liberation movement. Beginning in a 2013 statement by Juan Méndez, then UN Special Rapporteur on torture and other cruel, inhuman or degrading treatment or punishment, demands to end human rights violations in medical settings have been taken up by a variety of human rights mechanisms. UN Committees on the rights of children, women, and people with disabilities have now made relevant concluding observations to countries in every region. Landmark events include joint UN Agency statements on ending forced sterilization, and sexual health, human rights and the law, a 2015 UN expert meeting on ending human rights violations against intersex persons, a 2016 joint statement by human rights experts,[25] and a 2019 background note.[26] The Yogyakarta Principles plus Ten additionally provide a framework for protecting the right to bodily integrity, and the right to truth about human rights violations.[27] Attention to the human rights of people with intersex variations is a remarkably recent phenomenon, and reforms in response to address these concerns remain scarce. Few jurisdictions have yet acted to address these demands, with limited reporting of their impact.

The Abandonment of Traditional Norms

In the major colonial legal systems of Canon law and Islamic law, hermaphrodites were traditionally recognized as female or male depending on prevailing sex characteristics, expressed through an evaluation of secondary and primary sex characteristics, and sometimes reliant on method of urination.[28]

An increasing medicalization of intersex bodies from the nineteenth century took the treatment of intersex people out of the legal and social domain and into a realm where medical authority determined sex registration and consequential treatment. This transition can be seen in the Prussian Code of 1792 which, in Articles 22 and 23, specified that the sex of "hermaphrodites" be decided by parents, with the individual able to choose female or male sex at the age of majority; in the event of a dispute, a third party could request that the individual be examined by professionals to determine sex, and their decision took precedence over the choices of the individual and their parents.[29] Traditional approaches are preserved in, for example, allocations of

[25] Office of the High Commissioner for Human Rights (2016), "End violence and harmful medical practices on intersex children and adults, UN and regional experts urge," *United Nations*. Available online: http://www.ohchr.org/EN/NewsEvents/Pages/DisplayNews.aspx?NewsID=20739&LangID =E (accessed 24 October 2016).
[26] Office of the High Commissioner for Human Rights, "Background note."
[27] Australian Human Rights Commission, *Ensuring Health and Bodily Integrity: Towards a Human Rights Approach for People Born with Variations in Sex Characteristics* (Sydney: Australian Human Rights Commission, 2021).
[28] Ani Amelia Zainuddin and Zaleha Abdullah Mahdy, "The Islamic perspectives of gender-related issues in the management of patients with disorders of sex development," *Archives of Sexual Behavior* 46, no. 2 (2016): 353–360.
[29] Laurence Brunet and Salle Muriel, "Categorizing and attributing the sex of individuals: History of the science, law and ethics," in *Gender Testing in Sport: Ethics, Cases and Controversies*, ed. Sandy Montañola and Aurélie Olivesi (London; New York: Routledge, 2016), 69–70.

inheritance shares to men and women born with "ambiguous characteristics" in Pakistani law.[30]

The increasingly early medicalization of infants and children with intersex variations meant that clinicians in the UK had by 1969 to "imagine" the existence of intersex people who had not been subjected to medical interventions.[31] Accompanied with this, term hermaphrodite became associated with pejorative clinical diagnoses and a related narrowed biological definition.[32]

This transition from legal to medical authority eliminated a cultural and legal heritage in what in Robert Bevan's terms is a "destruction of memory."[33] The resulting lacuna[34] coincided with the growth of an LGBT movement, and anthropological research that sought to understand remaining non-Western conceptions of sex and gender, including constructions of third sexes and genders, and potentially explain the existence of Western queer people through an examination of the lives of non-Western minorities.[35] In her book on "the clinic and the colony," Lena Eckert[36] describes this as a colonization of "intersexualized" bodies. Morgan Holmes[37] argues that this research presumed the merits of third sex categories without considering how the various members of each category were valued in their societies. This appeal to the existence of non-Western minorities also failed to pay attention to the treatment of intersex people in both non-Western and Western cultures.

A Destruction of Memory

In recent years, attacks on "gender ideology" have focused attention not on the treatment of people with intersex variations, but on questions about the nature and meaning of sex, and of intersex. David Paternotte and Roman Kuhar[38] state that the "Catholic Church has been instrumental in the emergence and the development of the notion of 'gender ideology,'" describing "gender ideology" as "a term initially created to oppose women's and LGBT rights activism as well as the scholarship deconstructing essentialist and naturalistic assumptions about gender and sexuality." The term is an

---

[30] See sec. 7 (iii), Pakistan, *Transgender Persons (Protection of Rights) Act, 2018*.
[31] Christopher J. Dewhurst and Ronald R. Gordon, *The Intersexual Disorders* (London: Baillière, Tindall & Cassell, 1969).
[32] Elizabeth Reis, "Impossible hermaphrodites: Intersex in America, 1620–1960," *The Journal of American History* 95, no. 2 (2005): 411–441.
[33] Robert Bevan, *The Destruction of Memory: Architecture at War* (London: Reaktion Books, 2006).
[34] Miranda Fricker, *Epistemic Injustice: Power and the Ethics of Knowing* (Oxford: Oxford University Press, 2007), 192.
[35] Gilbert H. Herdt and Robert J. Stoller, "Sakulambei - A hermaphrodite's secret: An example of clinical ethnography," in *The Psychoanalytic Study of Society Volume 11*, ed. L. B. Boyer and W. Muensterberger (Hillsdale, NJ: Analytic Press, 1985), 115–156; Robert J. Stoller and Gilbert H. Herdt, "Theories of origins of male homosexuality: A cross-cultural look," *Archives of General Psychiatry* 42, no. 4 (1985): 399–404.
[36] Lena Eckert, *Intersexualization: The Clinic and the Colony* (New York: Routledge, 2017).
[37] Morgan Holmes, "Locating third sexes," *Transformations*, Regions of Sexuality, no. 8 (2004).
[38] David Paternotte and Roman Kuhar, "Disentangling and locating the 'global right': Anti-gender campaigns in Europe," *Politics and Governance* 6, no. 3 (2018): 6–19.

"empty signifier" with "flexible synonyms"[39] that marks feminism, sexual and reproductive rights including rights to abortion, recognition of transgender people, and same-sex marriage as alien to traditional values.

The existence of intersex people has been reinterpreted in this backlash in ways that disregard a long legal history and that instead associate the needs, circumstances and aspirations of an intersex population with the distinct needs, circumstances and aspirations of intersecting LGBT populations. Thus, in 2019, the Congregation for Catholic Education made a declaration on "gender theory" affirming the role of medicine, not only in determining sex but also in intervening "with a view to establishing the person's constitutive identity," stating that "where a person's sex is not clearly defined, it is medical professionals who can make a therapeutic intervention. In such situations, parents cannot make an arbitrary choice on the issue, let alone society." The declaration referred to the "suffering of those who have to live situations of sexual indeterminacy," without acknowledging the roles of social stigma and gender stereotypes in constructing such situations, nor the harms caused by unnecessary medical intervention. It also associated the term intersex with being transgender and "[e]fforts to go beyond the constitutive male-female sexual difference."[40] Together, these statements radically change the response of the church toward people with intersex variations, endorsing the role of medical authority in constructing normative identities through surgical and hormonal interventions, and rendering unaltered bodies impermissible.

Debating Sex

The existence of intersex people is treated by many in debate about "gender ideology" and the rights of transgender people as a slippery slope argument. On the one hand, appeals to the existence of intersex traits and people are typically relied upon in justifications of the rights of transgender people. For example, a syndicated article on the "myth that gender is binary" by Jeremy Colangelo refers to "disorders of sex development" and people with "ambiguous genitalia," presenting a contested position as fact: "scientists now describe sex as a spectrum,"[41] where people with intersex variations exemplify a status of being neither female nor male. More recently, a 2021 CNN news story on anti-trans rhetoric in UK media states, offhand: "Also, modern medicine views sex as a spectrum with many variables. Instersex [sic] people" exist.[42]

---

[39] Elżbieta Korolczuk and Agnieszka Graff, "Gender as 'Ebola from Brussels': The anticolonial frame and the rise of illiberal populism," *Signs* 43 no. 4 (2018): 797–821.

[40] Congregation for Catholic Education (2019), "'Male and female He created them' towards a path of dialogue on the question of gender theory in education."

[41] Jeremy Colangelo, "The myth that gender is binary is perpetuated by a flawed education system," *Quartz*, 21 June 2017. Available online: https://qz.com/1007198/the-myth-that-gender-is-binary-is-perpetuated-by-a-flawed-education-system/ (accessed 18 June 2021).

[42] Tara John, "Analysis: Anti-trans rhetoric is rife in the British media. Little is being done to extinguish the flames," *CNN*, 9 October 2021. Available online: https://www.cnn.com/2021/10/09/uk/uk-trans-rights-gender-critical-media-intl-gbr-cmd/index.html (accessed 10 October 2021).

The superficiality of this analysis is reinforced by a link from this text to a news story not on medical acceptance, but instead on a struggle for acceptance by athletes subjected to coercive and unconsented medical interventions to eliminate their perceived difference.[43] It is unclear if this reliance on the mere existence of intersex people omits acknowledgment of human rights abuses faced by people with intersex variations because such acknowledgment might undermine the human rights claim.

On the other hand, the status of people with intersex variations is collateral in positions, such as those expressed in a "Declaration on Women's Sex Based Rights,"[44] that seek to exclude transgender women from places for females and eliminate support systems for trans people. This declaration gives effect to a statement by Janice Raymond[45] that "the problem with transsexualism would best be served by morally mandating it out of existence." To this end, debate by signatories of this declaration often take mention of the existence of intersex people to indicate a belief in the idea that sex is a spectrum, and the supposition that people with intersex traits comprise a third sex.

Opponents of transgender inclusion have evolved multiple models of sex determination including a model based on chromosomes, where the existence of a Y chromosome is assumed to indicate male sex registration; a "gamete-producing developmental pathway" where bodies (irrespective of whether or not they will, do or have produced gametes) are aligned to situations where females produce large gametes and males produce small gametes; and a "cluster" approach that weighs different attributes.[46] These models fail to explain the legal and social status of people with intersex variations. No model of sex determination is capable of representing the diversity and complexity of lived experiences and legal registrations of people with intersex variations that exist in the world, or in any single region. These models instead reflect an undue emphasis on how to classify intersex people, and an ableist discourse where intersex people are defined in relation to idealized situations where actual physiological realities do not exist. In doing so, they exacerbate harm, and distract attention from the ways that people with intersex variations are stigmatized and subjected to violence, discrimination and harmful practices.

A Politics of Respectability

The rhetoric around "gender ideology" subjugates the interests of intersex people to the interests of larger intersecting populations, including the interests of parents, clinicians,

[43] Ivy Nyayieka, Christina Macfarlane and Jo Shelley, "Running as equals the elite athletes fighting for acceptance," *CNN*, 2021. Available online: https://www.cnn.com/interactive/2021/07/sport/athletics-testosterone-rules-negesa-imali-running-as-equals-dsd-spt-intl-cmd/ (accessed 10 October 2021).

[44] Women's Human Rights Campaign (n.d.), "Declaration on Women's Sex Based Rights". Available online: https://www.womensdeclaration.com/en/declaration-womens-sex-based-rights-full-text/ (accessed 9 October 2021).

[45] Janice Raymond (n.d.), "Fictions and facts about the transsexual empire." Available online: https://janiceraymond.com/fictions-and-facts-about-the-transsexual-empire/ (accessed 14 October 2021).

[46] Kathleen Stock, *Material Girls: Why Reality Matters for Feminism* (London: Hachette UK, 2021).

women, trans and same-sex-attracted people. In this environment, the legitimacy of the intersex movement and the rights of intersex people are granted only where they coincide with those larger demands.

This subjugation promotes choices of terminology perceived as respectable, or as fitting acceptable preconceptions. In this sense, the discursive role of intersex people as perceived in LGBT spaces (often accompanied by misconceptions about the population) has promoted a distancing by some non-LGBT individuals with intersex variations who choose to seek belonging and recognition as respectable in other social groupings. This subjugation prompts debates about intersex as a word, and about sex and gender, that can be understood as a form of destruction of memory, to eliminate alternative forms of community- and self-understanding. On social media this has led to uncomfortable situations that exemplify Evelyn Brooks Higginbotham's concept of respectability politics,[47] such that individuals with intersex traits and their parents appear pressured to accept models of sex determination that promote the self-perceived "normality" of themselves and those close to them, while discounting the status of others.

These difficult circumstances evince a discomfort with uncertainty and diversity of viewpoints. In this context, it is important to recognize that respectability and attempts to accommodate to clinical norms have not led to reforms that ensure medical practices meet fundamental human rights norms. On the one hand, acceptance of clinical terminology offers no escape from perceived failings of older language. For example, an international sports medicine "consensus statement" makes the surprising proposition that "DSD women" illustrate "the new realm of gender fluidity."[48] On the other hand, reforms aimed at protecting people with LGBT identities have not addressed the circumstances of people with stigmatized bodies.[49]

Distracted Attentions

Discourse on "gender ideology" perpetuates a status quo of neglect and human rights abuses affecting people with intersex variations. This is not simply an incidental effect; in an echo of legislation prohibiting female genital mutilation that enacted exemptions for surgeries on children with intersex variations, there is now evidence of legislation to restrict healthcare access by transgender youth that is accompanied by exemptions for surgeries on children with intersex variations. For example, legislation in Arkansas

[47] Evelyn Higginbotham, "The politics of respectability," in *Righteous Discontent: The Women's Movement in the Black Baptist Church, 1880–1920* (Cambridge: Harvard University Press, 1993), 185–229.
[48] Blair R. Hamilton et al., "Integrating transwomen and female athletes with differences of sex development (DSD) into elite competition: The FIMS 2021 Consensus Statement," *Sports Medicine* 51, (2021): 1401–1415.
[49] Morgan Carpenter, "Intersex human rights, sexual orientation, gender identity, sex characteristics and the Yogyakarta Principles plus 10," *Culture, Health & Sexuality* 23 no. 4 (2021): 516–532.

became "the first known trans medical care ban in the United States,"[50] while also exempting "services to persons born with a medically verifiable disorder of sex development" from the meaning of prohibited "gender transition procedures."[51]

Further, many commentators seeking to promote the rights of LGBT and intersex people fail to recognize that "disorders of sex development" refers to intersex people, with an impact on how they respond to anti-gender legislation. In discussion with a journalist for website *them*, Alicia Roth Weigel remarked that allies need "to invest in learning enough about intersex issues that when they read these bills, they realize that those pertain to intersex bodies … they need to invest sufficiently to be able to understand what our needs are as a community."[52]

Conclusions

It is possible that the intersex movement has only been able to exist because of the existence of the women's movement, disability and racial justice movements, and an LGBT movement. Intersex advocacy benefits from their challenges to dominant ideas about sex, gender and "normality," and their constructions of communities in the face of stigma, discrimination and even criminalization. However, legislative and other actions to address the rights of these intersecting or overlapping populations have to date been unable to address the particular needs and circumstances of people with intersex variations. Actions to effect protections for intersex people remain scarce and novel. The countervailing ideologies and analyses evident in current debates around "gender ideology" exemplify discomfort with uncertainty and difference, and this backlash to existing reforms make it all the more difficult to address the myriad challenges that remain. Nevertheless, the human rights of intersex people do not require a commitment to a particular view on the nature of sex, they rely on a commitment to fundamental human rights norms and standards. Human rights institutions and stakeholders can assist by promoting specific attention to intersex-specific human rights abuses and specific community resourcing needs, and by documenting abuses, disentangling misconceptions, and promoting practical reforms that implement human rights protections in medical and social settings.

Acknowledgments

The author would like to thank Sofia Gruskin, Christopher Jordens, Steph Lum, Mauro Cabral and Cody Smith for discussions regarding draft versions of this text.

[50] Sydney Bauer, "Attacks on trans health care target intersex people, too," *Them*, 10 September 2021. Available online: https://www.them.us/story/trans-health-care-attacks-target-intersex-people-too (accessed 19 September 2021).

[51] Robin Lundstrum (2021), *To Create the Arkansas Save Adolescents from Experimentation (SAFE) Act*.

[52] Bauer, "Attacks on trans health care."

4

Eppur si muove. Reflections on Human Rights and Trans Depathologization in ICD-11

Mauro Cabral Grinspan

The eleventh version of the International Classification of Diseases (ICD-11)[1] officially entered into force on January 1, 2022. It had been approved by the World Health Assembly in May 2019, after a revision and reform process that lasted almost a decade. The process carried out by the World Health Organization (WHO) not only updated already existing content; it also introduced new content. Among other changes, ICD-11 contains new chapters and diagnostic categories—including the chapter "Conditions Related to Sexual Health," and the category of "gender incongruence."

The WHO had concluded the ICD revision and reform process in May 2018; back then, the inclusion of that new chapter and that new category occupied a central place in the official communication produced by WHO itself; it was covered by traditional and social media, and incited a myriad of analytical and political reactions around the world.[2] Such a massive reaction was understandable: for the first time since 1978, when trans-related diagnoses were first added, trans people's existence was no longer classified as a mental disorder in the International Classification of Diseases.[3]

It is honestly tempting to hyperbolize the beginning of the ICD-11 implementation process, for example, expanding it to make it coincide, precisely, with the beginning of

---

[1] WHO. ICD-11. "International Classification of Diseases 11thth Revision." Retrieved from: https://icd.who.int/en.

[2] See, for example: "Being trans is not a mental disorder anymore: ICD-11 is officially released." Retrieved from: https://sxpolitics.org/being-trans-is-not-a-mental-disorder-anymore-icd-11-is-officially-released/18609

[3] However, it is included in the *Diagnostic and Statistical Manual of Mental Disorders* (DSM-5) published by the American Psychiatric Association (APA) in 2013. In the DSM-5 "gender identity disorder" was replaced by "gender dysphoria". According to the APA, "This change further focused the diagnosis on the gender identity-related distress that some transgender people experience (and for which they may seek psychiatric, medical, and surgical treatments) rather than on transgender individuals or identities themselves." The diagnostic focus on distress is compatible with WHO's language on "gender incongruence" in ICD-11. APA. Gender Dysphoria Diagnosis. Retrieved from: https://www.psychiatry.org/psychiatrists/cultural-competency/education/transgender-and-gender-nonconforming-patients/gender-dysphoria-diagnosis. See also: Davy, Zowie. The DSM-5 and the Politics of Diagnosing Transpeople. Arch Sex Behav2015 Jul;44(5):1165–76. doi: 10.1007/s10508–015–0573–6.

trans depathologization; however, and as I will argue throughout this chapter, both beginnings coincide in certain crucial points and diverge in others, equally crucial. In that sense, the singular moment dated January 2022 can function as a productive intersection between two related historical processes—those reforming psycho-medical classifications and those depathologizing trans people.

My goal in this text is to explore that intersection in three different ways. First, by analyzing some of the key opportunities and challenges posed to trans depathologization by the diagnostic category of "gender incongruence" and its location under the chapter "Conditions Related to Sexual Health" in ICD-11. Second, by mapping the present status of trans depathologization as a matter of rights and, particularly, of human rights. Third, by identifying the role of current anti-gender movements in the political contestation of those psycho-medical and legal reforms seeking to depathologize trans people.

*   *   *

Pathologization can be defined as the praxis of identifying a trait, an affect, a behavior, a body, a way of life, an individual or even an entire population as *inherently* disordered—that is to say, as pathological *in itself*.[4] Such an identification is just one side of the coin, provided that all traits, affects, behaviors, bodies, ways of life, individuals, and populations identified as pathological are normatively opposed to their namely healthy counterparts. The healthy/pathological dichotomy is markedly hierarchical, provided that "healthy" as historically constituted presents itself as the regulatory ideal—celebrating itself as desirable, defendable, and superior while demoting "pathological" as repudiable, attackable, and inferior.

Historically, trans pathologization must be placed within the unfolding of medicalization as a part of broader processes establishing medical jurisdiction over certain phenomena—for example, the very existence of individuals whose bodies, souls and/or sexual behavior contradict social and institutional mandates for womanhood and manhood. By proclaiming its ontological, epistemological and normative jurisdiction over them, medicine expropriated them from other domains, such as those of mythology, religion or criminal law. The process of medicalizing and pathologizing such individuals is recognized to have started at the end of the 19th century; however, and despite its dominance, it can also be identified as an unfinished process: even in present times, trans people can be *simultaneously* treated as monsters, sinners, criminals *and* pathological beings by different governments, institutions, and movements.

Medicalization and pathologization can be identified as *colonizing* processes, metaphorically but also literally. The process of establishing medical (and, later, psycho-medical) authority over trans lives has been historically dependent on establishing

[4] Kara, Sheherezade. *Gender is Not an Illness. How Pathologizing Trans People Violates Human Rights Law.* New York: GATE, 2017. Retrieved from: https://gate.ngo/gender-is-not-an-illness/. See also: Davy, Zowie. *Sex/Gender and Self-determination. Policy Developments in Law, Health and Pedagogical Contexts.* Bristol: Bristol University Press, 2021.

Western, white, and human geopolitical authority over the rest of the world.[5] As Julian Gill-Peterson demonstrates, the healthy/pathological border has always been inherently racialized, and perpetuated through domination, oppression, and exploitation.[6] The psycho-medical colonization of trans lives and, particularly, its extractive political economy, can be easily recognized today, for example, in the debates on "gender incongruence of childhood," as will be discussed below.

Trans resistance against pathologization can be traced back to the 70s and, with particular force, since the 90s onward.[7] As an emancipatory movement, trans depathologization has been focused not only on dismantling psycho-medical authority over trans people's lives, but also on liberating *all* bodies, identities, expressions, and sexualities from the social and institutional mandates reinforced by pathologization.

Depathologizing trans people has always existed within a complex political horizon, requiring the questioning of some foundational and cherished beliefs (such as those associated with the gender binary, its naturalness, and the role of psycho-medicine in protecting it). It entails identifying and deactivating the pervasive medicalization of legal frameworks and ensuring trans people's autonomy and self-determination a matter of law. It demands confronting the long history of geopolitical, racial, and socioeconomic injustice perpetrated by and through pathologization, imagining transformative and restorative responses, and finding the means to make them real.

1

Almost four years have passed since the World Health Organization presented a new version of the *International Classification of Diseases* and, since then, the world has learned that in ICD-11 being trans is no longer classified as a mental disorder. In this period, the same question has been posed again and again: were trans people depathologized by this change to the ICD? The same question is being asked right now: does effective entry into forces of ICD-11 mean that trans people are *finally* depathologized? The response to those questions keeps being one and the same: *yes, no, and maybe*. To explore this frustrating but nonetheless productive response, in this section I will examine some of the opportunities and challenges posed to trans depathologization by, first, the category of "gender incongruence" and, second, by its location under the field of sexual health.

---

[5] Vergeiro, Viviane. *Despatologizar é descolonizar*. GATE. Retrieved from: https://gate.ngo/es/viviane-vergueiro-despatologizar-es-descolonizar/. See also: Conrad, Peter. *The Medicalization of Society. On the Transformation of Human Conditions into Treatable Disorders*. Baltimore: The Johns Hopkins University Press, 2007.

[6] Gill-Peterson, Julian. *Histories of the Transgender Child*. Minneapolis and London: University of Minnesota Press, 2018.

[7] Suess, Amets, Espineira, Karine & Crego Walters, Pau. "Depathologization," in *Postposttranssexual. Key Concepts for a Twenty-First Century Transgender Studies*. *TSQ* Vol 1 (1–2):73–77, 2014. See also: Malatino, Hil. *Queer Embodiment. Monstrosity, Medical Violence, and Intersex Experience*. Lincoln: University of Nebraska Press, 2019.

*   *   *

Removing all diagnostic categories classifying gender diversity as a mental disorder within the ICD has historically been a key goal of trans depathologization movements;[8] this goal was achieved in ICD-11 with the removal of diagnoses such as "transsexualism," "gender identity disorder," "dual role travestism," "fetichistic travestitism," among others. In that sense, it is possible to offer a qualified response: *yes*, trans people have been effectively de-psycho-pathologized. However, achieving *full* depathologization has historically been identified as the removal of *all* diagnostic categories applicable to trans people. In that sense, it is also possible to offer a qualified response: *no*, trans people have not been fully depathologized—despite some substantial improvements. For example:

- Instead of diagnosing an individual's gender identity and/or expression as a disorder, "gender incongruence" is *only* focused on an individual's distress caused by the incongruence their experienced gender and the sex assigned to them at birth. In this sense, the new category operates two reductions: it can only be applied to those individuals expressing such a distress, which means that it does not apply to *all* trans people, and it does not necessarily apply over a trans individual's entire lifespan (e.g., when the distress ceases, the diagnosis should not be applied anymore).
- Unlike the previous diagnosis, "gender incongruence" does not assume a gender binary (e.g., it does not mention "opposite sexes").
- "Gender incongruence" has been defined as a "condition" which, as a matter of principle, can be considered to be a more benign entity than "disorder" or "disease."
- It has been classified as a condition related to sexual health—which, at least in theory, provides a less pathologizing location mental or behavioral disorders or other ICD Chapters.

While those improvements could be considered a promising advance when compared with the previous status quo, it is also imperative to identify some old and new problems associated with "gender incongruence." For example:

- To be diagnosable, the condition still requires trans people to express a certain level of suffering—which, as Tobias B. Wiggins rightfully argues about DSM diagnoses, perpetuates the cissexist assumption about trans lives as undesirable by definition.[9]
- The association between that suffering and the experience of "gender incongruence" seems to invoke congruence as a normative ideal. Given the pervasive role of pathologization in configuring social and institutional life,

---

[8] Missé, Miquel and Coll-Planas, Gerard (eds). *El género desordenado. Críticas en torno a la patologización de la transexualidad.* Barcelona and Madrid: EGALES, 2010.
[9] Wiggins, Tobias B. "A perverse solution to misplaced distress: Trans subjects and clinical disavowal," *TSQ* (2020) 7 (1): 56–76.

"gender incongruence" risks pathologizing those perceived as "incongruent" due to their gender expression and promoting gender conformity through gender affirming healthcare. In that sense, even when the category does not assume a gender binary, it risk reproducing it; in the same sense, the category is highly concerning for intersex people, as their bodies have been consistently identified as "incongruent" in terms of sex and gender and this new diagnosis could be used to justify normalizing interventions.

In ICD-11, "gender incongruence" has been divided into two diagnostic categories. One of them is called "gender incongruence of adolescence and adulthood" and the other is called "gender incongruence of childhood." The diagnosis focused on adolescents and adults has been (quite reluctantly) tolerated by many trans advocates on solidarity grounds—that is to say, as a way of securing access to legal gender recognition, gender affirming healthcare and coverage in those countries where needed.[10] The diagnosis focused on children has been strongly rejected by trans advocates, because, first, it pathologizes gender diversity in childhood and, second, there is neither a psycho-medical nor legal need to justify pathologizing it—such as access to coverage for hormonal treatments or surgical procedures.[11]

*   *   *

One of the most challenging trans-related issues in the ICD revision and reform process was finding the right location—or, at least, a *good enough* location- for the new diagnostic categories. While the ICD-11 chapter on mental and behavioral disorders was no longer acceptable, other proposed chapters brought their own problems. For example, those chapters focused on endocrine and/or genitourinary issues offered some advantages as possible locations—such as their close connection with gender affirming healthcare, and the secure coverage of their diagnosis. However, those chapters were also highly pathologizing, and carried the risks of identifying trans experiences as bio-anatomically determined by definition, and of gender affirming healthcare as potentially mandatory. For years, the chapter on "factors influencing

---

[10] See, for example, the *Joint Statement on the ICD-11 process for trans and gender diverse people* signed by Akahatá, APTN, GATE, ILGA, Iranti, RFSL, STP, TGEU and ULTRANS. Retrieved from: https://gate.ngo/icd-11-trans-process/ and the *Joint Statement Being Trans is not a mental disorder anymore: ICD-11 is officially released*, signed by GATE, Akahatá, TGEU, APTN, ILGA, PST*C, Iranti, and STP. Retrieved from: https://sxpolitics.org/being-trans-is-not-a-mental-disorder-anymore-icd-11-is-officially-released/18609.

[11] See, for example: GATE. *Critique and Alternative Proposal to the gender incongruence of childhood category in ICD-11*. Retrieved from: https://gate.ngo/critique-and-alternative-proposal-to-the-gender-incongruence-of-childhood-category-in-icd-11/https://www.thelancet.com/pdfs/journals/lanpsy/PIIS2215-0366(16)30043-8.pdf; Cabral, Mauro, Suess, Amets, Ehrt, Julia, Seehole, Tshegofatso J. and Wong, Joe. "Removal of gender incongruence of childhood diagnostic category: a human rights perspective," in *The Lancet Psychiatry*, May 2016. DOI: 10.1016/S2215–0366(16)30042–8; Winter, Sam, De Cuypere, Griet, Green, Jamison, Knudson, Gail. "The Proposed ICD-11 Gender Incongruence of Childhood Diagnosis: A World Professional Association for Transgender Health Membership Survey. October 2016." *Archives of Sexual Behavior* 45(7). DOI: 10.1007/s10508–016–0811–6.

health status or contact with health services" was considered a possibility; however, its benignity as a depathologizing location has to be weighed against how uncertain coverage for gender affirming procedures would be under it. The possibility of a stand-alone chapter focused on gender incongruence was also dismissed, as well as the possibility of a "starfish" model distributing different diagnostic codes through several chapters at the same time.[12]

The ICD-11 chapter "Conditions Related to Sexual Health" is a new chapter and includes only a small number of categories. It includes those associated with sexual dysfunction, those referred to sexual pain disorders, and "gender incongruence." Undoubtedly, it is a better location than the chapter on mental and behavioral disorders but, at the same time, it is necessary to identify some of the challenges that this location entails. For example:

- While locating "gender incongruence" under the field of sexual health implies its explicit emancipation from the field of mental health, it would be naive to presume sexual health to be necessarily and immediately a trans-progressive landscape. Actually, and through its history, sexology has proven its capacity to be extremely conservative—and even regressive- in its approach to bodies, sexualities, gender identities and gender expressions.
- In many regions of the world, there is a grave scarcity of sexual health professionals and, at the same time, many of them lack expert knowledge on trans issues.
- Sexual health and, particularly, sexual rights, are among the most contested areas in the contemporary political field and the identification of "gender incongruence" as a sexual health issue could have a deep negative effect on access to legal gender recognition, gender affirming treatment and its coverage.

Coming back to the question on the current status of trans depathologization that opened this section, this is the moment when *maybe* becomes, paradoxically, the most precise answer. Certainly, trans people have been de-psycho-pathologized in ICD-11 but making sexual health a *good enough* location will require maintaining, and even increasing, all forms of expert advocacy work, for example, on monitoring ICD implementation at the country level, engaging with professional associations, and ensuring full compliance of diagnostic guidelines and standards of care with human rights principles, norms.

2

Fifteen years ago, the *Yogyakarta Principles* (YPs) were published. The YPs had been elaborated to make clear and explicit the different ways in which existing international

[12] Drescher, Jack, Cohen-Kettenis, Peggy, Winter, Sam. "Minding the body: situating gender identity diagnoses in ICD-11," *Int Rev Psychiatry*, 2012 Dec;24(6):568–577.doi:10.3109/09540261.2012.741575.

human rights law could be applied to matters of sexual orientation and gender identity.[13] Even when pathologization is not specifically addressed in the YPs, depathologization is one of its core values. For example, the YPs defined gender identity as universal experience, "which may or may not correspond with the sex assigned at birth, including the personal sense of the body...", including, "if freely chosen, modification of bodily appearance or function by medical, surgical or other means." By introducing such a definition, the YPs affirmed that the distinction between healthy and pathological gender identities was not compatible with human rights standards. This depathologizing approach to gender identity issues was amplified through another two key references. Principle 3 on the right to recognition before the law affirmed that, according to human rights standards:

> Each person's self-defined sexual orientation and gender identity is integral to their personality and is one of the most basic aspects of self-determination, dignity and freedom. No one shall be forced to undergo medical procedures, including sex reassignment surgery, sterilization or hormonal therapy, as a requirement for legal recognition of their gender identity.

Principle 18 on protection from medical abuses affirmed that, under the same standards:

> No person may be forced to undergo any form of medical or psychological treatment, procedure, testing, or be confined to a medical facility, based on sexual orientation or gender identity. Notwithstanding any classifications to the contrary, a person's sexual orientation and gender identity are not, in and of themselves, medical conditions and are not to be treated, cured or suppressed.

While acknowledging the persistence of psycho-medical pathologization, the YPs urged States around the world to advance legal depathologization—that is to say, to depathologize sexual orientation and gender identity through the reform of laws and policies.

At the time the YPs were elaborated, trans people were living in conditions quite different from those of "self-determination, dignity and freedom." Many countries did not allow them to legally modify their gender markers; in other cases, modifying gender markers was subjected to long judicial processes, and/or conditioned to the fulfillment of a long list of requirements—including, for example, the obtention of psycho-medical diagnosis through extensive and invasive testing, mandatory bodily modifications, sterilization, the display of a cisheteronormative sexual orientation, gender identity and gender expression, and/or divorce.[14] Those people seeking to

---

[13] The Yogyakarta Principles on the Application of International Human Rights Law in Relation to Sexual Orientation and Gender Identity. Retrieved from www.yogyakartaprinciples.org

[14] See, for example: Grzywnowicz, Micah. "Consent signed with invisible ink: Sterilization of trans* people and legal gender recognition," in *Torture in Healthcare Settings: Reflections on the Special Rapporteur on Torture's 2013 Thematic Report.* American University.

access gender affirming healthcare had to go through intense psycho-medical *gatekeeping*, as only those conforming to diagnostic criteria would be allowed to access hormonal treatments and surgical procedures.

In 2012, ten years before the start of the ICD-11 implementation process, Argentina became the first country to pass a gender identity law fully compatible with human rights standards—that is to say, granting access to legal gender recognition based on self-determination, and without demanding any other requirement but a simple administrative procedure.[15] The same law granted access to gender affirming healthcare also based on self-determination, making informed consent the *only* valid requirement, and providing full healthcare coverage. Similar gender identity laws based on self-determination were soon passed in other countries, including Chile, Costa Rica, Denmark, Greece, Iceland, Ireland, Malta, Norway, Portugal, and Uruguay.[16] Just a few days before the official beginning of the ICD-11 implementation process, New Zealand and Switzerland approved gender identity laws based on the same principle.

Since the publication of the YPs, the international human rights system has made decisive steps towards identifying pathologization—and, particularly, trans pathologization—as a human rights issue. The second UN Independent Expert on Sexual Orientation and Gender Identity released an entire report focused on depathologization and legal gender recognition, where "the mandate holder concluded that the right to self-determine one's gender was a fundamental part of a person's freedom and a cornerstone of the person's identity," calling States to fulfill their human rights obligations by adopting gender identity laws and policies based on self-determination, accessed through simple administrative procedures, not connected with abusive requirements such as medical certification, surgery, treatment, sterilization and divorce, inclusive of nonbinary identities, and inclusive of minors.[17]

Advances in legal depathologization at the country level, as well as the increasing attention paid by the UN and regional systems to pathologization as a human rights issue, would seem to provide an optimistic landscape for trans depathologization. However, such an optimistic perspective must be confronted with a reality check, as advances toward trans depathologization are under the massive threat posed by anti-gender movements.

3

Back in May 2019, those of us following the World Health Assembly that approved the new *International Classification of Diseases* tried to imagine a world where ICD-11 was to start being implemented in 2022. Our world today does not look anything like that we could have imagined then—including, of course, the COVID-19 pandemic and its

---

[15] Retrieved from: https://gate.ngo/argentina-gender-identity-law-english-translation/

[16] GATE: Kara, Sheherezade. "Depathologizing gender identity through law." Retrieved from: https://gate.ngo/legal-depath-report-1/

[17] A/73/152, paras 75–78, quoted in A/HRC/47/27, para 36.

multiple social, political, and economic ramifications, but also the relentless anti-gender organizing against trans depathologization.

Over the past couple of years, an intense anti-gender opposition to trans depathologization has occurred—triggered by processes of legal reform, such as those taking place in the United Kingdom and Spain. That opposition appears based on a simple argument: trans people's self-determination would pose an extremely grave risk to *everyone*. Anti-gender activists argue that, for example:

- By allowing trans women and other people in the trans feminine spectrum to be legally recognized without a proper psycho-medical diagnosis could mean that (cis) men could require legal access to women-only spaces. The same (cis) men could perpetrate acts of violence against women without being properly prosecuted on a gendered basis.
- By allowing trans men and others in the trans masculine spectrum to be legally recognized without a proper psycho-medical diagnosis could mean that vulnerable (cis) women and, particularly, vulnerable (cis) lesbians, could be forced into manhood due to the prevalence of patriarchal mandates.
- By allowing nonbinary people to be legally recognized on the basis of their self-determination, sexual difference would be irreversible damaged.

These arguments not only share old and well-known cissexist biases against trans people;[18] they also represent a shared nostalgia for pathologization as a key organizer of individual, social and institutional life. In that sense, and similarly to other problematic contemporary movements (e.g., anti-vaxxers), anti-gender movements have a paradoxical relationship with science. While the restoration of psycho-medical authority is identified as an urgent protective measure necessary against the risks posed by trans people's self-determination, scientific evidence supporting trans depathologization is consistently dismissed by these same actors. For example, scientific evidence is denounced as grounded on for-profit scientific research, and/or as produced under the influence of a powerful queer, LGTB, gender and/or trans lobby, funded by Big Pharma and by the transgender healthcare industrial complex. One of the key arguments developed under this anti-science perspective is the linking of gender affirming healthcare with conversion therapies.

Anti-gender movements in the radical/critical spectrum position themselves as against conversion therapies focused on changing an individual's sexual orientation and support (cis) gay and lesbian depathologization. However, these same movements consider that gender affirming healthcare is, *in itself*, a form of conversion therapy whose goal is to transform (cis) gay and lesbian people into (trans) straight people.[19] At the same time, these movements advocate for the exclusion of trans people from conversion therapy bans—asserting that trans people and, particularly, trans children, *deserve* to have their gender identity tested and challenged by psycho-medical authority.

---

[18] Vincent, Ben, Erikainen, Sonja, and Pearce, Ruth (eds). "TERF Wars: Feminism and the fight for transgender futures," *The Sociological Review Monographs* 68, no. 4.
[19] LGB Alliance: Retrieved from https://lgballiance.org.uk/endconversiontherapy/.

The depathologization of trans adolescents and children have been a singular focus of anti-gender movements. A new category called "Rapid Onset Gender Dysphoria" (ROGD) has been introduced, as a way of classifying, studying, and treating them as suffering from an extreme form of social contagion produced through traditional and social media, sex education and peer influence.[20] Anti-gender advocacy against the use of puberty blockers has been based on two different but related arguments: on the one hand, a concern inspired by an increasing distrust in scientific evidence; on the other, a concern inspired by what seems to be an increasing sexual panic that associates puberty blockers with everything from grooming or delayed adulthood, to pedophilia. None of those arguments are specific to trans issues; quite the opposite, similar arguments characterize the status of public debates around the globe on issues as pressing as climate change, migration, disarmament, or vaccination.[21] And precisely because of their ubiquity, these arguments constitute an ominous landscape for trans depathologization.

*   *   *

Conclusions

Throughout its long history, trans advocacy to dismantle psycho-medical and legal barriers to self-determination has had to deal with a double realization: while reforming scientific classifications and legal regulations is and continues to be necessary, no reform will ensure, by itself, the fulfillment of trans people's human rights. January 2022 is an extraordinary moment in time to actualize, once again, that realization: while the beginning of the ICD-11 implementation process opens the possibility for moving trans depathologization forward, that possibility is nonetheless strongly compromised by a concentration of different forces.

Implementing ICD-11 implies an official beginning of trans de-psycho-pathologization; however, dismantling its deep social and cultural influences will require much more than legal and structural reform, or any other psycho-medical classification—rooted as they are on structural cissexism. New diagnostic categories, such as those based on "gender incongruence," carry with them a constitutive double bind: those categories look better when compared with a terrible past, while nonetheless carrying portions of that past into their present. Changes in terminology do not mask the reality: the long history of pathologizing gender diversity in childhood continues unfolding. Interrupting its continuity will require a sustained political effort. A similar

[20] Ashley, Florence. "A critical commentary on 'rapid-onset gender dysphoria,'" in Vincent, Ben, Erikainen, Sonja, and Pearce, Ruth (eds) "TERF Wars," 105–126. World Professional Association for Transgender Health (2018). "WPATH POSITION ON 'Rapid-Onset Gender Dysphoria (ROGD),'" Sept. 4 Retrieved from: http://www.wpath.org/policies.
[21] Wodak, Ruth. *The Politics of Fear. The Shameless Normalization of Far-Right Discourse*. 2nd Edition. Los Angeles & London: SAGE, 2021.

effort will be necessary to ensure global access to gender affirming healthcare in conditions fully compatible with socioeconomic justice.

Ten years ago, when a chapter on sexual health was proposed as a possible location for a new trans-related category, a joke circulated insistently: the only possibility worse than locating it under a chapter containing the word "sexual" would be to locate it under a chapter containing the word "gender." As happens with other jokes, this one was also partially true. The implementation of the ICD-11 chapter on sexual health will intrinsically depend on the political reality of sexual rights, and that reality has been, and is increasingly, under threat.

In spite of those challenges, the *eppur si muove* of trans depathologization is also true: the process of depathologizing trans identities is moving, slower than expected but deeper than imagined, shattering fossilized frameworks, and building expansive justice, demanding a daily combination of hope and caution, of analysis and strength. It moves and goes in circles, losing its way and then finding it again, abandoning old goals and creating new milestones, sometimes pushed by few and sometimes pushed by many. And, definitively, it is moving forward.

The attacks perpetrated by anti-gender movements against trans people position the entire human rights framework at a historical intersection. As those movements manifest every day, what is at stake at this moment is not only the right to legal gender recognition and/or to gender affirming healthcare in one jurisdiction or another; what is *really* at stake is who counts as a person; who has the right to *all* human rights, in a context where not all individuals are seen as equally human and where it seems there are not enough human rights for all. Trans depathologization is taking place, precisely, at that intersection.

Depathologizing trans people does not only mean removing diagnostic categories from psycho-medical classifications and from legal frameworks; it also means addressing and dismantling all the differences instituted, reinforced, and justified by classifying some people and their identities as normal and healthy and other people and their identities as abnormal and disordered. By questioning trans people's right to legal gender recognition based on their self-determination and calling for re-pathologization, anti-gender movements are defending a particular definition of "human." That definition is presented as based on the supposed naturalness of sex and of sexual difference and, therefore, it naturally reduces humanity to (cis) men and women. From that perspective, variations of sex characteristics, gender identities and gender expressions can only be understood as dangerous deviations from that natural order. The ontological difference defended by anti-gender movements is automatically expressed as a normative difference: as other-than-human, trans people are supposedly entitled to other-than-human rights. However, addressing and dismantling those differences and their consequences will require more than simply getting rid of psycho-medical and legal pathologization; it will require addressing the root causes and the pervasive consequences of trans pathologization within the human rights framework itself.

Historically, the intersection between trans people and human rights has often been reduced to "gender identity" issues—that is to say, reducing trans people's human rights to have their gender identities legally recognized, and to be protected against stigma, discrimination and violence. Despite the contributions to advancing both legal recognition and protection, such a reduction has also produced a series of negative long-lasting effects. For example, it has contributed to excluding attention to these human rights violations from initiatives focused on gender mainstreaming or mainstream sexual and reproductive rights agendas more generally.

Trans activists, organizations and networks, their allies, and many others in the human rights world, are working to ensure that being trans does not mean reduced or denied access to human rights. This work already includes full depathologization as a key goal; it must also include it as a key methodology. In other words, advancing trans people's depathologization as a matter of human rights requires, as a condition of possibility, to depathologize human rights—that is to put into question and dismantle the different ways in which pathologization creates and naturalizes different kind of humans and different kind of rights.

Section Four

Feminism and the "Triple Bind"

Introduction

Pardis Mahdavi

Being a feminist anywhere in the world right now is a high-stakes endeavor.

We are at a turning point in how we think about feminism, justice, and resistance. In the US, feminism is under attack from the Right, the Left, and from within—causing American feminists a "triple bind." As has historically been the case, the conservative Right attacks feminism by trying to incite a moral panic. Feminists are cast as scheming women tearing the fabric of family life by putting their careers and aspirations ahead of pro-creation or child-rearing, without a care for "life" as those in anti-abortion ranks would state. On the Left, feminism has also come under scrutiny in the backlash to #MeToo as well as recent efforts to restrict access to sexual and reproductive rights. Many on the Left criticize feminists for "going too far" and, insodoing, undermining the "causes" of the Left in presidential elections, for instance. And sadly, from within the feminist movement, the infighting has caused fracture, alienation, exile: in January of 2019, the Women's Marches almost did not take place, and those that did were highly controversial. Feminist support of various male or female presidential candidates for the 2020 race further exemplifies this infighting, with some declaring that true feminists would only back a woman. While conflict within a movement is okay, expected even, feminists today are having trouble fighting and then staying in solidarity. What it means to be a "true feminist" is up for debate in the US, and it is undermining a decades-long cause just as we approach the 100th anniversary of the 19th Amendment. Learning lessons from global feminism can help us think about the future of feminism as it engages with justice movements such as human rights.

Across the Atlantic, women are engaging in some of the same struggles as those of us here in the US. Transnational feminists are finding their feet through bonds formed between the threads of activism and shared struggles. Through the essays provided here, we can see that feminist human rights activists worldwide are also experiencing a "triple bind." These activists are simultaneously fighting patriarchal states, their religions, and fractures within other interconnecting justice movements. Notably, there have been tensions—as the authors in this section explore—between human rights movements and feminist movements transnationally. But there is much to be learned from the way that activists globally engage feminism. Notably, women in places like Iran, India, and Tunisia ground their feminism in solidarity at all costs. Movements such as the Arab Spring in 2010 and Green movement in Iran in 2009 showed how feminism and other civil and human rights movements were able to collaborate to bring about social change.

Coming together to share our struggles—different and similar as they are—is the best way to inspire the coming generations of feminists. The essays in this section provide a welcome opportunity for readers who are interested in the intersections of feminism and human rights to explore a different kind of feminism; one that is impactful, collaborative, and about sustainable change.

Through the stories presented here, we get an up-close look at the "challenges and opportunities found in a new kind of 'justice feminism'"—one rooted in societal and structural change. This new feminism, as the authors note, is one that is committed to upholding human rights for all. This commitment is not without its struggles, but a new way of thinking about human rights as a feminist endeavor and feminism as a human rights endeavor can help us re-think human rights at the intersections.

Feminism and human rights have been glossed as rudderless social justice movements. The remedy for this is a nuanced, story-driven look at activism by feminists who are at their core human rights activists. The authors in this section complicate this view.

Feminism globally is trying to define itself, figure out what to do next in this era of social media and fake news. But we don't need to start all over. This is where the work of these authors comes in. By calling attention to the presence of a strong feminist-driven resistance around the world, and a resistance that is messy at times and requires the resilience that comes from the bonds of friendship, that can inspire readers globally and help us view feminism in a more nuanced way.

Whose Gender Is It? Inclusion versus Exclusion in Global Feminist Movements

Lara Stemple

Broad global movements to advance human rights regularly intertwine with feminist movements, each influencing the other to varying degrees over time. And feminism, ever ripe with controversies both internal and external, has recently seen a resurgence of second-wave thinking that foregrounds women's victimhood. Reductive portraits sometimes paint women as the exclusive victims of interpersonal violence, leading to debates about excluded others.

When thinking of feminism and the "triple bind"—ideological battles with the right, with the left, and from within—as Pardis Mahdavi explores in this volume, it is the struggle within that I find most interesting, and confounding. Here I examine the turf wars taking place in some feminist, human rights, and humanitarian circles about who is entitled to our collective concern and whether we ought to police the use of terms like "gender" and "sex."

It is perhaps first worth reflecting on the particular political moment in which feminist activism now finds itself. The last few years have a seen an explosion of awareness about women's sexual victimization across a range of contexts. While the #MeToo movement has been exciting, massive, surprising, and potentially revolutionary, some of the movement's simplistic messages are less than helpful. For instance, "Believe Women" is meant to serve as a needed corrective to the decades of doubt female victims of sexual harassment and violence have routinely faced. Yet it also seems to imply that women are one-dimensional truth vessels, not complex, imperfect human beings.

"Believe Women" does little to assuage the concerns that many people (including feminist lawyers and scholars) have raised about inadequate due process in the wake of sexual misconduct charges on college campuses and elsewhere. It's unclear how "Believe Women" applies to female abusers and enablers (like those who facilitated the vast abuses committed by Jeffrey Epstein and Harvey Weinstein) or to male victims, such as the thousands of children around the world (predominantly boys) who were once routinely disbelieved when reporting abuse by Catholic clergy.

One might be unsurprised to find simplistic slogans like "Believe Women" in mass public discourse, but the resurgence of essentializing, purportedly feminist thinking can be seen in other contexts, including those concerning human rights-based advocacy and international policymaking. Work on human trafficking, sex work, armed conflict, and gender-based violence often reflect uncritical "rescue" tendencies, and contemporary organizers who identify as feminist are working to advance seemingly outdated ideas about women and gender in these and other contexts.[1]

"Women's Sex-Based Rights"

Some activists in Europe, the US, Australia, South Korea, Mexico, Brazil, and elsewhere are currently advancing a decidedly anti-trans agenda, many (though not all) identifying as TERFs, for trans-exclusive radical feminists.[2] TERFs decry the expanded use of the category "sex," which they view as biologically fixed, and dislike the term "gender identity," which allows for a fluidity they find offensive. For instance, in the retro "Declaration for Women's Sex-Based Rights" the signatories want feminist advocacy to be about cis-gendered women alone, and they claim that inclusive gender categories are a form of discrimination against women. They go so far as to turn this belief into a call to discriminate against others: "States should uphold the right of everyone to *describe others* on the basis of their sex rather than their 'gender identity,' in all contexts."[3] Here, a human rights-style call to action runs directly counter to fundamental notions of equality and self-determination that undergird the human rights movement.

Coalition of Feminists for Change (COFEM)

The seemingly reductive, non-intersectional "women only" thread can also be found in other, more influential emerging movements and groups. An instructive example is COFEM the Coalition of Feminists for Social Change, founded in 2017 and describing itself as "an advocacy collective of thought leaders, activists, practitioners and academics" working globally on violence against women. COFEM also resists expanded definitions of gender and is gaining some real traction among actors working in humanitarian and human rights spaces.[4]

COFEM's publications put forward a perspective, which, most prominently, challenges inclusive definitions of gender-based violence (GBV). COFEM presents the

---

[1] William Paul Simmons, "Paternal ignorance in human rights devalues knowledge of marginalized populations," *OpenGlobalRights (blog)*, 8 October 2020. Available online: https://www.openglobalrights.org/paternal-ignorance-in-human-rights-devalues-knowledge-of-marginalized-populations/.

[2] Viv Smythe, "I'm credited with having coined the word 'TERF.' Here's how it happened," *The Guardian*, 28 November 2018. Available online: https://www.theguardian.com/commentisfree/2018/nov/29/im-credited-with-having-coined-the-acronym-terf-heres-how-it-happened.

[3] Emphasis added, "Declaration on Women's Sex-Based Rights," *Women's Human Rights Campaign*, 2019. Available online: https://www.womensdeclaration.com/en/ (accessed September 24, 2020).

[4] "COFEM Knowledge Summit: Meet the Facilitators," *Coalition of Feminists for Social Change*, n.d. Available online: https://cofemsocialchange.org/initiatives-events/vawg-knowledge-summit/facilitator-profiles/ (accessed September 24, 2021).

belief that GBV *only* applies to women and girls as axiomatic; it asserts that the word "gender" itself should focus on the inequalities experienced by women and girls. They complain that "GBV is being (re)interpreted regularly to emphasize gender roles and identities as they affect *all* people, with these definitions often specifically calling attention to violence against males and violence against LGBTQ and other groups broadly (emphasis in original, page 3)."[5]

They call-out the European Union and USAID in particular for "deeply troubling" inclusivity.[6] COFEM dislikes one of the EU's definitions of GBV: "violence directed against a person because of that person's gender or as violence that affects persons of a particular gender disproportionately."[7] COFEM doesn't note that in most places the EU focuses on GBV against women and girls.

COFEM also complains that USAID describes GBV as an umbrella term for:

[A]ny harmful threat or act directed at an individual or group based on actual or perceived biological sex, gender identity and/or expression, sexual orientation, and/or lack of adherence to varying socially constructed norms around masculinity and femininity.

COFEM claims that such definitions are uncritical of and even caused by "the patriarchy," while conveniently excluding the very next portion of USAID's clear assertion that GBV roots are indeed found in "gender inequalities, patriarchy, and power imbalances."[8] This strategic omission from COFEM's critique of the USAID definition lets COFEM construct an imaginary world in which those concerned with sexual violence against men, boys, and/or LGBT+ persons simply fail to understand that sexual violence is informed by regressive, patriarchal, and misogynistic ideals.

Personally, I embrace the US government's rare "fuck the patriarchy" note, and I'd rather see it broadcast far and wide, not dubiously excised so as to claim that inclusive definitions are pro patriarchy. But COFEM wants the focus to remain on violence against women and girls alone, bemoaning that the topic is too "crowded" with others,[9] as if compassion, or fundamental human rights, were in limited supply.

COFEM further asserts that its particular version of GBV impacts all women "regardless of economic status, race and ethnicity."[10] But its use of "regardless" here is

[5] COFEM, "Funding: Whose priorities?" in *Coalition of Feminists for Social Change, Feminist Perspectives on Addressing Violence Against Women and Girls Series*, Paper No. 4, 2017.
[6] COFEM Secretariat, "Engaging men and boys - not at the cost of women and girls," *Coalition of Feminists for Social Change*, n.d. Available at: https://cofemsocialchange.org/engaging-men-and-boys-not-at-the-cost-of-women-and-girls/ (accessed September 29, 2021).
[7] COFEM Secretariat, "Engaging men and boys."
[8] "Gender-based violence prevention and response," U.S. Agency for International Development, last modified September 7, 2021. Available online: https://www.usaid.gov/what-we-do/gender-equality-and-womens-empowerment/reducing-gender-based-violence.
[9] "Violence against men and boys," *Feminist Pocketbook Tip Sheet 7. Coalition of Feminists for Social Change*, 2018: 1–4. Available online: https://cofemsocialchange.org/wp-content/uploads/2018/11/TS7-Violence-against-men-and-boys.pdf.
[10] "Violence against men and boys."

troubling. Surely the work that intersectional feminists have done to demonstrate the role that economic status, race, and ethnicity play in subordination, including gendered and sexualized subordination, cannot be dismissed so easily. GBV doesn't impact women "regardless" of their economic status, race, or ethnicity, but often in large part *because* of it. Consider the ways in which Black and Asian women are "othered" or exoticized to justify their exploitation.[11] Or the obstacles that a low-income immigrant woman faces when experiencing domestic violence while dependent on her spouse for legal status.[12]

In a different but related vein, consider the evidence that boys who are sexually abused in juvenile detention centers report that 94 percent of their victimizers are women. In this case, the boys' gender is seemingly less determinative than the racialized and socioeconomic factors that led to the boys' incarceration to begin with. In short, gender is one frequently subordinating factor, but it is not the only one.

COFEM claims *the* feminist mantle for themselves (excluding those of us who have persistently articulated feminist arguments for more inclusive understandings of gender), claiming that "expanded definitions of GBV fail largely to reflect feminist theory and principles."[13]

This entirely overlooks decades of work by feminist, long-experienced women's right advocates who are in favor of expanded approaches to men, boys, and LGBT+ victims, both because we view all victims as worthy of attention, and because feminism has a lot to say about these forms of abuse.[14] Look no further than prison contexts in which sexually dominant prisoners call the men they rape, "my woman" or "my bitch." Victimized inmates, who are sometimes virtually "owned" for years, can be expected to do laundry, adopt feminized ways of behaving, and remain submissive to "their man."[15] Yet, by COFEM's logic, a gender lens has no place here.

As far as the empirical landscape, while women experience more violence in many contexts, men experience alarmingly high rates as well, in some cases comparable rates to women, depending on the context, and LGBT+ persons are often at greatest risk of all.[16] This very fact is what has motivated many in the anti-violence field to include these populations in our work—not some imagined anti-women or anti-feminist agenda as critics fear.

COFEM's framing also overlooks feminist and intersectional critiques of essentializing portrayals of women as victims. Ratna Kapur and many others have argued for years that reductive victimization rhetoric in some forms of human rights advocacy is far from empowering for women; indeed, it reinforces racialized tropes about "Third World" women in need of outside rescue. The relentless drumbeat of

---

[11] Kimberlé Crenshaw, "We still have not learned from Anita Hill's testimony," *UCLA Women's Law Journal* 26 no. 1 (2019): 17–20.

[12] Kimberlé Crenshaw, "Mapping the margins: Intersectionality, identity politics, and violence against women of color," *Stanford Law Review* 43, no. 6 (2019): 1241–52.

[13] "Violence against men and boys."

[14] Lara Stemple, "Male rape and human rights," *Hastings Law Journal* 60, no. 3: 605–646.

[15] Don Sabo, Terry A. Kupers, and Willie London eds. *Prison Masculinities* (Philadelphia: Temple University Press, 2001).

[16] Smythe, "I'm credited with."

women as *the* victims thwarts feminisms' more emancipatory goals and reinforces global hierarchies.[17]

Complications

Consider this assortment of well-documented phenomena: Hegemonic masculinity norms drive homophobic violence throughout the world. Intersex infants undergo cosmetic genital surgeries to conform their appearance to a particular sex before they can consent.[18] Transfolk, native women, and disabled persons are at enormous risk of campus sexual victimization in the US despite the public emphasis on white, straight, able-bodied women.[19] Afghan and Pakistani men who practice bacha bazi sexually exploit boys who are forced to dress and dance in a feminine manner.[20] So the notion that gender-based violence is a concept applicable to one group, and one group only, thwarts more complicated analyses and denies reality. Yet this argument is gaining steam in some international circles.

At the same time, as resistance to progress on LBGT+ rights hardens in many parts of the world, women's rights NGOs are increasingly likely to see strong alliances with LGBT+ groups and agendas as a risk, rather than as an opportunity to advance shared interests. This division is especially counterproductive as paranoid politicians in Latin America, Europe and elsewhere crusade against so-called "gender ideology," simultaneously aiming to strip women and LGBT+ persons of fundamental rights.[21] Certainly religious conservatism in Eastern Europe is a bigger threat to women's rights than LBGT+ inclusion. So, when Poland's Catholic Church crusades against the whole of "gender ideology," isn't it more important to link arms in resistance than to engage in the proverbial circular firing squad?

All Survivors Project, an NGO working on the widespread problem of sexual violence against men, boys, and LGBT+ populations in armed conflict, has begun to see some progress on the international stage, including a Security Council resolution that addresses conflict-related sexual violence against both women and men. The organization uses feminist and human rights-informed approaches. But they've been blocked by some humanitarian groups from contributing to the work of the

---

[17] Ratna Kapur, "The tragedy of victimization rhetoric: Resurrecting the native subject in international/ postcolonial feminist legal politics," *Harvard Human Rights Law Journal*, 15, no. 1 (2002): 1–38.

[18] "I want to be like nature made me," *Human Rights Watch*, July 25, 2017. Available online: https://www.hrw.org/report/2017/07/25/i-want-be-nature-made-me/medically-unnecessary-surgeries-intersex-children-us.

[19] David Cantor, *Report on the AAU Campus Climate Survey on Sexual Assault and Misconduct* (Rockville: Westat, 2020).

[20] *Afghanistan* (Vaduz: All Survivors Project Foundation, 2017).

[21] Mariana Prandini Assis and Ana Carolina Ogand, "Bolsonaro, 'Gender Ideology' and hegemonic masculinity in Brazil," Al Jazeera, 31 October 2018. Available online: https://www.aljazeera.com/opinions/2018/10/31/bolsonaro-gender-ideology-and-hegemonic-masculinity-in-brazil/; Rachel Schmidt, "What battles over 'gender ideology' mean for Colombia's women human rights defenders," *OpenGlobalRights (blog)*, 4 February 2020. Available online: https://www.openglobalrights.org/gender-ideology-and-colombias-women-human-rights-defenders/.

gender-based violence coordination bodies. ASP has received pushback in other settings, specifically those addressing gender and armed conflict, where some argue that the inclusion of men and LGBT+ issues "dilutes the Women, Peace, and Security agenda." What to make of the "dilution" concern? It seems informed by an us-versus-them fear, implying that the right to be free from sexual violence is a finite commodity; if more than one group successfully claims the right, everyone will have it somewhat less.

On the other hand, money *is* a finite commodity, and much is made of resource competition. COFEM, for example, argues that broadened approaches risk leaving women and girls without services. It goes so far as to assert that, "Additional interventions, including research and engagement of men and boys, should not be funded [one wonders, not *at all*?] until core services [for women and girls] are widely available."[22] I've spent many years working in movements calling for resources and attention to a range of sexually victimized people, some of whom are men and boys. I've worked with academics and advocates in contexts as diverse as prisons, armed conflict and humanitarian settings, schools, and immigration detention. The near-total absence of donor funding for male victims in these contexts is a constant point of advocacy, of course. Yet never have I heard those working in these spaces call for funds to be transferred away from programming for women and girls and moved to programs for men and boys. Nor for LGBT+ programs. *No one seeks to get funding this way.* Nevertheless, the oft-repeated funding threat triggers alarm among chronically underfunded women's organizations, thereby generating buy-in for exclusionary strategies that claim "gender" for straight cis-women.

Dehumanization

Unfortunately, exclusionary strategies get much uglier than defensiveness around funding issues. Some TERFs use dehumanizing tactics that have been employed by human rights violators throughout history. For instance, political scientist Sheila Jeffreys proclaimed that transwomen "parasitically occupy women's bodies" at a 2018 event held at the UK House of Commons.[23] How, exactly, does one defend comparing members of an unquestionably marginalized group to parasites? In her earlier work, Jeffreys even claims that "transsexualism should be seen as a violation of human rights."[24] (The day that "wtf?" becomes acceptable shorthand in academic discourse cannot come soon enough.)

Jeffreys explains that "Transsexualism [prevents] the elimination of gender roles which lies at the basis of the feminist project. Transsexualism opposes feminism by

---

[22] COFEM, "Funding: Whose priorities?"

[23] Kashmira Gander, "Academic says trans women are parasites for 'occupying the bodies of the oppressed,'" *Newsweek*, 18 March 2018. Available online: https://www.newsweek.com/trans-women-are-parasites-occupying-bodies-oppressed-says-academic-846563.

[24] Sheila Jeffreys, "Transgender activism: A lesbian perspective," *Journal of Lesbian Studies* 1, no. 3–4 (1997): 55–74.

maintaining and reinforcing false and constructed notions of correct femininity and masculinity."[25] She and other TERFs criticize the appearance of transwomen, particularly those who are highly feminized. For example, one lawyer and trans activist invited to speak at a feminist event was publicly mocked as a blow-up doll.[26] Again the hateful strawman; deployment of cartoonish stereotypes to dehumanize and "other" whole populations is of course a technique deployed by racists, anti-Semites, and colonialists throughout history. Can one imagine the blowback should transwomen similarly make fun of the appearance of radical feminists like Jeffreys in order to make their political point? These radical feminists seem determined to ignore the varied, sometimes blended, sometimes nonbinary, sometimes fluid, and often exploratory range of trans identities that are upending the gender binary and—dare one say?— "radically" so.

To further her human rights argument, Jeffreys posits:

> It would now probably be quite well-accepted that lobotomy, as carried out in the fifties and sixties on lesbians and gays in mental hospitals to "cure" them, is unacceptable. Lobotomy would be seen, at least by gay activists, as state sanctioned and financed political surgery to cure a political problem. It could be likened to political psychiatry in the Soviet Union. I suggest that transsexualism should best be seen in this light, as directly political, medical abuse of human rights.

Lest this viewpoint be dismissed as stale due to its publication in 1997, Jeffreys asserts in her 2014 book that "Transgenderism is indeed transgressive, but of women's rights rather than an oppressive social system."[27] Wtf?

Erasure

None of this is to say that trans-inclusive efforts are flawless. The 2021 Lancet cover's declaration that, "Historically, the anatomy and physiology of bodies with vaginas have been neglected" clanked in the ear of many who support LGBT+ rights.[28] The outrage was swift, with one doctor in favor of inclusivity describing the phrase as misguided, insulting, and "a new low."[29] "Bodies with vaginas" sounds oddly devoid of humanity, and it fails to name the role that sexism toward women has played in the gross neglect of women's health needs over time. Editor-in-Chief Richard Horton apologized to

---

[25] Sheila Jeffreys, "Transgender activism."

[26] Shon Faye, *The Transgender Issue: An Argument for Justice* (London: Allen Lane, 2021).

[27] Sheila Jeffreys, *Gender Hurts: A Feminist Analysis of the Politics of Transgenderism* (London: Routledge, Taylor & Francis Group, 2014).

[28] Sophia Davis, "Periods on display," *The Lancet* 398, no. 10306 (2021): 1124–25. Available online: https://doi.org/10.1016/s0140-6736(21)01962-0.

[29] Bhvishya Patel, "Now the Lancet CANCELS women: Fury as leading medical journal runs 'dehumanising' and 'sexist' front-page describing females as 'bodies with vaginas' to placate trans lobby," *Daily Mail*, 26 September 2021. Available online: https://www.dailymail.co.uk/news/article-10029817/Fury-leading-medical-journal-describes-women-bodies-vaginas.html.

"readers who were offended," employing the widely derided pseudo-apology format, leaving it unclear where the medical establishment's language goes from here.[30]

The week prior, the ACLU published a quote from Ruth Bader Ginsburg on the anniversary of her death. The original quote read:

> The decision whether or not to bear a child is central to a woman's life, to her well-being and dignity. It is a decision she must make for herself. When government controls that decision for her, she is being treated as less than a fully adult human responsible for her own choices.

The ACLU's edited quote read:

> The decision whether or not to bear a child is central to a [person's] life, to [their] well-being and dignity.... When the government controls that decision for [people], [they are] being treated as less than a fully adult human responsible for [their] own choices.

In this case, the attempt at inclusivity changes the meaning of the original quote, which emphasizes that reproductive coercion and control is a form of subordination that overwhelmingly burdens women. Ginsburg wasn't referring to the need for all people to control their own reproductive destiny, as the revised quote reads. Cue the public outcry ("I am [person], hear me roar," quipped one headline); cue the expression of "regret" from Executive Director Anthony Romero, who also noted that not all people who seek abortion identify as women.

Reflecting on The Lancet and ACLU controversies, it's notable that both [people with penises] in charge of their respective institutions responded in such anodyne ways. It was a missed opportunity to offer a full-throated acknowledgment of the need to combat sexism and an assertion that inclusionary language doesn't need to obfuscate this. Rendering the word "women" taboo will do more to provide fodder for the right, alienate the middle, and divide us all, than it will to advance anyone's rights. It will quite often (though perhaps not always) be possible to both name sexism and reflect inclusion, and this should be a dual goal. In any event, these are conversations worth having, thoughtfully, and in good faith.

Instead, TERF activists like Jeffreys dismiss calls for fundamental human rights for trans people as "fashionable."[31] All Survivors Project, mentioned above, has also faced this accusation, despite the seriousness of conflict-related sexual violence and the dangerous settings in which they work. The group has been told by some women's organizations that funding for the group's work on sexual violence against men, boys, and LGBT+ persons will be easy to get because these populations/topics are "sexy" or "trendy."

---

30 Richard Horton, "A statement from Richard Horton, Editor-in-Chief, The Lancet," *The Lancet*, n.d. Available online: https://www.thelancet.com/25sept-cover-statement (accessed 29 September 2021).
31 Jeffreys, *Gender Hurts*, 61.

Setting aside how difficult it is to secure such funding in reality, it's curious to consider what the charge implies. It seems to imply more than mere popularity; rather it implies that these causes are trifling, flashy, or lacking in substance. On the one hand, one can well understand the frustration of NGOs who must frantically adapt to sometimes ill-considered donor-driven trends. On the other hand, one can scarcely get one's mind around the notion that the rape of a man by armed militants in the midst of a central African conflict is a fashionable issue. Certainly all advocates want attention to their cause, but the "fashionable" charge aims to trivialize the painstaking, low paid, and decidedly un-glamorous work of bringing neglected topics—indeed topics of stomach-churning brutality—to the fore.

Another tactic includes mischaracterizing work that applies gender analyses to broader populations by claiming that this work itself is a form of gender discrimination. For example, in her critique of an article advocating for gender-inclusive humanitarian work, Jeanne Ward writes, "It is well past time for a women-centred agenda to be received as legitimate, and those focusing on that agenda must not be subject to a replication of the gender-based discrimination against which they work."[32] But nowhere in the article does Ward describe being subject to gender-based discrimination; some people simply disagree with her. To my mind, hers is an attempt to silence reasonable and important debate around gender by asserting that those whose views merely differ from the author's are committing gender discrimination themselves.

Ward also misrepresents activities at the international level to make the argument that women are being harmed by broader approaches. For example, the US Institute for Peace and others held an international symposium on "Men, Peace, and Security" to compliment the women, peace, and security agenda already well underway on the global stage. Ward complains that the title of the symposium itself harms women and implies a troubling "shift in focus"[33] toward men. But the focus is on men *because* they commit violence and are architects of conflict; it was an explicitly feminist conference, as even a cursory look at the agenda confirms. One panel's description reads: "How Men Are Made: Cultures of Hyper Masculinities. An exploration of the social and cultural drivers of how men and boys develop exaggerated and violent identities."[34] Feminism, anyone? Ward seems to fear that any discussion of men harms women, even a discussion about why men harm women. Do she and others who dislike such discussion believe that we will address gendered harms by pretending men do not exist?

Several years ago, I attended a Human Rights Watch event focused on sexual violence in the Democratic Republic of Congo (DRC), and one of the organizers was Joanne Mariner, who once, on another assignment, drafted a book-length report on sexual violence against men in US prisons and jails. The panelists, including men and women from the DRC, spoke at length about sexual violence against women and

---

[32] Jeanne Ward, "It's not about the gender binary, it's about the gender hierarchy: A reply to 'letting go of the gender binary,'" *International Review of the Red Cross* 98, no. 901 (2016): 275–298.

[33] Jeanne Ward, "It's not about the gender binary."

[34] Maria Butler et al., "How men are made: Cultures of hyper masculinities," Panel at the Men, Peace and Security Symposium, Washington, D.C., October 28, 2013.

girls during the ongoing conflict. Given Mariner's expertise and fair mindedness, I awaited the portion that would include male victims. In many contexts the "men can be victims, too" acknowledgment is reserved for the end, almost as an afterthought, but in this case, it never came. And so I asked about it during the Q and A, creating a lengthy and uncomfortable silence. This was followed by two Congolese men speaking hesitantly and then more openly about the reality and frequency of male rape and the pain involved in acknowledging it. One man had tears in his eyes and halted as he spoke. He did not say, or could not say, whether he or someone he loves had been victimized.

The erasure of male victimization matters even more in humanitarian settings on the ground. One challenge for organizations inching toward service provision for male survivors of conflict-related sexual violence is assessing the scope of the problem. Efforts have recently begun to serve every survivor, male or female, who presents for services, but the hesitancy of men to do so is profound. One study found that men and boys in the DRC comprise 4–10 percent of the total number of survivors of sexual violence who seek medical treatment,[35] a data point that allows humanitarian orgs to maintain that sexual violence in conflict is overwhelmingly a women's issue. Unsurprisingly, COFEM cites to this survey in its literature. But a population-based study (not requiring anyone to present to a clinic), found that 30 percent of women and 22 percent of men in the DRC reported conflict-related sexual violence, a much narrower divide.[36] If we only measure who shows up to clinic to assess the need, we miss those too ashamed or afraid to come, and the data suggest that these are more likely to be men. Yes, the patriarchy confers subordination upon women, but the men who are emasculated by rape can also be so constrained by its rigid norms that they suffer profound physical and psychological harm in private.[37]

Interconnectedness

Setting aside the deep stigma of male rape, healthcare avoidance in general is a macho norm that has been documented in other contexts. For example, turning to HIV, a largely heterosexual pandemic as far as sub-Saharan Africa is concerned, one finds that men in that region are less likely to know their HIV status, less likely to receive treatment for the disease, and more likely to get lost to follow-up care than women. What does this have to do with feminism and gender equality? The International Men and Gender Equality Survey found that men with less gender-equitable attitudes toward women are also less likely to seek HIV services, which in turn makes them and

[35] Séverine Autesserre, "Dangerous tales: Dominant narratives on the Congo and their unintended consequences," *African Affairs* 111, no. 443 (2012): 202–222.

[36] Kirsten Johnson et al., "Association of sexual violence and human rights violations with physical and mental health in territories of the Eastern Democratic Republic of the Congo," *JAMA* 304, no. 5 (2010): 553–562.

[37] Maria Stern, Marysia Zalewski, Elisabeth Prugle, and Paula Drumond, ed., *Sexual Violence against Men in Global Politics* (Routledge, 2018).

their sexual partners more vulnerable.[38] Likewise, research has found that men's embrace of harmful masculinity norms encourages sexual risk-taking, entitled attitudes toward women's sexual availability, and a propensity for alcohol abuse. A feminist-informed disruption of these norms is critical, and benefits both women and men in inextricable ways.[39]

Global work on HIV embraced the fact that women's equality is key to HIV prevention, thanks to tireless feminist efforts over decades. And many of those efforts, as well as language in international instruments on HIV, have called for the need to engage men to transform regressive attitudes toward gender equality.[40] Occasionally, however, such messaging seems to paint men as uniformly uncaring or unchanging, labeling them as "the problem." These simplistic takes can overlook a growing body of literature demonstrating that gender roles and relations are not fixed, vary widely, and can and do sometimes change quickly. Failure to recognize this can undermine efforts to mobilize men around the concern they feel for the women and girls in their lives and their own desires to get out from under relentless pressure to "be a man." Moreover, approaches that paint men only as holders of power and privilege miss other intersecting vulnerabilities to HIV that affect men in minority populations, including men who are inmates, who inject drugs, who are migrants, who are poor, and who have sex with other men.

Meanwhile, turning to US developments, Trump-appointed Supreme Court Justice Neil Gorsuch penned the 2020 holding in *Bostock v. Clayton County*, which found that the prohibition of employment discrimination "based on sex" also bars discrimination based on sexual orientation and gender identity. When the drafters of Title VII used the phrase "based on sex" 56 years prior to Bostock, protecting gay and trans rights were hardly front of mind. Nevertheless, the court ruled 6–3 that firing people who are gay or transgender *is* a form of sex-based discrimination. This LGBT+ victory, a surprising one given the court's rightward tilt, mirrors earlier decisions by the Court of Justice of the European Union and by high courts in Belize, Colombia, New Zealand, Thailand, and elsewhere, where the judiciary has decided that prohibitions on sex discrimination ought to also prohibit discrimination on the basis of sexual orientation and/or gender expression.

Spoiling the party, some radical feminists complain when "sex" is interpreted in ways that advance LGBT+ agendas. But when definitions of sex and gender are interpreted in ways that expand rights for more people, particularly for people who do not conform to traditional, regressive notions of who women and men should love, or how people should identify and present themselves, this is a clear win for feminist principles.

---

[38] Gary Barker, et al., "Evolving men: Initial results from the International Men and Gender Equality Survey," *IMAGES International Center for Research on Women*. Available at: http://www.icrw.org/publications/evolving-men.

[39] Dean Peacock et al., "Men, HIV/AIDS, and Human Rights," *JAIDS Journal of Acquired Immune Deficiency Syndromes*, S119-S125, 51 no. 3 (2009): 1–12.

[40] Rachel Jewkes, Michael Flood, and James Lang, "From work with men and boys to changes of social norms and reduction of inequities in gender relations: a conceptual shift in prevention of violence against women and girls," *The Lancet* 385 no. 9977 (2015):1580–89.

Of course, following *Bostock's* win for gay and trans rights, *Dobbs* dealt a devastating blow to women's rights in 2022, dismantling the privacy rights that had protected abortion access and calling into question the future of reproductive and sexual rights for all. Now would seem an especially good time for a united front among the many of us who prize the ability to fully actualize ourselves in our bodies, as we see fit. Much more should be made of the coherent and even obvious inseverability of bodily integrity, freedom of choice, sexual autonomy, and demands for equitable treatment regardless of gender, sexual orientation, and identity.

Unfortunately, reductive "women-only" discourses increasingly aim to lock down the meaning of gender, just as they lock *out* other claimants seeking justice, dangerously dividing us. This must be rejected by those of us seeking more inclusive ways of tackling harms with gendered components. It's time to embrace approaches that push hard for gender equality and leave no one behind; the two are not mutually exclusive. Only in this way can we actualize a robust, non-divisive call for human rights for all people.

2

"What Can Intersectional Approaches Reveal about Experiences of Violence?"

Dolores Trevizo

The recent resurgence of second-wave feminist perspectives articulated in "The Declaration on Women's Sex-Based Rights" denounce gender analyses for decentering women, or for distinguishing "gender" from "sex." That this "declaration" received such broad support (from 256 organizations) is unsurprising, given that movements for change tend to trigger countermovements when they impinge on the material, cultural, or symbolic interests of those who benefit from the status quo. Using the devictimization of murdered or disappeared men in Mexico as an example, I argue that intersectional approaches do a better job of understanding all forms of violence, including sexual violence, than do these second-wave feminist analyses. The latter, in contrast, may contribute to injustice in part by relying on essentialist tropes that ignore the complexity of social reality.

In response to the "The Declaration on Women's Sex-Based Rights," Laura Stemple argues that the competition for material resources explains why some second-wave feminists tend see women's victimhood as more worthy of sympathy and, thus, material resources than men's victimization. William Paul Simmons provides an additional explanation when he observes not only that certain analyses resonate as "true" because they fit well-accepted narratives, but that some may even contribute to injustice by defining some people as "inferior knowers."

To further illustrate how tropes can contribute to injustice, I offer examples from Mexico where well over 200,000 people have died while tens of thousands have disappeared since the war against the drug cartels began (in late 2006) (Reuters Staff, April 26, 2018; Booth, November 29–2012). According to the data, while the overwhelming majority of those murdered or disappeared are men (by other men), public opinion sees women and children as the most likely victims of such crimes. This misconception is partly explained by the patriarchal trope that "women and children" (often read as "women as children") are always in need of extra protections. Not surprisingly, this trope also reinforces the view of men as saviors or protectors—roles associated with some of the very forms of power that various feminisms seek to challenge (and that would be better addressed by recognizing the vulnerability of all people in the context of generalized violence and impunity).

Worse, the indifference to the tens of thousands of missing and murdered men is possible because poor and Indigenous men are denied a place in the existing conceptual framework that determines who is worthy of sympathy. Indeed, the missing men are often suspected of involvement in drug trafficking, as if there could be no explanation of the violence inflicted on them but their own criminality. The Ayotzinapa youth—who were detained by Mexican police and then disappeared in 2014—escaped such "devictimization" in part because they were defined as students. To be clear, the empathy gap toward male victims of violence is not unique to Mexico. It is evident in the support of death squads in Brazil. It is also evident in the callousness of the "false positives" scandal in Colombia during President Álvaro Uribe's term (2002–2010) when soldiers "inflated their kill counts by luring and then murdering [male] civilians, who postmortem were dressed and staged to look as if they had been killed in combat" (Trevizo 2016, p. 256). As Rachel Schmidt observed in a recent personal communication, "even the term 'false positive' erases the violence of these murders" (Schmidt comments to Trevizo September 4, 2020; also September 15, 2020). To refer to the Colombian military's extrajudicial killings of thousands of poor or mentally impaired male civilians as the "false positives scandal" centers the officers' motives for murder, rather than the thousands of male victims (see Daniels 2018), human beings loved and mourned by friends and family. By decentring male murder victims the popular frame also reinforces the gender trope embraced by second-wave feminists that only women can be victims.

And while there are countless examples of men's devictimization from many parts of the globe, I want to be clear that violence and sexual exploitation are indeed gendered, even if their victims are people of all genders. The way that women are killed in Mexico—the fact that they are routinely "overkilled" *and* sexually mutilated— crystallizes the patriarchal entitlement that some men have about women's bodies, as well as the misogyny of their effort to put women in their "sexual place". The feminicides in Mexico exemplify what happens when patriarchal entitlement intersects with chronic and generalized violence. But the men whose bodies are dissolved in acid by a cartel's "*pozolero*," or whose beheaded corpses are displayed on overpasses, also die painful and inhumane deaths even if their bodies are not sexualized as frequently, or in the same way, as feminized bodies. Therefore, even though violence is gendered, the feminicides are inextricably linked to the generalized violence produced by the interplay of patriarchy, neoliberal capitalism, and a weak criminal justice system. If the impunity that has prevailed since the country transitioned to electoral democracy in 2000 has freed criminals to profit from terrorizing society, an intersectional lens exposes the unequal impact of the terror. The wealthy can better shelter behind their high security walls, some with private security guards and many with surveillance devices. The poor do not have such protections and neither do the people expelled from their homes for their non-conforming sexual or gender identities.

An intersectional lens illuminates the fact that a number of social dynamics play out at once in acts of violence. Intersectional approaches not only assume the basic insights of the sociological trifecta—race, class, gender—but they unpack how multiple variables intersect in any particular instance. Black feminists developed this method to examine the full context and social significance of action. Because the perpetrators of violence are not abstracted from society, they too recognize at least some of the social characteristics of their victim(s) (such as, young-old, men-women, ethnic/racial/ religious other, etc.); in some cases, these very social characteristics may well have motivated their sexual violence in the first place. Because sexual violence is infused with meaning, it is more than a raw act of power enacted on a person against their will. As such, the rape of men is no less significant or dehumanizing.

In sum, an intersectional lens avoids the "essentialism" trap of second-wave feminism by unpacking the ways that violence results from how distinct forms of othering intersect. Further, by virtue of being anti-reductionist, intersectional analyses can lead to political alliances. As Kate Hunt suggested at a (2019) workshop at Occidental College on "cross-cutting approaches to human rights," precisely by attending to variation, intersectional analyses create opportunities for political coalitions among people whose circumstances are similar or approximate, rather than identical.

To conclude, the resurgent second-wave feminist positions articulated in the "Declaration on Women's Sex-Based Rights" are arguments that were rejected in the 1980s for drawing too sharp a definition of women (as white, middle-class, heterosexual, cisgendered, etc.,). Clearly, only some women benefit materially, symbolically and politically from this focus. In contrast to such reductive arguments, intersectional methodologies illuminate all gender identities by interrogating all socially meaningful axes of power and inequality. Intersectional methods illuminate the variation in human suffering, with gender being only one of several factors shaping people's experiences with violence—all of them worthy of empathy, resources, advocacy, and policy solutions. Rather than erase women, intersectional analyses foreground their experiences in all their variation, including along a gender continuum.

3

Speaking Feminism to Rights: Intersections of Ethos and Praxis

Alison Brysk

Feminism and human rights have been in dialogue throughout their evolution. How has feminism influenced and been influenced by human rights framing? The ethos of human rights has expanded the reach and leverage of feminism, while the ethos of feminism has shaped the communicative action of human rights. At the same time, the practice of feminism has advanced women's human rights, while campaigns for human rights and gender justice have strengthened each other—and inspired linked backlash. Feminist responses to these challenges have provided important lessons for the promotion of rights, justice, and equity in a globalizing world.

The ethos of human rights is embodied in the 1948 Universal Declaration claim that we are "All human beings are born free and equal in dignity and rights.... And should act towards one another in a spirit of brotherhood." The rights enumerated in the international regime constitute a universal entitlement to claim self-determination, equity, and community in every sphere of social relations. Human rights propose that the exercise of authority is legitimated and bounded by its impact on human dignity. Rights are enacted through a growing body of norms, movements, and institutions to protect, respect, and fulfill this standard across all levels of social order.

Feminism begins with the idea of equal rights for women—a natural subset of human rights norms in principle that is challenged in practice by patriarchal legacies, intertwined hierarchies of power and privilege, and assertions of cultural relativism. But feminism goes beyond the struggle for equity and self-determination within the human rights agenda to assert the importance of personal and private power relations as a source of gender inequity, question the naturalization of socially assigned gender roles and binaries, and contest the limits and transformation of historic hegemonic structures of law and governance as sources of rights and self-determination. This can expand the range of legal claims within rights discourse beyond civil rights and international law to areas such as family law, legal pluralism, and gendered nationality and immigration status practices. But it also directs social attention and mobilization to gendered issues of public policy, personal security, mobility and public space, and cultural representation.

The initial intersection of feminism and human rights comes in the framing of "women's rights as human rights." The emergence of this claim in the 1990s moved women's rights from protection of a vulnerable population to a quest for gender justice and began a movement from public sphere equity to self-determination crossing the global and local, public and private. The framing of women's rights as human rights articulated feminist analysis with the human rights norm articulated at the Vienna Conference that rights are interdependent, indivisible, and intersectional.[1]

Although women's rights as human rights was first articulated globally by Charlotte Bunch[2] and later forwarded at the 1994 Beijing Women's Conference by US Secretary of State Hilary Clinton, it originated from Philippine activists[3] and began to bridge between global and local audiences. The participation and networking of increasing numbers of more grassroots representatives of the Global South over the generation of global gatherings from the 1975 Mexico City World Conference on Women through the Nairobi, Copenhagen, and Beijing gatherings—alongside the 1994 Cairo World Population Conference attended by a record number of NGOs—shifted the focus of international efforts from prior protectionism toward empowerment and a more integrated full-spectrum rights frame.

Women's rights as human rights are both universal and gendered, expanding both framings. Women's rights include equal access to all of the political and social rights outlined in the Universal Declaration, International Covenant on Civil and Political Rights (ICCPR), and International Covenant on Economic Social and Cultural Rights (ICESCR)—as well as equitable treatment in gendered reproductive and social roles proposed in the CEDAW Convention on the Elimination of Discrimination Against Women and the Declaration on the Elimination of Violence Against Women.

Women and sexual and gender (SOGI) minorities are systematically disadvantaged in fulfillment of universal rights to physical integrity, political freedoms and participation, labor and social rights—as well as to self-determination in marriage, sexuality, and reproduction. One out of three women in the world has experienced gender-based violence, there is a persisting "gender gap" in women's employment and income worldwide, and child or forced marriage affects millions of women each year. These disadvantages are linked and interdependent through social structures of patriarchy and its institutionalization in "gender regimes" of law, markets, mobility, and disciplinary violence that govern gender roles and rules. Within these gendered patterns of rights shortfalls, intersectional identities of race, class, origin, and citizenship status compound vulnerabilities and complicate responses.[4]

---

[1] "World Conference on Human Rights 14-25 June 1993, Vienna," United Nations, n.d. Available online: https://www.un.org/en/conferences/human-rights/vienna1993.

[2] Charlotte Bunch, "Women's Rights Are Human Rights," *Human Rights Quarterly* 12, no. 4 (1990): 486–498.

[3] Valerie Hudson, *The Hillary Doctrine: Sex and American Foreign Policy* (New York: Columbia University Press, 2015), 336.

[4] Alison Brysk, *The Struggle for Freedom from Fear: Contesting Violence Against Women at the Frontiers of Globalization.* (New York: Oxford University Press, 2018); Patricia Hill Collins and Sirma Bilge, *Intersectionality* (Malden: Polity Press, 2016).

Women's rights follow issue-specific patterns rooted in reproductive relations, and gender relations are "the first political order" that underlies the distribution of all power.[5] The World Health Organization defines reproductive rights as the right to choose sexual activity and pregnancy; sexual health; and freedom from sexual violence. These rights are enabling rights for women's rights to life, liberty, livelihood, physical integrity, health, and education and are intertwined with political repression and economic exploitation. Feminist mobilization for these rights crosses another intersection to show the consequences of patriarchy as a social system for world order, peace, and development.

The intersection of feminist and human rights campaigns has shifted global understandings and policies across international law, security, economics, and governance. Such campaigns are forms of communicative action that operate through dynamics of voice, frames, media, and bridging publics that constitute a politics of persuasion. Women's rights campaigns around femicide, contemporary slavery, and rape as a war crime centered new voices and introduced new claims and frames[6]—such as the protagonist role of Latin American movements on femicide, new claims for sex workers' and migrant rights contesting contemporary slavery, and the innovative international coalition that formed to advocate for inclusion of rape as a war crime at the International Criminal Court. Rights-based campaigns around these issues diffused the feminist ethos that "the personal is political" and expanded the scope of the human rights regime to social structures of patriarchal abuse.[7] Feminist reframing of formerly "cultural" issues such as FGM and child marriage as rights issues strengthened the connection between health rights and feminist self-determination. The appeal of such campaigns was based in part on interdependence arguments for rights with development and security that resonated across the rights regime.[8]

The constructive intersection of feminist and human rights movements has empowered struggles for recognition, representation, responsibility, and resistance— and fostered greater awareness of the linkages among these pathways to change.[9] Recognition of hidden or marginalized groups such as sex workers revealed by a feminist analysis has strengthened campaigns against femicide, trafficking and police

---

[5] Valerie Hudson, Donna Lee Bowen, and Perpetua Lynne Nielsen, *The First Political Order: How Sex Shapes Governance and National Security Worldwide* (New York: Columbia University Press, 2020).

[6] Alison Brysk, *Speaking Rights to Power: Constructing Political Will* (New York: Oxford University Press, 2013).

[7] Alison Brysk, *Human Rights and Private Wrongs* (New York: Routledge Press, 2005).

[8] Madeline Baer and Alison Brysk, "New Rights for Private Wrongs: Female Genital Mutilation and Global Framing Dialogues," in *The International Struggle for New Human Rights*, ed. Clifford Bob (Philadelphia: University of Pennsylvania Press, 2008); Alison Brysk, "Changing hearts and minds: sexual politics and human rights," in *The Persistent Power of Human Rights: From Commitment to Compliance*, ed. Thomas Risse, Steve Ropp, and Kathryn Sikkink (Cambridge: Cambridge University Press, 2013); Amanda Murdie, Baekkwan Park, Jacqueline Hart and Margo Mullinax, "Building momentum: changes in advocacy discourse around early child marriage, 2011-2017," in *Contesting Human Rights: Norms, Institutions, and Practice*, ed. Alison Brysk and Michael Stohl (Northampton: Edward Elgar Publishing, 2019).

[9] Alison Brysk, "Introduction: Contesting Human Rights-Pathways of Change," in *Contesting Human Rights: Norms, Institutions, and Practice*, ed. Alison Brysk and Michael Stohl (Northampton: Edward Elgar Publishing, 2019).

abuse, and fostered intersectional struggles for health rights, racial justice, and gender diversity (see Stemple this volume). First-wave liberal feminist claims for representation—from parliaments to peace accords—expanded to broader campaigns for gender equity throughout global governance, that carry interdependent consequences for political, economic, health, and even environmental rights.[10] Feminist understandings of responsibility for abuse by private actors above and below the state have infused the rights regime—from Human Rights Watch expansion of its mandate through its Women's Rights division to international court rulings requiring states' "due diligence" to prevent and protect from domestic violence to an international treaty on the rights of domestic workers.

The feminist ethos that arises from these campaigns intersects with and informs the reconstruction of the beleaguered liberal rights regime through an ethic of care and notions of intimate labor. In the 21st century, the international human rights regime struggles as equity is decoupled from freedom, the liberal world order cannot compensate for the collapsing claims of citizenship, and cosmopolitan universalism is rejected as an identity and rhetoric of responsibility.[11] An alternative feminist ethic of care rooted in relational feminism redefines rights: from juridical claims to developmental capacities that must be recognized and nurtured as the basis for social life. The ethic of care can shift a doctrine of state-based cosmopolitan connection to a social norm of empathetic compassion, addressed to a multi-level systemic social responsibility for flourishing. Such feminist understandings of recognition and relationship underpin the expansion of the human rights regimes and movements for Indigenous peoples, migrants, disability, and environmental justice.[12]

The pattern of contemporary populist and national backlash is an ironic testament to the intersecting efficacy of human rights and feminism, as aspiring authoritarians target modernizing gender regimes and the protagonist role of women in civil resistance. From Poland to Turkey, the Philippines to Brazil, India to the US, attacks on democracy, civil liberties, and minorities and migrants are intertwined with attacks on the bodies, rights, and sexuality of women and SOGI minorities.[13] But feminist rights advocates respond to repression with a combination of norm translation, intersectional

---

[10] Alison Brysk and Aashish Mehta, "Do rights at home boost rights abroad? Sexual equality and humanitarian foreign policy," *Journal of Peace Research* 51, no. 1 (2014); Alison Brysk and Miguel Fuentes Carreño, "Why Feminism Is Good for Your Health," *New Security Beat*, August 2020. Available online: https://www.newsecuritybeat.org/2020/08/feminism-good-health/?utm_source=feedburner&utm_medium=email&utm_campaign=Feed%3A+TheNewSecurityBeat+%28New+Security+Beat%29.

[11] Alison Brysk, *The Future of Human Rights* (Malden: Polity Press, 2018).

[12] Alison Brysk, "Making Rights Rhetoric Work: Constructing Care in a Post-Liberal World," in *The Changing Ethos of Human Rights*, ed. Alison Brysk, Hoda Mahmoudi, and Kate Seaman (Northampton: Edward Elgar Publishing, 2021).

[13] Valentine Moghadam and Gizem Kaftan, "Right-wing populisms north and south: Varieties and gender dynamics," *Women's Studies International Forum* 75 (2019): 102244; Weronica Grzebalska and Andrea Peto, "The gendered modus operandi of the illiberal transformation in Hungary and Poland," *Women's Studies International Forum* 68 (2018): 164–172; Alison Brysk, "Global Dynamics of Authoritarian Populism," *University of California, Santa Barbara Global E-Journal*, 18 February 2020. Available online: https://www.21global.ucsb.edu/global-e/february-2020/global-dynamics-authoritarian-populism.

resistance, and renewed campaigns for reproductive rights that define the gender regime.[14] Brazilians mobilize across all sectors of society to protest the assassination of Marielle di Franco as a Black queer feminist defender of democracy and campaign against rape culture, while Polish women make common cause with civil libertarians as they rally for abortion rights. Persecuted Philippine journalist Maria Ressa spearheads resistance as she reveals repression and is honored with the Nobel Prize, while the International Criminal Court takes up the case, as the Philippine women's rights movement has brought worldwide recognition to the patterns of labor exploitation for transnational domestic workers.

From the global to the grassroots, feminism and human rights have grown together. Despite some differences in the movements' origins, lenses, and priorities that have resulted in periodic divergences, it is the intersections of feminism and human rights that have proven the most visionary and effective. The lesson for all rights struggles is precisely the value of this type of dialectical engagement that goes beyond tactical alliance to mutual learning and mobilization. A feminist ethos of rights and the rights-based praxis of feminism are the best basis for enhancing justice, equity, and dignity for all.

---

[14] Philip Ayoub, "Tensions in rights: navigating emerging contradictions in the LGBT rights revolution," in *Contesting Human Rights: Norms, Institutions, and Practice*, ed. Alison Brysk and Michael Stohl (Northampton: Edward Elgar Publishing, 2019).

Why Does Sexual Difference Matter in the Legal Paradigm of Equality? Human Rights Violations of Migrant Women in Immigration Detention in Mexico

Alethia Fernández de la Reguera Ahedo

To have a right as a woman is not to be free of being designated and subordinated by gender.[1]

Migration is marked by gender. Forced migration of Central American women to Mexico comprises of different forces than that of their male counterparts. "Gender is one of the fundamental social relations anchoring and shaping immigration patterns, and immigration is one of the most powerful forces disrupting and realigning everyday life."[2] While there is a context of structural violence and poverty that expels people from their places of origin, in the case of women, the type of violence they face usually begins in the family and community. Central American women flee their countries because of violence exercised by the State, a type of gendered structural violence occurring in the public and private realms.[3] This compels the migration of thousands of women yearly.

The Encuesta Nacional de Personas Migrantes en Tránsito por México [National Survey of Migrants in Transit Through Mexico] shows that in 2016 the main push factors for women from Honduras, El Salvador and Guatemala to migrate to Mexico were insecurity and violence (46 percent) followed by economic reasons (32 percent).[4] Fearing exposure to sexual violence during the migratory journey, 8 out of 10 women reported leaving their country accompanied.

---

[1] W. Brown, "Suffering the Paradoxes of Rights." In *Left Legalism / Left Critique*, eds., W. Brown and J. Halley, 420–434, (Durham: Duke University Press, 2002), 422.

[2] Hondagneu-Sotelo. "Gendering Migration: Not for 'feminists only'—and not only in the household," (No. CDM Working Paper #05–02f, 2005).

[3] A. Varela, "La trinidad perversa de la que huyen las fugitivas centroamricanas: violencia feminicida, violencia de estado y violencia de mercado." *Debate Feminista*, 53, (2017): 1–17.

[4] UNAM, C.-I. *Los desafíos de la migración y los albergues como oasis. Encuesta Nacional de Personas Migrantes en Tránsito por México* (Cd. de México, 2017).

It is common for women to hire the services of smugglers or unscrupulous middlemen recruiters. Women are often abandoned en route, which exposes them to greater risks including being victims of human trafficking, kidnapping by organized crime and extortion by authorities. In 2021, the Instituto Nacional de Migración [National Migration Institute] (INM) reported 307,679 detentions and 114,366 deportations (80.5 percent and 96 percent from Guatemala, Honduras, El Salvador and Nicaragua respectively). In this period a total of 100,064 women were taken to immigration detention centers in Mexico.[5]

Between 2017 and 2019 I conducted ethnographic research at the border between Mexico and Guatemala. I engaged in participant observation specifically in the city of Tapachula at the Estación Migratoria Siglo XXI, which is one of the biggest and most important detention centers[6] in the country with capacity for nearly 960 irregular immigrants. It is the place that brings together large groups of migrants detained throughout the country prior to being deported across Mexico's southern border. The project included participant observation and in-depth interviews with (active and former) immigration agents and officers, immigrants, governmental officials, staff from international organizations and NGOs.[7] I continuously visited the Estación Migratoria Siglo XXI in Tapachula, Chiapas and interviewed immigrants who had been previously detained and at the time of the interview were asylum seekers assisted by NGOs. My goal was to understand the scope of immigration agents' subjectivities in immigration policy enforcement within the management of a detention center. I sought to explain to what extent the stigmas, fears, desires and life stories of immigration agents—first responders—impact the destiny of forced migrants arriving in Mexico. I decided to conduct this research at the Estación Migratoria Siglo XXI because it is one of the biggest detention centers in the country which receives thousands of people who are detained throughout Mexican territory before being deported. My entry was possible thanks to an alliance with the Centro de Derechos Humanos Fray Matías de Córdova A.C. a non-profit organization that provides psycho-legal assistance to people in detention. I was able to conduct interviews with people inside and outside the detention center. I usually prioritized cases of migrant women who required psycho-legal assistance because they were migrating with their children, seeking asylum or were in prolonged detention.

In this chapter I analyze from a feminist critical theory of the State and law, a specific form of discrimination or "soft" violence exercised by the State against migrant women

5   Unidad de Política Migratoria, *Boletín Mensual de Estadísticas Migratorias 2021*, (Centro de Estudios Migratorios, 2021).
6   In this chapter I indefinitely use the terms immigration station, detention center and migrant prison because in practical terms immigration stations function as prisons.
7   I carried out 14 interviews and participant observations at the offices of the National Immigration Institute in Tapachula, Mexico City, and Tijuana; more than 30 interviews with migrants in detention, three interviews with former public officials, six interviews with staff from different agencies, such as: *Comisión Mexicana de Ayuda a Refugiados* [Mexican Commission for Refugees], *Comisión Nacional de Derechos Humanos* [National Commission for Human Rights], *Comisión Estatal de Derechos Humanos de Chiapas* [Chiapas State Commission of Human Rights], and Office of the United Nations High Commissioner for Refugees.

in detention. I reflect on the paradoxes raised by various theorists on the valuation of sexual differences both in legal frameworks and in public policies to achieve equality and its effects on the exercise of human rights of migrant women.

The chapter consists of four sections plus the introduction and conclusion. In the first section I present a brief overview of Mexico as a country of immigration detention, followed by a section on State violence, specifically the institutional gender-based violence I observed at the Estación Migratoria Siglo XXI in Tapachula, Chiapas. A third section presents some elements to discuss how the law reproduces gender subordination and I briefly point out some conceptual elements to understand Wendy Brown's human rights paradox.[8] Finally, in the last section I discuss the dichotomous representations of femininity, stigmatization and the lack of protection that migrant and racialized women face in Mexico.

Detention of female migrants in Mexico

Mexico has one of the largest immigration detainee systems in the world with about 60 detention centers (30 immigration detention centers and 24 temporary detention centers).[9] Most of them were installed between 2000 and 2010; the ones with the largest accommodation capacity are: Tapachula (960 persons), Acayucan (836 persons) and Iztapalapa (430 persons). In accordance with Article 3 of the 2011 Migration Law, an immigration station is a physical facility established by the Instituto Nacional de Migración to "temporarily host foreigners that fail to prove regular migratory status, until their migratory situation is resolved." These centers operate on a continuum between prisons and refugee camps. The prison model, together with the proliferation of new detention centers, structures a system that orders, restricts and criminalizes migrants in the region.

Reports from civil society organizations, CNDH [National Human Rights Commission] and the INM's Consejo Ciudadano [Citizen Council] show that unsanitary conditions are a common characteristic at immigration stations. The most repeated complaints in these reports are overcrowding, lack of privacy, lack of water, infestations, and limited access to cleaning kits. Additionally, women are provided with only one sanitary pad a day, and one or two diapers a day for babies. Severe illness is common while in detention.[10]

From my first interactions with women in detention, I identified that the conditions of stay were very precarious. In addition to expressing their concerns about the

[8] W. Brown, *Estados del agravio: poder y libertad en la modernidad tardía.* (Madrid: Lengua de trapo, 2019).

[9] Global Detention Project, *Immigration Detention in Mexico: Between the United States and Central America. Global Detention Project Country Profile,* (2021).

[10] Comisión Nacional de los Derechos Humanos. *Informe Especial. Situación de las Estaciones Migratorias en México, hacia un Nuevo Modelo Alternativo a la Detención,* (Ciudad de México, 2019); Consejo Ciudadano del Instituto Nacional de Migración. *Personas en detención migratoria en México. Misión de Monitoreo de Estaciones Migratorias y Estancias Provisionales del Instituto Nacional de Migración,* (Cd. de México, 2017); A. Fernández de la Reguera, *Detención migratoria. Prácticas de humillación, asco y desprecio,* (Ciudad de México, UNAM, 2020); A. Macías Delgadillo, Hernández Méndez, A., Carreño Nigenda, C., Martínez Medrano, D., Castro Lobato, M., Oehler Toca, M., and Cano Padilla, S. *La Ruta del Encierro. Situación de las personas en detención en estaciones migratorias y estancias provisionales,* (Ciudad de México: Sin Fronteras, 2013).

uncertainty of their immigration proceedings and/or effective access to asylum applications, the main complaints they had were the lack of privacy, the unsanitary conditions of the place, and the lack of access to medicines, diapers, sanitary napkins, and pregnancy tests. Most women interviewed experienced illness especially gastrointestinal problems, skin conditions, or respiratory problems because of high daytime temperature and low nighttime temperature, unhealthy food, and/or unsanitary conditions of the spaces they inhabit in detention centers.

> We just looked at the pile of mats and as we grabbed one mat, they stank so badly. The mats were full of lice, urine, everything! I mean, it stank, and the bad smell was noticeable because they were all piled up. Later, we saw that there were rats there. There were large rats on top of the mats, and well, we couldn't sleep at all that night. (Woman from El Salvador in immigration detention, 23 years old.)
>
> This week they gave my baby rotten fruit with worms. When I asked the guard if she would change it, she rudely took it away. (Woman from Honduras in immigration detention, 24 years old.)
>
> To us women, they give us almost nothing for personal care, for shaving, things like that, they don't allow in any of that in. I never combed my hair in the 17 days I was there; they don't even allow in a comb. (Honduran woman in immigration detention, 19 years old.)

Articles 225 and 226 of the Migration Law Regulations stipulate that the human rights of all persons must be respected in immigration detention centers and that there must be no discrimination on the basis of gender. Likewise, the Regulations indicate respect for the human rights of different vulnerable groups, among them pregnant women in migration detention centers (art. 225), the adoption of protection measures for migrant women, especially pregnant women when they are "presented" before the authorities, such as giving priority to theur stay in specialized institutions (art.230) and the regularization of their migration status when their degree of vulnerability cannot be a factor contributing to their deportatio (art.144).

The question is why, despite having this legal framework and a supposed human rights approach, in practice, immigration detention processes highlight the body as the site of inscription for immigration policies,[11] resulting in practices of control, cruelty and dehumanization. Migration detention centers function as total institutions[12] or spaces of discipline within their own functioning divided between those who guard and those who are detained. In these places, immigration agents usually work under assumptions of ambiguity that allow for their discretion to take precedence—in other words, with the power to act according to the dictates of their own judgment and conscience. On a daily basis, street level bureaucracy responds to a state of exception that operates in a gray space between politics and law. In migration detention

---

[11]   D. Fassin, "The biopolitics of otherness." *Anthropology Today*, 17, no. 1 (2001): 3–7.
[12]   E. Goffman, *Internados*, (Buenos Aires: Amorrortu editors, 2001).

centers norms are suspended or applied according to whether or not it is convenient to political intention.[13]

State Violence: A Gender Violence

In 2018 migrant caravans coming from Central America in transit through Mexico were at the center of the migration agenda, on the one hand due to the increasing border controls and the impossibility of applying for asylum in the United States, and on the other hand because it was a strategy employed by the most vulnerable people to move with lower costs and greater visibility, thereby avoiding the risks of human trafficking and clandestine crossings.[14] As a result of increased media coverage, there are several examples of recent events (raids and mass detentions) on social networks where INM personnel can be seen capturing and beating migrants at strategic points along the Suchiate River, in the border between Mexico and Guatemala, preventing the entry of men, women and children into Mexican territory. These images are aligned with a growing global discourse that stereotypes and criminalizes migrants as a threat to national security;[15] and reinforces an adverse reception context, which generates greater vulnerabilities especially for women, children and adolescents, the elderly and people with disabilities.

Given increasing border control measures and the presence of the National Guard in migration control and verification operations since 2019, women are more exposed to human rights violations, including sexual violence by the authorities.[16] Migrant women face a continuum of violence from the place of origin to the place of transit and destination. In my research I have prioritized the analysis of women's experiences during immigration detention, however I acknowledge the importance of conducting research in transit points to understand the scope of institutional violence suffered by migrant women.

This type of violence is a "[...] a form of dynamically symbolic State metapolitical violence, which has structured over the long term a system of values that discriminates, differentiates and excludes through the ideological strategies of invisibility, concealment, denial, omission and stereotyping."[17] On a daily basis, the interaction between migration agents and detained women generates practices of institutional violence that range from the subtle, such as denying access to a sanitary napkin, to denying access to due process. These practices have real consequences to safeguard human rights, especially when authorities lack a feminist perspective in the procedures of asylum application;

---

[13] Fernández de la Reguera, Detención migratoria. Prácticas de humillación, asco y desprecio.
[14] L. Gandini, Fernández de la Reguera, A., and Narváez Gutiérrez, J. C. *Caravanas*, (Ciudad de México: SDI, IIJ, UNAM, 2020).
[15] C. Minca, "Geographies of the camp." *Political Geography*, 49, (2015): 74–83; Ramadan, A. "Spatialising the refugee camp." *Transactions of the Institute of British Geographers*, 38, (2013): 65–77.
[16] Amnesty International. "La nueva Guardia Nacional de México está rompiendo su juramento de respetar los derechos humanos." *Noticias*, (2020, November).
[17] L. A. Maya Restrepo, "Racismo institucional, violencia y políticas culturales. Legados coloniales y políticas de diferencia en Colombia," *Historia Crítica Edición Especial*, (2009): 218–245.

or when a woman is left in indefinite detention after she filed an appeal with the migration authority; or denied the right to a gynecological examination; or when authorities do not guarantee safety conditions to a woman at risk of meeting her perpetrator.

Clearly there is a missed opportunity for human rights discourses and practices to be inclusive of feminism. In the framework of the 2011 constitutional human rights reform in Mexico, feminist demands for the right to justice and the right to a life free of violence have not been fully integrated. Guaranteeing women's human rights obliges States to recognize and transform the paternal ignorance.[18] In the practice of human rights, or in other words to uproot the perception of granting victims a conception of rights imposed by dominnat groups.

Law, the State and Gender

The 2011 Migration Law is a relatively recent legislation. It is aligned with the constitutional human rights reform of that same year that incorporates in its Art. 1 the obligations of all authorities, within the scope of their competencies, to respect, protect, promote and guarantee the human rights of all persons. This includes the judicial and legislative powers (federal and local), the executive powers (federal, local and municipal), especially with regard to public policies.[19] The 2011 Migration Law recognizes and guarantees the human rights of migrants, especially the rights to health and education regardless of their immigration status. However, it is necessary to study which symbolic interpretations have been constructed at the institutional and local level by the actors in charge of applying this Law.

Far from integrating a feminist approach, Mexico's Migration Law incorporates a limited human rights approach. Even though migration policy programs in both, former and current administrations (2012–2018 and 2018–2024) have integrated the gender perspective within their main objectives, throughout my research experience, I have observed that in practice, most of the provisions of the Law and its Regulations on gender perspective are hardly fulfilled. What I have identified is that usually three actions are complied with: the separation of spaces between men and women, the management of women's areas in detention in charge of female personnel, and training on gender issues.

Feminist theory in legal studies has analyzed how law reproduces gender. According to Carol Smart, a British feminist legal theorist, law is a gendered technology that legally and discursively constructs the category of woman, which tends to reinforce gender inequalities.[20] Her critique of the supposed neutrality of gender in law refers to

18 W. Simmons, Boynton, J., and Landman, T. "Facilitated Communication, Neurodiversity, and Human Rights." *Human Rights Quarterly*, 43, no. 1, (2021): 138–167.
19 P. Salazar Ugarte, Caballero Ochoa, J. L., and Vázquez, L. D. *La Reforma Constitucional sobre Derechos Humanos. Una guía conceptual*, (Ciudad de México: Instituto Belisario Domínguez, Senado de la República, 2014).
20 C. Smart, "La mujer en el discurso jurídico." In *Mujeres, Derecho penal y criminología*, ed. E. Larrauri, 167–189, (Madrid: Siglo XXI, 1994).

the constitutive tension of the norm that reproduces sexual difference as a form of subordination, both in its practical and symbolic dimensions. For her part, the Italian jurist Tamar Pitch (2003) has made a critique of the real benefits that women may obtain through law, and their expectations of a legal system where women exist in terms of their gender roles, for example as wives or mothers, or included in the categories of implicitly masculine subjects.[21]

An example of the former can be found in Mexico's Migration Law which establishes pregnant women as a vulnerable group, and the State's obligation to create additional protection measures for them, especially when they are detained. However, in practice these protection measures are in effect limited to access to essential medical care only. I have documented cases of detained pregnant women who are denied medication or translation services when they do not speak Spanish.[22] I also documented a case of a woman who was taken from the immigration detention center in Tapachula to a hospital to give birth and two days later was returned to her cell with her newborn baby. In reality, pregnant women are exposed to greater risks in immigration detention, given the unsanitary conditions, poor food, lack of privacy, and deficient medical service. The 2011 Migration Law does not contemplate co-responsibility for care work on the part of the State as part of the protection measures. Instead of protection, what stands out is the discourse that stereotypes and punishes women for the irresponsibility of migrating while pregnant.

The tension between human rights and women's rights increases in a scenario where the State, whether from the right wing, center or left, is constantly and publicly discrediting feminist discourses and demands in Mexico. It is of utmost urgency to integrate the feminist perspective into human rights discourses and practices, so that they are not experienced as a confrontation or in *conflicto* with one another, but as a fundamental axis to guarantee the effectiveness of protection mechanisms for migrant women, since sexual difference does make an important difference in access to rights.

From current human rights frameworks, women, the LGBT+ population and other minorities are conceived as subjects of rights from a partial understanding of the social risks and vulnerabilities they face. They are an example of the ethical non-recognition of the other[23] as a subject of rights. From a feminist perspective, non-recognition is based on a legal, political, economic, cultural and social order that generates and reproduces deep inequalities and a conception of rights adjusted to the patriarchal system. My research proves that having a Migration Law with a supposed human rights approach is not sufficient to protect migrant women from gender injustices and systematic violations of human rights. The law is a minimum basis that must be accompanied by a migration policy with a gender and human rights approach, budgets and political will to safeguard women's human rights.

American political scientist and philosopher Wendy Brown says that in the face of the powers that subordinate women, human rights are a form of mitigation rather than

---

[21] T. Pitch, *Un derecho para dos*, (Madrid: Editorial Trotta, 2003).
[22] Fernández de la Reguera, Detención migratoria. Prácticas de humillación, asco y desprecio.
[23] C. Taylor, *El multiculturalismo y la política del reconocimiento*, (México: Fondo de Cultura Económica, 1993).

a resolution.[24] Still, they are something that women cannot reject. "Given the still precarious and fraught conditions of women's existence in a world ordered by a relentless construction and exploitation of sexual difference as subordination, certainly rights appear as that which we cannot not want."[25] She points to a discussion on how and why rights are created that is more relevant than ever, especially to analyze under what conditions women can exercise them, and whether or not they succeed in overcoming gender injustices.

In view of this, it is imperative to reflect on Brown's paradox of human rights: "the more highly specified rights are as rights for women, the more likely they are to build that fence insofar as they are more likely to encode a definition of women premised on our subordination in the transhistorical discourse of liberal jurisprudence."[26] As long as the conception of the female subject of law continues under the principles of subordination so deeply rooted in the liberal discourse, despite achieving the greatest specificity in favor of women, these rights will have a greater chance of achieving only the regulation of the conditions of subordination. On the other hand, the more gender-neutral or gender-inequality-neutral the rights are conceived, the more likely they are to reinforce male privileges without disrupting the specific needs of women, people with non-gender identities, racialized people, etc.[27] This paradox has no simple solution. Feminism confronts this paradox on a daily basis through various strategies, including affirmative actions to compensate for conditions of discrimination and inequality. However, on many occasions these actions do not achieve their main objective, which is why it is necessary to build forms of citizen equality that recognize sexual difference, and that allow us to contextualize and weigh its effects on the exercise of human rights.

Does the culture that stigmatizes migrant women outweigh the culture and institutionalization of human rights? My research suggests the answer is yes. In the particular case of migrant women, sexual difference does represent risks and gender-based human rights violations during transit and immigration detention. The sexual difference of menstruating, gestation, childbirth and breastfeeding does make a difference in how women experience institutional violence because they are migrants, poor, racialized, mothers, and pregnant or menstruating women. Their status as women exposes them to greater risks and additional stigma because they are considered irresponsible for migrating with their children, pregnant or for having left their children in their countries. Motherhood is a gender mandate that weighs heavily on migrant experiences. A woman who leaves her country transgresses the mandate to stay at home to care for her children. A woman who has to leave her country with her children is also stigmatized, accused of exposing them to the risks of cross-border transit, and recently in the face of restrictive immigration policies in the United States, it is believed that Central American women leave with their children in order to have a better chance of applying for asylum. The stigma of migrating as mothers is present in both the sending and receiving communities.

---

[24] Brown, "Suffering the Paradoxes of Rights."
[25] Brown, "Suffering the Paradoxes of Rights."
[26] Brown, "Suffering the Paradoxes of Rights."
[27] Brown, "Suffering the Paradoxes of Rights."

Human rights have been adopted as a discourse at all levels of the Instituto Nacional de Migración but have become a cliché.[28] And in order to understand how a law mutates in the local context I conclude that for the street bureaucrats in Tapachula, human rights represent greater obstacles to their work, as they have to generate extra reports and take more training. In this sense and for the case studied, sexual difference is recognized in the legislation, at least in the case of pregnant women in detention, but the necessary measures to guarantee the right to health and non-detention are not generated, so they are exposed to even greater risks under the veil of a law with an alleged human rights and gender approach.

Which Femininity is Protected by the State?

Latin American feminisms have had important historical conquests in terms of rights, but more than ever young women express rage and pain in the face of the injustices and indifference of the State.[29] Just as Brown says, women have justified reasons to distrust the State's protection policies.[30] Taking as a starting point the conception about women needing the protection of men, which has served as a basis for the exclusion of women in public life; there is also a symbolic relationship that associates femininity with the privileged classes, for example the delicacy of white women in opposition to racialized migrant women. I return, therefore, to the concept of parental ignorance[31] to illustrate how the State is less willing to listen to the demands of the groups it considers to be beneficiaries of social assistance. In this case, the State ignores feminist demands by conceiving women's rights as a consideration nor an obligation for a historically subordinated group.

According to American anthropologist Sherry Ortner, in various cultures the symbols of femininity are constructed from a dichotomy that structures two opposing symbolic axes: on the one hand the pure, virgin woman, the mother, the goddess of fertility; and on the other hand, Eve, Mary Magdalene, the witch and the prostitute.[32] State protection policies reinforce this division and classify women by differentiating those who are constructed as vulnerable and in need of protection from those who generate their own vulnerability, that is, who are invulnerable because of their own sexual availability.[33]

According to Brown:

> Protection codes thus become key technologies for regulating privileged women, while intensifying the vulnerability and degradation of those who have been left

---

[28] Fernández de la Reguera, *Detención migratoria. Prácticas de humillación, asco y desprecio.*

[29] M. Lamas, *Dolor y Política. Sentir, pensay y hablar desde el feminism*, (Ciudad de México: Oceano, 2021).

[30] Brown, *Estados del agravio.*

[31] Simmons et al., "Facilitated Communication, Neurodiversity, and Human Rights."

[32] S. B. Ortner, "Is Female to Male as Nature is to Culture." In *Women, Culture and Society*, eds., M. Z. Rosaldo and L. Lamphere, 67–87, (Stanford, 1974).

[33] Brown, *Estados del agravio.*

on the side of intemperance, once that wall separating light from dark, women from prostitutes, good girls from bad girls has been built.[34]

Central American migrant women are racialized and stigmatized usually as sex workers because of, on the one hand, the latent risk of suffering sexual violence in transit, and on the other hand, the high possibilities of being employed in sex work to survive both in transit and in the places of destination. From the State, the idea of blaming migrant women for having left their country and having done so without resources, money, papers or support networks, is very present both in practice and in public discourse, especially among public officials.

Stigma has fatal consequences for women in detention, as sexual violence is normalized even by State agents. In my fieldwork I have documented how common it is that when women enter a migratory detention center they are not asked if they have suffered sexual violence during transit.[35] On a recent visit to the Migrant Detention Center in Mexico City, I interviewed a woman who had suffered sexual violence by the National Guard during her arrest and had not reported it in the interviews conducted once she entered the detention center; however, the immigration authorities had not asked her if she had been a victim of sexual violence or any crime in Mexican territory. This means that the protocols established to provide care to migrant women in Mexico are not being complied with. This is, on the one hand, due to the normalization of violence against women, and on the other hand, because if a woman reports having suffered sexual violence in Mexican territory, the law stipulates that she is entitled to immigration regularization through a visa for humanitarian reasons. Once again, this example shows that the human rights of migrant women are subject to the migration policy of control, deterrence and deportation.

Duncan Kennedy, the American critical legal theorist, discusses the social scripts that tolerate sexual abuse of women, which generate a tolerated residue of abuse that benefits men and represents higher costs for women. "The social scripts of harassment include, along with the roles of the provocateur and the woman who does not know how to take care of herself, the roles of the vindictive deceiver, the delusional hysteric, and the 'overly' susceptible woman who systematically misinterprets innocent male behaviors."[36] These same scripts carry over to migrant women: "they are irresponsible," "they asked for it," "they are husband-stealing women," and so on. The scripts are also reproduced by State agents, since gender is an element that shapes subjectivities, which adds to the culture of subordination and criminalization of migrant women that generates opposing representations: either victims or victimizers, but not as subjects of rights.

One of the contributions of feminist critical theory of the State has been to demonstrate the complexity and abstraction of gender in State structures, in such a

---

[34] Brown, *Estados del agravio*, p. 305.
[35] Fernández de la Reguera, Detención migratoria. Prácticas de humillación, asco y desprecio.
[36] D. Kennedy, *Abuso sexual y vestimenta sexy*, (Ciudad de México: Siglo XXI, 2016), 37.

way that it is not easily observable.[37] Based on this assumption, the analysis of gender in the State should focus on the types of power, its uses and privileges that operate as a result and reproduction of the structures of male domination. It is necessary to analyze the State not as an abstract entity, but in its most immediate relations with the subjects of rights, for example in the daily interaction between a State agent and a migrant woman, where State practices are observable, in the contact between the street bureaucrat and the person who requires a service or protection.

Conclusions

The analysis of the effectiveness of human rights compliance requires the use of various methodologies and analytical techniques provided by social and anthropological research. Political ethnography[38] opens the possibility of a deep immersion in State institutions to analyze power and gender relations. In migration, as in many other priority human rights issues, political will and budgets must be accompanied by a deep understanding of all the various levels at which patriarchy constructs the State.

In this chapter I have analyzed how both subtle and more direct institutional violence by State agents against migrant women in detention centers are human rights violations that occur on a daily basis in an institutional environment that operates under a discourse of "strict adherence to human rights" based on a Migration Law and its Regulations. My objectives were, on the one hand, to demonstrate the importance of knowing the local contexts and the culture of gender and racism in which interactions between the State and migrants take place, and on the other hand, to reflect on how and to what extent sexual difference should be emphasized in human rights in order to achieve substantive gender equality. In the case of migrant women, and applying the paradox of Brown's rights, it is necessary to emphasize this difference but to prevent the differentiation itself from being another form of subordination of women. Ten years after the constitutional reform of human rights in Mexico, the feminist critique of law is today more relevant than ever in order to transform the patriarchal essence of law. The recognition of the need to establish gendered rights to be included in the normative paradigm of equality should be the basis to stop mitigating female subordination and instead undermine and transform it from a diverse and inclusive culture of human rights.

---

[37] R. L. Segato, *Las estructuras elementales de la violencia. Ensayos sobre género entre la antropología, el psicoanálisis y los derechos humanos*, (Buenos Aires: Prometeo Libros, 2010).

[38] J, Kubik, "Ethnography of Politics: Foundations, Applications, and Prospects." In *Political Ethnography What Immersion Contributes to the Study of Power*, ed. E. Schatz, (Chigago: The University of Chicago Press. 2009).

Snapshot #7: Feminism and Its Discontents: A Conversation with Gloria Steinem and Gloria Feldt

Interviewer: Pardis Mahdavi

The braiding between feminism and human rights has loosened over the past several years and feminism as a movement has changed drastically in the past three decades. I sat down with feminist icons Gloria Steinham and Gloria Feldt to get their take on the challenges and opportunities facing feminism in the twenty-first century. The conversation shed light on messaging and pathways for change that involve re-braiding social movements like feminism, human rights, social justice, and civil rights.

Pardis Mahdavi: What do you think are the biggest issues facing the feminist movement right now, as we sit here in 2021?

Gloria Feldt: Having made a study of women's relationship with power and realizing how much power we actually have, the question in my mind is, why are we not operating from power at this point? Why are we operating still from fear?

We have a sense that we can't do it we can't be heard and we're not going to be heard, so how do we get over that hump because I feel like we're at a real inflection point where if we don't act we really can go back in this country to where we were 200 years ago. And this is not a dystopian novel this is, real possibility and I do not understand what keeps women from operating from the power that we actually have That is my question. It is my existential question to the world.

Gloria Steinem: Well, I think that sometimes we do, I mean we have done this. Like in underground abortion movements, movements against domestic violence that depended on a rescue system of mainly women rescuing other women and driving them to other states, you know we've had this power, we've done this work. But, from time to time, maybe we got too overconfident in our ability to change the dominant system and so began to put too much time into working *within* the system. By that I mean you know we've spent 50 years just trying to get women into the Constitution.

And we're still doing that right, but, you know you maybe we were wrong to have given up our underground networks.

Pardis Mahdavi: So that is interesting to me because I actually think the underground networks, at least in the places I work, are alive and well. So, in places like Iran, Afghanistan, even India even Turkey, it seems like the underground is working to support feminism and justice. But the question for me is: how do we tell the story of transnational feminism and the underground and build bridges—like an underground network to help all boats rise together.

Gloria Steinem: Unfortunately, I think, women in Western countries here and in Europe may believe they don't need these kind of underground networks, so that in itself is a useful message to challenge. The more that these networks are described the better able women in other countries are to learn from them.

I mean we now have an underground network in Texas that we thought we didn't need anymore, probably, but it resembles the underground network we had in the 70s, and clearly we need it.

Gloria Feldt: Okay, but can I just ask this: I mean underground networks are important and I'm not saying we shouldn't have them because you always have to help the people who are in need of immediate help. But isn't that a defensive posture? A defensive action rather than a use of power?

Gloria Steinem: Of course, that goes without saying, but I'm saying that over time we may have put too much faith in negotiating within the system and so we have lost our focus on alternative ways of organizing.

Pardis Mahdavi: More subversive ways?

Gloria Steinem: Yes exactly.

Pardis Mahdavi: So, another one of my questions was: How has/have the feminist movement or movements changed in the past three decades?

Gloria Steinem: Well, you know we started out of rescuing each other, I would say, you know, because in instances of domestic violence, we were literally driving women from one state to the next secretly because there were no shelters, there were no laws. Or if there were laws they weren't really enforced, because the police seem to think that their power is stopped at the at the family door.

So we were doing everything ourselves, and also learning from other women and other countries, I believe that England, for instance, had the first kind of underground network of women rescuing each other from domestic violence, and then we started to try to do that as well.

Then we also began to focus on the electoral system and try to get women or feminist men into positions of power where they could change the practices and we could eventually change the laws. But what I'm saying now is perhaps we ended up giving too much faith in working through the system, as opposed to outside the system, and we need to return to the underground network kind of safety and strategy.

I also do think it's harder because our successes in the feminist movement have made it harder for us to strategize together, because there is so much diversity. Unfortunately, we also have focused on divisions among us, economic and racial divisions among women for instance.

Pardis Mahdavi: Part of the "triple bind."

Gloria Feldt: You know, the feminist movement came in and it is true that many women are safer now than they were before. But now we have to think about this question of safety. Now we have the two pandemics of COVID and the pandemic of racism. Well, this has questioned safety, but it has also given us a moment of disruption that is our opportunity to come together and move forward faster. And I'm not going to claim that I know exactly how to do that.

But I will say that I think if we could in some way gather enough of the groups together and enough of the organizations; it seems like these moments of disruption are the times when you can get new ideas into the system and, just as we have been talking about, start to change the mainstream.

Here is an example of big change in the mainstream: this administration talks about childcare as infrastructure, which has never happened before and I never expected to hear those two words in the same sentence in my lifetime. So, I would just love to get other people's thinking about how could we take this moment on and embrace it, because I think this can also be a moment of rebirth of the feminist movement. And, I hope that it is also a moment when we can bridge the whatever racial gaps have been there, because I think a lot of that narrative has been a narrative that has been put out to keep us apart frankly. And, to be honest, I think women of color are going to save the world.

So how do we, how do we harness the moment and push for change?

Gloria Steinem: Partly by doing what you're doing, saying what you are saying. I mean ever since the first public opinion poll about the women's movement and women's liberation as a phrase which was in the 1970s Black women have been many times more likely to support it than white women. Yet, the public portrayal of the women's movement is way more white than Black and that's one of the problems.

Gloria Feldt: But how did that happen, Gloria, because I, you know all the pictures, I see of you in the 60s and early 70s you've always made a point to be in solidarity with Black women, so how did that narrative get spun?

Gloria Steinem: Well, I, it seems to me as a media person that the press was a big part of spinning the narrative. They painted a picture of white women as the leadership of the women's movement and Black men as the leadership of the civil rights movement. That left Black women out of everything for 20 years. For example, I would be speaking at an event with Dorothy Pitman Hughes, you know, we always did speeches together. And then inevitably at the press conference—even if it was just a campus press conference—the reporters would ask me questions about the women's movement and Dorothy questions about the Civil Rights movement. And we would kind of let it happen for a bit, but then we would say wait a minute, hello? We are both here for the absolute same reason. So the more we can take over the media, the more we have to. We *have to* use new media to set this right. We have to explain that women of color have always been more supportive of the changes that feminism proposes than white women. And we have to strategize about this because it's clearly one of the biggest misapprehensions about what feminism is.

Pardis Mahdavi: Agreed. So then how do we keep in conversation women of color and transnational feminists? I see myself as kind of straddling those two worlds. I identify as Iranian-American, but I also identify as a transnational feminist and have been deeply enmeshed in feminism of the Global South. I do think that the feminism that brought about like the Green movement in Iran, the Arab Spring, and the movements to repeal Section 377 in India—these were all important roots of like #MeToo. And yet we don't talk about the feminism of the Global South or the feminism led by women of color in the US It seems like some people here have internalized the white supremacist scarcity model—and that scares me. That we fear uplifting other voices because we might be shut out? So how do we resist that?

Gloria Steinem: Well, in my case, I mean I learned feminism in India, because when I graduated from college I, in an effort, not to get married, I moved to India for two years. And that is where I learned feminism. Those women used to say feminists taught Gandhi everything he knew.

Gloria Steinem: So I mean part of the answer to your question is we need more public consciousness. We need to be explicit about saying that we have neglected racial representation and we have neglected global representation—even though the two overlap.

Gloria Feldt: I mean, one of the leadership contingency tools that I have in my new book is a belief in the infinite pie. And I could not agree more that it's that scarcity mentality of the patriarchy and a general part of the narrative of our history that we have always had that it's about fighting and you have to keep your piece of the pie because if you uplift someone else that takes away from you.

But the truth is, you can make more pies! If I help you and your help me, there is more for all of us. We just need to find a way to instill that way of thinking.

Pardis Mahdavi: This is very true. So I want to come back to the question of the intersection of human rights and feminism.

Gloria Steinem: I mean many feminists started out in the human rights movement, and then when we felt that they were not doing anything for women, unless women were in jail and counted as prisoners, they and we branched out.

Gloria Feldt: Similarly, I started out in the civil rights movement but felt like "where is the concern for women?" I mean it's like but wait a minute, if there are civil rights, women must have them too. And then I looked around and wondered, why are the women doing all the frontline work and the men are getting all the leadership roles and all the credit?

Seems like a major gap there.

Pardis Mahdavi: Do you think we—as feminists—are just inherently threatening to what we might call the 'mainstream'?

Gloria Steinem: Right now, I think we're especially threatening because the birth rate is down and also in about 20 minutes, this is not going to be a majority white country right and the ultra-right wing is very aware of that so it's part of the reason for their focus, for their being threatened.

Pardis Mahdavi: Yes, I was listening to that podcast: The Tanning of America, that talks about how America is getting 'browner' and more diverse. So do you think that it's a double threat to be a woman of color? A woman bringing the birthrate down and the tanning of America?

Gloria Steinem: Well yeah it's sort of the same thing, because there are fewer white babies being born to make up for the brown babies. But I think we need to be positive about it, which we haven't been. We might feel positive about it, but I think we haven't stated enough that this is great we're going to look more like the rest of the world we're going to have better food, we're going to be better for this diversity.

Pardis Mahdavi: So I hear a call for change, a change in feminism, in discourse, in human rights. How do we make this change?

Gloria Steinem: I think we do it with specificity, from the bottom up and we take lessons from transnational feminists. I mean in India, the woman who is the leader of

West Bengal, Mamata Bannerjee, she is the most popular leader in India. And the state of Kerala, in the South, as you know, has a tradition of female leadership and matriarchy and, incidentally, was the only part of India, with no COVID cases. Right, so when we talk about India, we should talk about these women, not Modhi. I think we give Modhi and men like him power by talking about him. Let's shift the narrative. Let's talk about the positive gains women are making.

Gloria Feldt: To me women's rights—whether it's sexual rights or reproductive rights or any women's rights are human rights. I don't not separate them out, I speak of them together as one thing. I speak of women's human and civil rights period.

Gloria Steinem: Right, because if you don't, you're not addressing half the human race. And if you don't talk about all human's rights, well you are the adversary, and we can start calling the adversary masculinized maybe. Here is the thing: we have wombs. We have them, men don't. And all along throughout history the clashes have been about controlling our wombs. That is a big part of the patriarchy—it is what frightens the adversary. The ability of women to reproduce frightened men throughout history— they couldn't understand how it happened. This is why we became goddesses. But it was a kind of magic to them that they didn't understand because they—the adversaries— couldn't do it. So they had to kill us. We were the only animals who bled and did not die. So we were—and maybe still are—a threat.

Pardis Mahdavi: So maybe it's time to put aside our fears and to show the adversary that we are not a threat but that we are all humans with rights.

Gloria Feldt: It's not just time. It's past time.

Conclusion: Human Rights in Motion

Huss Banai

In the concluding paragraph of his global history of human rights struggles, *A World Divided: The Global Struggle for Human Rights in the Age of Nation-States*, the late historian Eric D. Weitz noted:

> For all the partial advances, for all the contradictions, all the sheer opposition— human rights remain our best hope for the future. Their advocates sometimes espouse utopian aspirations. A restrained perspective is more appropriate and effective. Human rights will never be implemented in the all-embracing fashion of declarations like the UDHR; they will always face opponents, some quite strong. Yet human rights provide a powerful affirmation of the human spirit. They require that people be respected and afforded recognition no matter what their specific gender, nationality, or race. They demand that all people have access to the basic necessities of life, and have the freedom to express themselves, to work and build and create as they wish, to join with others as they desire, and to be free of the scourge of violence and forced displacement. Those *are* our fundamental human rights. We should demand nothing less from the worlds we inhabit.[1]

These pronouncements are representative of perspectives held by many scholars and practitioners who have devoted their time and labor to the advancement of human rights. At their core, they are about the indivisibility of human rights ideals from lived experiences and struggles that, in their diversity, stand as a "powerful affirmation of the human spirit." They also reflect, crucially, the unpleasant and tragic reality that human rights are not universally valued by, or valid to, everyone. The complementary relationship between historical, contemporary, and futuristic social imaginaries that enjoins various human rights struggles from different domains of life has always had to contend with an assortment of transhistorical movements opposed to that very relationship. The latter are not just myriad tyrannies and structural inequities, but also a constellation of beliefs, actors, and narratives that regard human rights as a threat to material interests and established hierarchies at the local, regional, and global levels.

This volume addresses itself to the zones of contention between human rights and their opponents in these early, troubled years of the twenty-first century. The sheer

[1] Eric D. Weitz, *A World Divided: The Struggle for Human Rights in the Age of Nation-States* (Princeton, NJ: Princeton University Press, 2019), p. 429–30.

scale and pace of abuses brought on by unregulated greed, unbound militarism, resurgent xenophobia, rapid climate change, ever-disruptive technologies, rising anti-democratic coalitions, and countless other derivative causes of human misery, have all but obliterated the comforting sense of arrival at history's end that framed much thinking about human rights not too long ago. The singular, combined, and uneven promotion of and violation of human rights today require more exacting methods of inquiry that complement mainstream scholarship and practice with cross-cutting and intersectional perspectives. The eclectic range of chapters—and the empirical "snapshots" that accompany them in each section—in this book each take up this challenge by demonstrating how struggles for human rights in different domains, times, and locations engage with each other, and how those intersections, in turn, inform our understanding of the boundaries of discourse and practice today. They do so by employing interdisciplinary and pluralistic methodologies that treat the pursuit of human rights as fundamentally dynamic and contextual.

Beyond Binaries

The four sections into which the contributions to this volume are organized feature an array of complementary and contrasting arguments, reflections, concepts and themes, and exploratory lines of thought that, contra conventional desires for consensus or synthesis, aim to highlight—even celebrate—the many irresolvable tensions and contradictions at the heart of human rights struggles. As noted in the Introduction, this approach is indeed deliberate (a feature and not a bug, in the parlance of our times). Foremost among these tensions are a series of binaries—universal vs. particular, global vs. local, national vs. international, community vs. individual, radical vs. reformist, critical vs. mainstream—around which debates about, and topics in, human rights have traditionally been framed.

The six chapters that comprise the first section of the book address these binaries most directly in their critical reconsideration of cosmopolitan impulses and justifications that inform and frame much contemporary thinking about human rights. As Joe Hoover asks, "It is important to think carefully about what makes cosmopolitanism distinctive, to ask: what other desires does it bring with it?" For Hoover, since its inception as a Stoic ethical precept, cosmopolitanism has been "haunted" by "the desire for order," which too often has provided moral cover for unjust exercises of power—be they imperial, hegemonial, or supranational. The ordering impulses of cosmopolitan thinking, he notes, are best exemplified in the "malignant" universal rationality of cosmopolitanism's chief ideological champion, liberalism. The latter banding undermines the development of a genuinely "pluriversal" human rights alternative and "presents many profound challenges for those moved by, and hoping to advance, cosmopolitan ideals."

The specter of *liberal* cosmopolitanism also looms over Michael Goodhart's intervention. He argues that human rights were not "*born* cosmopolitan" but "were apotheosized into a cosmopolitan Human Rights Project, which became the third element of a new cosmopolitan trinity alongside liberal democratization and neoliberal globalization." This trinity can be especially oppressive in its imposition of a singular liberal morality that not only subsumes pluralism but also massively undermines social and economic rights at the local level. In place of this hegemonic liberal-cosmopolitan project, Goodhart proposes an "emancipatory" framework he calls "Right to City" (or R2C). Instead of cosmopolitanism's "universal, transcendent, liberal, and international" frameworks for human rights, R2C's conceptual matrix is "place-based, political, radical, and people-centered." The self-aware political quality of this alternative framework, Goodhart proposes, has the benefit of already being and "thriving all around us. To see and embrace it, we must forget cosmopolitanism, with its inherent hostility to place-based, politicized, radical, and people-centered politics. The future of human rights is local."

Kristi Heather Kenyon's chapter argues in a distinctly powerful manner for situating human rights struggles at the level of local communities. As she argues, "[c]ommunity is the place where we experience mutual recognition, interconnection and consequent empathy." To recognize local communities as important sites for the interaction, contestation, and interconnection of rights, however, is not to deny their ongoing dialectic with international forces and movements. As Kenyon notes in references to various international treaties and transnational movements, community-based struggles demonstrate the contextualization of global discourses and practices. A similar contextual understanding informs my own chapter in this section, in which I caution against dispensing with cosmopolitanism simply on account of its liberal interpretations. Cosmopolitanism's original statement by Diogenes the Cynic is less a statement about a shared universal morality based on reason, I argue, than it is a call to prioritize recognition and empathy toward others above one's own worldly attachments. The latter reading forms the basis of what I call "Everyday Cosmopolitanism"—a fairly mundane, daily occurrence between individuals within, across, and between communities at both the local and global levels. It is universally recognizable only in the manner in which it forces the observer to continually understand and contextualize the specific circumstances attending to particular struggles for human rights.

Everyday intersectional issues in contemporary local, national, and global politics very much inform the chapters by LaDawn Haglund and Shareen Hertel. In the face of mounting global challenges—the COVID-19 pandemic, transnational racism, anti-democratic movements, climate change, etc.—Haglund asks, "What role might human rights play in defending democratic institutions and basic human dignity not only from the onslaught of right-wing xenophobia and racism but also from the ravages of capitalism?" She agrees with Hoover and Goodhart that (liberal) cosmopolitanism is an inadequate framework within which to address the sheer scale of "structural and cultural violence" at the core of challenges to human rights today. Haglund's own contextual examination in the chapter focuses on the "transformative potential of human rights mechanisms and strategies in urban areas" in relation to the SDG Cities movement. Shareen Hertel's chapter offers her perspective on the structural reasons behind vaccine hesitancy and disproportionate access to them in the wake of the COVID-19 global pandemic. For Hertel, the challenge of "forging solidarity" around vaccines is directly linked to the economic inequities that structure everyday interactions between people and institutions, which can only be understood and mitigated within a rights-based framework (specifically, economic rights). As she argues, "Each one of us can claim such [economic] rights, but they are bound up with our individual and collective duties to one another. Recognition of our mutual interdependence is thus linked to creating the stable systems that make equitable economic rights fulfillment possible. Without that stability, we are all at risk."

Beyond the State

The chapters in the second section of this volume build on the themes developed in the previous section and specifically address themselves to the double burden imposed on rights-based struggles by the state: as both a sight of resistance to global rights regimes and a vehicle for rights abuses within countries. These burdens, as the contributors demonstrate, have activated local actors and communities—specifically, urban activists and city governments—as principal drivers of change and meaningful implementation of international human rights norms. In her chapter, Gaea Morales argues that "especially where national governments either withdraw from international commitments, or simply fall short in the protection of people and the environment, cities act not just as rebels, but as rocks." Cities can not only act as important counterweights to the authority of national governments in instances when rights frameworks are deliberately flouted by state authorities, but more importantly can be anchors that weight down and localize international norms. Morales's chapter provides a robust theoretical framework for the three contributions that follow, each of which offers context-specific empirical case studies of how local actors may serve as important interlocutors and implementers of international human rights objectives.

In their contribution, Sergio Chaparro Hernández and Nelson Camilo Sánchez argue that "a local discussion of fiscal policy from a human rights perspective has enormous potential for creating more democratic, ecologically responsible social local polities with sufficient capacity to respond to authoritarian attacks on democracy and rights." Establishing the linkages between international human rights declarations—such as the Gwangju Guiding Principles for a Human Rights City—and local political movements working toward their targeted implementation—as in the case of the movement behind "participatory budgeting" in Porto Alegre, Brazil—Hernández and Sánchez demonstrate how local movements behind "fiscal justice" can bypass the stifling politicking of national governments in order to achieve meaningful rights-based changes at the city level. Another compelling instance of localization of international norms is presented in the chapter by Yohanna Abdou, Shehu Sarkin Fada, Paulo E. Hansine, Jone A. José, and William Paul Simmons. Their case studies detail the specific "vernacularization" (i.e., translation) of the UN Principles and Guidelines as part of leprosy de-stigmatization campaigns in Niger, Nigeria, and Mozambique. The authors, some of whom have been affected by leprosy themselves, demonstrate how through community-based participatory action research tools such as "participatory video" conferences, they were able to support marginalized communities through familiar vernaculars.

Anthony Tirado Chase's chapter also casts a critical eye on the state-level capture of an essential tool of human rights practice: truth and reconciliation/accountability mechanisms for addressing past injustices. The existing frameworks for this norm, Chase points out, are deeply flawed not merely because of their limited scope and application under the auspices of state institutions, but also because the substance behind such processes holds special resonance for local communities with histories of injustice unrelated to intractable conflict. A case in point is "Truth-in-LA," a local effort (involving Chase himself) to institute truth and accountability processes for the City of Los Angeles, whose long-standing history of racial strife and police violence—similar to many other US cities, of course—is now a subject of a renewed local-national-global reckoning in the wake of the 2020 Black Lives Matter protests. Although it is too early to gauge the effectiveness of such efforts, Chase argues that they are a compelling model for constructing hybrid rights-based practices out of global and local norms: "When 'local' cities are transnationally constituted, the local becomes an insufficient conceptualization of grassroots practices. These practices are often informed by global "cosmopolitan" norms, just as such norms can be (and must be) informed by grassroots practice."

An instructive historical case study of the *campesino* social movement in Montes de María, Colombia forms the core of the closing chapter in this section by Pablo Abitbol Piñeiro. His analytical narrative testifies to a complex, multilayered relationship between fractured social ties (due to persistent cycles of violence) and vulnerable resistance movements straining for durable bonds of solidarity. Abitbol Piñeiro points to seven "institutional legacies of violence"—state capture, extractive economies, adaptive structures of macro-criminality, criminal family ties and social networks, failed reintegration processes of ex-combatants and military personnel, social norms and political culture, and psychosocial traumas affecting individuals and communities— whose interaction produces the "socio-psychological normalization of clientelist, corrupt and violent practices in rural territories." Yet despite these adverse impacts, peace-building efforts have gone some distance in incorporating international norms of transitional justice into promising "mandates for a reorientation of drug policy, democratic aperture, and rural reform." Montes de María makes for an especially illuminating case study by demonstrating how even under the circumstances in which state functions have been surrendered to clientelist, corrupt, and violent aims, zones of resistance can still function as important incubators for rights-based struggles, if they remain inclusive, participatory, and open to change.

Beyond Insularity

In the third section, the focus broadens beyond insular notions of rights to considerations of sexual rights as a category that must be continually and critically examined not only for how they intersect with social, economic, cultural, and political factors, but also for how they are intricately linked to the scope and depth of other categories of rights. The contributions here, in other words, compel us to reconsider the categorical and disciplinary silos where sexual and other human rights at the global and local levels are often stored. Similar to the first two sections, these chapters reject false binaries and resist the arbitrary enclosures and contortions of global human rights norms by states. But they also improve on those qualities by eschewing any static conceptions of rights in their critical accounting of the location, scope, and substance of sexual rights.

Rajat Khosla and Kate Gilmore's chapter focuses on "the role of power in the contexts of sex, sexuality, and sexual and reproductive health." They expand on radical theories of power—such as Steven Lukes's three-dimensional and "varietal" approaches to understanding power—in order to demonstrate how sexual rights as human rights can "invert" power on established hierarchies and reactionary/conservative forces. "Under human rights," Khosla and Gilmore argue, "the 'must dos,' that power would otherwise impose on us, are transformed into obligations placed back on power itself, and on the State in particular, to positively respect and uphold our rights. It is the State that 'must do' that." Inverting power in this manner, of course, requires constant vigilance and proactive engagement with shifting international norms, national agendas, and local power hierarchies. Using intersex variations as an example, the following chapter by Morgan Carpenter provides a concrete illustration of the precarity, but also the inverting power, of human rights protections. Carpenter's intervention provides us with both a rich historical overview of the entangled relationship between intersexual bodies and different colonial, imperial, hegemonic, and state-centric orders that have rendered intersex variations a "disorder" and have actively worked toward their erasure in the public sphere. Although the intersex movement has over time benefited enormously from the "challenges to dominant ideas about sex, gender and 'normality'" lodged by various gender-based, capabilities-oriented, and racial justice movements, Carpenter argues that "[a]ctions to effect protections for intersex people remain scarce and novel." In this regard, the existing local and global human rights regimes must venture out of their respective silos and work toward extending the scope and depth of their frameworks.

The broadening of existing human rights frameworks around gender also touches significantly upon matters of sexual health. Mauro Cabral's chapter examines efforts at, and opportunities for, "trans depathologization" through the World Health Organization's process of revising the category of "gender incongruence" in its eleventh edition *International Classification of Diseases* (ICD-11). Cabral argues that the "medicalization and pathologization" of trans people must be seen as part of complex historical "colonizing processes" that rely on the stability of mainstream gender norms and practices in order to maintain existing power asymmetries. In this context, the WHO's revision of ICD-11 becomes all the more important because it enjoins the depathologization of transsexual health with other long-standing human rights struggles against powerful anti-gender movements and coalitions at local, national, and global levels. Cabral distills the essence of the struggles thus: "what is *really* at stake is who counts as a person; who has the right to *all* human rights, in a context where not all individuals are seen as equally human and where it seems there are not enough human rights for all. Trans depathologization is taking place, precisely, at that intersection."

Momin Rahman and Adnan Hossain's chapter seeks to move beyond established categories and thought silos within the existing scaffolding of international queer rights. They do so by introducing a conceptual framework they call "homocolonialism," which refers to "a political process through which LGBTQ2+ human rights are deployed and then resisted as part of both an actual and perceived neo-colonial dynamic." They explore this dynamic in the case of Bangladesh, a Muslim-majority postcolonial state that still retains many colonial-era legal statutes such as the prohibition again same-sex sexualities under its existing penal code. A key challenge facing these developments, however, is "to assess whether a demand for LGBTQ2+ rights is an *enabling* resource for local movements or whether it creates disabling levels of resistance." As with the previous chapters, their own prescriptive answer is to focus on cultivating existing local communities and building on the progress at hand, and to "avoid prompting homocolonialist outrage from national governments and cultural/ religious movements that further narrows the possibilities of identifying sexual diversity with local forms."

Beyond the Mainstream

The last section of this volume addresses a topic that has been a long-standing subject of human rights endeavors across the globe: feminism and challenges to it from political forces on the Left, the Right, and from within—its so-called "triple bind." While the challenges associated with the triple bind have always attended feminist politics and social movements, the sheer global scale of these challenges today are unprecedented. As feminists across the globe struggle to sustain and expand the scope of human rights in the face of mounting reactionary, conservative, and xenophobic forces at the local, state, and international levels, it is imperative that the bonds as well as the boundaries of solidarity between different rights-based movements are clarified, elaborated, and deepened. Undertaking this task requires moving beyond mainstream templates for social and political action: a de-centering impulse that can always provide an account of itself, yet also avoids the temptations of stable and solid identities.

The problems associated with stable, mainstream categories of "women" and "girls" is explored in the chapter by Lara Stemple in her case study of the Coalition of Feminists for Social Change (COFEM) an "advocacy coalition" that opposes broadening the definition of gender and limits its activism to issues related to violence against women. Through a detailed and comparative critique of COFEM's aims and work, Stemple demonstrates both the power and poverty of mainstream challenges to feminism from within. Such anti-intersectional, "reductive 'women-only' discourses," she warns, "increasingly aim to lock down the meaning of gender, just as they lock *out* other claimants seeking justice, dangerously dividing us." Indeed, this is precisely what Cabral and Carpenter in the previous section demonstrated in their chapters on the rights of intersex and of trans people, respectively. The "locking down and out" of gender, in each case, at bottom reflects the conservation of a particular set of power relations that bring coherence and material benefits to the mainstream.

Dolores Trevizo's chapter builds on Stemple's critique of some mainstream feminist organizations' lack of attention to intersectionality by offering a broad outline of an intersectional feminist lens on gender-based violence. As she explains in the case of drug cartel-fueled violence in Mexico, "while the overwhelming majority of those murdered or disappeared are men (by other men), public opinion sees women and children as the most likely victims of such crimes." These misperceptions persist due to highly entrenched structures of patriarchy that serve to "decenter" male murder victims and instead reinforce "the gender trope embraced by second-wave feminists that only women can be victims." To Trevizo, this reductive reading can only be countered by an intersectional approach that disturbs the stability of gender norms and roles that mainstream feminist perspectives reify and perpetuate.

The case of the institutional abuse of Central American female migrants in Mexico's state detention centers forms the backdrop for a critical consideration of the rights of displaced women in Alethia Fernández de la Reguera Ahedo's chapter. The application of state violence on the basis of sexual differences, as the chapter documents, is a systematic practice in the case of migrant women, whose agency is severely diminished by their displaced status as compared to their male counterparts. Ahedo shows how migrant women are subjected, in the eyes of Mexican Migration Law, to "greater risks and additional stigma because they are considered irresponsible for migrating with their children, pregnant or for having left their children in their countries." She additionally draws on the works of critical theorist Wendy Brown and the critical legal scholar Duncan Kennedy to argue that "[i]t is necessary to analyze the State not as an abstract entity, but in its most immediate relations with the subjects of rights, for example in the daily interaction between a State agent and a migrant woman, where State practices are observable, in the contact between the street bureaucrat and the person who requires a service or protection."

Moving beyond mainstream feminist perspectives that favor stable gender categories necessitates an understanding of the intersection of gender and human rights, which is examined in the chapter by Alison Brysk. She offers an upbeat assessment of this relationship, on the main: "The constructive intersection of feminist and human rights movements has empowered struggles for recognition, representation, responsibility, and resistance—and fostered greater awareness of the linkages among these pathways to change." But as others have cautioned, the resilience of national and international power hierarchies, combined with the considerable challenges posed by the "triple bind," render human rights inherently contingent, even unstable. This final section regarding the future of human rights and feminisms around the globe is intimately connected to arguments that have coursed through previous sections.

* * *

All sections of this book are united by their considerations of the dynamics between the global, transnational, national, and local in constructing rights-based approaches to issues under consideration. They each shed light on the essential importance of context-specific rights movements and networks of solidarity both on behalf of and against human rights. It is at the intersections of those levels and processes that momentum can be built that take advantage of new political, social, cultural, and economic openings to shift both predominant norms and problematic practices. Beyond the staid conceptual binaries, the stifling enclosers of state prerogatives, the insularities imposed by siloed struggles, and the privileged perspectives of the mainstream, the power and promise of human rights lies at the intersections.

Bibliography

Acuto, Michele. "City Leadership in Global Governance." Global Governance: A Review of Multilateralism and International Organizations 19, no. 3 (2013): 481–498. doi:10.1163/19426720-01903008.

Afghanistan. Vaduz: All Survivors Project Foundation, 2017.

AIS Support Group Australia, Intersex Trust Aotearoa New Zealand, Organisation Intersex International Australia (2017). "Darlington Statement." Available online: https://darlington.org.au/statement (accessed 10 April 2018).

Alkon, Cheryl. "5 Things to Know About This Summer's Birth Control Ruling." Everyday Health, 17 July 2020. Available online: https://www.everydayhealth.com/womens-health/things-to-know-about-this-summers-birth-control-ruling/ (accessed 17 September 2021).

Amiel, Sandrine. "Istanbul Convention: Poland moves a step closer to quitting domestic violence treaty." Euronews, 4 January 2021. Available online: https://www.euronews.com/2021/04/01/istanbul-convention-poland-moves-a-step-closer-to-quitting-domestic-violence-treaty (accessed 29 June 2021).

Angier, Natalie. "Intersexual Healing: An Anomaly Finds a Group." The New York Times, 4 February 1996. Available online: http://www.nytimes.com/1996/02/04/weekinreview/ideas-trends-intersexual-healing-an-anomaly-finds-a-group.html (accessed 2 December 2014).

Asampong, Emmanuel, Joseph Osafo, Jeffrey Bart Bingenheimer, Clement Ahiadeke. "Adolescents and parents' perceptions of best time for sex and sexual communications from two communities in the Eastern and Volta Regions of Ghana: implications for HIV and AIDS education." BMC Int Health Hum Rights 13, no. 40 (2013).

Assis, Mariana Pradini and Ana Carolina Ogand. "Bolsonaro, 'Gender Ideology' and Hegemonic Masculinity in Brazil." Al Jazeera, 31 October 2018. Available online: https://www.aljazeera.com/opinions/2018/10/31/bolsonaro-gender-ideology-and-hegemonic-masculinity-in-brazil/.

Atrakouti, Amal. "GHANA: 'The "Anti-Gay" Bill Will Have Far-Reaching Consequences If We Do Not Fight It Now.'" Civicus, 27 October 2021. Available online: https://www.civicus.org/index.php/media-resources/news/interviews/5406-ghana-the-anti-gay-bill-will-have-far-reaching-consequences-if-we-do-not-fight-it-now.

Attoh, Kafui A. "What Kind of Right Is the Right to the City?" Progress in Human Geography 35, no. 5 (2011): 669–685.

Attorney General's Department. "Review of Australia's Female Genital Mutilation Legal Framework - Final Report," 2013.

Australian Human Rights Commission. Ensuring Health and Bodily Integrity: Towards a Human Rights Approach for People Born with Variations in Sex Characteristics. Sydney: Australian Human Rights Commission, 2021.

Autesserre, Séverine. "Dangerous tales: Dominant narratives on the Congo and their unintended consequences." African Affairs 111, no. 443 (2012): 202–222.

Ayoub, Philip. "Tensions in rights: navigating emerging contradictions in the LGBT rights revolution." In Contesting Human Rights: Norms, Institutions, and Practice, eds., Alison Brysk and Michael Stohl. Northampton: Edward Elgar Publishing, 2019.

Ayoub, P. and Paternotte, P. (2020). "Europe and LGBT Rights: A Conflicted Relationship." In Michael J. Bosia, Sandra M. McEvoy, and Momin Rahman, eds., *The Oxford Handbook of Global LGBT and Sexual Diversity* Politics. New York: Oxford University Press.

Baer, Madeline and Alison Brysk. "New Rights for Private Wrongs: Female Genital Mutilation and Global Framing Dialogues." In *The International Struggle for New Human Rights*, eds., Clifford Bob. Philadelphia: University of Pennsylvania Press, 2008.

Baraka, Ajamu. "'People-Centered' Human Rights as a Framework for Social Transformation." (10 December 2013 2013). Accessed 22 September 2021. https://www.ajamubaraka.com/peoplecentered-human-rights-as-a-framework-for-social-transformation.

Barber, Benjamin R. *If Mayors Ruled the World: Dysfunctional Nations, Rising Cities.* Yale University Press, 2013.

Barkataki, P. S. Kumar, and PS Rao. "Knowledge of and Attitudes to Leprosy among Patients and Community Members: A Comparative Study in Uttar Pradesh, India" *Leprosy Review* 77, no. 1 (2006): 62–68.

Barker, Gary, Manuel Contreras, Brian Heilman, Ajay Singh, Ravi Verma, Marcos Nascimento. "Evolving men: Initial results from the International Men and Gender Equality Survey." IMAGES International Center for Research on Women. Available at: http://www.icrw.org/publications/evolving-men.

Barnett, Michael, and Martha Finnemore. *Rules for the World: International Organizations in Global Politics.* Cornell University Press, 2004.

Bartolini, Stefano. "On Time and Comparative Research." *Journal of Theoretical Politics* 5, no. (1993): 131–167. https://doi.org/10.1177/0951692893005002001.

Batha, Emma. "Post-Soviet countries urged to fix laws that let rapists off hook." *Reuters,* 16 January 2019. Available online: https://www.reuters.com/article/us-europe-asia-law-women-idUSKCN1PB00Q (accessed 17 September 2021).

Bauer, Sydney. "Attacks on Trans Health Care Target Intersex People, Too." *Them,* 10 September 2021. Available online: https://www.them.us/story/trans-health-care-attacks-target-intersex-people-too (accessed 19 September 2021).

Baxi, Upendra. *The Future of Human Rights.* 3 ed. New Delhi: Oxford University Press, 2008.

Bennett, Andrew, and Colin Elman. "Society for Political Methodology Complex Causal Relations and Case Study Methods: The Example of Path Dependence." *Political Analysis* 14, no. 3 (2006): 250–267. https://doi.org/10.1093/pan/mpj020.

Betsill, Michele M., and Harriet Bulkeley. "Cities and the Multilevel Governance of Global Climate Change." *Global Governance* 12, (2006).

Bevan, Robert. *The Destruction of Memory: Architecture at War.* London: Reaktion Books, 2006.

Bhambra, Gurminder K. "Cosmopolitanism and Postcolonial Critique." Chap. 18 In *The Ashgate Research Companion to Cosmopolitanism*, eds., Maria Rovisco and Magdalena Nowicka, 313–28. Farnam, UK: Ashgate, 2011.

Blanc, Ann K. "The Effect of Power in Sexual Relationships on Sexual and Reproductive Health: An Examination of the Evidence." *Studies in Family Planning* 32, no. 3 (2001): 189–213. Available online: http://www.jstor.org/stable/2696304.

Bollyky, Thomas J., Lawrence O. Gostin, Margaret A. Hamburg. "The Equitable Distribution of COVID-19 Therapeutics and Vaccines," *JAMA* 323, no. 24 (2020): 2462–2463. doi:10.1001/jama.2020.6641.

Boonstra, Wiebren J. "Conceptualizing power to study social-ecological interactions." *Ecology and Society* 21, no. 1 (2016): 21

Bosia, M. J. (2015). "Strange Fruit: Homophobia, the State, and the Politics of LGBT Rights and Capabilities." *Journal of Human Rights* 13 (2014): 256–273.

Bosia, M. J. (2020). "Global Sexual Diversity Politics and the Trouble with LGBT Rights." In Michael J. Bosia, Sandra M. McEvoy, and Momin Rahman, eds., *The Oxford Handbook of Global LGBT and Sexual Diversity Politics*. New York: Oxford University Press.

Bosia, M. J. and Weiss, M. (2013), "Political Homophobia in Comparative Perspective." In Meredith Weiss and Michael J. Bosia, eds., *Global Homophobia: States, Movements, and the Politics of Oppression*. Urbana Champagne: University of Illinois Press.

Bouie, Jamelle. "If You Skip the Vaccine, It Is My 'Damn Business,' *The New York Times*, 14 August 2021, A18.

Brenner, Neil. "Global Cities, Glocal States: Global City Formation and State Territorial Restructuring in Contemporary Europe." *Review of International Political Economy* 5, no. 1 (1998): 1–37. https://doi.org/10.1080/096922998347633.

Brown, W. "Suffering the Paradoxes of Rights." In *Left Legalism / Left Critique* eds., W. Brown and J. Halley, 420–434. Durham: Duke University Press, 2002.

Brown, Wendy. "'The Most We Can Hope For . . .': Human Rights and the Politics of Fatalism." *The South Atlantic Quarterly* 103, no. 2 (2004): 451–63.

Brown, W. *Estados del agravio: poder y libertad en la modernidad tardía*. Madrid: Lengua de trapo, 2019.

Brunet, Laurence and Salle Muriel. "Categorizing and Attributing the Sex of Individuals: History of the Science, Law and Ethics." In *Gender Testing in Sport: Ethics, Cases and Controversies*, eds., Sandy Montañola and Aurélie Olivesi, 69–60. London; New York: Routledge, 2016.

Brysk, Alison. *Human Rights and Private Wrongs*. New York: Routledge Press, 2005.

Brysk, Alison. *Speaking Rights to Power: Constructing Political Will*. New York: Oxford University Press, 2013.

Brysk, Alison. *The Future of Human Rights*. Malden: Polity Press, 2018.

Brysk, Alison. *The Struggle for Freedom from Fear: Contesting Violence Against Women at the Frontiers of Globalization*. New York: Oxford University Press, 2018.

Brysk, Alison. "Changing hearts and minds: sexual politics and human rights." In *The Persistent Power of Human Rights: From Commitment to Compliance*, eds., Thomas Risse, Steve Ropp, and Kathryn Sikkink. Cambridge: Cambridge University Press, 2013.

Brysk, Alison. "Global Dynamics of Authoritarian Populism." University of California, *Santa Barbara Global* E-Journal, 18 February 2020. Available online: https://www.21global.ucsb. edu/global-e/february-2020/global-dynamics-authoritarian-populism.

Brysk, Alison. "Introduction: Contesting Human Rights-Pathways of Change." In *Contesting Human Rights: Norms, Institutions, and Practice*, eds., Alison Brysk and Michael Stohl. Northampton: Edward Elgar Publishing, 2019.

Brysk, Alison. "Making Rights Rhetoric Work: Constructing Care in a Post-Liberal World." In *The Changing Ethos of Human Rights*, eds., Alison Brysk, Hoda Mahmoudi, and Kate Seaman. Northampton: Edward Elgar Publishing, 2021.

Brysk, Alison and Aashish Mehta. "Do rights at home boost rights abroad? Sexual equality and humanitarian foreign policy." *Journal of Peace Research* 51, no. 1 (2014).

Brysk, Alison and Miguel Fuentes Carreño. "Why Feminism Is Good for Your Health." *New Security Beat*, August 2020. Available online: https://www.newsecuritybeat. org/2020/08/feminism-good-health/?utm_source=feedburner&utm_medium=email&utm_campaign=Feed%3A+TheNewSecurityBeat+%28New+Security+Beat%29.

Bunch, Charlotte. "Women's Rights Are Human Rights." *Human Rights Quarterly* 12, no. 4 (1990): 486–498.

Butler, Maria, Madeline Di Nonno, Natko Geres, Jok Madut Jok, Henry Myrttinen, and William Reno. "How Men Are Made: Cultures of Hyper Masculinities." Panel at the Men, Peace and Security Symposium, Washington, D.C., October 28, 2013.

Cabrera, Luis. "Review Article: World Government: Renewed Debate, Persistent Challenges." *European Journal of International Relations* 16, no. 3 (2010): 511–530. https://doi.org/10.1177/1354066109346888. https://journals.sagepub.com/doi/abs/10.1177/1354066109346888.

Cahill, Caitlin, Indra Rios-Moore, and Tiffany Threatts. "Different Eyes/Open Eyes: Community-Based Participatory Action Research." In *Revolutionizing Education : Youth Participatory Action Research in Motion*, eds., Julio Cammarota and Michelle FineNew York: Routledge, 2008.

Calder, Kent E., and Mariko de Freytas. "Global Political Cities as Actors in Twenty-First Century International Affairs." *SAIS Review of International Affairs* 29, no. 1 (2009): 79–96. https://doi.org/10.1353/sais.0.0036.

"Campaigns to Undermine Sexuality Education in the (US) Public Schools." American Civil Liberties Union, n.d. Available online: https://www.aclu.org/other/campaigns-undermine-sexuality-education-public-schools (accessed 17 September 2021).

Cantor, David. Report on the AAU Campus Climate Survey on Sexual Assault and Misconduct. Rockville: Westat, 2020.

Carnes, Nicholas and Noam Lupu. "The White Working Class and the 2016 Election," *Perspectives on Politics* 19, no.1 (2021): 55–72.

Carpenter, Morgan. "Intersex Human Rights, Sexual Orientation, Gender Identity, Sex Characteristics and the Yogyakarta Principles plus 10." *Culture, Health & Sexuality* 23 no. 4 (2021): 516–532.

Carpenter, Morgan. "Intersex Variations, Human Rights, and the International Classification of Diseases." *Health and Human Rights* 20, no. 2 (2018): 205–214.

Carpenter, Morgan. "The 'Normalisation' of Intersex Bodies and 'Othering' of Intersex Identities." In *The Legal Status of Intersex Persons*, eds., Jens M. Scherpe, Anatol Dutta, and Tobias Helms, 445–514. Cambridge: Intersentia, 2018.

Carrara, Sérgio. "Moralidades, racionalidades e políticas sexuais no Brasil contemporâneo." *MANA* 21, no. 2 (2015): 323–345.

Castán Broto, Vanesa, and Harriet Bulkeley. "A Survey of Urban Climate Change Experiments in 100 Cities." *Global Environmental Change* 23, no. 1 (2013): 92–102. https://doi.org/10.1016/j.gloenvcha.2012.07.005.

Chakrabarty, Dipesh. *Provincializing Europe: Postcolonial Thought and Historical Difference.* Princeton, NJ: Princeton University Press, 2000.

Chang, Wei, Lucía Díaz-Martin, Akshara Gopalan, Eleonora Guarnieri, Seema Jayachandran, Claire Walsh. "What works to enhance women's agency: Cross-cutting lessons from experimental and quasi-experimental studies." J-PAL Working Paper, 2020: 87. Available online: https://www.povertyactionlab.org/sites/default/files/research-paper/gender_womens-agency-review_2020-march-05.pdf (accessed 19 September 2021).

Chang, Wei. "Decision-Making Power for Women and Girls: Evaluating Interventions In Sexual And Reproductive Health In Sub-Saharan Africa." PhD diss., Gillings School of Global Public Health, University of North Carolina at Chapel Hill, 2020. Available online: http://search.proquest.com.ezp-prod1.hul.harvard.edu/dissertations-theses/decision-making-power-women-girls-evaluating/docview/2436898223/se-2?accountid=11311

Cheah, Pheng. *Inhuman Conditions*. Harvard University Press, 2009.

Christie, A., Brooks, J. T., Hicks, L. A., Sauber-Schatz, E. K., Yoder, J. S., Honein, M. A., and CDC COVID-19 Response Team (2021). Guidance for Implementing COVID-19 Prevention Strategies in the Context of Varying Community Transmission Levels and Vaccination Coverage. MMWR. Morbidity and mortality weekly report 70(30): 1044–1047. https://doi.org/10.15585/mmwr.mm7030e2.

Chua, Lynette J. "The Vernacular Mobilization of Human Rights in Myanmar's Sexual Orientation and Gender Identity Movement" *Law & Society Review* 49, no. 2 (2015): 299–332.

Coates, Ta-Nehisi. "The Case for Reparations." *The Atlantic*. May 14, 2021. https://www. theatlantic.com/magazine/archive/2014/06/the-case-for-reparations/361631/

COFEM. "Funding: Whose priorities?" In *Coalition of Feminists for Social Change, Feminist Perspectives on Addressing Violence Against Women and Girls Series*, Paper No. 4, 2017.

"COFEM Knowledge Summit: Meet the Facilitators." Coalition of Feminists for Social Change, n.d. Available online: https://cofemsocialchange.org/initiatives-events/ vawg-knowledge-summit/facilitator-profiles/ (accessed September 24, 2021).

COFEM Secretariat. "Engaging Men and Boys - Not at the Cost of Women and girls." Coalition of Feminists for Social Change, n.d. Available at: https://cofemsocialchange. org/engaging-men-and-boys-not-at-the-cost-of-women-and-girls/ (accessed September 29, 2021).

Colangelo, Jeremy. "The Myth That Gender Is Binary Is Perpetuated by a Flawed Education System." Quartz, 21 June 2017. Available online: https://qz.com/1007198/the-myth-that-gender-is-binary-is-perpetuated-by-a-flawed-education-system/ (accessed 18 June 2021).

Cole, David and Daniel Mach. "Vaccine Mandates Protect Freedom," *The New York Times*, 5 September, SR 5, 2021.

Colgrove, James. *State of Immunity: The Politics of Vaccination in Twentieth Century America*. Berkeley, CA: University of California Press, 2006.

Collins, Patricia Hill and Sirma Bilge. *Intersectionality*. Malden: Polity Press, 2016.

Comisión Nacional de los Derechos Humanos, 2019. *Informe Especial. Situación de las Estaciones Migratorias en México, hacia un Nuevo Modelo Alternativo a la Detención.* Ciudad de México.

Congregation for Catholic Education. "'Male and Female He Created Them' Towards a Path of Dialogue on the Question of Gender Theory in Education." 2019.

Consejo Ciudadano del Instituto Nacional de Migración. *Personas en detención migratoria en México. Misión de Monitoreo de Estaciones Migratorias y Estancias Provisionales del Instituto Nacional de Migración*. Cd. de México, 2017.

Cooke, Bill and Uma Kothari. *Participation: The New Tyranny?* New York: Zed Books, 2001.

Corrales, J. (2020). "The Expansion of LGBT Rights in Latin America and the Backlash." In Michael J. Bosia, Sandra M. McEvoy, and Momin Rahman, eds., *The Oxford Handbook of Global LGBT and Sexual Diversity Politics*. New York: Oxford University Press.

Council of Europe. "Text of the Istanbul Convention." n.d. Available online: https://www. coe.int/en/web/istanbul-convention/text-of-the-convention

Cowan, Benjamin A. *Securing sex: morality and repression in the making of the cold war in Brazil*. Chapel Hill: The University of North Carolina Press, 2016.

Crenshaw, Kimberlé. "Mapping the Margins: Intersectionality, Identity Politics, and Violence against Women of Color." *Stanford Law Review* 43, no. 6 (2019): 1241–1252.

Crenshaw, Kimberlé. "We Still Have Not Learned from Anita Hill's Testimony." *UCLA Women's Law Journal* 26 no. 1 (2019): 17–20.

Cruz, Alice. "Battling Exclusion: Giving a Voice to Women Affected by Leprosy" OpenGlobalRights. Available at: https://www.openglobalrights.org/battling-exclusion-giving-a-voice-to-women-affected-by-leprosy/, 2018.

Cruz, Alice. Factsheet of the Special Rapporteur on the Elimination of Discrimination against Persons Affected by Leprosy and Their Family Members, 2020. Available at: https://www.ohchr.org/Documents/Issues/Leprosy/Factsheet_ACruz2021.pdf

Daly, Michael, Andrew Jones, and Eric Robinson. "Public Trust and Willingness to Vaccinate Against COVID-19 in the US From October 14, 2020, to March 29, 2021," *JAMA* 325, no. 23 (2021): 2397–2399. doi:10.1001/jama.2021.8246.

Davis, Sophia. "Periods on Display." *The Lancet* 398, no. 10306 (2021): 1124–1125. Available online: https://doi.org/10.1016/s0140-6736(21)01962-0.

"Declaration on Women's Sex-Based Rights." Women's Human Rights Campaign, 2019. Available online: https://www.womensdeclaration.com/en/ (accessed September 24, 2020).

Dellatolla, A. (2020). "Sexuality as a Standard of Civilization: Historicizing (Homo) Colonial Intersections of Race, Gender, and Class." *International Studies Quarterly* 64 (1): 148–158.

Department of Health. "Newborn Bloodspot Screening Condition Assessment Summary Congenital Adrenal Hyperplasia (CAH)." 2020. Available online: https://www.health.gov.au/sites/default/files/documents/2020/02/newborn-bloodspot-screening-condition-assessment-summary-congenital-adrenal-hyperplasia_0.pdf (accessed 4 August 2021).

Destrooper, Tine. "Localization 'Light': The Travel and Transformation of Nonempowering Human Rights Norms." In *Human Rights Transformation in Practice*, eds., Tine Destrooper, and Sally Engle Merry. Philadelphia: University of Pennsylvania Press, 2018.

Dewhurst, Christopher J. and Ronald R. Gordon. *The Intersexual Disorders*. London: Baillière, Tindall & Cassell, 1969.

Douzinas, Costas. *Human Rights and Empire: The Political Philosophy of Cosmopolitanism*. New York: Routledge-Cavendish, 2007.

"Draconian abortion laws kill women and girls." Amnesty International, 18 August 2015. Available online: https://www.amnesty.org/en/latest/news/2015/08/draconian-abortion-laws-kill-women-and-girls-1/; (accessed 17 September 2021)

Dragić, Sanja. "On the Concept of the 'Human Rights Backlash.'" Paper presented at the Imagining the Human, Vienna, 2019.

Dreger, Alice. "Twenty Years of Working toward Intersex Rights." In *Bioethics in Action*, eds., Francois Baylis and Alice Dreger. Cambridge University Press, 2018.

Dreier, Sarah K., James D. Long, and Stephen J. Winkler. "African, Religious, and Tolerant? How Religious Diversity Shapes Attitudes Toward Sexual Minorities in Africa." *Politics and Religion* 13 no. 2 (2019): 273–303. Available online: https://doi.org/10.1017/S1755048319000348.

Duke University Center for Global Development. US Emergency Plan for Global COVID-19 Relief: Urgent Action to End the Pandemic Globally and Accelerate US Recovery and Security. Durham, NC: Duke University, 2021. Accessible via: https://healthpolicy.duke.edu/sites/default/files/2021-08/US%20Emergency%20COVID%20Plan_FINAL_For%20Distribution.pdf

Eade, John. *Living the Global City: Globalization as a Local Process*. Routledge, 1997.

Ebenso, Bassey, Aminat Fashona, Mainas Ayuba, Mike Idah Gbemiga Adeyemi, Shehu S-Fada. "Impact of Socio-Economic Rehabilitation on Leprosy Stigma in Northern Nigeria: Findings of a Retrospective Study" *Asia Pacific Disability Rehabilitation Journal* 18 no. 2 (2007): 98–119.

Eckert, Lena. *Intersexualization: The Clinic and the Colony*. New York: Routledge, 2017.

Escobar, Arturo. "Beyond the Third World: Imperial Globality, Global Coloniality and Anti-Globalisation Social Movements." *Third World Quarterly* 25, no. 1 (2004/02/01 2004): 207–230.

Fassin, D. "The biopolitics of otherness." *Anthropology Today*, 17, no. 1 (2001): 3–7.

Faye, Shon. *The Transgender Issue: An Argument for Justice*. London: Allen Lane, 2021.

Felice, William F. and Diana Fuguitt. *Human Rights and Public Goods: The Global New Deal*. Lanham, MD: Rowman & Littlefield, 3rd edition, 2021.

Ferguson, Yale H., and Richard W Mansbach. "Technology and the Transformation of Global Politics." Geopolitics 4, no. 3 (1999): 1–28.

Fernández de la Reguera, A. *Detención migratoria. Prácticas de humillación, asco y desprecio.* Ciudad de México: UNAM, 2020.

Finnemore, Martha. "Norms, Culture, and World Politics: Insights from Sociology's Institutionalism." *International Organization*, 325–47, 1996.

Forman, Lisa and Jillian Clare Kohler "Global health and human rights in the time of COVID-19: Response, restrictions, and legitimacy," *Journal of Human Rights* 19, no. 5 (2020): 547–556, DOI: 10.1080/14754835.2020.1818556

Françoise Baylis and Alice Dreger. *Bioethics in Action*. Cambridge: Cambridge University Press, 2018.

Fricker, Miranda. *Epistemic Injustice: Power and the Ethics of Knowing*. Oxford: Oxford University Press, 2007.

Galea S, Abdalla SM. "COVID-19 Pandemic, Unemployment, and Civil Unrest: Underlying Deep Racial and Socioeconomic Divides," *JAMA* 324, no. 3 (2020): 227–228. doi:10.1001/jama.2020.11132.

Gander, Kashmira. "Academic Says Trans Women Are Parasites for 'Occupying the Bodies of the Oppressed.'" Newsweek, 18 March 2018. Available online: https://www.newsweek.com/trans-women-are-parasites-occupying-bodies-oppressed-says-academic-846563.

Gandini, L., Fernández de la Reguera, A., and Narváez Gutiérrez, J. C. *Caravanas*. Ciudad de México: SDI, IIJ, UNAM, 2020.

García Chueca, Eva. "Human Rights in the City and the Right to the City." In *Global Urban Justice: The Rise of Human Rights Cities*, eds., Barbara Oomen, Martha F Davis and Michele Grigolo, 103–120. Cambridge: Cambridge University Press, 2016.

Gaventa, John. "Linking the prepositions: using power analysis to inform strategies for social action." *Journal of Political Power* 14, no. 1 (2021): 109–130.

Gavrielides, Theo. "Bringing Race Relations Into the Restorative Justice Debate." *Journal of Black Studies* 45, no. 3 (2014): 216–246. doi:10.1177/0021934714526042.

Geisinger, Alex and Michael Ashley Stein. "A Theory of Expressive International Law" *Vanderbilt Law Review* 60 (2007): 77–131.

"Gender-Based Violence Prevention and Response." U.S. Agency for International Development, last modified September 7, 2021. Available online: https://www.usaid.gov/what-we-do/gender-equality-and-womens-empowerment/reducing-gender-based-violence.

Gest, Justin, Tyler Reny, and Jeremy Mayer. "Roots of the Radical Right: Nostalgic Deprivation in the United States and Britain," *Comparative Political Studies* 51, no. 3 (2018): 1694–1719.

Global Detention Project. *Immigration Detention in Mexico: Between the United States and Central America. Global Detention Project Country Profile*, 2021.

Goffman, E. *Internados*. Buenos Aires: Amorrortu editores, 2001.

González, Eduardo, and Kelebogile Zvobgo. "As America Seeks Racial Justice, It Can Learn From Abroad." Foreign Policy. March 14, 2021. https://foreignpolicy.com/2021/03/14/racial-justice-truth-reconciliation-commissions-international/

Goodale, Mark, and Sally Engle Merry, eds. *The Practice of Human Rights: Tracking Law Between the Global and the Local*. New York: Cambridge University Press, 2007.

Goodhart, Michael. "Revisiting interdependence in times and terms of crisis," *Journal of Human Rights* 19, no. 5 (2020): 520–527, DOI: 10.1080/14754835.2020.1814709.

Goodhart, Michael. "Human Rights Cities: Making the Global Local." Chap. 8 In *Contesting Human Rights: Norms, Institutions and Practice*, eds., Alison Brysk and Michael Stohl, 142–158. Cheltenham, UK: Edward Elgar Publishing, 2019.

Goodhart, Michael. "How Do Human Rights Matter?". Chap. 2 In *Why Human Rights Still Matter in Contemporary Global Affairs*, eds., Mahmood Monshipouri, 27–42. New York: Routledge, 2020.

Greenwood, Davydd J. and Morten Levin. *Introduction to Action Research: Social Research for Social Change*. Thousand Oaks, CA: Sage Publications, 2007.

Grigolo, Michele. "Towards a Sociology of the Human Rights City." In *Global Urban Justice: The Rise of Human Rights Cities*, eds., Barbara Oomen, Martha F Davis and Michele Grigolo, 276–293. Cambridge: Cambridge University Press, 2016.

Grzebalska, Wronica and Andrea Peto. "The gendered modus operandi of the illiberal transformation in Hungary and Poland." *Women's Studies International Forum* 68, (2018):164–172.

Gupte, Manish. "Women's experiences with family planning." *Health Millions* 2, no. 3 (1994):33–6.

Haglund, LaDawn and Rimjhim Aggarwal. "Test of Our Progress: The Translation of Economic and Social Rights Norms Into Practice," *Journal of Human Rights* 10, no. 4 (2011):494–520, DOI: 10.1080/14754835.2011.619409.

Haglund, LaDawn. "Human Rights Pathways to Just Sustainabilities," *Sustainability* 11, no. 12 (2019): 3255. https://doi.org/10.3390/su11123255

Haglund, LaDawn and Robin Stryker. *Closing the Rights Gap: From Human Rights to Social Transformation*. Berkeley, CA: University of California Press, 2015.

Hall, Peter A., and Rosemary C. R. Taylor, 1996. "Political Science and the Three New Institutionalisms." *Political Studies* 44, no. 5 (1996): 936–957.

Hamilton, Blair R., Giscard Lima, James Barrett, Leighton Seal, Alexander Kolliari-Turner, Guan Wang, Antonia Karanikolou, Xavier Bigard, Herbert Löllgen, Petra Zupet, Anca Ionescu, Andre Debruyne, Nigel Jones, Karin Vonbank, Federica Fagnani, Chiara Fossati, Maurizio Casasco, Demitri Constantinou, Bernd Wolfarth, David Niederseer, Andrew Bosch, Borja Muniz-Pardos, José Antonio Casajus, Christian Schneider, Sigmund Loland, Michele Verroken, Pedro Han, Wen-Jui and Jake Hart. "Job precarity and economic prospects during the COVID-19 health crisis," *Social Science Quarterly* (2021), available via: https://onlinelibrary.wiley.com/doi/full/10.1111/ssqu.13031.

Harvey, David. "The Right to the City." *The City Reader* 6 (2008): 23–40.

Harvey, David. *Rebel cities: from the right to the city to the urban revolution*. London: Verso, 2013.

Heikkinen, Milja, Aasa Karimo, Johannes Klein, Sirkku Juhola, and Tuomas Ylä-Anttila. "Transnational Municipal Networks and Climate Change Adaptation: A Study of 377 Cities." *Journal of Cleaner Production* 257, (2020), https://doi.org/10.1016/j.jclepro.2020.120474.

Herdt, Gilbert H. and Robert J. Stoller. "Sakulambei - A Hermaphrodite's Secret: An Example of Clinical Ethnography." In *The Psychoanalytic Study of Society* Volume 11, eds., L. B. Boyer and W. Muensterberger, 115–156. Hillsdale: Analytic Press, 1985.

Hertel, Shareen. "Mobilizing empathy for a truly cosmopolitan human rights," *Open Global Rights*, 30 September 2020. Available via https://www.openglobalrights.org/do-sub-state-actors-complicate-how-we-think-of-cosmopolitanism/.

Hertel, Shareen. "A New Route to Norms Evolution: Insights from India's Right to Food Campaign." Social Movement Studies 15, no. 6 (2016): 610–621.

Hertel, Shareen and Lance Minkler. *Economic Rights: Conceptual, Measurement, and Policy Issues*. New York: Cambridge University Press, 2007.

Higginbotham, Evelyn. "The Politics of Respectability." In *Righteous Discontent: The Women's Movement in the Black Baptist Church, 1880–1920*, 185–229. Cambridge: Harvard University Press, 1993.

Holmes, Morgan. "Locating Third Sexes." *Transformations, Regions of Sexuality*, no. 8 (2004).

Hondagneu-Sotelo. *Gendering Migration: Not for "feminists only"-and not only in the household* (No. CDM Working Paper #05-02f), 2005.

Hoover, Joe. "The Human Right to Housing and Community Empowerment: Home Occupation, Eviction Defence and Community Land Trusts." *Third World Quarterly* 36, no. 6 (2015/06/03 2015): 1092–109. https://doi.org/10.1080/01436597.2015.1047196. http://dx.doi.org/10.1080/01436597.2015.1047196.

Hopgood, Stephen. *The Endtimes of Human Rights Ithaca*, NY: Cornell University Press, 2013.

Horton, Richard. "A statement from Richard Horton, Editor-in-Chief, The Lancet." *The Lancet*, n.d. Available online: https://www.thelancet.com/25sept-cover-statement (accessed 29 September 2021).

Hossain, A. (2017). "The Paradox of Recognition: *Hijra,* Third Gender and Sexual Rights in Bangladesh." *Culture, Health and Sexuality*, 19 (12: 1418–1431).

Hossain, A. (2019). "Section 377, Same-Sex Sexualities and the Struggle for Sexual Rights in Bangladesh." *Australian Journal of Asian Law*, 20 (1): 1–11.

Hossain, A. (2021). *Beyond Emasculation: Pleasure and Power in the Making of Hijra in Bangladesh*. Cambridge: Cambridge University Press.

Houk, Christopher P., Ieuan A. Hughes, S. Faisal Ahmed, Peter A. Lee. "Summary of Consensus Statement on Intersex Disorders and Their Management." *Pediatrics* 118, no. 2 (2006): 755.

Howard, Brian. "AD362: Africans Tolerant on Ethnic, Religious, National, but Not Sexual Differences." *AfroBarometer*, 19 May 2020, https://doi.org/10.1057/s41290-017-0036-8.

Hudson, Valerie, Donna Lee Bowen, and Perpetua Lynne Nielsen. *The First Political Order: How Sex Shapes Governance and National Security Worldwide*. New York: Columbia University Press, 2020.

Hudson, Valerie. *The Hillary Doctrine: Sex and American Foreign Policy*. New York: Columbia University Press, 2015.

Human Rights Watch 2020. https://www.hrw.org/news/2020/05/18/global-report-card-lgbtq-rights-idahobit

Ibhawoh, Bonny. *Imperialism and Human Rights: Colonial Discourses of Rights and Liberties in African History*. SUNY Press, 2008.

IDEA, The International Association for Integration, Dignity, and Economic Advancement, IDEA. 2008. "Report on Stigma and Discrimination Facing People Challenged by Leprosy: A Compilation of Submissions from IDEA Members from Sixteen IDEA Branches" On File with the Authors.

ILGA (2020). *State-Sponsored Homophobia: Global Legislation and Overview Update.* https://ilga.org/state-sponsored-homophobia-report-2020-global-legislation-overview.

Institutions and Civil Society Shape the Modern State. Cambridge: Cambridge University Press. doi:10.1017/9781108672337.

International, Amnesty. "La nueva Guardia Nacional de México está rompiendo su juramento de respetar los derechos humanos." *Noticias*, 2020, November.

International Labour Organization/ILO June 2020. Research Brief: The Effects of COVID-19 on trade and global supply chains. Geneva: ILO. Available via https://www.ilo.org/wcmsp5/groups/public/---dgreports/---inst/documents/publication/wcms_746917.pdf

International Leprosy Association. n.d. History of Leprosy. Available at: https://leprosyhistory.org/about.

"I Want to Be like Nature Made Me." Human Rights Watch, July 25, 2017. Available online: https://www.hrw.org/report/2017/07/25/i-want-be-nature-made-me/medically-unnecessary-surgeries-intersex-children-us.

Jain, Mahima. "The 'shadow pandemic' of domestic violence." *BMJ*, 374, no. 2166 (2021).

Jeffreys, Sheila. *Gender Hurts: A Feminist Analysis of the Politics of Transgenderism.* London: Routledge, Taylor & Francis Group, 2014.

Jeffreys, Sheila. "Transgender Activism: A Lesbian Perspective." *Journal of Lesbian Studies* 1, no. 3–4 (1997): 55–74.

Jewkes, Rachel, Michael Flood, and James Lang. "From work with menand boys to changes of social norms and reduction ofinequities in gender relations: a conceptual shift inprevention of violence against women and girls." *The Lancet* 385 no. 9977 (2015):1580–1589.

John, Tara. "Analysis: Anti-Trans Rhetoric Is Rife in the British Media. Little Is Being Done to Extinguish the Flames." CNN, 9 October 2021. Available online: https://www.cnn.com/2021/10/09/uk/uk-trans-rights-gender-critical-media-intl-gbr-cmd/index.html (accessed 10 October 2021).

Johnson, Kirsten, Jennifer Scott, Bigy Rughita, Michael Kisielewski, Jana Asher, Ricardo Ong, Lynn Lawry. "Association of Sexual Violence and Human Rights Violations With Physical and Mental Health in Territories of the Eastern Democratic Republic of the Congo." *JAMA* 304, no. 5 (2010): 553–562.

Jones, Tiffany, Bonnie Hart, Morgan Carpenter, Gavi Ansara, William Leonard, and Jayne Lucke. *Intersex: Stories and Statistics from Australia.* Cambridge: Open Book Publishers, 2016.

JoyNews. "Group of 18 Lawyers and Academic Mount Spirited Attack against Anti-LGBTQ Bill- (4-10-21)." 4 October 2021, video, 10:37. Available online: https://www.youtube.com/watch?v=TK19g3UCGc8.

Kafkadesk Budapest Office. "Hungarian Parliament speaker's homophobic comments spark outrage." Kafadesk, 19 May 2019. Available online: https://kafkadesk.org/2019/05/19/hungarian-parliament-speakers-homophobic-comments-spark-outrage/ (accessed 17 September 2021).

Kaiser Family Foundation 2021. KFF COVID-19 Vaccine Monitor: September 2021. Available via: https://www.kff.org/coronavirus-covid-19/poll-finding/kff-covid-19-vaccine-monitor-september-2021/

Kant, Immanuel. *Kant's Political Writings.* Translated by H.B. Nisbet. Eds., Hans Reiss. Cambridge: Cambridge University Press, 1970.

Kapur, Ratna. "The Tragedy of Victimization Rhetoric: Resurrecting the Native Subject in International/Postcolonial Feminist Legal Politics." *Harvard Human Rights Law Journal*, 15, no. 1 (2002): 1–38.

Karkazis, Katrina and Morgan Carpenter. "Impossible 'Choices': The Inherent Harms of Regulating Women's Testosterone in Sport." *Journal of Bioethical Inquiry* 15, no. 4 (2018): 579–587.

Karkazis, Katrina and Rebecca M. Jordan-Young. "The Powers of Testosterone: Obscuring Race and Regional Bias in the Regulation of Women Athletes", *Feminist Formations* 30, no. 2 (2018): 1–39.

Kennedy, D. *Abuso sexual y vestimenta sexy*. Ciudad de México: Siglo XXI, 2016.

Kirk, Edwin P., Royston Ong, Kirsten Boggs, Tristan Hardy, Sarah Righetti, Ben Kamien, Tony Roscioli, David J. Amor, Madhura Bakshi, Clara W. T. Chung, Alison Colley, Robyn V. Jamieson, Jan Liebelt, Alan Ma, Nicholas Pachter, Sulekha Rajagopalan, Anja Ravine, Meredith Wilson, Jade Caruana, Rachael Casella, Mark Davis, Samantha Edwards, Alison Archibald, Julie McGaughran, Ainsley J. Newson, Nigel G. Laing and Martin B. Delatycki. "Gene Selection for the Australian Reproductive Genetic Carrier Screening Project ('Mackenzie's Mission')." *European Journal of Human Genetics* 29, (2021): 79–87.

Konczal, Mike. *Freedom from the Market: America's Fight to Liberate Itself from the Grip of the Invisible Hand*. New York: New Press, 2021.

Korolczuk, Elżbieta and Agnieszka Graff. "Gender as 'Ebola from Brussels': The Anticolonial Frame and the Rise of Illiberal Populism." *Signs* 43 no. 4 (2018): 797–821.

Krasner, Stephen D, "Review: Approaches to the State: Alternative Conceptions and Historical Dynamics." *Comparative Politics* 16, no. 2 (1984).

Kubik, J. Ethnography of Politics: Foundations, Applications, and Prospects. In E. Schatz (Ed.), *Political Ethnography What Immersion Contributes to the Study of Power*. Chigago: The University of Chicago Press, 2009.

Lal, Shaneel. "It is time for New Zealand to end gay conversion practices." The Guardian, 5 September 2021. Available online: https://www.theguardian.com/world/commentisfree/2021/sep/06/it-is-time-for-new-zealand-to-end-gay-conversion-practices (accessed 17 September 2021).

Lamas, M. *Dolor y Política. Sentir, pensay y hablar desde el feminismo*. Ciudad de México: Oceano, 2021.

Lauer, Claudia and Meghan Hoyer. "Almost 1,700 priests and clergy accused of sex abuse are unsupervised." Associated Press, 4 October 2019. Available online: https://www.nbcnews.com/news/religion/nearly-1-700-priests-clergy-accused-sex-abuse-are-unsupervised-n1062396 (accessed 17 September 2021).

Law, Anwei Skinsnes. *Kalaupapa: A Collective Memory*. Honolulu: University of Hawai'i Press, 2012.

Lee, Peter A., Anna Nordenström, Christopher P. Houk, S. Faisal Ahmed, Richard Auchus, Arlene Baratz, Katharine Baratz Dalke, Lih-Mei Liao, Karen Lin-Su, Leendert H. J. Looijenga 3rd, Tom Mazur, Heino F. L. Meyer-Bahlburg, Pierre Mouriquand, Charmian A Quigley, David E. Sandberg, Eric Vilain, Selma Witchel, Global DSD Update Consortium. "Global Disorders of Sex Development Update since 2006: Perceptions, Approach and Care." *Hormone Research in Paediatrics* 85, no. 3 (2016): 170.

Lee, Taedong. "Global Cities and Transnational Climate Change Networks." *Global Environmental Politics* 13, no. 1 (2013): 108–127. https://doi.org/10.1162/GLEP_a_00156.

Lefebvre, Henry. *Writings on Cities*. Edited and Translated by Eleonore Kofman and Elizabeth Lebas, Oxford: Blackwell, 1996.

Libal, Kathryn and Prakash Kashwan. "Solidarity in times of crisis," *Journal of Human Rights* 19, no. 5 (2020): 537–546, DOI: 10.1080/14754835.2020.1830046.

Li Bassi, Luca. 2021. "Allocating COVID-19 Vaccines Globally: An Urgent Need. *JAMA Health Forum* 2 no. 2 (2021): e210105. doi:10.1001/jamahealthforum.2021.0105.

Lukes, Steven. *Power: A Radical View.* New York: NYU Press, 1974.

Lundstrum, Robin. *To Create the Arkansas Save Adolescents from Experimentation (SAFE) Act.* 2021.

Macías Delgadillo, A., Hernández Méndez, A., Carreño Nigenda, C., Martínez Medrano, D., Castro Lobato, M., Oehler Toca, M., and Cano Padilla, S. *La Ruta del Encierro. Situación de las personas en detención en estaciones migratorias y estancias provisionales.* Ciudad de México: Sin Fronteras, 2013.

Mandavilli, Apoorva. "A U.N. Declaration on Ending AIDS Should Have Been Easy. It Wasn't." *The New York Times*, 8 June 2021. Available online: https://www.nytimes.com/2021/06/08/health/unaids-declaration-patents.html; (accessed 22 August 2021).

Manonelles Marqueta, Francisco Arroyo, André Pedrinelli, Konstantinos Natsis, Evert Verhagen, William O. Roberts, José Kawazoe Lazzoli, Rogerio Friedman, Ali Erdogan, Ana V. Cintron, Shu-Hang Patrick Yung, Dina C. Janse van Rensburg, Dimakatso A. Ramagole, Sandra Rozenstoka, Felix Drummond, Theodora Papadopoulou, Paulette Y. O. Kumi, Richard Twycross-Lewis, Joanna Harper, Vasileios Skiadas, Jonathan Shurlock, Kumpei Tanisawa, Jane Seto, Kathryn North, Siddhartha S. Angadi, Maria Jose Martinez-Patiño, Mats Borjesson, Luigi Di Luigi, Michiko Dohi, Jeroen Swart, James Lee John Bilzon, Victoriya Badtieva, Irina Zelenkova, Juergen M. Steinacker, Norbert Bachl, Fabio Pigozzi, Michael Geistlinger, Dimitrios G. Goulis, Fergus Guppy, Nick Webborn, Bulent O. Yildiz, Mike Miller, Patrick Singleton and Yannis P. Pitsiladis. "Integrating Transwomen and Female Athletes with Differences of Sex Development (DSD) into Elite Competition: The FIMS 2021 Consensus Statement." *Sports Medicine* 51, (2021): 1401–1415.

Marcuse, Peter. "Rights in Cities and the Right to the City?". In *Cities for All: Proposals and Experiences Towards the Right to the City*, eds., Ana Sugranyes and Charlotte Mathivet, 87–98. Santiago, Chile: Habitat International Coalition, 2010.

Mathivet, Charlotte. "The Right to the City: Keys to Understanding the Proposal for 'Another City Is Possible'." In *Cities for All: Proposals and Experiences Towards the Right to the City*, eds., Ana Sugranyes and Charlotte Mathivet, 21–26. Santiago, Chile: Habitat International Coalition, 2010.

Maya Restrepo, L. A. "Racismo institucional, violencia y políticas culturales. Legados coloniales y políticas de diferencia en Colombia." *Historia Crítica Edición Especial*, (2009): 218–245,

Meyer, John W, and Brian Rowan. 1977. "Institutionalized Organizations: Formal Structure as Myth and Ceremony." *American Journal of Sociology* 83, no. 2 (1977): 340–363.

Meyer, John W, John Boli, George M Thomas, and Francisco O Ramirez. "World Society and the Nation-State." *American Journal of Sociology* 103, no. 1 (1997): 144–81. https://doi.org/10.1086/231174.

Milne, E-J, et al. *Handbook of Participatory Video.* AltaMira Press, 2012.

Minca, C. "Geographies of the camp." *Political Geography*, 49, (2015):74–83.

Moghadam, Valentine and Gizem Kaftan. "Right-wing populisms north and south: Varieties and gender dynamics." *Women's Studies International Forum* 75 (2019): 102244.

Moon, Suerie. "Power in global governance: an expanded typology from global health." *Global Health* 15, no. 74 (2019).

Morefield, Jeanne. "Trump's Foreign Policy Isn't the Problem." *The Boston Review*, 8 January 2019. https://bostonreview.net/war-security/jeanne-morefield-trump%e2%80%99s-foreign-policy-isn%e2%80%99t-problem.

Moyn, Samuel. *Not Enough: Human Rights in an Unequal World.* Cambridge, MA: Harvard University Press, 2018.

Munhazim, A. Q. (2020). "LGBT Politics in South Asia: Ground Rules, Underground Movements." Chp. 15 in Bosia, M., McEvoy, S. and Rahman, M. (eds), *The Oxford Handbook of Global LGBT and Sexual Diversity Politics.* New York: Oxford University Press.

Murdie, Amanda, Baekkwan Park, Jacqueline Hart, and Margo Mullinax. "Building momentum: changes in advocacy discourse around early child marriage, 2011–2017." In *Contesting Human Rights: Norms, Institutions, and Practice*, eds., Alison Brysk and Michael Stohl. Northampton: Edward Elgar Publishing, 2019.

Mutua, Makau. *Human Rights: A Political and Cultural Critique.* University of Pennsylvania Press, 2002.

Nabeel, G. (2020). "Rainbow Flags over Baghdad fan debate, spur fear", https://www.al-monitor.com/originals/2020/05/iraq-lgbt-culture-justice.html.

Nagar, Richa. *Muddying the Waters: Coauthoring Feminisms across Scholarship and Activism.* Urbana: University of Illinois Press, 2015.

Neocosmos, Michael. "Can a Human Rights Culture Enable Emancipation? Clearing Some Theoretical Ground for the Renewal of a Critical Sociology." *South African Review of Sociology* 37, no. 2 (2006): 356–79.

Nevens, Frank, Niki Frantzeskaki, Leen Gorissen, and Derk Loorbach. "Urban Transition Labs: Co-Creating Transformative Action for Sustainable Cities." *Journal of Cleaner Production* 50, (2013): 111–22. https://doi.org/10.1016/j.jclepro.2012.12.001.

Newman, Peter. "Global City Planning." In *Future of Sustainable Cities: Critical Reflections*, eds., J. Flint and M. Raco, 2011.

Nijman, Janne. "The Future of the City and the International Law of the Future." In *Law of the Future and the Future of the Law*, Torkel Opsahl Academic, 2011.

Nijman, Janne. "Renaissance of the City as Global Actor: The Role of Foreign Policy and International Law Practices in the Construction of Cities as Global Actors." In *The Transformation of Foreign Policy: Drawing and Managing Boundaries from Antiquity to the Present*, Oxford University Press, 2016.

Niño-Zarazúa, Miguel, Laurence Roope, and Finn Tarp. "Global Inequality: Relatively Lower, Absolutely Higher," *The Review of Income and Wealth*, Special Issue 63, 4 (2017): 661–648.

Nyamu-Musembi, Celestine and Andrea Conrwall. "What is the human rights-based approach all about?: perspectives from international development agencies." Institute of Development Studies, 2004. Available online: https://opendocs.ids.ac.uk/opendocs/handle/20.500.12413/4073

Nyayieka, Ivy, Christina Macfarlane and Jo Shelley. "Running as Equals the Elite Athletes Fighting for Acceptance", CNN, 2021. Available online: https://www.cnn.com/interactive/2021/07/sport/athletics-testosterone-rules-negesa-imali-running-as-equals-dsd-spt-intl-cmd/ (accessed 10 October 2021).

Office of the High Commissioner for Human Rights. "End Violence and Harmful Medical Practices on Intersex Children and Adults, UN and Regional Experts Urge." United Nations. 2016. Available online: http://www.ohchr.org/EN/NewsEvents/Pages/DisplayNews.aspx?NewsID=20739&LangID=E (accessed 24 October 2016).

Office of the High Commissioner for Human Rights. "Background Note on Human Rights Violations against Intersex People." United Nations. 2019. Available online: https://www.ohchr.org/EN/Issues/Discrimination/Pages/BackgroundViolationsIntersexPeople.aspx (accessed 25 October 2019).

Office of the High Commissioner for Human Rights. "Draft Bill on 'Proper Sexual Rights and Ghanaian Family Values Bill 2021'—An Analysis by UN Independent Human Rights Experts | United Nations in Ghana." United Nations, 9 August 2021. Available online: https://ghana.un.org/en/139914-draft-bill-proper-sexual-rights-and-ghanaian-family-values-bill-2021-analysis-un-independent; https://ghana.un.org/en/139914-draft-bill-proper-sexual-rights-and-ghanaian-family-values-bill-2021-analysis-un-independent.

Ortner, S. B. Is Female to Male as Nature is to Culture. In *Women, Culture and Society*, M. Z. Rosaldo and L. Lamphere, eds., 67–87. Stanford, 1974.

Pagden, Anthony. "Human Rights, Natural Rights, and Europe's Imperial Legacy." *Political Theory* 31, no. 2 (April 2003): 171–199.

Page, Scott E. "Path Dependence." *Quarterly Journal of Political Science* 1 (2005): 87–115.

Paine, Thomas. *The Rights of Man.* online: University of Groningen, 1791/2. http://www.let.rug.nl/usa/documents/1786-1800/thomas-paine-the-rights-of-man/text.php.

Paiva, Vera, Marcos R. V. Garcia, Ivan França-Jr, Cristiane Gonçalves da Silva, L. G. Galeão-Silva, Júlio Assis Simões, José Ricardo Ayres, Research Group on Youth's Health and Human Rights. "Youth and the COVID-19 crisis: lessons learned from a human rights-based prevention program for youths in São Paulo, Brazil." *Global Public Health. An International Journal for Research, Policy and Practice* 16, no. 8–9 (2021): 1454–1467.

Paiva, Vera and Valeria N. Silva. "Facing negative reactions to sexuality education through a Multicultural Human Rights framework." *Reproductive Health Matters* 23, no. 46 (2015): 96–106, 20.

Pakistan, Transgender Persons (Protection of Rights) Act, 2018.

Patel, Bhvishya. "Now the Lancet CANCELS women: Fury as leading medical journal runs 'dehumanising' and 'sexist' front-page describing females as 'bodies with vaginas' to placate trans lobby." *Daily Mail*, 26 September 2021. Available online: https://www.dailymail.co.uk/news/article-10029817/Fury-leading-medical-journal-describes-women-bodies-vaginas.html.

Paternotte, David and Roman Kuhar. "Disentangling and Locating the 'Global Right': Anti-Gender Campaigns in Europe." *Politics and Governance* 6, no. 3 (2018): 6–19.

Peacock, Dean, Lara Stemple, Sharif Sawires, and Thomas J. Coates. "Men, HIV/AIDS, and Human Rights." *Journal of Acquired Immune Deficiency Syndromes*, S119–S125, 51 no. 3 (2009): 1–12.

Peck, Jamie. *Austerity Urbanism: The Neoliberal Crisis of American Cities.* New York: Rosa Luxemburg Stiftung, May 2015.

Peterson, P.E. *City Limits.* University of Chicago Press, 1981.

Pew Research Center (2013). "The Global Divide on Homosexuality: Greater Acceptance in More Secular and Affluent Countries." June 4, 2013. http://www.pewglobal.org/2013/06/04/the-global-divide-on-homosexuality/.

Phillips, Susan, Lynell George, Alex Walsh, Marissa López, William Deverell, Sahra Sulaiman, Richard White, John Rechy, Alex Ross, Eugene W. Moy, D.J. Waldie, Janna Ireland, Guadalupe Rosales, Catherine Gudis, Edward Cella, Sam Sweet, Christopher Hawthorne, Tyree Boyd-Pates, and Mike Davis. *Civic Memory Working Group.* http://civicmemory.la/.

Pierson, Paul. *Politics in Time.* Princeton University Press, 2004.

Piketty, Thomas. *Capital in the 21st Century.* Translated by Arthur Goldhammer. Cambridge, MA: Harvard University Press, 2013.

Pitch, T. *Un derecho para dos.* Madrid: Editorial Trotta, 2003.

Porras, Ileana M. "The City and International Law: In Pursuit of Sustainable Development." *Fordham Urban Law Journal* 36, no. 3 (2008): 537–601. https://doi.org/10.1525/sp.2007.54.1.23.

Posner, Eric. *The Twilight of International Human Rights Law*. New York: Oxford University Press, 2014.

Posthumus, Daniel, and Kelebogile Zvobgo. "Democratizing Truth: An Analysis of Truth Commissions in the United States." *International Journal of Transitional Justice*, October 20, 2021. doi:10.1093/ijtj/ijab029.

Prempeh, Matthew Opoku. "Promotion of Proper Human Sexual Rights and Ghanaian Family Values Bill, 2021." Available online: https://cdn.modernghana.com/files/722202192224-0h830n4ayt-lgbt-bill.pdf.

The President's Advisory 1776 Commission. *The 1776 Report*. The National Archives (online: 2021). https://trumpwhitehouse.archives.gov/wp-content/uploads/2021/01/The-Presidents-Advisory-1776-Commission-Final-Report.pdf.

Quarcoo, Ashley, and Medina Husaković. "Racial Reckoning in the United States: Expanding and Innovating on the Global Transitional Justice Experience." Carnegie Endowment for International Peace. October 26, 2021. https://carnegieendowment.org/2021/10/26/racial-reckoning-in-united-states-expanding-and-innovating-on-global-transitional-justice-experience-pub-85638.

Rahman. M. (2014). *Homosexualities, Muslim Cultures and Modernity*. Basingstoke, UK: Palgrave Macmillan.

Rahman, M. (2020). "Queer Muslim Challenges to the Internationalization of LGBT Rights: Decolonizing International Relations Methodology Through Intersectionality." Chp. 27 in Bosia, M., McEvoy, S. and Rahman, M., eds., *The Oxford Handbook of Global LGBT and Sexual Diversity Politics*. New York: Oxford University Press.

Ramadan, A. Spatialising the refugee camp. *Transactions of the Institute of British Geographers*, 38, (2013) 65–77.

Rancière, Jacques. "Who Is the Subject of the Rights of Man?". *South Atlantic Quarterly* 103, no. 2/3 (2004): 297–310.

Raymond, Janice (n.d.). "Fictions and Facts about the Transsexual Empire." Available online: https://janiceraymond.com/fictions-and-facts-about-the-transsexual-empire/ (accessed 14 October 2021).

Reality Check Team. "African Diaspora: Did Ghana's Year of Return Attract Foreign Visitors?" BBC News, 30 January 2020. Available online: https://www.bbc.com/news/world-africa-51191409.

Reich, Robert. *Saving Capitalism: For the Many, Not the Few*. New York: Penguin, 2015.

Reis, Elizabeth. "Impossible Hermaphrodites: Intersex in America, 1620–1960." *The Journal of American History* 95, no. 2 (2005): 411–441.

Risse, T., S. C. Ropp and K. Sikkink. Eds. *The Power of Human Rights: International Norms and Domestic Change*. Cambridge: Cambridge University Press, 1999.

Rixen, Thomas, Lora Anne Viola, and Michael Zürn. *Historical Institutionalism and International Relations*. Oxford University Press, 2016, https://doi.org/10.1093/acprof.

Robin, Corey, "Check Your Amnesia, Dude: On the Vox Generation of Punditry," *Crooked Timber*, 21 July 2016, https://crookedtimber.org/2016/07/21/check-your-amnesia-dude-on-the-vox-generation-of-punditry/.

Rubin, Gayle. "Thinking sex: notes for a radical theory of the politics of sexuality." In *Deviations: A Gayle Rubin Reader*, 137–181. London: Duke University Press, 2011. First published in Vance, Carole. Pleasure and Danger: exploring female sexuality. Boston: Routledge, 1984.

Sabo, Don, Terry A. Kupers, and Willie London, editors. *Prison Masculinities*. Philadelphia: Temple University Press, 2001.

Salazar Ugarte, P., Caballero Ochoa, J. L., and Vázquez, L. D. *La Reforma Constitucional sobre Derechos Humanos. Una guía conceptual.* Ciudad de México: Instituto Belisario Domínguez, Senado de la República, 2014.

Sampson, Lyneette. "Critical Pedagogy Through Participatory Video: Possibilities for Post-Colonial Higher Education in the Caribbean" In *Democracy 2.0: Media, Political Literacy and Critical Engagement.* eds., Paul R. Carr, Michael Hoechsmann, and Gina Thésée. London: Brill, 2018.

Santoro, Michael and Robert Shanklin. "Human rights obligations of drug companies," *Journal of Human Rights* 19, no.5 (2020): 557–567, DOI: 10.1080/14754835.2020.1820315

Santos, Boaventura de Sousa. "Human rights as an emancipatory script? Cultural and political conditions." *In Another knowledge is possible? Beyond Northern epistemologies,* eds., Boaventura de Sousa Santos. London: Verso, 2007.

Sarah, Robert. "Herald Top 10: Cardinal Sarah: 'As a bishop, it is my duty to warn the West.'" *The Catholic Herald*, 31 December 2019. Available online: https://catholicherald.co.uk/herald-top-10-cardinal-sarah-as-a-bishop-it-is-my-duty-to-warn-the-west/ (accessed 22 August 2021).

Sardinha, LynnMarie and Héctor E. Nájera Catalán. "Attitudes towards domestic violence in 49 low- and middle-income countries: A gendered analysis of prevalence and country-level correlates." *PLOS ONE* 13, no. 10 (2018).

Sassen, Saskia. "The Global City: Strategic Site/New Frontier." *American Studies,* 7 (2000): 9–95.

Sassen, Saskia. "Local Actors in Global Politics." Current Sociology 52, no. 4 (2004): 649–670. https://doi.org/10.1177/0011392104043495.

Schmidt, Rachel. "What Battles Over 'Gender Ideology' Mean for Colombia's Women Human Rights Defenders." *OpenGlobalRights* (blog), 4 February 2020. Available online: https://www.openglobalrights.org/gender-ideology-and-colombias-women-human-rights-defenders/.

Scruggs, Lyle 2018. "Public opinion and economic human rights: Patterns of support in 22 countries," *Journal of Human Rights* 17, no. 5 (2018): 568–588, DOI: 10.1080/14754835.2017.1422705.

Segato, R. L. *Las estructuras elementales de la violencia. Ensayos sobre género entre la antropología, el psicoanálisis y los derechos humanos.* Buenos Aires: Prometeo Libros, 2010.

Sellers, Jefferey M., Anders Lidström, and Yooil Bae. *Multilevel Democracy: How Local Institutions and Civil Society Shape the Modern State.* Cambridge University Press, 2020.

Sellers, Jefferey M. *The SAGE Handbook of Governance State-Society Relations.* SAGE Publications, 2011. https://doi.org/10.4135/9781446200964.n9.

Sellers Jefferey, M. *Governing from Below : Urban Regions and the Global Economy.* Cambridge University Press, 2002.

Sen, Gita, Aditi Iyer, Sreeparna Chattopadhyay and Rajat Khosla. "When accountability meets power: realizing sexual and reproductive health and rights." *International Journal for Equity in Health* 19, 2020: 111.

Sermrittirong, Silatham, et al., "The Effectiveness of De-stigmatising Interventions" International Journal of Tropical Disease and Health 4, no. 12 (2014): 1218–1232.

Sermrittirong, Silatham and Wim H. Van Brakel. "Stigma in Leprosy: Concepts, Causes and Determinants" *Leprosy Review* 85 (2014): 36–47.

Shameem, Naureen, Alejandra Sardá-Chandiramani, Alex McCarthy, Ana Inés Abelenda, Anthea Taderera, Felogene Anumo, Fenya Fischler, Fernando D'Elio, Gillian Kane, Hyshyama Hamin, Inna Michaeli, Isabel Marler, Lola Guerra, María Luisa Peralta, Mirta Moragas Mereles, Paula Sánchez-Mejorada, Varyanne Sika, Verónica Vidal Degiorgis. "Rights at Risk—Time for Action: The Observatory on the Universality of Rights Report." Association for Women's Rights in Development, 2021.

Shaw, Jacqueline. "Beyond Empowerment Inspiration: Interrogating the Gap between the Ideals and Practice Reality of Participatory Video." In *The Handbook of Participatory Video,* eds., E. J. Milne, C. Mitchell, and N. de Lange, Altamira Press, 2012.

Simmons, W., Boynton, J., and Landman, T. 2021. Facilitated Communication, Neurodiversity, and Human Rights. *Human Rights Quarterly*, 43, no. 1 (2021): 138–167.

Simmons, William Paul. "Making the Teaching of Social Justice Matter." In *Real Social Science*, eds., Bent Flyvbjerg, Todd Landman, and Sanford Schram. Cambridge University Press, 2012.

Simmons, William Paul. "Paternal Ignorance in Human Rights Devalues Knowledge of Marginalized Populations." *OpenGlobalRights* (blog), 8 October 2020. Available online: https://www.openglobalrights.org/paternal-ignorance-in-human-rights-devalues-knowledge-of-marginalized-populations/.

Slaughter, Anne-Marie. *A New World Order*. Princeton: Princeton University Press, 2004.

Smart, C. "La mujer en el discurso jurídico." In *Mujeres, Derecho penal y criminología*, ed., E. Larrauri, 167–189. Madrid: Siglo XXI, 1994.

Smialek, Jeanna and Madeleine Ngo. "Top Fed officials say the labor market needs more time to heal", *The New York Times*, 27 September, 2021. Available online: https://www.nytimes.com/2021/09/27/business/economy/fed-labor-market-interest-rates.html

Smith, Courtney B. "The Politics of Global Consensus Building: A Comparative Analysis." *Global Governance* 5, no. 2 (1998): 173–201.

Smythe, Viv. "I'm Credited with Having Coined the Word 'Terf'. Here's How It Happened." *The Guardian*, 28 November 2018. Available online: https://www.theguardian.com/commentisfree/2018/nov/29/im-credited-with-having-coined-the-acronym-terf-heres-how-it-happened.

Sneed, Tierney. "McKayla Maroney: 'FBI made entirely false claims about what I said.'" CNN, 16 September 2016. Available online: https://edition.cnn.com/2021/09/15/politics/gymnasts-senate-judiciary-committee-larry-nassar-hearing/index.html; (accessed 17 September 2021).

Spruyt, Hendrik. "War, Trade, and State Formation". In *The Oxford Handbook of Comparative Politics*. University of Oxford Press, 2009.

Sriram, Veena, Stephanie M Topp, Marta Schaaf, Arima Mishra, Walter Flores, Subramania Raju Rajasulochana, Kerry Scott. "10 best resources on power in health policy and systems in low- and middle-income countries." *Health Policy and Planning* 33 no. 4 (2018): 611–621.

Stanimirova, Gabriela. "The Domino Effect of Normalizing Violence Against Women: Why Turkey's Withdrawal from the Istanbul Convention Has Become the Norm Rather Than the Exception." *Global Risk Insights*, 21 May 2021. Available online: https://globalriskinsights.com/2021/05/the-domino-effect-of-normalizing-violence-against-women-why-turkeys-withdrawal-from-the-istanbul-convention-has-become-the-norm-rather-than-the-exception/

Stemple, Lara. "Male Rape and Human Rights." *Hastings Law Journal* 60, no. 3 (2009): 605–646.

Stern, Maria, Marysia Zalewski, Elisabeth Prugle, and Paula Drumond, eds. *Sexual Violence against Men in Global Politics*. Routledge, 2018.

Stock, Kathleen. *Material Girls: Why Reality Matters for Feminism*. London: Hachette UK, 2021.

Stoller, Robert J. and Gilbert H. Herdt. "Theories of Origins of Male Homosexuality: A Cross-Cultural Look." *Archives of General Psychiatry* 42, no. 4 (1985): 399–404.

Suy, Kahofi Jischvi. "Homosexuality: a crime in several African countries." BBC, 12 November 2019. Available online: https://www.bbc.com/afrique/region-48618256 (accessed 17 September 2021).

Tamang, Jyotsna. "Foreign ideology vs. national priority: impacts of the US Global Gag Rule on Nepal's sexual and reproductive healthcare system." *Sex Reprod Health Matters* 28, no. 3 (2020):1831717.

Taylor, C. *El multiculturalismo y la política del reconocimiento*. México: Fondo de Cultura Económica, 1993.

"Texas Senate Bill 8 (2021–2022 87th Legislature)." 2021. Available online: https://legiscan.com/TX/text/SB8/id/2395961.

Thelen, Kathleen. "Historical Institutionalism in Comparative Politics." *Annu. Rev. Polit. Sci.* 2 (1999): 369–404.

Thiel, M. (2021). *The European Union's International Promotion of LGBTI Rights Promises and Pitfalls.* New York: Routledge.

Truong, Michelle and Susan Y. Wood. "Unconscionable: When Providers Deny Abortion Care." International Women's Health Coalition, 2018.

UNAM, C.-I. *Los desafíos de la migración y los albergues como oasis. Encuesta Nacional de Personas Migrantes en Tránsito por México*. Cd. de México, 2017.

Unidad de Política Migratoria, S. *Boletín Mensual de Estadísticas Migratorias 2021.*

United Nations Committee on Economic, Social and Cultural Rights. "General Comment 22: The right to sexual and reproductive health. E/C.12/GC/22." United Nations, 2016.

United Nations General Assembly. "UN Transforming our World: The 2030 Agenda for Sustainable Development. A/RES/70/1." United Nations, 21 October 2015.

United Nations Office of the High Commissioner for Human Rights (2012). *Born Free and Equal: Sexual Orientation and Gender Identity in International Human Rights Law*, https://www.ohchr.org/Documents/Publications/BornFreeAndEqualLowRes.pdf.

Urueña, René. *No Citizens Here: Global Subjects and Participation in International Law*. Leiden: Martin Nijhoff, 2012.

van Klinken, Adriaan and Ezra Chitando. *Public Religion and the Politics of Homosexuality in Africa*. New York: Routledge, 2016.

Varela, A. 2017. La trinidad perversa de la que huyen las fugitivas centroamricanas: violencia feminicida, violencia de estado y violencia de mercado. *Debate Feminista*, 53, (2017): 1–17.

Vida, Bianka. "New waves of anti-sexual and reproductive health and rights strategies in the European Union: the anti-gender discourse in Hungary." *Sexual and Reproductive Health Matters* 27, no. 2 (2019): 13–16.

Vinjamuri, Leslie. "Human Rights Backlash." Chap. 5 In *Human Rights Futures*, eds., Stephen Hopgood, Jack Snyder and Leslie Vinjamuri, 114–134. Cambridge: Cambridge University Press, 2017.

"Violence Against Men and Boys." Feminist Pocketbook Tip Sheet 7. Coalition of Feminists for Social Change, 2018: 1–4. Available online: https://cofemsocialchange.org/wp-content/uploads/2018/11/TS7-Violence-against-men-and-boys.pdf.

Vora, Komal and Shubha Srinivasan. "A Guide to Differences/Disorders of Sex Development/Intersex in Children and Adolescents." *Australian Journal of General Practice* 49, no. 7 (2020): 418.

Walsh, Shannon. "Critiquing the Politics of Participatory Video and the Dangerous Romance of Liberalism" *Area* 48, no. 4 (2016): 405–411.

Ward, Jeanne. "It's Not about the Gender Binary, It's about the Gender Hierarchy: A Reply to 'Letting Go of the Gender Binary.'" *International Review of the Red Cross* 98, no. 901 (2016): 275–298.

Weber, Max. "Politics as a Vacation." *American Journal of Cultural Sociology* 5, no. 3 (2017): 307–321.

Weidler, Erica M., Maria E. Linnaus, Arlene B. Baratz, Luis F. Goncalves, Smita Bailey, S. Janett Hernandez, Veronica Gomez-Lobo, Kathleen van Leeuwen. "A Management Protocol for Gonad Preservation in Patients with Androgen Insensitivity Syndrome." *Journal of Pediatric and Adolescent Gynecology* 32, no. 6 (2019): 605–11.

Women's Human Rights Campaign (n.d.). "Declaration on Women's Sex Based Rights." Available online: https://www.womensdeclaration.com/en/declaration-womens-sex-based-rights-full-text/ (accessed 9 October 2021).

"Women Unjustly Imprisoned in El Salvador." Center for Reproductive Rights, 26 January 2021. Available online: https://reproductiverights.org/center-reproductive-rights-women-unjustly-imprisoned-el-salvador/ (accessed 17 September 2021).

Wong, Wendy H. and Eileen A. Wong "What COVID-19 revealed about health, human rights, and the WHO," *Journal of Human Rights* 19, no. 5 (2020): 568–581, DOI: 10.1080/14754835.2020.1819778.

Workers' Rights Consortium Report 2020. "My children don't have food. I can withstand this hunger, but they cannot." What the crisis means for people who make collegiate apparel. Washington, DC: Workers' Rights Consortium. Available via: https://www.workersrights.org/wp-content/uploads/2020/06/My-children-dont-have-food_June-2020.pdf

"World Conference on Human Rights 14–25 June 1993, Vienna." United Nations, n.d. Available online: https://www.un.org/en/conferences/human-rights/vienna1993.

World Health Organization (WHO). n.d. "Leprosy Elimination" Available at: http://www.afro.who.int/en/clusters-a-programmes/dpc/neglected-tropical-diseases/programme-components/1729-leprosy-elimination-lep.html.

Young, Katharine G. "The idea of a human rights-based economic recovery after COVID-19," *International Journal of Public Law and Policy* 6, no. 4 (2020): 390–415. DOI: 10.1504/IJPLAP.2020.114810.

Zainuddin, Ani Amelia and Zaleha Abdullah Mahdy. "The Islamic Perspectives of Gender-Related Issues in the Management of Patients With Disorders of Sex Development." *Archives of Sexual Behavior* 46, no. 2 (2016): 353–360.

Index

www.ingramcontent.com/pod-product-compliance
Lightning Source LLC
Chambersburg PA
CBHW071353290326
41932CB00045B/1775